Daniela E. Casartelli, Silvio Cruschina, Pekka Posio and Stef Spronck (Eds.)
The Grammar of Thinking

Trends in Linguistics
Studies and Monographs

Editors
Chiara Gianollo
Daniël Van Olmen

Editorial Board
Walter Bisang
Tine Breban
Volker Gast
Hans Henrich Hock
Karen Lahousse
Natalia Levshina
Caterina Mauri
Heiko Narrog
Salvador Pons
Niina Ning Zhang
Amir Zeldes

Editor responsible for this volume
Daniël Van Olmen

Volume 379

The Grammar of Thinking

From Reported Speech to Reported Thought
in the Languages of the World

Edited by
Daniela E. Casartelli, Silvio Cruschina,
Pekka Posio and Stef Spronck

DE GRUYTER
MOUTON

ISBN 978-3-11-221504-3
e-ISBN (PDF) 978-3-11-106583-0
e-ISBN (EPUB) 978-3-11-106603-5
ISSN 1861-4302

Library of Congress Control Number: 2023936689

Bibliographic information published by the Deutsche Nationalbibliothek
The Deutsche Nationalbibliothek lists this publication in the Deutsche Nationalbibliografie;
detailed bibliographic data are available on the internet at http://dnb.dnb.de.

© 2025 Walter de Gruyter GmbH, Berlin/Boston
This volume is text- and page-identical with the hardback published in 2023.
Typesetting: Integra Software Services Pvt. Ltd.
Printing and binding: CPI books GmbH, Leck

www.degruyter.com

Contents

Daniela E. Casartelli, Silvio Cruschina, Pekka Posio & Stef Spronck
1   Introduction —— 1

Part I: Contrasting reported speech and reported thought

Tatiana Nikitina & Ekaterina Aplonova
2   The morphosyntax of reported speech and reported thought: A preliminary survey —— 15

Eva-Maria Remberger
3   To want, to think, to say: The development of WANT in German from volitional to reportative modal —— 41

Karolina Grzech
4   Reporting speech and thought in Upper Napo Kichwa —— 73

Malte Rosemeyer & Pekka Posio
5   On the emergence of quotative *bueno* in Spanish: A dialectal view —— 107

Part II: Pathways from saying to thinking

Sophia Fiedler
6   Thinking out loud? *Je me suis dit* 'I said to myself' and *j'étais là* 'I was there' in French talk-in-interaction —— 141

Denys Teptiuk
7   Self-quotations of speech and thought, and how to distinguish them —— 171

Nino Amiridze
8   When *saying* becomes *thinking*: A case of the Georgian autonomous quotative *metki* —— 207

Prapatsorn Tiratanti & Pholpat Durongbhan
9   Reported thought embedded in reported speech in Thai news reports —— 239

Part III: **Reported thought as a category in its own right**

Anja Hennemann
10 Complementizer deletion in structures of reporting on thinking in Argentinian Spanish and Brazilian Portuguese —— 263

Daniela E. Casartelli
11 Towards a typology of reported thought —— 291

Index —— 317

Daniela E. Casartelli, Silvio Cruschina, Pekka Posio & Stef Spronck
1 Introduction

1 From reported speech to reported thought

Speakers routinely discuss the words of others, whether they have actually heard these words being spoken or merely attribute them, with constructions as in (1)–(4):

(1) Sasha said: "This will be a beautiful day."
(2) Sasha said that it would be a beautiful day.
(3) Sasha thought: "This will be a beautiful day."
(4) Sasha thought that it would be a beautiful day.

The first two of these sentences are examples of reported speech, traditionally divided into direct speech (1), which purports to represent an utterance without significant modification by the current speaker, and indirect speech (2), which has no such implications (Coulmas 1986). While many questions remain in the study of reported speech, it has received relatively wide attention, including in several influential volume-length treatments (e.g. Lucy 1993) and in many individual studies.

This cannot be said for reported thought, as exemplified by (3) and (4). As these example sentences show, expressions of reported thought parallel those of reported speech in many ways, at least in English and most other commonly described languages. We could therefore label (3) 'direct thought' and (4) 'indirect thought' and this classification is straightforward on structural grounds: in both (1) and (3) deictic pronouns and tense are indexing the *origo* of the subject of the matrix clause and in the written form they include quotation marks, both (2) and (4) appear to involve complementation with an embedded proposition, and the only distinction between the two pairs of examples of reported speech and reported thought is the choice of the lexical verbs *say* and *think*.

But what does 'direct thought' mean and what would motivate its choice over 'indirect thought'? While authors have frequently remarked that direct speech is rarely actually a 'verbatim' representation of some one's words (see Vandelanotte 2009: 118–130 for discussion), the question of what it means to reflect someone's thoughts *as they were thought*, instead of by approximation, seems absurd. There is an obvious, fundamental difference between the usage context of reported speech and reported thought: a thought, by its very definition, remains unspoken. No one has direct access to a thought apart from the person who thinks it, the so-called 'cognisant' (apart from the exceptional case of omniscient narrators in a literary text).

https://doi.org/10.1515/9783111065830-001

Therefore, the main questions of the reported speech literature, that primarily deal with the representation and manipulation of utterances and the coordination of the perspectives of multiple speakers and hearers, are irrelevant for understanding reported thought. As a consequence, the phenomenon remains largely unstudied.

This is not to suggest that reported thought has gone completely unmentioned in studies of reported speech. Authors have, roughly, dealt with it the phenomenon in one of three ways:

a) assuming that reported thought is mostly equivalent to reported speech (the equivalence assumption);
b) assuming that reported thought is derived from reported speech (the derivation assumption);
c) assuming that reported thought is irrelevant for understanding reported speech and can therefore be ignored in studies on the latter phenomenon (the dissimilarity assumption).

As the initial examples in (1)–(4) illustrated, the equivalence assumption is not unreasonable, especially for languages like English. From a syntactic viewpoint, structures involving reported speech and reported thought are often similar (Palmer 1986: 135; Spronck & Nikitina 2019). Moreover, the predicates used in reported speech (e.g. *say*, *tell*) and reported thought (e.g. *think*) behave as bridge verbs allowing for a number of syntactic phenomena, including extraction across wh-questions, embedded V2 in Germanic languages, and complementizer deletion (Erteschik-Shir 1973; Vikner 1995; Cocchi & Poletto 2002; Dor 2005; see also Salvesen & Walkden 2017). Apart from these syntactic similarities, across nearly all continents languages have been found that do not even make a lexical distinction between 'say' and 'think' (Larson 1978; Saxena 1988; Rumsey 1990; Reesink 1993; Güldemann 2008; Spronck 2015), resulting in an even greater structural resemblance between reported speech and reported thought.

The derivation assumption is also quite plausible. On the one hand, it serves as a diachronic explanation for the equivalence assumption (a reported speech expression often constitutes the source construction for reported thought in languages in which the two are indistinguishable, cf. Spronck & Casartelli 2021). This explanation is made even stronger by the fact that no language has so far been demonstrated to show the opposite development path, i.e. from reported thought to reported speech. On the other hand, even languages in which the verbs of speech and thought are consistently distinguished, speech verbs are routinely used to express mental states (Pascual 2014), as in expressions like 'I said to myself. . .' or 'Her smile spoke volumes'.

A particularly interesting psychological motivation for the derivation assumption lies in Vygotsky's (1987) notion of 'inner speech', which interprets thought as a form of speaking to oneself (cf. Vološinov 1973). In a more recent study, Mercier & Sperber (2017) build on this idea by proposing that our human ability to reason is a consequence of internalizing dialogue, with conscious thought being no more than practicing how we are going to explain our judgements and intentions before vocalizing them. Where expressions of reported thought are diachronically or structurally based on reported speech constructions, they mirror this process of internalization in a remarkably iconic way.

The dissimilarity assumption can be adopted for many reasons, for example: a traditional formal semantic analysis of quotation may choose to exclude reported thought because it does not involve statements with a verifiable truth-value and for a similar reason a functionalist account of quotative meaning (cf. Boye 2012) may disregard reported thought since it does not involve a fully embedded illocution or speech act.

Such analyses build on an important observation: the fact that there *are* empirical and theoretical differences between reported speech and reported thought. These emerge, for example, in the differences in the syntactic structure of complement clauses involved in reported speech and reported thought: authors have pointed out that the complements of thought predicates seem to lack an independent illocutionary force, while speech predicates select for clauses with a full structure licensing root phenomena (Hooper & Thompson 1973; Heycock 2006). Such distinctions also lead to different diachronic processes leading to (semi-)grammaticalized constructions, parenthetical expressions, evidential or epistemic adverb(ial)s (cf. English *methinks*, Spanish *dizque*, Greek *leí*), discourse markers and modal particles, and grammatical elements such as complementizers (Cruschina & Remberger 2008; Thompson & Mulac 1991; Posio 2014; Cruschina 2015; Wiemer 2018, and references therein).

Furthermore, reported speech and thought may involve different complementizers (see, e.g. Ledgeway 2005), or have different moods in the embedded clause (see, e.g., Laca 2013), and behave differently with respect to other phenomena such as negation raising (Horn 1989) and the omission of complementizers in spontaneous speech (e.g., Posio & Pesková 2020).

Therefore, while none of the assumptions that previous authors have taken to the discussion of reported thought are necessarily false for the purposes of the respective studies, or even mutually exclusive, they have often tipped the balance to studying reported speech instead of reported thought. This is where the current volume aims to rebalance the scales, not by assuming that reported thought is the same, derived or even necessarily different in all languages from reported speech, but by asking the question: what happens if we study reported thought as an autonomous research topic? In the chapters of this volume, authors take up this challenge from a range of backgrounds, theoretical persuasions and linguistic sub-disciplines.[1]

2 Overview of the volume

Bringing together linguists from different frameworks, specializations and methodological approaches, this volume aims to turn the spotlight on the often ignored sibling of reported speech, while illustrating the many different linguistic manifestations of reported thought. In doing so, on the one hand, it continues the trend towards the joint analysis of categories of cognition and perspective, which in recent years has gained a strong presence in typology, syntax, semantics, and pragmatics (cf. Speas & Tenny 2003; Aikhenvald 2004; Cornillie 2009; Traugott 2010; Boye 2012; Cruschina 2015; Gentens et al. 2019). On the other hand, it also assesses in detail, for the first time, as far as we are aware, to what extent we can qualify reported thought as a separate linguistic category in its own right and how, exactly, it relates to reported speech/quotation and (other) attitudinal expressions. By examining semantic, pragmatic and morpho-syntactic properties of reported thought in relation to reported speech, as well as the historical linguistic processes that lead to their emergence the present volume aims to contribute to the understanding of the two notions, their cross-linguistic range and their limitations, and to foster debate across theoretical divides and approaches.

The volume is divided into three sections: *Contrasting reported speech and reported thought* (part I), *Pathways from saying to thinking* (part II) and *Reported thought as a category in its own right* (part III). The four chapters in part I, broadly, take a contrastive perspective to reported thought and speech, highlighting the differences and communalities between the two. From a variety of perspective this section first brings into view how reported thought might be *different* from reported speech. The chapters in the second part all explore phenomena that either occur at the border of reported speech and thought or that represent a (diachronic) bridging context between them. Finally, part III abandons the comparison with reported speech altogether and considers the specific idiosyncrasies of reported thought.

---

[1] The following chapters represent a selection of the talks presented at workshop *The grammar of thinking: Comparing reported thought and reported speech across languages*, organized within the 53rd Annual Meeting of the *Societas Linguistica Europaea* (SLE 2020), University of Bucharest, 26–29 August 2020. Due to the pandemic, the conference took place online.

2.1 Contrasting reported speech and reported thought

Part I starts with the chapter 'The morphosyntax of reported speech and reported thought: A preliminary survey' by Tatiana Nikitina and Ekaterina Aplonova. In it the authors present a detailed corpus analysis of eight genetically and geographically diverse languages, examining structural and lexical properties of reported speech and thought. They identify three types of relationships between reported speech and reported thought: (i) reported thought is expressed by the same constructions used to convey reported speech, (ii) reported thought is expressed by means of reported speech constructions with special lexical markers (e.g., verbs of thinking), and (iii) reported thought is expressed by dedicated constructions that have no equivalents among constructions expressing reported speech. Despite the formal differences in the expression of reported speech and thought, Nikitina and Aplonova find that the two phenomena share important similarities in their sample. They also uncover theoretical and empirical aspects of reported thought constructions that distinguish them in relevant ways and conclude by stating that while reported speech is a cross-linguistic category, reported thought should not be treated as one.

The chapter 'To want, to think, to say: The development of WANT in German from volitional to reportative modal' by Eva-Maria Remberger deals with the development of a volitional verb (German *wollen* 'want') into a verb encoding a saying component and reported evidentiality. According to the author, this development is mediated by a thought or belief component, thus shedding light on a new aspect of the complex relationship between (reported) thought and speech. In her reconstruction of the modal shift, the intermediate step between the bouletic conversational background (volitional modality) and the reportative conversational background (reported evidentiality) is characterized by a doxastic conversational background (of belief or thought) which is already present in the root interpretation of the volitional modal and which then yields the reportative evidential function.

The analysis of the grammaticalization process of the reportative volitional verb shows that the reportative component of this construction is non-at-issue (only the content of what is said is at issue) and non-eventive, in that it does not introduce into the discourse a speech event that can be referred to. These characteristics are in line with the evidential function, since evidential marking does not contain or make reference to a speech act event. Even if there is no speech act event, and hence there is no utterance context, the volitional constructions with the reportative meaning still include the author of the source of information (i.e. the syntactic subject of the volitional verb). Indeed, the reportative component is anchored to this subject of the reportative modal. Once the bouletic modal base is lost, together with the volitional event, the doxastic modal base takes over. In this intermediate stage the syntactic subject still serves as an anchor for the evaluation time of the modal, which cannot be shifted to the speaker. The co-existence of the epistemic state of the speaker ('what the speaker knows') with the doxastic state of the subject-argument of the main clause ('what the subject believes') explains the rise of reportative evidentiality ('what the subject says').

Karolina Grzech's chapter 'Reporting speech and thought in Upper Napo Kichwa' introduces an intriguing interaction between marking of epistemic access in the Amazonian language Upper Napo Kichwa (Quechuan, Ecuador) and reported speech and thought. Since the language has dedicated morphemes for signalling whether knowledge is shared or exclusively known to the speaker, the data Grzech introduces provides a unique perspective on how the two strategies may differ in this respect in actual spontaneous interaction. The epistemic enclitics used in reportative constructions in this language permit speakers to express multiple perspectives when conveying reported speech and thought. These particles express the delimitation of the reported speech and thought and separate it from the speakers' perspective, limiting the speakers' responsibility or commitment towards the propositional contents of the stretch of reported discourse.

In the chapter 'On the emergence of quotative *bueno* in Spanish: a dialectal view' by Malte Rosemeyer & Pekka Posio, the relationship between reported speech and reported thought is investigated with respect to the distribution of the discourse marker *bueno* in Spanish. Among its many functions, ranging from the expression of agreement to the expression of disagreement, the element *bueno* (literally meaning 'good') has developed the function of quotative marker occurring at the beginning of reported discourse. Adopting a cross-dialectal perspective, based on in a multi-dialect corpus of spoken Spanish, this paper provides both quantitative and qualitative evidence for the hypothesis that *bueno* is grammaticalizing into a quotative marker. In this emerging function, *bueno* does not completely replace other quotative markers (e.g. the verb *decir* 'say'), but it is used together with them, also in the group of dialects with the most frequent and productive uses of *bueno*, where this element is most frequently used at the beginning of reported discourse. The emergence of the quotative function may in fact be due to this frequent collocation of *bueno* with other quotative markers and to a hearer-based reanalysis of the resulting structure.

In the analysis of *bueno* as a quotative marker, the authors use the term *reported discourse* to subsume both reported thought and reported speech. Once the investigation turns to a more specific verification of possible differences in the use of *bueno* in association with reported thought and reported speech, the conclusion is that these two dimensions are not systematically distinguished in Spanish. Some evidence is found suggesting that in the dialects with a particularly productive use of *bueno* some speakers tend to associate it with reported thought rather than speech, but the authors admit that it is nevertheless difficult to arrive at sound generalizations and that this tendency may in fact be dependent on the specific discourse context or may even reflect the speakers' individual preferences. In turn, the lack of a systematic distinction between reported thought and reported speech may be taken as evidence for the assumption that, in Spanish, reported thought is presented similarly to reported speech, as if speaking equalled thinking that is reported to an interlocutor.

2.2 Pathways from saying to thinking

With the chapter 'Thinking out loud? *Je me dis* 'I tell myself' and *j'étais là* 'I was there' in French talk-in-interaction' we move to part II. In this paper, Sophia Fiedler examines two constructions that are used to introduce direct reported thought in spoken, colloquial French, *je me suis dit* 'I said to myself' and *j'étais là* 'I was there'. Drawing on data from video recordings of students discussing over coffee breaks, Fiedler uses methods from Conversation Analysis and Interactional Linguistics to uncover the regularities in the uses of these constructions. In addition to speech, the analysis takes into account the bodily conduct of the speakers, including gaze, gestures, postures, and facial expressions while speaking. The results shows that the two constructions are used differently: the speakers use *j'étais là* to take an affective stance in the ongoing conversation, and the use of this device is regularly accompanied by verbal, prosodical and bodily reenactments. The other construction, *je me suis dit*, is used to take a rational stance by making available to the interlocutors a conclusion or a decision that accounts for previous actions. Unlike *j'étais là,* the construction *je me suis dit* is not accompanied by bodily reenactment.

These functional differences are reflected in the distribution of these constructions: *je me suis dit* occurs during rational explanations or tellings about past actions, while *j'étais là* appears in more emotionally charged tellings and depicts the speaker's reactions to previous stretches of talk or action. While presenting data from two constructions specializing to the expression of reported thought, the paper contributes to the growing body of research on the interface of grammar, conversation and bodily conduct in interaction.

In Denys Teptiuk's chapter 'Self-quotations of speech and thought, and how to distinguish them', the relationship between reported thought and speech is tackled in relation to the ambiguity between the two dimensions that can emerge in quotations and self-quotations. The author analyses non-standard written speech in six Finno-Ugric languages, as well as in Russian and in English for comparative purposes. In this chapter, reported thought is mainly understood as the (re)presentations of "internal/inner speech", which stands in opposition to the previously verbalized category of reported speech.

Since the constructions that turn out to be ambiguous with respect to the representation of speech and thought are characterized by event-un(der)specification, the author selects and analyses specific quotative indexes where such ambiguity is expected in different constructions with distinct features: constructions with generic speech verbs that can also introduce reported thought, constructions with an equational verb and etymologically non-reportative quotative markers, constructions with a non-clausal use of (self-)quotative particles, and turn-taking constructions with ellipsis of the speech/mental verb. The results show that the ambiguity between speech and thought appears more frequently in self-quotations, even though the context and characteristics as addressivity of speech and egocentricity of thought may help to resolve this ambiguity. Because of the egocentric nature of reported thought, which, unlike reported speech, is directed to the reporters themselves and not to the interlocutors, there are also more cases of reported thoughts in self-quotations than in quotations. By contrast, quotations mostly report speech rather than thoughts. All this contributes to the higher ambiguity of self-quotations between an interpretation of reported speech and reported thought.

Nino Amiridze's chapter 'When *saying* becomes *thinking*: A case of Georgian *metki*' examines reported thought in Georgian, which has two particularly interesting features: like many Caucasian languages, Georgian has an intricate set of restrictions on indexical expressions that characterize reported speech and thought constructions. The author comments on how these may be used to distinguish the two phenomena. However, what motivates the appearance of the chapter in this part of the volume is the second property of Georgian reported thought: reported thought constructions are introduced by a morphosyntactically independent quotative marker *metki*, deriving from an enclitic marker (=*metki*) whose origin is in a matrix clause containing a speech verb (*me vtkvi* 'I said'). Thus, Georgian data provides an example of both grammaticalization and lexicalization of a verb of speech into a marker of reported thought.

The chapter 'Reported thought embedded in reported speech in Thai news reports' by Prapatsorn Tiratanti and Pholpat Durongbhan explores the domain of speech and thought reports in Thai news articles. The authors cross-examine televised and written news reports of the major news outlets in Thailand. Their analysis reveals that reported thoughts in written news reports are not always inferences drawn by the journalist based on reported speech from the televised report. Several examples in the author's data show that the original speaker in the televised news report did explicitly reference their own thoughts. Reported thoughts in the televised news report are indicated by the matrix verb that expresses thought, rather than speech. This is reflected in the written news article, where the journalist transfers the structure of the original thought report from the televised news report. This is what the authors refer to as a thought report embedded in reported speech.

The grammatical structure of Thai only allows for a distinction between thought and speech reports depending on the matrix verb in the main clause. Contrastive examples show that thought reports are distinguished from speech reports on the basis of the matrix verb that takes the report as its complement. Reported thought and speech are two closely related functional domains that are distinguished on the basis of the matrix verb in the main clause in Thai.

2.3 Reported thought as a category in its own right

The chapter 'Complementizer deletion in structures of reporting on thinking in Argentinian Spanish and Brazilian Portuguese' by Anja Hennemann examines subject and complementizer expression in Spanish and Portuguese mental verb constructions (*yo*) *pienso* (*que*) and (*eu*) *acho* (*que*) 'I think that'. In both languages and constructions, the first-person singular pronominal subject, as well as the complementizer, can be deleted. While the variable expression of subjects has received a lot of attention in previous research, complementizer deletion has not yet been the object of systematic studies. Hennemann uses corpus data from Argentina and Brazil representing written, informal language that can be conceptualized as closer to orality than formal written texts where complementizer deletion is thought to be more common. She discusses whether the phenomenon is best accounted for in terms of grammaticalization, pragmaticalization, or constructionalization. Complementizer deletion tends to occur in particle-like constructions with certain discourse functions and remains relatively rare in clausal constructions where the mental predicate acts as the verb of a main clause with the stretch of reported speech or thought figuring as the complement.

Daniela Casartelli's chapter 'Towards a typology of reported thought' is an innovative piece of research looking at the typology of the expression of reported thought and whether it can be distinguished from reported speech in the languages of the world. The study is based on a morphosyntactic analysis of a sample of 100 languages. The results of the study show that some languages do distinguish between reported thoughts and reported speech. Casartelli also distinguishes between five different morphosyntactic sub-types of reported thought: (i) those relying uniquely on the use of the verb 'think' in the matrix clause, (ii) serial verb constructions with clausal complements, (iii) converbs used in addition to the complement-taking verb, (iv) quotative markers in the reported clause, and (v) verbalized nouns symbolizing the represented thought. This paper makes an important contribution to the typological study of reported thought, an exciting yet so far under-researched field.

References

Aikhenvald, Alexandra Y. 2004. *Evidentiality*. Oxford: Oxford University Press.
Boye, Kasper. 2012. *Epistemic meaning: A crosslinguistic and functional-cognitive study*. Berlin & Boston: De Gruyter Mouton.
Buchstaller, Isabelle & Ingrid Van Alphen (eds.). 2012. *Quotatives: Cross-linguistic and cross-disciplinary perspectives*. Amsterdam & Philadelphia: John Benjamins.
Cocchi, Gloria & Cecilia Poletto. 2002. Complementizer deletion in Florentine: The interaction between merge and move. In Claire Beyssade, Reineke Bok-Bennema, Frank Drijkoningen & Paola Monachesi (eds.), *Romance languages and linguistic theory 2000*, 55–56. Amsterdam: John Benjamins.
Cornillie, Bert. 2009. Evidentiality and epistemic modality. On the close relationship between two different categories. *Functions of Language* 16(1). 9–43.
Coulmas, Florian (ed.). 1986. *Direct and indirect speech*. Berlin: Mouton de Gruyter.
Cruschina, Silvio. 2015. The expression of evidentiality and epistemicity: Cases of grammaticalization in Italian and Sicilian. *Probus* 27(1). 1–31. (doi:10.1515/probus-2013-0006)
Cruschina, Silvio & Eva-Maria Remberger. 2008. Hearsay and reported speech: Evidentiality in Romance. *Rivista di Grammatica Generativa* 33. 99–120.
Dor, Daniel. 2005. Toward a semantic account of *that*-deletion in English. *Linguistics* 43(2). 345–382.
Erteschik-Shir, Nomi. 1973. *On the nature of island constraints*. MIT. (PhD thesis.)
Gentens, Caroline, Maria Sol Sansiñena, Stef Spronck & An Van linden (eds.). 2019. *Pragmatics*. Vol. 29. Amsterdam & Philadelphia: John Benjamins.
Güldemann, Tom. 2008. *Quotative indexes in African languages: A synchronic and diachronic survey*. Berlin: Mouton de Gruyter.
Güldemann, Tom & Manfred von Roncador (eds.). 2002. *Reported discourse: A meeting ground for different linguistic domains*. Amsterdam & Philadelphia: John Benjamins.
Heycock, Caroline. 2006. Embedded root phenomena. In Martin Everaert & Henk van Riemsdijk (eds.), *The Blackwell companion to syntax*, vol. II, 174–209. Boston & Oxford: Blackwell.
Hooper, Joan B. & Sandra A. Thompson 1973. On the applicability of root transformations. *Linguistic Inquiry* 4(4). 465–497.
Horn, Laurence R. 1989. *A natural history of negation*. Chicago: University of Chicago Press.
Theo Janssen & Wim van der Wurff (eds.). *Reported speech: Forms and functions of the verb*. 1996. Amsterdam & Philadelphia: John Benjamins.
Laca, Brenda. 2013. Temporal orientation and the semantics of attitude verbs. In Karina Veronica Molsing & Ana Maria Tramunt Ibanos (eds.), *Time and TAME in language*, 158–180. Newcastle: Cambridge Scholars Publishing.
Larson, Mildred Lucille. 1978. *The functions of reported speech in discourse*. Dallas: Summer Institute of Linguistics.
Ledgeway, Adam. 2005. Moving through the left periphery: The dual complementiser system in the dialects of southern Italy. *Transactions of the Philological Society* 103. 336–396.

Lucy, John A. (ed.). 1993. *Reflexive language: Reported speech and metapragmatics*. Cambridge: Cambridge University Press.
Mercier, Hugo & Dan Sperber. 2017. *The enigma of reason*. Cambridge, MA: Harvard University Press.
Palmer, Frank R. 1986. *Mood and modality*. Cambridge: Cambridge University Press.
Pascual, Esther. 2014. *Fictive interaction: The conversation frame in thought, language, and discourse*. Amsterdam & Philadelphia: John Benjamins.
Posio, Pekka. 2014. Subject expression in grammaticalizing constructions. The case of *creo* and *acho* 'I think' in Spanish and Portuguese. *Journal of Pragmatics* 63. 5–18. (doi: 10.1016/j.pragma.2013.07.001)
Posio, Pekka & Andrea Pesková. 2020. Le dije yo, digo: Construccionalización de los introductores cuotativos con el verbo decir en español peninsular y argentino. *Spanish in context* 17(3). 391–414.
Reesink, Gerard P. 1993. "Inner speech" in Papuan languages. *Language and Linguistics in Melanesia* 24. 217–225.
Rumsey, Alan. 1990. Wording, meaning and linguistic ideology. *American Anthropologist* 92(2). 346–361.
Salvesen, Christine M. & George Walkden. 2017. Diagnosing embedded V2 in Old English and Old French. In Eric Mathieu & Robert Truswell, (eds.), *Micro-change and macro-change in diachronic syntax*, 168–181. Oxford: Oxford University Press.
Saxena, Anju. 1988. On syntactic convergence: The case of the verb 'say' in Tibeto-Burman. In Shelley Axmaker, Annie Jaisser, & Helen Singmaster *Proceedings of the fourteenth annual meeting of the Berkeley Linguistics Society*, 375–388. Berkley: Berkeley Linguistics Society.
Speas, Peggy & Carol Tenny. 2003. Configurational properties of point of view roles. In Anna Maria Di Sciullo (ed.), *Asymmetry in grammar*, 315–343. Amsterdam & Philadelphia: John Benjamins.
Spronck, Stef. 2015. *Reported speech in Ungarinyin: Grammar and social cognition in a language of the Kimberley region, Western Australia*. The Australian National University. (PhD thesis.) (http://hdl.handle.net/1885/733712596)
Spronck, Stef & Daniela Casartelli. 2021. In a manner of speaking: How reported speech may have shaped grammar. *Frontiers in Communication* 6. 1–22. (doi:10.3389/fcomm.2021.624486)
Spronck, Stef & Tatiana Nikitina. 2019. Reported speech forms a dedicated syntactic domain. *Linguistic Typology* 23(1). 119–159.
Thompson, Sandra A. & Anthony Mulac. 1991. A quantitative perspective on the grammaticalization of epistemic parentheticals in English. In Elizabeth Closs Traugott & Bernd. Heine (eds.), *Approaches to grammaticalization*, 313–339. Amsterdam & Philadelphia: John Benjamins.
Traugott, Elizabeth Closs. 2010. (Inter)subjectivity and (inter)subjectification: A reassessment. In Kristin Davidse, Lieven Vandelanotte & Hubert Cuyckens (eds.), *Subjectification, intersubjectification and grammaticalization*, 29–71. Berlin & New York: De Gruyter Mouton.
Vandelanotte, Lieven. 2009. *Speech and thought representation in English: A cognitive-functional approach*. Berlin/New York: De Gruyter Mouton.
Vikner, Sten. 1995. *Verb movement and expletive subjects in the Germanic languages*. Oxford: Oxford University Press.
Vološinov, Valentin N. 1973. *Marxism and the philosophy of language*. Translated by Ladislav Matejka & I. R. Titunik. New York/London: Seminar Press.
Vygotsky, Lev S. 1987. *Thinking and speech. The collected works of lev vygotsky*. Vol. 1. New York, NY: Plenum Press.
Wiemer, Björn. 2018. *Catching the elusive: Lexical evidentiality markers in Slavic languages (a questionnaire study and its background)*. Berlin: Peter Lang.

Part I: **Contrasting reported speech and reported thought**

Tatiana Nikitina & Ekaterina Aplonova

2 The morphosyntax of reported speech and reported thought: A preliminary survey

Abstract: This study addresses the relationship between the reporting of speech and the reporting of thought based on a set of annotated data from several typologically diverse languages. The context-based approach we adopt allows us to explore the relationship between reported speech and reported thought without relying on specific lexical or constructional cues.

We identify three types of relationship between reported speech and reported thought. First, in all our languages, reported speech constructions can be *recruited* for the expression of reported thought; such uses can only be identified based on context. Second, in some of the languages, we find expressions that are best described in terms of *speech-to-thought coercion*: in a construction normally associated with reported speech, a verb of thinking or another lexical marker triggers a reported thought interpretation. Such an interpretation is sometimes at odds with the construction's original properties, since situations of thinking and speaking differ in a number of linguistically relevant ways. For example, situations of thinking do not involve an addressee, and that difference accounts for the seemingly superfluous use, in some languages, of expressions such as "think inside one's head" or "think to oneself", which serve to reconcile the construction's argument properties (an implied addressee) with its coerced interpretation. Speech-to-thought coercion also explains why, despite the absence of an addressee in the verb's argument structure, it is possible to refer to addressees within thought reports. Finally, in some languages, reported thought constructions are attested that have no equivalent among expressions of reported speech.

We conclude, based on the structural diversity of reported thought expressions, that reported thought cannot be treated as a uniform cross-linguistic concept in a way similar to reported speech (Spronck & Nikitina 2019), and that conceptualization of thought processes varies across languages in ways that make direct comparison impossible.

Acknowledgements: This project has received funding from the European Research Council (ERC) under the European Union's Horizon 2020 research and innovation programme (grant agreement No 758232). We would like to thank our fellow project members for their assistance, in particular Elena Perekhvalskaya, Abbie Hantgan-Sonko, Lacina Silué, and Guillaume Guitang. We are also grateful to our language consultants and assistants: Alexander Savelyev, Fizaliya Makhianova, and Sekou Coulibali. Moreover, we would like to thank Valentin Vydrin for his comments on the Bambara data.

https://doi.org/10.1515/9783111065830-002

1 Introduction

Recent years have seen an upsurge of interest in the properties of speech reports, yet it remains an open question whether and to what degree the findings extend to attitude reports, and in particular to reported thought. In this study we neither assume reported thought to be a subtype of reported speech nor approach it as an a priori unrelated phenomenon (see Introduction to this volume); rather, we adopt a data-driven comparative approach and explore correspondences in the ways different types of reported content are encoded cross-linguistically.

To address the relationship between the expression of speech and the expression of thought, we survey a set of annotated data from several typologically diverse languages, extracted from the multilingual SpeechReporting corpus of traditional storytelling (Nikitina et al. 2022). The corpus consists of traditional narratives annotated for instances of reported speech and reported thought using the ELAN-CorpA software and tools (Chanard 2019); the same annotation principles are applied across the datasets, making it easy to extract and directly compare the relevant data from different languages. Although the survey is based on a small convenience sample that is not intended to be representative of cross-linguistic diversity, the same approach can be applied, in future studies, to an extended sample of languages, to test the suggested typology against data from more languages in a rather precise way.

Table 1 lists the languages explored systematically in this study based on corpus data. In addition, we use occasional examples from the Bambara Reference Corpus (Vydrin et al. 2011–2018), without exploring systematically the encoding of reported thought in that language.

Table 1: Our dataset.

Language	Genetic affiliation	Country	References
Bashkir	Turkic	Russia	Aplonova (2021)
Ben Tey	Dogon	Mali	Hantgan-Sonko (in prep.)
Chuvash	Turkic	Russia	Nikitina (2022)
Gizey	Chadic	Cameroon	Guitang (2022)
Joola Eegimaa	Atlantic	Senegal	Hantgan-Sonko (2021)
Mwan	Mande	Côte d'Ivoire	Perekhvalskaya (in prep.)
Udihe	Tungusic	Russia	Perekhvalskaya (2020; 2021)
Wan	Mande	Côte d'Ivoire	Nikitina (2012; in prep.)

The database of traditional storytelling has been manually annotated for instances of reported speech and thought. The annotation was done independently of this study (Nikitina et al. 2019). The distinction between reported speech and reported thought was based on the natural reading of the report in the context of a particular story, according to native speaker interpretation. The annotation was therefore not tied to particular lexical or morphosyntactic markers, and we were able to identify instances of reported thought without reference to specific words or constructions. This approach distinguishes our study from previous studies that focus on specific lexical expressions and translational equivalents of English mental activity verbs (Fortescue 1990; Persson 1993; Onishi 1997; Stanwood 1997; Viberg 2004, inter alia) or on specific construction types (cf. the survey of thought complements in Australian languages by McGregor 2021). One of our findings follows directly from the lack of assumption that the notion of thinking must be expressed in any particular way: we find that a significant proportion of instances of reported thought do not involve any specialized lexical items, and they instantiate a variety of construction types beyond what could be observed if data were searched for specific words or syntactic relations.

Methodologically, our approach departs from the tradition of building a typology by comparing individual languages or defining idealized language profiles. We aim instead at classifying the entire set of strategies used across languages to encode the same two functions: reported speech and reported thought. In doing so we assume that the notions of reported speech and reported thought are universal, even though they need not be universally distinguishable at the level of grammar or lexicon (Spronck and Nikitina 2019, Goddard and Wierzbicka 2019). Consistent with this assumption, in all our datasets we find extensive examples of reported speech and sporadic examples of reported thought (though as we discuss in the conclusion, languages may be found where reporting of thought is subject to cultural restrictions).

Instead of attempting to classify the languages, we explore our data through a typology of morphosyntactic *strategies* available to speakers for the encoding of reported thought. The strategies are defined in terms of their availability, in the same language, for the encoding of reported speech. They fall into three major types. A strategy that is attested in all of the languages and is likely universal involves encoding reported thought by unaltered expressions associated with reported speech (Sections 2). The opposite strategy involves using constructions that are specialized for the encoding of reported thought, and unattested in speech reports (Section 3). Finally, the third strategy involves using expressions normally associated with reported speech but with modifications, such as after substituting a verb of thinking for the verb of speaking. This third strategy is only attested in some of the languages, and it is the one that we find most interesting from a grammatical point of view, as it creates a partial overlap in the morphosyntactic properties of reported speech and reported thought. We propose to analyze this strategy as an instance of *coercion*, and we believe that it may explain a number of attested asymmetries between reported speech and reported thought as well as a number of otherwise puzzling characteristics of reported thought expressions (Section 4).

It has become customary in certain traditions of research on reported discourse to classify strategies in terms of their degree of "(in)directness", attributing a central role to the use of indexical elements and other shifters. We do not pay much attention to this parameter in this study, because we believe that a Eurocentric direct/indirect distinction – either binary or gradual – does not apply to some of our languages (Nikitina and Bugaeva 2021). We adopt instead a stratified typology, as sketched out in (Nikitina and Vydrina 2020): the construction's syntax is considered independently of the use of indexical expressions. The behavior of indexical expressions is assumed to depend on language-specific lexical properties of the words involved (pronouns, adverbs, etc.), and not on syntactic configurations in which they appear.

We also do not treat here extended uses of verbs of speaking and verbs of thinking, or of constructions in which such verbs appear (Spronck & Casartelli 2021). It is sometimes difficult, for example, to draw a strict boundary between the notions of thinking and intention or between thinking and perception, and the same expressions are commonly used across languages to encode these and other kinds of inner states. We restrict ourselves to expression types used to describe mental activity in general, without additional entailments of emotions and desire (as in English constructions with 'want'), a specific degree of conviction (as in English constructions with 'believe') or the presence of a perceptual stimulus (as in English constructions with 'feel').

Although our study is based on corpus data, it is limited to general observations and does not explore the frequencies of different strategies. Notwithstanding the large number of clear cases, some reports are ambiguous between reported speech and reported thought, and they are distributed unevenly across languages and speakers. This complication prevents us, at this point, from relying on quantitative information, which may be misleading in the case of individual languages and may also not be directly comparable across the languages.

In sum, despite all these limitations, the approach we adopt allows us to explore the relationship between reported speech and reported thought without relying on specific lexical or constructional cues. We find that in all languages in our sample, speakers have access to multiple morphosyntactic strategies for the encoding of reported thought, ranging from the use of unaltered expressions for reported speech to highly specialized constructions associated with reported thought and coerced expressions combining reported thought interpretation with inherited properties of reported speech constructions.

2 Reported speech expressions *recruited* for reported thought

In all of our languages reported thought can be encoded *as if* it were speech, i.e. with verbs of speaking or other markers of speech and by constructions normally associated with speaking. In such uses, a dedicated speech reporting expression is *recruited* for the expression of "inner speech" (Vygotsky 1987), and it is only the broader context that makes it clear that the words were thought rather than uttered.

Examples (1a-c) illustrate the recruitment of reported speech constructions for the expression of mental activity in Udihe, Wan, and Bashkir. We have chosen these examples because it is relatively uncontroversial, in context, that the reported thoughts were not spoken aloud or at least not intended to be heard by anyone around. In (1a), a character named Old Kanda is considering his chances against a competitor, planning an adversary act unbeknownst to the protagonist; the report is followed by a matrix clause with the verb *guŋ* 'say'. In (1b), the character is reflecting upon a troubling issue while staying on her own in the savannah; the report is introduced by a matrix clause with a morphologically defective verb *gé* 'say'. In (1c), the protagonist is preparing for a meeting with the local ruler; the report is followed by a general-purpose quotative verb (*ti*) and a full-fledged lexical verb *äjt* 'say'. In all these contexts, the reports are clearly meant to describe mental activity rather than acts of communication, but the constructions and the choice of verbs are typical of speech reports. In isolation, the examples would be interpreted as describing the characters' speech, and it is only due to contextual clues that the quoted portions (in brackets) are understood not to be uttered aloud.

(1) a. [*nii   baja-ni   wac'a   bihi-ni   baja-we-ni   kieu*
person   property-P.3   a.little   be-3sg   property-ACC-P.3   all
*zawa-zeŋe-i] Kand'a   mafa   **guŋ-ki-ni**   [Udihe; Tungusic]*
take-FUT-1SG Kanda   old.man   say-PST-3SG
'He has few things, I will take all the goods, - thought (= said) Old Kanda.'

b. *ɓé   è   gé   [dèŋbī   pɔ́   é   ɓā   gēē   wò*
then   3SG.SUBJ   say   remainder   thing   DEF   LOG   here+3SG   make
lé   sīēŋ́   yā   ɓé   zà   gó]   [Wan; Mande]
PROG   stick   with   that   matter   in
'And she thought (= said): As for why that thing does not leave me, it's because I keep hitting it with a stick.'

c. *nimä   ti-p   äjt-er-men   [nimä   ti-p   tanəš-tər-ər-mən]*
   what   QV-CV   say-CAUS-1SG   what   QV-CV   know-CAUS-POT-1SG
   ti-p   äjt-ä   inde   [Bashkir; Turkic]
   QV-CV   say-IPFV   FOC
   '"What would I say, how will I present myself?", – he thinks (= says).'

Not only are the examples clearly understood in context as encoding thought rather than speech, but the relevant verbs of speaking are also normally not ambiguous between speech and thought (for example, the verbs in 1a-c are not used in elicitation to translate expressions with reported thought). The phenomenon of recruiting reported speech expressions for expressing reported thought may be more difficult to assess for languages with systematic lexical ambiguity between 'say' and 'think' (as reported, for example, for a number of Australian languages; Spronck 2015, McGregor 2021).

Besides verbs of speaking, other speech-introducing elements can be used to introduce reported thought. In examples (2a-c) from Gizey, Bashkir, and Chuvash, thought is reported by means of a construction with a (non-verbal) quotative marker (in the case of Gizey) or by a highly grammaticalized quotative verb, without the support of a full-fledged lexical verb of speaking (in the case of Bashkir and Chuvash). The quotative marker always precedes the report in Gizey (2a), but follows it in Bashkir (2b). The two instances of the quotative verb in Chuvash (2c) illustrate the pattern of multiple marking of the same clause, widely attested with reported speech in some languages (such as Chuvash and Wan). Note also that example (2a) describes "mistaken belief"; such descriptions are particularly common among contexts favoring reported thought interpretations (see Introduction).

(2) a. *ʔàl   nàʔ   ʧĩl=ām   hān   vèt=tā   dùléj   ʧĩl=ām*
       QUOT   3SF   bite.PFV=3SM   DEM   hare=DEF   CNJ   bite.PFV=3SM
       hān   gɔ̄ɔ̄rī=nā   [Gizey; Chadic]
       DEM   stone=DEF
       'While she thought she bit the hare, it was instead the stone she bit.'
   b. *[quj   it-e-n   aša-j-əm]   **ti-p***   [Bashkir; Turkic]
       lamb   meat-P.3-ACC   eat-HORT-1SG   QV-CV
       'He thought (= said): I will eat the meat.'
   c. *[jomax   ɕi-n-tɕ-i]   **t-et***   *[asam-lə   starik*
       fairy.tale   top-P.3-LOC-NMLZ   say-CV   magic-PROPR   old.man
       *pol-ma-r-ë=și   ku]   **t-et***   [Chuvash; Turkic]
       be-NEG-PST-3   Q   say-CV
       'Isn't this magical old man, [he] thinks (= says), from a fairy tale? [he] thinks (= says).'

2 The morphosyntax of reported speech and reported thought: A preliminary survey — 21

Another illustration of universal flexibility in the interpretation of reported speech as reported thought comes from examples where the report is not introduced by anything. Across languages, speech reports appear in discourse without any overt matrix clause, especially in the context of vivid oral narration (cf. Spronck 2017 on "defenestration"). In examples (3a,b), from Ben Tey and Mwan, reports that are not introduced by any overt matrix clause are interpreted, in context, as expressing thought rather than speech: they are not addressed to anyone and not intended to be heard.

(3) a. ɔⁿhɔ́   í   dɔ́ɔ́-rɛ̀   dè   [Ben Tey; Dogon]
       INTJ   1SG   arrive-PFV when
       (thinking) 'Uhhuh, when I have arrived (there) <...>'
   b. sètrá̠   pēgéé   yāā   ùzù-né=mū   wlá-à
       Satan   and   3SG.POSS   spirit-DIM=PL   enter-PRS
       yéē   yrē   wéŋ   é   nɔ́ɔ̀   àmā-à   [Mwan; Mande]
       3SG   place   honest   ART   place   for.sure-Q
       (thinking) 'Has Satan and his spirits entered the holy place?'

In sum, we observe that all expression types available for the encoding of reported speech can also be used, in discourse, to encode reported thought, including secret thoughts that are clearly understood as unspoken. It is important to remember, however, that while in many cases the context helps distinguish speech from thought, some reports remain vague as to whether or not speaking was actually involved. Such is, for example, the report in (4), where the context provides no clue as to whether it represents a phrase the characters uttered while crying or rather describes their confused internal state that caused the crying.

(4) aṣṣë-pe   aməṣë   makər-sa   jol-tɕ-ë-ɕ   vot
    father.P.3-INSTR   mother.P.3 cry-CV.COORD remain-PST-3-PL   so
    xajxi-sker   mëlle   kom   pek   [Chuvash; Turkic]
    that-NMLZ   what.ADVBZ   this:OBL   like
    'The father and the mother remained, crying: Here, what, how come [it is] like that?'

The widespread flexibility in the interpretation of such examples suggests to us that the use of reported speech expressions for the encoding of characters' inner states is a matter of a universally available rhetorical strategy and should not depend much on the grammar of a particular language.

3 *Exclusive* thought-reporting strategies

This strategy is the opposite of the one discussed above, i.e. the opposite of *recruitment* of reported speech constructions for the expression of thought. Across languages, construction types are used to report mental activity that have no equivalent among expressions of reported speech. In fact, expressions of reported thought show an extraordinary degree of structural diversity, both within our sample languages and cross-linguistically.

In Wan, for example, all types of reported speech expressions can be recruited to express thought, but in addition, a number of structures are associated with thought reports that cannot be used to report speech. In (5a) the content of thinking is cross-referenced in the thought-introducing clause by an oblique argument: "their belly is on (it)". In (5b), it is cross-referenced by the subject: "it occurs to him that. . .". There are no equivalents to such expressions among those used to report speech.

(5) a. à̰má̰ŋ   kā   á   mì   mɔ̄ɔ̄   gōŋā   má   [Wan; Mande]
       3PL.INDP belly COP   side   LOG.PL:POSS hut+DEF   it.is
       'They thought the hut was for them.' (Literally, 'Their belly is on [it]: It is our hut.')
   b. è   wò   á   lὲŋ   dóō   ka̰   ŋ̀   gà   [Wan; Mande]
       3SG.SUBJ make RSLT to   QUOT   1PL.EXCL   PRF   go
       'She thought that we left.' (Literally, 'It happened to [her] that we left.')

In Chuvash, too, all expressions for reporting speech can be used to report thought, but additional construction types are attested exclusively with reported thought. The examples in (6a,b) illustrate the use of future participles with the noun for mental activity 'thought' (the noun is represented by two different dialectal variants, and it is marked for possession in one example but not in the other).

(6) a. akəş-ën   katɕtɕ-a   kaj-as   şokkəş   kër-se
       sister.P.3-GEN fiance-ACC/DAT   go-PC.FUT   thought   enter-CV.COORD
       kaj-at^j   [Chuvash; Turkic]
       go-PRS.3SG
       'The sister becomes possessed by the idea of getting married.' (Literally, 'His sister's thought of getting married enters [her].')

b. ɕij-as   šokəš-ë   te   ɕokkə   on-a   [Chuvash; Turkic]
   eat-PC.FUT thought-P.3 PRT EX.NEG 3SG.OBL-ACC/DAT
   'She is not even thinking of eating him.' (Literally, 'The thought of eating him does not even exist [to her].')

Summing up, we have seen that in representing reported thought, speakers can use expressions normally associated with reported speech, leaving it to the listener to figure out that the thought was never actually spoken (Section 2), or they can use expression types that have little or nothing in common with reported speech constructions, including nominal predicates with body part nouns ('head', 'belly', 'inside') or existential predicates with nouns for mental activity ('thought').

4 *Coercion* between speech and thought

4.1 Lexically specialized expressions

We now turn to a strategy that we believe explains some seemingly unmotivated properties of reported thought constructions in some of the languages. Like the recruitment strategy, it involves the use of the same morphosyntactic construction type as in speech reports, but the report is now *lexically specified* to represent thought rather than speech. This is commonly done through substitution of a verb of thinking for the verb of speaking (in languages that have such specialized verbs), but we will see that there are other strategies widely available across languages. Due to the substitution there is also no ambiguity as to whether the report represents speech or thought. We propose to treat such examples as instances of *speech-to-thought coercion*: in a construction normally associated with reported speech, a lexical element associated with thinking triggers a reported thought interpretation.

As commonly observed for other instances of coercion (Lauwers & Willems 2011), the examples form a continuum stretching from cases where the speech reporting construction easily accommodates the new reading, to cases of a serious mismatch between the construction's properties and the resulting interpretation. The coercion analysis, accordingly, may seem unnecessary for the former but proves essential for the latter.

In the simplest case of speech-to-thought coercion, coercion is triggered by a verb of thinking, substituted for the verb of speaking most commonly associated with the reporting construction. The resulting examples could be alternatively analyzed as involving a construction underspecified for a speech vs. thought interpretation, where the interpretation depends directly on the choice of the verb. In Udihe, for example, a number of different structures can introduce reported speech, and a mental activity verb can be substituted for the verb of speaking in all of them. Examples (7a-c) illustrate the most typical reported speech constructions, here featuring a verb of thinking. In (7a), the content of the report follows the matrix clause; in (7b), the same two parts occur in the reverse order; and (7c) is a typologically rare framing construction where exactly the same verb appears both before and after the report (this construction is used to report either speech or thought, cf. the example with reported speech in 8) (Perekhvalskaya 2020).

(7) a. zuu   b'ata-ziga   **meisi-li-he-ti**   [ebede   bi-mi   ono
       two   boy-PL   think-INC-PST-3PL   like.this be-GER how
       bagdi-za-fi   minti]   [Udihe; Tungusic]
       live-OPT-1PL 1PL.INCL
       'Two boys thought: Given how we are now, how will we live (in the future)?'

   b. [timanaŋi xeŋde-ze-mi   bi]   **meisi-he-ni**   zuktigi   ŋen-ie-ni
       tomorrow   go-OPT-1SG   1SG   think-PST-3SG   house-DIR   go-IMP-3SG
       'I will go tomorrow – he thought and went home.'

   c. jagdig'a   **meisi-he-ni**   [aziga-ŋi-i   mene   die-le-i
       hero   think-PST-3SG   girl-POSS-P.1   REFL   place.further-LOC-P.1
       ambugi-zeŋe-i]   **meisi-he-ni**
       put-FUT-1SG   think-PST-3SG
       'The guy thought: I shall put my daughter further from the fire – he thought.'

(8) jagdig'a   **xauntasi-hə-ni**   [aja   si   əmus'ə   bi-hi-jəu]   **xauntasi-hə-ni**
    hero   ask-PST-3SG   well   2SG   one   be-2SG-Q   ask-PST-3SG
    'The guy asked: Well, are you living alone? – he asked.'

An important question that the coercion analysis raises concerns the direction of coercion. In many examples, such as (7a-c), it is natural to assume that the construction is primarily associated with speaking but the use of a verb of thinking can trigger coercion to a reported thought interpretation. It is also theoretically possible that a construction specialized for reporting thought might be able to accommodate speech verbs, resulting in a coerced reported speech interpretation. Particularly promising in this respect are constructions that are disproportionately frequent with thought reports. In Chuvash, for example, combinations of a matrix clause with a report not followed by a quotative verb (9a) are overall rather rare (Nikitina et al. 2023), yet they are disproportionately frequent with verbs of thinking (9b).

(9) a. snatɕtɕët   Ivan   **kal-at**   kil-e   il-se
       it.means   Ivan   speak-PRS.3SG   home-ACC/DAT   take-CV.COORD
       kaj-ər   mën… mën   kirlë,   pötöm-pe   il-se
       go-IMP.2PL   what   what   needed   all-INSTR   take-CV.COORD
       kaj-ər   kil-e   [Chuvash; Turkic]
       go-IMP.2PL   home-ACC/DAT
       'That's it, Ivan says: Take [it] home, take home all you need…'
   b. nu   vot   ɕak   jəməkk-i   ëntë   **ɕot-l-at**ʲ
       well so   this   little.sister-P.3   PRT   thought-VBLZ.PRS.3SG
       mëlle   kaj-sa   kor-as=pətʲ   on-ta
       what.ADVBL   go-CV.COORD   see-PC.FUT=is.needed   3SG.OBL-LOC
       'And now, that little sister is already thinking how to reach there, to take a look [at how they live].'

Similarly, nominalized reports are disproportionately associated in Chuvash with reported thought, even though reported speech is also attested with nominalizations. In (10a), a future participle clause appears as a nominalized argument of the verb 'think', with the accusative/dative case marker. In (10b), a nominalization serves as an argument of the verb 'speak'. (The examples differ in the order of the two parts of the construction, but given the relatively free word order of Chuvash, this difference is irrelevant.)

(10) a. patşa   pol-ass-a   **ɕot-la-ma-n**
        tsar   be-PC.FUT-ACC/DAT   thought-VBLZ-NEG-PC.PST
        ta   [Chuvash; Turkic]
        PRT
        'We did not even think that you would become a tsar.'
    b. nu   **ɕar-la-maɕ**   xaj   völ   akkəşn-e
        well IDPH-VBLZ-NEG.PRS.3SG   that.one s/he   elder.sister.P.3-ACC/DAT
        ɕöl-n-in-e
        save-PC.PST-NMLZ-ACC/DAT
        'Well, he does not tell (= does not make noise), that one, that he had saved her sister.'

Such asymmetries in the distribution could correspond to the possibility of coercion from thought to speech but they could also be a result of competition between several reported speech constructions, some of which favor coercion to reported thought to a greater degree than others. Examples of constructions that are disproportionately associated with reported thought while also admitting verbs of speaking are in fact very rare in our data. We cannot address the question of directionality of coercion based on such limited evidence and we leave it to future studies.

The coercion strategy does not imply the use of specialized verbs of mental activity. The same interpretation can be triggered by lexical items other than verbs, such as nouns and adverbs. For example, in (11a), from Gizey, the verb is a general verb of speaking but a body part term is substituted for its normally agentive subject, to designate the internalized nature of "speaking". The most typical body parts referred to in such expressions are head, liver, heart, as well as abstract organs of cognition such as mind and soul. Another common strategy is modifying the speech verb by a locative adjunct, again to specify that "speaking" takes place inside one's mind or body, as in (11b) from Mwan.

(11) a. **nàm ʔàr=àm** d=ūm là nàm bùr gàŋgā
3SM eye-3SM tell.PFV=3SM QUOT2 3SM lie.IMP down
nɔ̄ lì=t gɛ̀ʼ [Gizey; Chadic]
DEM do.PFV=how Q
'He thought he should lie down.' (Literally, 'His mind/eye told him that why would he not lie down.')

b. mú yáá pē-lē **mā mú kpéé** yē
3PL.EMPH RETR say-GER surface 3PL in there
mɛ̄ɛ̄ é dèlè ɓé jà̰ é wó-zīí
person ART who 3SG word ART do-PROG
gèé [Mwan; Mande]
like.this
'People said inside themselves: Who is saying these words?'

Unlike the recruitment strategy discussed in Section 1, the coercion strategy is not universal. For example, it is not attested in Wan, where a verb of thinking cannot be substituted for the verb of speaking, and no other lexical coercion triggers are attested with reported speech constructions.

4.2 Addressee-related phenomena explained by coercion

A coercion analysis actually predicts some of the characteristics of reported thought that may otherwise seem puzzling. The coerced interpretation is at odds with the construction's formal properties, since situations of thinking and speaking differ in a number of linguistically relevant ways (see Teptiuk 2022, inter alia, for a recent discussion). The conflict between meaning and grammar sometimes results in seemingly inconsistent or superfluous expressions. To illustrate this point, we sketch here three types of phenomena related to the non-communicative nature of thinking. Such phenomena call for explanation, and an explanation is suggested by the coercion analysis: while lexically specified as referring to thinking, the examples inherit certain properties from expressions of reported speech on which they are modelled.

4.2.1 Addressee of the report appears in the report but not in the matrix clause

In language after language, we encounter examples of unambiguous thought reports referring to an imaginary addressee, by means of second person pronouns and address terms (12a,b).

(12) a. min **hine** šul šešqolaq-tar-ə-ndan höjrä-p <...> ti-p
1SG 2SG.ACC that ear-PL-P.3-ABL catch-CV QV-CV
ujla-γan ikän [Bashkir; Turkic]
think-PC.PST be.PC.PST
'And I will catch you by your ears <...> – that is what she was thinking.'
b. mën=ke=xa **es=ke** kom pek
what=PRT=PRT 2SG=PRT this:OBL like
şot-l-atʲ [Chuvash; Turkic]
thought-VBLZ-PRS.3SG
'How [come] you [are] like that? - he is thinking.'

In (12a,b), we have deliberately chosen examples that represent regular statements not addressed to anyone in the conventional sense of the term. The reports, in particular, do not feature imperatives; that is important because reported imperatives could perhaps be dismissed as part of a performative act intended to influence the behavior of an imaginary interlocutor. In (13), the verb of thinking is in the imperative (here, an unmarked form of the verb), and the report is addressed to a second person (as evidenced by a second person marker on the verb 'beat'), as if the character were addressing himself in the second person.

(13) mëlle ɕap-**an**=xa ëntë, **şot-la-sa**
what.ADVBZ beat-PRS.2SG=PRT PRT thought-VBLZ-CV.COORD
pəx=xa [Chuvash; Turkic]
look=PRT
'How will you beat [him], think [for yourself]!'

In example (14), we see an interesting combination of third person and second person reference. The remark comes from the bear who discovers that he has been cheated upon by the fox. The first clause refers to the fox in the third person, while the second clause – promising to find and kill her – is seemingly addressed to the fox (by that time long gone). The optative form of the verb is used within the speech report in the meaning of proximate future ('you will [soon] be killed by me').

(14) tukca site-ni sul'ai mine-we ebede camna-a-**ni**
hare child-3SG fox 1SG-ACC so cheat-PST-3SG
alide bagi-e min-du uu-ze-**hi** [Udihe; Tungusic]
somewhere live-PRS 1SG-DAT be.killed-OPT-2SG
'The bastard (literally, "child of a hare") fox has cheated me so. No matter where [you] live, you will be killed by me.'

Surprisingly, such examples never refer to the same addressee within the matrix clause, and such reference is in general not allowed. Characters are never described as "thinking *to*" hares or foxes, even though they refer to them freely as interlocutors in their thoughts. In Udihe, in particular, addressees are encoded by a directional case (more recently, under the influence of Russian, by the dative, Elena Perekhvalskaya pers. comm.). Neither directional nor dative arguments combine with verbs of mental activity (the topic of thinking – in expressions 'think *about* x' – is only very rarely expressed, and is marked by the accusative).

The restriction may seem trivial given that conceptually, thinking does not involve an interlocutor: unlike speaking, it is an inherently solitary activity. Yet we see clearly in the examples above that an interlocutor *can* be present, hence the restriction cannot be explained by considerations of conceptual nature. Neither can it be explained by peculiarities of the argument structure of verbs of thinking. It could be hypothesized, for example, that verbs of mental activity do not license an addressee for lexical reasons. That supposition, however, is not supported by the data: some languages allow the role of addressee to be encoded with verbs of thinking, yet require that addressee to be reflexive. If one can 'think to oneself' and at the same time refer to an addressee within the thought report, why should it not be possible to "think *to a fox*"?

Reference to addressees in thought reports illustrates a mismatch between the presence of a pragmatic role and the impossibility to express that role outside the report, with a verb of thinking. The coercion account explains this mismatch: second person reference is possible within the report because of the construction's association with the pragmatic role of addressee, inherited from speech reports. Since the verb of thinking is not associated with a semantic role of addressee, it does not allow the same referent to be encoded in the matrix clause introducing the report. As a result of the mismatch, the fictive interlocutor of a mental activity can be expressed as addressee within thought reports but not in matrix clauses that introduce them.

4.2.2 Superfluous arguments

A similar explanation accounts for cases of seemingly superfluous reference to an addressee in the matrix clause of coerced thought reports. While we do not have clear examples in our data, they are attested in well-studied languages in expressions such as English *think to oneself*. From a purely semantic point of view, the presence of an overt addressee in the matrix clause of a thought report is superfluous, since mental activity involves no addressee, and the addressee, if expressed, can only be co-referential with the subject. Such uses can be explained by a discrepancy between the construction's coerced interpretation and its retained "speech-like" morphosyntax.

By the same logic, locative adverbials may appear in thought reports to specify, superfluously, that the activity is taking place entirely in one's mind (head, heart, stomach…), rather than between two interlocutors. Locative expressions such as 'in one's head' and 'inside oneself' (15a,b) serve as substitutes for addressee phrases, and again, serve to reconcile the construction's argument properties (an implied addressee) with its coerced interpretation.

(15) a. **nàm   kāk   ɗʒè   ɗʒìbēr   j=ám-ū   ʔā là   hjɛ̄ɛ̄ɛ̄**
       3SM   sit.PFV POSS   think.IPFV   head=3SM-PPV QUOT1 INTJ
       sī=n   ɗʒèē-n   dè   ɬ=úm   līj=t
       person=ART.SM POSS-DEM   PROS   take.IPFV=3SM place=ART
       k=ɔ́m   mɛ̄j   nàm lí   dɔ̄w-n
       PREP=3SM   EMPHADD   3SM do.IPFV POSS-DEM
       lī=t   gē   [Gizey, Chadic]
       do.PFV=how   Q
       'He sat there, thinking in his head: Hey, this man is going to take all his land; what is he going to do?'
    b. *a   ko   a   yɛrɛ   kɔnɔ   a   fɔ   ne*
       3SG   QUOT   3SG REFL   inside 3SG say   1SG.EMPH
       na   to   fugari-ya   la   ka   n   teri-kɛ   to
       FUT   leave slacker-ABSTR PP INF 1SG friend-male   leave
       wara bolo   [Bambara, Mande]
       lion hand
       'He said inside himself: I will stay in doing nothing and I will leave my friend in the paws of a lion.'

4.2.3 Unusual interpretation of addressee marking

Our last example of unusual treatment of addressees that can be explained by coercion comes from Bambara (Vydrin et al. 2011–2018). With speech reports, the addressee argument of the verb *fɔ* 'say' can be introduced by two postpositions: *ye* and *ma*.

(16) a. cɛ   bɛ   a   fɔ   **muso**   **ma**   e   kelen   tɛ
man IPFV 3SG say woman   PP   2SG one   NEG
muso   *ye*   [Bambara; Mande]
woman   PP
'A man says to a woman: You are not the only woman here.'
b. sa   de   ye   a   fɔ   **muso**   **ye**   ko   <...>
snake FOC PFV.TR 3SG say woman   PP   QUOT
'The snake said this to a woman: ...'.

Since mental activity does not involve an addressee in the usual sense, we would not expect addressee-introducing postpositions to be found with the verb 'think' (or if they are, their arguments should be restricted to reflexive pronouns). In fact, however, the addressee-introducing postposition *ma* does appear with the verb *miiri* 'think', but on a very different reading: it is interpreted, in a rather exceptional way, as introducing the topic of thinking ('think about x'), i.e. the postposition is used to express an aboutness relation (17). The other addressee-introducing postposition, *ye*, does not seem to be allowed in the same role with mental activity verbs, as far as we can tell based on consultations with native speakers. This suggests that the two roles are distinct, and the fact that the two different interpretations are available with *ma* 'to, about' (depending on the verb) is likely due to a semantic change.

(17)   ni   i   ye   i   miiri   sanu   girinya
if   2SG PFV.TR REFL think   gold   weight
ma   [Bambara; Mande]
PP
'If you thought **about** the weight of gold...'

With the verb *fɔ* 'say', the topic of conversation is usually introduced by a different postposition, *la*, while the direct object (the third singular pronoun *a* in 18a) refers to what was actually said. The same postposition can introduce the topic of thinking but in that case no direct object is required (18b).

(18) a. dɔ=w   bɛ   a   fɔ   aw   la   ko: <...>
       some=PL IPFV 3SG   say   2PL   PP   QUOT
       'Some people say this about you: ....'
   b. n   bɛ   miiri   **matigi**   la
       1SG IPFV think   lord   PP
       'I think about God.'

The difference in the interpretation of Bambara postpositions with verbs of thinking and speaking is summarized in Table 2. The difference that is crucial for us concerns the interpretation of *ma*.

Table 2: Postpositions introducing addressees and topics in Bambara.

	ye	ma	la
miiri 'think'	n/a	topic of conversation ('about x')	
fɔ 'say'		addressee	topic of conversation ('about x')

Examples where the indirect object of 'think' is introduced by an addressee postposition, but interpreted as a topic of thinking, are exceptional from a language-internal point of view. They can be explained, on the other hand, if the presence of the postposition is treated as a "legacy" of constructions with a speech verb.

A similar phenomenon is reported by McGregor (2021) for an Australian language Warrwa, where the generic verb 'say, do, think' hosts an oblique pronominal marker that can cross-reference either the addressee of a speech event or the topic spoken about (see also Spronck 2015 on Ngarinyin). With expressions of reported thought, however, it can only cross-reference the topic, and corpus data suggests that such interpretation is dispreferred with reported speech. The fact that the same marking is available for the encoding of addressees and topics, and the two interpretations are unevenly distributed between readings involving speech and readings involving thinking suggests how the curious split in the interpretation of *ma* 'to, about' may have developed in Bambara.

4.3 Structural consequences of coercion

We have argued that the speech-to-thought coercion account sheds light on a number of phenomena involving unexpected behavior of addressees, superfluous use of reflexive addressees and locative adverbials, and unusual interpretations of addressee-encoding markers. Such phenomena have not, to the best of our knowledge, been previously discussed in typological literature, and we believe they should be treated together as instantiations of a general tendency.

The coercion account also helps reconcile existing evidence on the relationship between reported speech and reported thought. If the account is on the right track, we should expect speech-to-thought coercion strategies to result in slight differences between reported speech and reported thought with respect to a number of content-related phenomena. Mental activity differs from typical acts of communication in a number of ways other than the set of participants involved; for example, they tend to differ in aspectual characteristics and volitionality, and the content of thinking differs epistemologically from the content of speaking. Hence, the coerced expressions may show a reduced set of possibilities, as compared to reported speech, in the expression of categories such as tense-aspect-mood, evidentiality, factivity, as well as categories related to information structuring. A number of such phenomena are discussed in this volume (see the chapters by Remberger and Grzech).

One difference along these lines that we already mentioned concerns the weaker tendency to use quotative verbs in thought reports than in speech reports in Chuvash. The low-frequency construction without a quotative verb is strongly associated with thought reports, even though it is occasionally also attested with speech reports (ex. 9a vs. 9b). The distribution asymmetry is probably related to the fact that quotative verbs are grammaticalized from verbs of speaking, and as such are associated primarily with speech situations. Expressions of mental activity are not subject to the same constraints, or do not become subject to them at the same time as speech reports.

Our limited data does not allow us to perform a full-scale analysis of the suggested differences, but the case of overt reference to addressees suggests that they should be mostly of a statistical nature. Even though the role of addressee is absent from the argument structure of verbs of thinking, the coerced nature of the expression may lead speakers to refer overtly to an "addressee" of the mental activity. We believe that other conceptual differences between thinking and speaking, too, need not always be directly reflected in the behavior of the coerced constructions, and properties may emerge in such constructions that cannot be accounted for by the grammar of mental activity verbs alone.

Further differences, not discussed in this paper, may be related to the way expressions with verbs of speaking and verbs of thinking develop additional uses. Verbs of speaking, for example, regularly grammaticalize into specialized quotative markers and markers of intentionality (Güldemann 2008, Matić and Pakendorf 2013, inter alia), while expressions with verbs of thinking seem more likely to develop into epistemic markers (see Aimer 2005 for a literature review). When both types of expression give rise to discourse markers, they tend to be associated with rather different meanings (cf., for example, the difference between the responsibility-diminishing function of *I think* and the responsibility-enhancing effect of *I say* in English). Our approach allows for treating such diachronic asymmetries along with synchronic ones, without assuming too categorical a difference between reported speech and reported thought.

5 Conclusion

In our attempt at a constructional typology of reported thought expressions, we have reached the following tentative conclusions.

Reported speech and reported thought are intimately related, in a way that can be described by an *implicational statement*: constructions available in a given language for the expression of reported speech are also universally available for the expression of reported thought, but not vice versa. In other words, languages seem to allow their speakers to represent thought *as if it were* speech. Our subcorpora differ in the frequency of such representations, but these differences are likely a matter of rhetorical preference rather than grammar (for example, we note considerable variation among narratives by different speakers of the same language).

At the same time some languages have highly specialized constructions for encoding reported thought which cannot be used to encode reported speech or constructions that are derived from reported speech constructions. So overall, we have identified three strategies used by speakers in our data to report thought:

– Reported speech constructions are *recruited wholesale* for the expression of thought; this strategy is attested in all of our languages and may be universal.
– Languages use specialized reported thought constructions that have no equivalent among expressions of reported speech; this strategy of using *exclusive* morphosyntax is attested in all of our languages, and it may be universal.
– Reported speech and reported thought can be related through coercion: a construction normally associated with reported speech can change its interpretation in the presence of a lexical trigger (a verb of thinking, a body part term, an adverbial). This strategy is not universal, and the details of its use vary across languages (just like the lexical means used as the triggers also vary). We have evoked the theoretical possibility of coercing specialized reported thought constructions to a reported speech interpretation but we currently have no data that would allow us to explore it.

All languages in our sample use *more than one* morphosyntactic strategy to express reported thought, and some use all three. The co-existence of multiple strategies points, on the one hand, to a universal connection between the concepts of thinking and speaking, and on the other hand, to their universal distinguishability. In the same language, reported speech can either be represented as speech or encoded by very different morphosyntactic means; in addition, it can be represented as speech at the morphosyntactic level yet specified to describe "inner speech" by additional lexical means.

This complexity corresponds well with the heterogeneity of mental processes commonly subsumed under "thinking". Lexical studies often assume that expressions of mental activity belong to a universal semantic domain built around a cross-linguistically comparable core notion (Fortescue 1990; Goddard 2003, inter alia). Our constructional approach reveals considerable heterogeneity not only across languages, but also in the range of available options in a given language. This heterogeneity is perhaps not surprising given that "thinking" subsumes a variety of phenomena ranging from unintentional information processing to deliberate planning and organized problem solving, and some of these mental activities can be facilitated by strategic language use in the form of "self-talk" or private speech (Vygotsky 1934). It seems natural that languages offer their speakers a variety of tools for referring to different kinds of mental processes, in ways that sometimes conflate thought with speech and sometimes treat it in a radically different way. Future typologies will need to address the ways mental activities are categorized across languages and the ways such categorization corresponds to morphosyntactic expression.

These conclusions can only be regarded as tentative, however, due to the nature of our data. Our convenience sample is far from representative, both in terms of linguistic families and geographic areas. For example, as noted by a reviewer, the sample does not include languages from the Pacific, and a systematic study of such languages would be essential to testing our predictions because of their tendency to avoid reporting people's thoughts, due to the cultural belief in the "opacity of other minds" (Robbins & Rumsey 2008; Rumsey 2008, 2013). Would such languages still conform to our generalizations in the rare cases when speakers do report thoughts? We cannot answer this question, because we do not have comparable annotated data for languages of this type. We speculate, however, that even speakers of languages where reporting others' thoughts is avoided may still have at their disposal some thought reporting strategies analogous to the ones we explored in this paper.

For example, in Schieffelin (2007) the Papua New Guinean language Bosavi is described as lacking resources for reporting private thoughts, leading to innovation and calquing from Tok Pisin during Bible translation. Such resources are present, however, in traditional story genres where the reported thoughts belong to fictional characters; they were just not used in Bible translation because of their association with "genres of the past", which pastors sought to avoid (Schieffelin 2007: 150). The textual examples analyzed by Schieffelin, moreover, show that the expressions used to translate reports of private thoughts from Tok Pisin were ultimately very similar to the ones we find in our corpus: 'be thinking one's thoughts', 'be thinking in one's heart', and 'thoughts came'; translators are also reported often to hesitate between the verbs 'think' and 'say'.

Similarly, as discussed by Rumsey (2013), speakers of the Papua New Guinean language Ku Waru avoid attributing thoughts to others, but the language still provides them with resources to attribute thoughts to themselves (the examples analyzed by Rumsey involve a serial verb construction consisting of the verb *nyi-* 'say' and the verb *pilyi-* 'hear, sense'; this construction seems to be specialized for reporting thoughts as opposed to speech). And the tendency to report thoughts by means of expressions normally associated with reported speech is discussed, for Papuan languages, by Himmelmann & Riesberg (forthc.); these are the expressions that we suggest represent universal rhetorical strategies. These observations lead us to expect that our generalizations should hold across a more representative sample of languages, including languages from areas known for special cultural attitude to talking about other people's mind.

To conclude, the dual status of reported thought – the fact that it can be represented, within the same language, exactly like speech or much unlike speech – suggests that reported thought should not be treated as a cross-linguistic syntactic category in a way similar to reported speech (Spronck and Nikitina 2019). Conceptualization of thought processes varies across languages in ways that make direct comparison difficult, and we have not been able to pin down any formal universals pertaining to the morphosyntactic expression of reported thought. Our only universal claims describe the relationship of expressions of reported thought to expressions of reported speech, more specifically: thought reports are universally encoded in discourse as if they were speech reports (but not vice versa). We hope that further research into the grammar of thinking will shed more light on this relationship in a larger set of languages.

Abbreviations

ABL	ablative case
ABSTR	abstract noun
ACC	accusative case
ADVBL	adverbalizer
ART	article
CAUS	causative

CNJ	conjunction
COP	copula
CV	converb
COORD	coordinative
DAT	dative case
DEF	definite
DEM	demonstrative
DIM	diminutive
DIR	directional
EMPH	emphatic
EMPHADD	emphatic additive
EX.NEG	negative existential
FOC	focus
FUT	future
GEN	genitive
GER	gerund
HORT	hortative
IDPH	ideophone
IMP	imperative
INC	inchoative
INCL	inclusive
INDP	independent series of pronouns
INF	infinitive
INSTR	instrumental case
INTJ	interjection
IPFV	imperfective auxiliary
LOC	locative case
LOG	logophoric pronoun
NEG	negation
NMLZ	nominalization
OBL	oblique case
OPT	optative
P.1	possessive marker of first person
P.3	possessive marker of third person
PFV	perfective
PL	plural
POSS	possessive
POT	potential
PP	postposition
PPV	prepausal vowel
PREP	preposition
PRF	perfect
PROG	progressive
PROPR	property marker
PROS	prospective
PRS	present tense
PRT	particle

PST	past
Q	question
QUOT	quotative particle
QV	quotative verb
REFL	reflexive
RETR	retrospective
RSLT	resultative
SF	singular feminine
SG	singular
SM	singular masculine
SUBJ	subject pronoun
VBLZ	verbalization

References

Aijmer, Karin. 2014. Pragmatic markers. In Karin Aijmer & Christoph Rühlemann (eds.), *Corpus Pragmatics: A handbook*, 193–276. Cambridge: Cambridge University Press.

Aplonova, Ekaterina. 2021. A narrative corpus of Bashkir. In Tatiana Nikitina, Ekaterina Aplonova, Izabela Jordanoska, Ekaterina Biteeva, Abbie Hantgan-Sonko, Guillaume Guitang, Olga Kuznetsova, Elena Perekhvalskaya & Lacina Silué (eds.), *The SpeechReporting Corpus: Discourse Reporting in Storytelling*. CNRS-LLACAN & LACITO.

Chanard, Christian. 2015. ELAN-CorpA: Lexicon-aided annotation in ELAN. In Amina Mettouchi, Martine Vanhove & Dominique Caubet (eds.), *Corpus-based Studies of Lesser-described Languages: The CorpAfroAs Corpus of Spoken AfroAsiatic Languages*, 311–332. Amsterdam: John Benjamins.

Fortescue, Michael. 1990. Thoughts about thought. *Cognitive Linguistics* 12(1). 15–45.

Goddard, Cliff. 2003. Thinking across languages and cultures: six dimensions of variation. *Cognitive Linguistics* 14(2–3). 109–140.

Goddard, Cliff & Anna Wierzbicka. 2019. Reported speech as a pivotal human phenomenon: Commentary on Spronck and Nikitina. *Linguistic Typology* 23(1). 167–175.

Güldemann, Tom. 2008. *Quotative Indexes in African Languages: A Synchronic and Diachronic Survey*. Berlin: Mouton de Gruyter.

Guitang, Guillaume 2022. A narrative corpus of Gizey. In Tatiana Nikitina, Ekaterina Aplonova, Izabela Jordanoska, Ekaterina Biteeva, Abbie Hantgan-Sonko, Guillaume Guitang, Olga Kuznetsova, Elena Perekhvalskaya & Lacina Silué (eds.), *The SpeechReporting Corpus: Discourse Reporting in Storytelling*. CNRS-LLACAN & LACITO.

Hangtan-Sonko, Abbie. in prep. A narrative corpus of Dogon Ben Tey. In Tatiana Nikitina, Ekaterina Aplonova, Izabela Jordanoska, Ekaterina Biteeva, Abbie Hantgan-Sonko, Guillaume Guitang, Olga Kuznetsova, Elena Perekhvalskaya & Lacina Silué (eds.), *The SpeechReporting Corpus: Discourse Reporting in Storytelling*. CNRS-LLACAN & LACITO.

Hangtan-Sonko, Abbie. 2021. A narrative corpus of Jóola Eegimaa. In Tatiana Nikitina, Ekaterina Aplonova, Izabela Jordanoska, Ekaterina Biteeva, Abbie Hantgan-Sonko, Guillaume Guitang, Olga Kuznetsova, Elena Perekhvalskaya & Lacina Silué (eds.), *The SpeechReporting Corpus: Discourse Reporting in Storytelling*. CNRS-LLACAN & LACITO.

Lauwers, Peter & Dominique Willems. 2011. Coercion: Definitions and challenges, current approaches, and new trends. *Linguistics* 49(6). 1219–1235.

Matić, Dejan & Brigitte Pakendorf. 2013. Non-Canonical SAY in Siberia: Areal and genealogical patterns. *Studies in Language* 37. 356–412.

McGregor, William B. 2021. Thought complements in Australian languages. *Language Sciences* 86. 101398.

Nikitina, Tatiana, Abbie Hantgan and Christian Chanard. 2019. *Reported speech annotation template for ELAN (The SpeechReporting Corpus).* Villejuif-Paris: LLACAN.

Nikitina, Tatiana. 2022. A corpus of traditional stories in Chuvash. In Tatiana Nikitina, Ekaterina Aplonova, Izabela Jordanoska, Ekaterina Biteeva, Abbie Hantgan-Sonko, Guillaume Guitang, Olga Kuznetsova, Elena Perekhvalskaya & Lacina Silué (eds.), *The SpeechReporting Corpus: Discourse Reporting in Storytelling.* CNRS-LLACAN & LACITO.

Nikitina, Tatiana, Ekaterina Aplonova & Leonardo Contreras Roa. 2023. The use of interjections as a discourse phenomenon: A contrastive study of Chuvash (Turkic) and Wan (Mande). In Alessandra Barotto & Simone Mattiola (eds.), Discourse Phenomena in Typological Perspective, 65–89. Amsterdam: John Benjamins.

Nikitina, Tatiana. In prep. A corpus of Wan. In Tatiana Nikitina, Ekaterina Aplonova, Izabela Jordanoska, Ekaterina Biteeva, Abbie Hantgan-Sonko, Guillaume Guitang, Olga Kuznetsova, Elena Perekhvalskaya & Lacina Silué (eds.), *The SpeechReporting Corpus: Discourse Reporting in Storytelling.* CNRS-LLACAN & LACITO.

Nikitina, Tatiana, Ekaterina Aplonova, Izabela Jordanoska, Ekaterina Biteeva, Abbie Hantgan-Sonko, Guillaume Guitang, Olga Kuznetsova, Elena Perekhvalskaya & Lacina Silué (eds.). 2022. *The SpeechReporting Corpus: Discourse Reporting in Storytelling.* Villejuif-Paris: CNRS-LLACAN & LACITO. Available at http://discoursereporting.huma-num.fr/index.html

Nikitina, Tatiana & Anna Bugaeva. 2021. Logophoric speech is not indirect: Towards a syntactic approach to reported speech constructions. *Linguistics* 59(3). 609–633.

Nikitina, Tatiana & Alexandra Vydrina. 2020. Reported speech in Kakabe: Loose syntax with flexible indexicality. *Folia Linguistica* 54(1). 133–166.

Onishi, Masayuki. 1997. The grammar of mental predicates in Japanese. *Language Sciences* 19(3). 219–233.

Perekhvalskaya, Elena. 2020. Reportativnaja reč v udegejskom jazyke i shire. [Reported speech in Udihe and beyond]. *Voprosy Jazykoznanija* 2020(1). 84–103.

Perekhvalskaya, Elena. 2021. *A narrative corpus of Udihe.* In Tatiana Nikitina, Ekaterina Aplonova, Izabela Jordanoska, Ekaterina Biteeva, Abbie Hantgan-Sonko, Guillaume Guitang, Olga Kuznetsova, Elena Perekhvalskaya & Lacina Silué (eds.), *The SpeechReporting Corpus: Discourse Reporting in Storytelling.* CNRS-LLACAN & LACITO.

Perekhvalskaya, Elena. In prep. A narrative corpus of Mwan. In Tatiana Nikitina, Ekaterina Aplonova, Izabela Jordanoska, Ekaterina Biteeva, Abbie Hantgan-Sonko, Guillaume Guitang, Olga Kuznetsova, Elena Perekhvalskaya & Lacina Silué (eds.), *The SpeechReporting Corpus: Discourse Reporting in Storytelling.* CNRS-LLACAN & LACITO.

Persson, Gunnar. 1993. Think in a panchronic perspective. *Studia Neophilologica* 65(1). 3–18.

Robbins, Joel & Alan Rumsey. 2008. Introduction: Cultural and linguistic anthropology and the opacity of other minds. *Anthropological Quarterly* 81(2). 407–420.

Rumsey, Alan. 2008. Confession, anger and cross-cultural articulation in Papua New Guinea. *Anthropological Quarterly* 81. 455–472.

Rumsey, Alan. 2013. Intersubjectivity, deception and the 'opacity of other minds': Perspectives from Highland New Guinea and beyond. *Language & Communication* 33(3). 326–343.

Schieffelin, Bambi B. 2007. Found in translating: reflexive language across time and texts. In Miki Makihara & Bambi B. Schieffelin (eds.) *Consequences of Contact: Language ideologies and sociocultural transformations in Pacific societies*, 140–165. New York: Oxford University Press.

Spronck, Stef. 2015. *Reported speech in Ungarinyin: Grammar and social cognition in a language of the Kimberley region, Western Australia*. Doctoral dissertation, Australian National University.

Spronck, Stef. 2017. Defenestration: deconstructing the frame-in relation in Ungarinyin. *Journal of Pragmatics* 114. 104–133.

Spronck, Stef & Daniela Casartelli. 2021. In a manner of speaking: How reported speech may have shaped grammar. *Frontiers in Communication* 6. 624486.

Spronck, Stef & Tatiana Nikitina. 2019. Reported speech forms a dedicated syntactic domain: Typological arguments and observations. *Linguistic Typology* 23(1). 119–159.

Stanwood, Ryo. 1997. The primitive syntax of mental predicates in Hawaii Creole English: A text-based study. *Language Sciences* 19(3). 209–217.

Teptiuk, Denys. 2022. Person alignment in reported speech and thought: The distribution and typology of participant roles (based on six Finno-Ugric languages). *Linguistic Typology at the Crossroads* 2(2). 39–92.

Viberg, Åke. 2004. The lexical typological profile of Swedish mental verbs. *Languages in contrast* 5(1). 121–157.

Vydrin, Valentin, Kirill Maslinsky, Jean Jacques Méric & Andrij Rovenchak. 2011–2018. Corpus Bambara de Référence. http://cormand.huma-num.fr/

Vygotsky, L. S. [1934] 1987. Thinking and speech. In Robert W. Rieber & Aaron S. Carton (eds.), *The Collected Works of Lev Vygotsky*, Vol. 1, 39–285. New York: Plenum Press. (Originaly published in 1934).

Eva-Maria Remberger

3 To want, to think, to say: The development of WANT in German from volitional to reportative modal

Abstract: In this paper, I claim that the development of WANT in German from a volitional modal verb to a reportative modal is multidimensional, requiring discussion on all grammatical levels, including pragmatics. I first discuss the properties of some propositional attitude verbs such as THINK and BELIEVE, SAY and WANT. I then describe the main grammatical properties of volitional and reportative WANT-constructions in German, at the levels of both semantics and morphosyntax. Particular attention is then paid to two dimensions of pragmatics, at-issueness and eventiveness. I apply some tests proposed in the literature to the reportative modal WANT, which in German clearly encodes a not-at-issue and non-eventive reportative component. Finally, I sketch a grammaticalisation as well as pragmaticalisation path for reportative WANT. The most important finding is that in WANT-constructions a doxastic conversational background is present, connected to volitional modality (sitting in the appropriate functional category). This doxastic conversational background then takes over and leads, in the final step, to a reportative evidential interpretation.

1 Introduction: Speech and thought reporting

In this paper, I will explore one aspect of the complex relationship between (reported) thought and speech, namely the development of a verb encoding volition into a verb encoding a saying component. I will claim that this development is mediated by a thought or belief component, which then results in an interpretation as an externalised thought component in the form of reportative evidentiality. The particular construction discussed here is given in (1), where the German volitional verb WANT,[1] *wollen*, grammaticalises to a reportative modal:

(1) Ein Zeuge will ihn gesehen haben.
 a witness wants him seen have
 'A witness says/claims that he has seen him.'

---

[1] I use small caps to refer to the prototypical verb as present in many languages.

Here, WANT acts as a second-hand evidential reportative modal, and the source of the information encoded in the proposition 'A witness has seen him' is identified by the syntactic subject of WANT, i.e. the witness herself. Since WANT acts as a kind of subject control verb here,[2] the subject of WANT is coreferential with the subject of the proposition encoded in the infinitive.[3] In what follows, I will translate this kind of reportative meaning sometimes by 'self-reportedly', sometimes by 'x claims'. A parallel development is found with the German modal *sollen* (roughly 'shall') but in this construction, unlike with reportative WANT, the source of the reported information remains unknown ("third-hand evidence (hearsay)", cf. Willett 1988).[4]

As above, I will claim that the intermediate step in the development of WANT from a verb encoding intention or volition to a verb encoding a saying report is its interpretation as a thought or belief report.[5] This brings us to the distinction between inner and outer speech. In Sauerland and Alexiadou (2020) it is claimed that in speech production "thought structure is generated first; the thought structure is then realised using language to communicate the thought, to memorise it, or perhaps with other purpose".[6] Sauerland (2020) says that "inner speech should not be viewed solely as an internalization of outer speech". However, although propositional thought is not the same as inner speech, as thoughts are not sentences,[7] "(re-)internalized" speech might serve to support to memorisation. At this point propositional attitude verbs, i.e. cognitive verbs, like KNOW, THINK and BELIEVE, and *verba dicendi*, like SAY, come into play, and these will often be used as a point of comparison in this paper. Of course, there are also some fundamental differences between cognitive verbs and *verba dicendi*, since the latter usually refer to a speech act including its utterance context, whereas something like a "thought act" is far

---

2 In German, the external subject of the embedded infinitive is coreferential with the subject of volitional WANT. However, the analysis of WANT as a reportative modal seems to involve a kind of restructuring or reanalysis (cf. Section 5), such that we may no longer call it a control verb in the canonical sense.

3 With the reportative meaning, it is impossible for WANT to have a finite complement clause, cf. (4b), below.

4 Note that in evidential systems, as in the categorisation proposed by Willett (1988), there is also the evidential category of "folklore" or "common knowledge"; this evidential marking is often found in fairy tales or similar productions of oral history. German *sollen* cannot be used with this evidential interpretation, since it clearly encodes that there is a source for the proposition ('somebody says'), whereas this is not the case with the text types just mentioned, where the evidential meaning is more like 'it is commonly transmitted oral knowledge'.

5 Note, however, that the report is not-at-issue and non-eventive, cf. Section 4.

6 Cf. also Sauerland & Alexiadou (2020): "We view the relationship between the thought structure and the corresponding signal as one of compression."

7 Cf. also Lobina (2020): "Linguistic production, either inner or outer speech, may not *ipso facto* be an act of thinking but instead simply constitute a reflection of it."

less tangible.[8] I will leave the general discussion aside at this point and concentrate on the particular phenomenon exemplified in (1).

This paper is structured as follows: In Section 2, the behaviour of propositional attitude verbs is compared with the use of German WANT. Section 3 discusses the grammar of volitional and reportative WANT at the semantic and morphosyntactic level. Section 4 is dedicated to the pragmatic properties of the reportative modal WANT in German; it will be shown that, as proposed by Bary and Maier (2021) for reportative evidentials, reportative WANT encodes a saying report that is not-at-issue and non-eventive. In Section 5, I summarise the grammaticalisation process of reportative WANT at all levels of grammar, including the pragmatic level, i.e. its pragmaticalisation. In this section, the claim that there is an intermediate step involving a doxastic modal base is derived from the semantic, morphosyntactic, and pragmatic properties of the construction discussed in Section 3 and 4. This development, roughly representing a pathway from WANT to SAY via THINK, gives this paper its title.[9]

2 Propositional attitude verbs

Propositional attitude verbs are characterised by differences in syntactic behaviour and semantic properties, which are also subject to remarkable crosslinguistic variation.[10] The propositional attitude verb SAY features in several constructions, all of which involve a saying report. For reported speech, and to a lesser extent for reported thought, several typologies have been proposed (e.g. Keizer 2009, Mortara

---

[8] But see Schlenker (2004: 279) for an interesting approach, where he separates the *Context of Speech* into two separate branches, i.e. the *Context of Thought* and the *Context of Utterance*. Whereas the *Context of Utterance* includes speaker, hearer, time of utterance and world of utterance, his *Context of Thought* includes a thinker, a time of thought and a world of thought. This separation allows him to distinguish between a *here* of expression and a *here* of intention (Schlenker 2004: 279), necessary for the interpretation of indexicals in free indirect discourse, on the one hand, and the historical present, on the other.
[9] Note that, although this work often refers to insights from formal semantics and pragmatics, the aim is to provide a general view of the grammaticalisation of the German reportative modal WANT in the sense of an interplay of several modules of grammar rather than offering a new semantic formalisation proper.
[10] Cf. e.g. White et al. (2018), in particular Section 2, where some crosslinguistic tendencies for these verbs are observed, but mainly only on the basis of English examples. In their semantic distinction, THINK and SAY are "representational nonfactives", whereas WANT is a "preferential nonfactive" (421). Note, however, that there are several fundamental differences between English and German in this group of verbs, particularly at the morphosyntactic level.

Garavelli 1995, Cappelen and Lepore 2012).[11] Some of these are illustrated in (2), namely direct speech (2a), indirect speech (2b), a parenthetically expressed saying event (2c), and an assertion marked by a reportative evidential adverb (derived from a verb of saying in the case of *reportedly*, (2d)):

(2) a. John says: "I haven't seen my sister for years."
    b. John says that he hasn't seen his sister for years.
    c. He hasn't seen his sister for years, John says.
    d. Allegedly/reportedly, John hasn't seen his sister for years.

Similar types can be observed for thinking reports (cf. 3):

(3) a. John thinks: "I haven't seen my sister for years."
    b. John thinks that he hasn't seen his sister for years.
    c. He hasn't seen his sister for years, John thinks.
    d. As far as he thinks, John hasn't seen his sister for years.

The behaviour of reportative WANT constructions differs in several respects (cf. 4); in particular, they do not seem to comply with the syntactic structure of speech and thought reports, e.g. there is no such thing as a "direct want report" (cf. 4a):

(4) a. *Hans will: "Ich habe meine Schwester seit Jahren
       H.   wants   I   have   my   sister   for   years
       nicht gesehen."
       not   seen
       'Hans hasn't seen his sister for years, he claims.'
    b. Hans will, dass er seine Schwester nicht mehr sieht.
       H.   wants that he his   sister   not   more sees
       'Hans wants (it so) that he doesn't see his sister anymore.'
    c. *Er hat seine Schwester seit Jahren nicht gesehen,
       he has his   sister   for years not   seen
       will Hans.
       wants H.

Direct discourse is not allowed with WANT (4a), nor is indirect discourse: A sentence like (4b) is grammatical, but has a clear volitional interpretation. WANT is

---

[11] For sake of simplicity, the examples for THINK and SAY in (2) and (3) will be in English, and only the later examples will be in German.

also not allowed in a parenthetical position, even with a volitional interpretation (4c).[12] WANT, however, can be used as a volitional control verb (cf. 5a). It is in this context, i.e. with an embedded infinitive, that the interpretation as a reportative modal arises (cf. 5b).

(5) a. Er   will   seine Schwester seit Jahren nicht mehr sehen.
       he   wants   his   sister   for years not   more see
       'He doesn't want to see his sister for years.'
   b. Er   will   seine Schwester seit Jahren nicht mehr gesehen
       he   wants   his   sister   for years not   more seen
       haben.
       have
       'Hans, self-reportedly, hasn't seen his sister for years.'

However, BELIEVE, THINK and SAY can embed infinitive clauses and act as control verbs. The difference between these and WANT-constructions is that the latter have a bare infinitive (cf. 6a) while in the former the infinitive is introduced by *zu* 'to' (cf. 6b-d).

(6) a. Peter will   Maria gesehen haben.
       P.   wants   M.   seen   have
       'Peter claims to have seen Maria.'
   b. Peter glaubt, Maria gesehen zu haben.
       P.   believes M.   seen   to have
       'Peter believes that he saw Maria.'
   c. Peter denkt,   Maria gesehen zu haben.
       P.   thinks   M.   seen   to have
       'Peter thinks that he saw Maria.'
   d. Peter sagt,   Maria gesehen zu haben.
       P.   says   M.   seen   to have
       'Peter says that he saw Maria.'

Another interesting aspect is the use of SAY, THINK and BELIEVE as bridge verbs (7a-c), which is impossible with WANT (7d); furthermore, in German (unlike in other languages), WANT cannot embed a clause in the subjunctive (see also (4b), where

---

12 Not even if the non-parenthetical part is in a simultaneous or posteriority relation to WANT, cf. (i):

(i) *Er   sieht seine Schwester nie   wieder, will   Hans.
      he   sees   his   sister   never again   wants H.

volitional WANT would not allow the subjunctive),[13] whether as a volitional or as a reportative modal, whereas the subjunctive is allowed and even preferred with THINK and BELIEVE:

(7) a. Hans sagt, er hat/habe seine Schwester seit
       H.   says he has/has$_{SUBJ}$ his sister for
       Jahren nicht gesehen.
       years not   seen
       'Hans says he hasn't seen his sister for years.'
    b. Hans denkt, er habe/?hat seine Schwester seit
       H.   thinks he has$_{SUBJ}$/has his sister for
       Jahren nicht gesehen.
       years not   seen
       'Hans thinks he hasn't seen his sister for years.'
    c. Hans glaubt, er habe/?hat seine Schwester seit
       H.   believes he has$_{SUBJ}$/has his sister for
       Jahren nicht gesehen.
       years not   seen
       'Hans believes he hasn't seen his sister for years.'
    d. *Hans will, er hat/habe seine Schwester seit
       H.   wants he has/has$_{SUBJ}$ his sister for
       Jahren nicht gesehen.
       years not   seen
    e. Hans will, dass die Welt gerettet wird
       H.   wants that the world saved become
       /*?werde.
       become$_{SUBJ}$
       'Hans wants the world to be saved.'

There are additional peculiarities in the semantics of SAY and cognitive verbs like THINK and BELIEVE. Brasoveanu and Farkas (2007) have shown that cognitive verbs are better interpreted with the help of a function that is proposition-based rather than world-based.[14] That means that a function *dox(x,w)* "associates a set of propositions to a sentient individual x in w, namely the propositions x takes as true of w." This gives us a doxastic modal base, which is individually anchored (for the *individual anchor*, cf. Farkas 1992) to the external argument (i.e. the subject) of

---

[13] It might embed the subjunctive in a highly archaic register.
[14] Or "content-based", cf. Kratzer (2016).

the cognitive verb. Brasoveanu and Farkas (2007) then show that saying reports are more complex than believe reports: Saying reports require a "faithfulness of meaning dimension", since they refer to a "source speech act", which is an event with an author and a context, including presuppositions, implicatures and a particular linguistic form. Thus, faithfulness must not only be given to the at-issue content of the assertion, but also to the non-literal content. The source speech act contains a complex linguistic expression, which is not a single "single proposition $S_{at\text{-}issue}$, but in turn has a form S_{form} (necessary to account for quotation) and a multidimensional content <S_{presup}, $S_{at\text{-}issue}$, S_{implic}>; the pair <$S_{at\text{-}issue}$, S_{implic}> constitutes the assertive change of the speech act" (Brasoveanu and Farkas 2007: 13). In conclusion, what is reflected by the formalisation for SAY given by Brasoveanu and Farkas (2007) is the fact that SAY does not embed just propositional content, but includes an utterance context of a source speech act that contains this content.[15]

This observation, at first sight, recalls Jakobson's well-known characterisation of evidentiality as encoding three events:[16]

> En/Ens/Es) EVIDENTIAL is a tentative label for the verbal category which takes into account three events – a narrated event, a speech event, and a narrated speech event (Ens), namely the alleged source of information about the narrated event. The speaker reports an event on the basis of someone else's report (quotative, i.e. hearsay evidence), of a dream (revelative evidence), of a guess (presumptive evidence) or of his own previous experience (memory evidence). (Jakobson 1971 [1957]:135)

However, there is a huge difference between evidential marking and the report of a speech act proper; as will be shown (cf. Section 4), the notion of "event" is not appropriate for reportative evidentiality or hearsay marking. Evidential marking does not contain a speech act event that can be referred to. The evidentially marked proposition, and thus also the proposition embedded by reportative WANT, is not complex in the sense of Brasoveanu and Farkas (2007). However, while there is no utterance context, since there is no speech act event, constructions with reportative WANT still include the author of the source of information (i.e. the syntactic subject of WANT). We will look more closely at the grammar of volitional and reportative WANT in the next section.

---

[15] The propositional content is contextualised in an embedded utterance context, which offers the possibility of introducing second level conversational backgrounds.
[16] En = narrated event; Ens = narrated speech event; Es = speech event.

3 The grammar of volitional and reportative WANT

With regard to the semantics of WANT, I will follow, at least in principle, the classical approach to modals proposed by Kratzer (Section 3.1); however, I will not offer further discussion of possible worlds semantics or of any other particular formal semantic theories. Instead, I will use the time-relational approach introduced by Reichenbach (1947) and further extended by Vikner (1987) among others (cf. also Klein 1994, Giorgi and Pianesi 1997, Demirdache & Uribe-Etxebarria 2000), combined with modal semantics (cf. Section 3.1). In morphological terms, the inventory of verbal forms for reportative WANT is reduced (cf. Section 3.2). A cartographic approach, in particular Cinque (1999), will briefly be referred to (cf. Section 3.2) in the discussion of the syntactic positions of the different interpretations of WANT.

3.1 The semantic level

The semantic ingredients of modality, following the classical account by Kratzer (1977, 1981, 1991) and others are 1) the modal relation (necessity or possibility); 2) a (possibly empty) modal base and further ordering sources; 3) the source of modality; 4) the goal of modality. Note that modal bases and ordering sources are constituted by different types or partitions of conversational backgrounds (cf. Kratzer 1991), so I will often refer to conversational backgrounds if the distinction between modal base and ordering source is not required. In what follows, these components will be described in more detail for the volitional verb WANT (see also Remberger 2010, 2011, for an earlier approach to WANT).

The modal relation encoded in WANT is necessity, which becomes particularly clear at the diachronic level (see e.g. the origin of Engl. *want*) and in cases where volitionality, i.e. necessity anchored to a sentient individual, is lost (e.g. in deontic existentials, cf. Remberger 2013). The modal base or conversational background, against which the modal expression is evaluated, has been the topic of some debate. It has been noted in the literature (Heim 1992, von Fintel 1999) that desire reports differ from belief reports in that there is a volitional or bouletic conversational background ('that what is wanted, desired, preferred in w'), which serves as an ordering relation for a doxastic model base, or, as Hacquardt (2006) puts it, a model of 'the subject's belief'. This assumption comes from the idea (see in particular Heim 1992)[17] that what is wanted by the subject should be based on her beliefs, i.e.,

---

[17] Cf. Heim (1992: 202): "*Want*-sentences are felicitous in contexts where it has already been established that the subject believes the presuppositions of its complement. [...] *want*-sentences are

as Giorgi and Pianesi (1997: 266, fn. 24) put it, that besides the volitional-intentional semantics of WANT, "a verb such as *want* requires the subject to believe it possible for the embedded proposition to become true". On the other hand, not everything in the subject's beliefs is also wanted, i.e. both conversational backgrounds are not, or not necessarily, in an overlapping relation. A bouletic ordering imposed on a doxastic modal base has the effect that the set of worlds or situations of the modal base (belief worlds) in which the proposition in the infinitival clause is true are more desirable than the set of worlds or situations in which the proposition in the infinitival clause is false.[18]

Giannakidou (2007) simply assumes an epistemic modal base for WANT. In Remberger (2011: 21), I assumed that for WANT there are two conversational backgrounds, a bouletic conversational background and an epistemic (knowledge-based), or, preferably, doxastic (belief- or thought-based, cf. *dox(x,p)* by Brasoveanu and Farkas 2007 mentioned in Section 2) conversational background. While the bouletic conversational background, which serves as an ordering source (following Kratzer 1991: 648) or provides "the ranking of possible worlds in terms of desirability" (following Heim 1992: 197), it is this doxastic modal base that will be relevant for the development of German WANT into a reportative modal.[19]

A particular feature of WANT is that it has an argument structure that includes a theta role for an animate, intentional, sentient external argument.[20] This argument position is not implicit, as Kratzer (1991) claims arguments in root modals would be, but syntactically explicit. This means that the doxastic modal base and the bouletic ordering source are both anchored not to the speaker, but to the subject of the modal. The subject of WANT represents the individual anchor connected to the modal meaning and is thus the source of modality (it is for x that it is necessary that p, considering what x believes or thinks and what would be preferable).

Finally, the goal of modality is the scope proposition of WANT, i.e. the proposition encoded in the complement clause, which is anchored to the matrix clause encoded by WANT. Note that modality in general includes a "non-anteriority restriction" (cf. Quer 1998: 50), i.e. the scope proposition of WANT can only be simul-

---

interpreted with respect to a doxastic modal base: to want Φ means to find the Φ-worlds among those worlds compatible with one's beliefs more desirable than comparable non-Φ-worlds compatible with one's beliefs."
18 At this point I would like to thank an anonymous reviewer for his or her clarifying observations on ordering relations/ordering sources, a point that in a former version of this paper was confused.
19 According to Kratzer (1991: 648), the modal base in this case is not epistemic (nor doxastic), but circumstantial "('in view of the relevant facts')".
20 For several proposals on the nature of this theta role in the literature, see the overview in Remberger (2010: 167, fn. 17).

taneously anchored to the matrix reference time or be in a relation of posteriority. Note also that an epistemic or doxastic modal base must in any case be coindexed with the modal evaluation time.

3.2 The morphosyntactic level

The verbal form of evidential WANT can encode only simple tenses, i.e. only one time relation T1 in the sense of Vikner (1987) can be expressed. Note that a combination of two complex times in WANT-constructions is in principle possible for volitional WANT, but often not very natural (cf. (8); see also (12) and (30) further below for the modal MÜSSEN 'must'). An embedded simple infinitive makes the interpretation ambiguous, cf. (9). Nevertheless, an example like (10) can only have a canonical volitional meaning;[21] the evidential interpretation does not arise:[22,23]

(8) Hans hätte gestern angekommen sein wollen.
 H. had yesterday arrived be want
 'H. would have wanted to have arrived.'

(9) Peter will krank sein.
 P. wants ill be
 'Peter, self-reportedly, is ill.'
 'Peter wants to be ill.'

---

21 Note that the same is true for passive constructions where only the volitional reading is available in German.
22 You might note that all examples provided in this paper are in the third person singular. However, other persons are possible, in principle, although the appropriate contexts must be created. Third person (singular and plural) is by far the most common person for evidential *want*-constructions in German. Nevertheless, second and even first person examples might be found, cf. (i), and (ii):

(i) Ach ja, und ich will ihn nicht gesehen haben?
 oh yes and I want him not seen have
 'What do you say, that I claim not to have seen him?'

(ii) Du willst ihn ja nicht gesehen haben!
 you want him yes not seen have
 'It's you who claims not to have seen him.'

23 Note that this is not the participle *gewollt*, but the *infinitivo pro participio* form (*Ersatzinfinitiv*), particular to German modal verbs. The same is true in (10), and, for *müssen* instead of *gemusst*, in (12) and (30).

(10) Peter hat krank sein wollen.
     P.   has ill   be   want
     *'Peter, self-reportedly, was ill.'
     'Peter wanted to be ill.'

Furthermore, negation clearly refers to the proposition encoding the event in the infinitive, i.e. the saying component encoded in the reportative modal cannot be negated (whereas with volitional WANT the "volitional act" can be negated):[24]

(11) Peter will   ihn nicht gesehen haben.
     P.   wants him not   seen   have
     'Peter, self-reportedly, hasn't seen him./Peter claims not to have seen him.'
     *'Peter doesn't claim to have seen him.'

This is an important difference compared to the epistemic uses of MUST and CAN, where negation is usually interpreted as belonging to the embedded clause, but can in principle also be interpreted as a negation of the modal's necessity or possibility.[25] This difference between reportative WANT and epistemic modals in German is probably due to the presence of the subject of WANT as an individual anchor for the evaluation of the modal; another possible explanation is that the reportative component does not allow negation – in fact there is no such thing as "negative evidentiality" in the sense that a source of information for the assertion is negated – whereas modality comes in duals (cf. Kratzer 1991) and certainly can be negated (see the modal equivalences, as e.g. $\Diamond \neg p \sim \neg \Box p$ etc.).[26]

---

24 Negated infinitive WANT constructions are usually ambiguous, since in German, the negation *nicht* can be interpreted in both the matrix and the subordinate clause. However, if there is a double negation, it becomes clear that both verbs can be negated, cf. (i):

(i) Ich will nicht nicht heiraten.
    I   want not   not   get-married
    'I don't want not to get married.'

25 See the following example, which is ambiguous in German (contrary to English) in the written form (but can be disambiguated by intonation):

(i) Hans muss das Kind nicht bemerkt haben.
    H.   must the child not   noted   have
    'Hans must not have noticed the child./It is necessarily the case that Hans hasn't noticed the child.'
    'It is not necessarily the case that Hans has noted the child.'

26 Again, I thank an anonymous reviewer for pointing out these important differences as far as negation is concerned. The reviewer also proposes that it might be that the reportative meaning is

The fact that morphologically complex tenses are impossible with reportative WANT was interpreted not only as evidence of a reduced tense-event structure in Remberger (2010, 2011), but also as an important syntactic property of modal verbs in general, namely that they appear – and are interpreted – in a higher syntactic position in their derived (epistemic or reportative) meanings. Hacquard (2010), for example, states that the modals have two positions in the clausal structure proposed by Cinque (1999), cf. (14): root modals are situated immediately above the VP, whereas epistemic readings of modals arise in a position immediately above tense. In the low position, the event variable of the modal is interpreted in the second time relation E/R, i.e. the relation between Reference time and Event time (or as Hacquard 2010: 82 puts it "aspect binds the modals event variable"), whereas in the high position it is interpreted in the first time relation S/R, i.e. the relation between Speech time and Reference time (or as Hacquard 2010: 82 puts it "its event variable gets bound by the default topmost speech event binder"). In embedded contexts the modal gets interpreted in the second time relation of the matrix clause (or as Hacquard 2010: 82 puts it "the modal's event variable gets bound by the aspect of the *matrix*").

However, I will depart from Hacquard's (2010) analysis of event anchoring in several respects (cf. Section 5): First, I use a Reichenbachian approach (Reichenbach 1947), further elaborated by Vikner (1987), taking into account the time relations between speech time and reference time S/E and between reference time and event time R/E. In order not to be too restrictive, it might also be better to talk about situations (cf. Kratzer 2021, Zucchi 2015) rather than times, i.e. a speech situation S (the contextualised moment of the utterance) that is related to a reference situation R introduced by tense, which then is related to the event situation E.[27] Situations are more flexible in allowing partial events or including contextual information that does not belong to the argument structure. Note that Hacquard (2020)

---

more similar to non-at-issue uses of the verb SAY, as given later in this article in the examples (26) and (27), where SAY certainly cannot be negated without resulting in a pragmatically unacceptable answer.

There seem to be several extremely interesting questions open for further research, such as the difference between German and English (cf. fn. 10), and the fact that German WANT does not lose its anchoring to a subject; other languages do allow WANT to lose the subject anchoring, resulting in a purely deontic meaning, such as the deontic existentials in Sardinian and Italian (cf. Remberger 2013) and, as reported in an interesting example from colloquial English, an epistemic meaning (from Verplaetse 2003: 158):

(i)   A: Do you have coolers?
       B: Coolers? They wanna be on one of the top shelves somewhere.

27 As Vikner (1987) has already shown, it is important that S and E are not directly related to each other, but mediated by R.

assumes that modal bases (conversational backgrounds) are projected from "event arguments", whereas it might be better to assume that it is "situations" and "situation participants" that serve as anchors for modal interpretation (cf. also Kratzer 1991: 24). Second, I assume that there is generally no "modal" event to be bound in the epistemic interpretation of modals. The main reason for this assumption is that epistemic modal constructions, such as the reportative constructions with WANT, do not allow the modal to appear in morphologically complex tenses. The example in (12) again shows that the analytic form of the modal (*hätte . . . müssen*) is possible in principle, but only with the deontic root interpretation. The epistemic interpretation is only allowed with the modal in a simple tense (13):

(12) Hans hätte gestern angekommen sein müssen.
 H. had yesterday arrived be must
 'H. would have had to have arrived yesterday.'

(13) Hans muss gestern gearbeitet haben.
 H. must-PRES.3SG yesterday worked have
 'H. must have worked yesterday.' (cf. Remberger 2010: 16, ex. (10))

In my approach, then, the second time relation of the (matrix) modal is simply deleted, since the modal encodes not an event, but an evaluation at speech time (anchored to a participant of the speech situation). This deletion is reproduced in syntactic structure, i.e. epistemic modals are not only distinguished from their root counterparts by syntactic position and scope, but also by the syntactic structure they govern. Epistemic modals thus are somehow "more grammaticalised" than root modals.

The situation for WANT, this most particular of all modal verbs, is somewhat different from other modals like MUST and CAN, since, as already noted in the context of negation, in its volitional interpretation it needs – syntactically – a sentient, intentional external argument, which – semantically – is automatically the source of modality. We have seen that even in its reportative use the anchor to the subject as the source of the reportative information is conserved (i.e. it does not shift to the speaker). Furthermore, as we have already discussed, for WANT in its root or volitional interpretation a conversational background in the form of a doxastic modal base (also anchored to the subject) can be assumed. Other modals of necessity might be assumed to be root or epistemic and thus to occupy the corresponding positions in Cinque's (1999) hierarchy, namely $Mod_{epistemic}$ and $Mod_{necessity}$; modal WANT, however, is interpreted in a lower position for its volitional use ($Mod_{volitional}$) – maybe later combined by movement with higher Mod$_{necessity}$ – and in a higher position for its reportative use (Mood$_{evidential}$), but continues to provide a subject position.[28]

(14) Cinque's (1999) hierarchy (relevant syntactic functional categories are marked in bold)
frankly Mood$_{speech\ act}$ – *fortunately* Mood$_{evaluative}$ – **allegedly Mood$_{evidential}$** – **probably Mod$_{epistemic}$** – *once* T$_{(Past)}$ – *then* T$_{(Future)}$ – *perhaps* Mood$_{irrealis}$ – **necessarily Mod$_{necessity}$** – *possibly* Mod$_{possibility}$ – *usually* Asp$_{habitual}$ – *again* Asp$_{repetitive(I)}$ – *often* Asp$_{frequentative(I)}$ – **intentionally Mod$_{volitional}$** – *quickly* Asp$_{celerative(I)}$ – *already* T$_{(Anterior)}$ – *no longer* Asp$_{terminative}$ – *still* Asp$_{continuative}$ – *always* Asp$_{perfect}$ *just* – Asp$_{retrospective}$ – *soon* Asp$_{proximative}$ – *briefly* Asp$_{durative}$ – *characteristically* Asp$_{generic/progressive}$ – *almost* Asp$_{prospective}$ – Mod$_{obligation}$ – Mod$_{permission/ability}$ – *completely* Asp$_{Completive}$ – Voice – Asp$_{celerative(II)}$ – Asp$_{repetitive(II)}$ – Asp$_{frequentative(II)}$ · · ·

Furthermore, if we consider an even more fine-grained, discourse-oriented syntactic left periphery such as that proposed by Speas and Tenny (2003), Speas (2004, 2010) and Hill (2007), we need to assume further syntactic projections for the representation of speech acts and speech act participants and a sentient domain that might be relevant for saying events and maybe also for reportative WANT. Unfortunately, for reasons of space I cannot discuss these approaches in detail here.[29]

Let us now take a look at some pragmatic dimensions for saying reports in general and reportative WANT in particular in the next section.

4 The pragmatics of reportative WANT in German

In this section, I will first present the typology for saying reports offered in Bary and Maier (2021) (Section 4.1), in order then to apply the tests that they developed for at-issueness (Section 4.2) and eventiveness (Section 4.3) to data for reportative WANT in German. Section 4.4 summarises the findings.

---

28 Note that in Cinque's (1999) hierarchy, there is a position Mod$_{epistemic}$ but no position for doxastic modality. However, knowledge-based modality and belief- or thought-based modality are different in nature (cf. also Brasoveanu & Farkas 2007).
29 Speas (2004, 2010), an approach to evidentiality where time relations and situations play a role, seems to offer some particularly valuable ideas that should be applied to the analysis of the interplay of syntax, semantics and pragmatics in the development of evidential interpretations. I must leave this to further research in another paper.

4.1 Saying reports in Bary and Maier (2021)

In the analysis of the German reportative modal WANT, I will base part of my analysis on the typology recently developed by Bary and Maier (2021) (see also Brasoveanu and Farkas 2007, Murray 2017, in particular ch. 2). The main point in their approach is that two dimensions are used as criteria for a systematic classification of the vast range of what can be called reported speech, including direct speech, quotatives, indirect speech, free indirect discourse, parenthetical uses of speech verbs, reportative evidential morphemes, reportative mood, lexical adverbial means and reportative modals (cf. the selected examples in (2) above). Since this paper is concerned with reportative WANT, the examples given in Bary and Maier (2021) for reportative modals (mostly the Dutch reportative modal *schijnen*) will serve as a model for categorisation. The two pragmatic dimensions of saying reports concern 1) at-issueness vs. not-at-issueness, and 2) eventiveness vs. non-eventiveness. At-issueness "concerns the distinction between reports where the fact that something is said is at-issue versus reports where not the reportative component but the content of what is said is at-issue" (Bary and Maier 2021: 4). Direct discourse and indirect discourse are usually cases in which the reporting event, not the content of the report, is at-issue (but see ex. 26 and 27); reportative evidentials are usually cases in which the reporting component is not-at-issue, whereas the proposition marked by the reportative evidential is the at-issue content. As for eventiveness, not all types of reporting introduce a speech event into the discourse, i.e. an event that could be modified e.g. by the manner of speaking or could be anaphorically referred to. Direct and indirect discourse (as well as quotatives, e.g. Spanish quotative *que*, cf. Etxepare 2008, 2010) clearly introduce such a speech event, whereas reportative evidentials do not.

Bary and Maier (2021) developed several tests for the distinction of the two dimensions, which we will apply, where appropriate, to the use of reportative WANT in German (cf. Sections 4.2 and 4.2).

4.2 Tests for at-issueness

The *In Situ Interpretation Test* (modelled on ex. (3)[30] and (47) in Bary and Maier 2021, respectively)[31] checks whether the saying report encoded by reportative *want*

---

[30] In contrast to Dutch *schijnen*, with German *wollen* the subject is clearly the source of the report. Dutch *schijnen* seems to correspond to German reportative *sollen*.
[31] To clearly get the reportative meaning of WANT it is better to use a past infinitive and therefore to shift the conditional into the past.

is the at-issue content of an utterance, by verifying whether the saying report can be interpreted in situ in the protasis of a conditional or not:

(15) *Wenn Peter krank gewesen sein will, dann war er krank.
    if   P.   ill   been   be   wants then was he ill

(16) *Wenn Sonja angekommen sein will, sag mir bitte Bescheid.
    when S.   arrived   be wants tell me please note

The interpretation of (15), at least in my intuition as a native speaker, does not allow the reporting component to be interpreted in the protasis of the conditional (it is not 'If Peter says that he was ill, then he was ill.', but rather not interpretable),[32] i.e. the saying event does not seem to be at-issue in the modal reportative. The same holds for (16): It does not mean 'When Sonja says that she has arrived, please tell me.'

The *What Makes You Think Test* (modelled on ex. (5) and ex. (48) in Bary and Maier 2021, respectively) controls for entailment: Can the saying component be the reason for an assumption or is it the content of the saying that entails the assumption (and is thus at-issue)?

(17) A: What makes you think that Mary was ill?
    B: #Sie will die Grippe gehabt haben.
       she wants the flu   had   have
       'She had the flu, self-reportedly.'

(18) A: What makes you think that John went fishing yesterday?
    B: #Er will gestern   fischen gegangen sein.
       he wants yesterday fishing gone   be
       'He, self-reportedly, went fishing yesterday.'

The answer of B in (17) is not a pragmatically felicitous answer to A's question, since it cannot mean that the reason why B thought that Mary was ill was her telling him. In B's answer it is not the reporting component that is at-issue, but Mary's illness, which makes B's answer somehow tautological (B thinks that Mary is ill

---

32 The volitional interpretation for WANT should be possible in this case; however, it is quite difficult to get with an embedded past infinitive. An interpretation like 'If Peter has the intention to have been ill, e.g. at least three days before next Christmas, then he was ill' does not really make sense.

because she is ill). The same holds for Bs answer in (18): There is no at-issue saying event that could be the reason for B's thinking that John went fishing.

The *Challengeability Test* (modelled on ex. (6) and ex. (49) in Bary and Maier 2021, respectively) tries to challenge an assertion, i.e. the at-issue part of the utterance. In the following examples the saying component itself cannot be challenged, only the content of the saying:

(19) A: Sie   will   unschuldig gewesen sein.
         she   wants innocent   been   be
      'She was innocent, self-reportedly.'
      B: Nonsense, she is guilty, regardless of what she told you.
      B': #Nonsense, she may have been innocent, but she would never say that.

(20) A: Sie   will   krank   gewesen sein.
         she   wants ill   been   be
      'She was ill, self-reportedly.'
      B: Nonsense, I don't know what you heard from her, but she is very healthy.
      B': #Nonsense, she didn't say that, though she might be sick.

In both (19) and (20), the answer B' is inappropriate, since it challenges the truth of the saying event, which is supposedly encoded in the reportative modal. But since the reporting component is not at-issue, this challenge is not pragmatically well-formed. It is the content of the speech reporting, which represents the at-issue part in the discourse. A further example makes the challengeability of the content of the saying component even clearer:

(21) Sie   will   zuhause gewesen sein, aber sie war nicht zuhause.
      she   wants at-home been   be   but   she was not   at-home
      'She claims to have been at home, but she wasn't at home.'

(22) *Sie will   zuhause gewesen sein, aber gesagt hat   das   Hans.
      she   wants at-home been   be   but   said   has   this H.
      'She says to have been at home, but it was Hans who said this.'

The content of the saying can clearly be contradicted (cf. 21), but the saying event cannot be contradicted (i.e. by doubting the authorship of the saying, as in 22).

4.3 Tests for eventiveness

The *Modification Test* (modelled on ex. (9) in Bary and Maier 2021) refers to the modification of an event, e.g. by manner attribution or by the addition of explicit temporal or local coordinates. As (23) shows, the saying component in reportative WANT cannot be modified and thus is not eventive:

(23) #Peter will die Türe mit tiefer Stimme geschlossen haben.
      P. wants the door with deep voice closed have
      'Peter, self-reportedly with a deep voice, had closed the door.'

(24) Peter will die Türe gestern geschlossen haben.
      P. wants the door yesterday closed have
      'Peter, self-reportedly, had closed the door yesterday.'

The sentence in (23) is marked and could only mean that Peter somehow closed the door by using his deep voice, not that there was a saying event in which he used his deep voice. (24) is perfect, but only with *yesterday* modifying the closing event, not Peter's saying.

Finally, the *What Happened Next Test* (modelled on ex. (10) in Bary and Maier 2021) checks whether the saying component or its content is at-issue by explicitly asking for an event (so it combines both properties, the at-issue and eventiveness properties):[33]

(25) A: Did anyone dare say anything? / What happened next?
      B: Peter will das Haus verlassen haben.
         P. wants the house left have
         'Peter, self-reportedly, had left the house.'

(25) can only be interpreted in the sense that Peter's leaving was what happened next, not his claiming that he did (although it is his claim that he did).

Note, however, that even in indirect speech with the verb SAY, i.e. a construction that usually encodes an at-issue saying event, it is possible to have a "pragmatic backgrounding" of the saying event to a not-at-issue status (cf. Bary and Maier 2021: 37, for ex. 26, also White et al. 2018: 422, for ex. 27):

---

[33] Here, I do not discuss the *Anaphoricity Heuristics* (Bary & Maier 2021: 14) for reportative *want*, but I am sure that the tendency to find explicitly mentioned speech acts in the context of reportative *want* is also a feature of German.

(26) A: Why is John not at the meeting?
    B: Mary said that he is ill.

(27) A: Where is Jo?
    B: Bo said that she's in Florida.

This is a hint to how the verb SAY might grammaticalise into a hearsay marker, a phenomenon that is well-known in several Romance languages (cf. Cruschina and Remberger 2008), but will not be discussed any further here.

4.4 The categorisation of German WANT reportatives

As has been shown in Sections 4.2 and 4.3, German WANT reportatives do not contain an eventive reporting component and the reporting component is not-at-issue. In Bary and Maier's (2021) framework, this means that the reportative component is supplemental content in a second semantic dimension (it belongs to "thetical syntax" as Kaltenböck et al. 2011 would put it).[34]

(28) Peter will das Haus verlassen haben.
    At-issue: Peter has left the house.
    Not-at-issue Peter said that he left the house

Not only reportative modals, but also reportative evidentials such as those as found in Quechua (cf. Faller 2002), are not-at-issue non-eventive reports (Bary and Maier 2021, 24). For all saying reports expressing reportative evidentiality (e.g. Dutch *schijnen* but also evidential morphemes in evidentiality marking languages like Quechua), Bary and Maier introduce an operator HEARSAY(), which takes the at-issue proposition in its scope, cf. (29):

(29) T(schijnen) = λp_{st} p   (Bary and Maier 2021: 26)
    HEARSAY(p)

However, as we have seen for WANT, we must also consider the individual anchor of the reportative evidentiality, i.e. the subject of WANT. Therefore, in the follow-

---
[34] "Thetical syntax" or "thetical grammar", in contrast to "sentence grammar", is a notion introduced by Kaltenböck et al. (2011): they derive it from "parenthetical", but extend it to other linguistic elements that are somehow extra-clausal and thus not interpreted inside the clause but at the level of discourse.

ing analysis, which tries to trace the grammaticalisation and pragmatisalisation of the German reportative *wollen*, I prefer to model reportative evidentiality with the help of the notion of conversational backgrounds (and not operators).

5 The grammaticalisation and pragmatisalisation path of the reportative modal WANT

In this section, the grammaticalisation path of reportative WANT will be traced and an analysis that takes all levels of grammar into account will be presented. Since pragmatic features and syntactic-semantic features at the interfaces also play a role in this process, we can call part of this development pragmaticalisation. Particular attention will be paid to the relation of volition to thought and reportative evidence.

Summarising the observations of the preceding Sections 3 and 4 we can state the following:
- The reportative component of WANT-constructions is not at-issue.
- The reportative component of WANT-constructions is not an event that can be referred to.
- The verbal form of reportative WANT can encode only one time relation; it cannot encode aspect.
- The meaning of reportative WANT cannot be in the scope of negation.
- The reportative component is anchored to the subject of the reportative modal.
- The volitional/bouletic conversational background is changed to a reportative/ evidential conversational background.

Following Hacquard (2010), in principle, "modals are relative to an event – rather than a world – of evaluation, which readily provides a time (the event's running time) and (an) individual(s) (the event's participants)." She also distinguishes between "three types of events a modal can be relativized to" (Hacquard 2010:82), one of them being the "event of evaluation". This notion is somewhat misleading in the context of our discussion (as was the "narrated speech event" mentioned in Jakobson, cf. Section 2), since we used the term event/eventiveness in a different sense, based on the observations made by Bary and Maier (2021). I would thus propose to change the notion of "event of evaluation" to "time" or better still to "situation of evaluation"; this allows me to integrate the time-relational system proposed by Reichenbach (1947) and Vikner (1987) into my analysis as well as permitting to consider the contextual information of situations. In this sense, Hacquard's speech event could refer to the speech situation S of the modalised proposition (and, as a consequence, also to the relation between speech situation and reference situation S/R), and her VO-event could refer to the reference situation R of the modalised proposition (and as a consequence also to the relation between reference situation and event situation R/E); her "attitude event (which anchors it to the attitude holder and the attitude time)", instead, roughly refers to – at least in my account – the particular relation for the evaluation of the modal itself, as I will explain in what follows. Modal bases and ordering sources can be anchored to participants of the situation.

In Remberger (2011), I assumed that in German (as in English) the shift from a root modal construction to a higher modal interpretation, such as the epistemic interpretation of MÜSSEN, is due to the loss of one of the time-situational relations that can in principle be morphologically encoded by tense in the modal verb (ex. (12) is repeated here as (30)):[35]

(30) Hans hätte gestern angekommen sein müssen.
 H. had yesterday arrived be must
 'H. would have had to have arrived yesterday.'
 $S,R_M \bullet E_M\_R_M$ | Anchor= $E_M,R_E \bullet E_E\_R_E$ with E_E/R_E_S (gestern)
 (cf. Remberger 2010: 13, ex. (6b))

In (30), both the second time-situational relation T2 of the modal matrix and the second time-situational relation of the embedded proposition T2 morphologically encode an anteriority relation. In an epistemic context, aspect, i.e. the second time-situational relation of the modal (R_M/E_M) is lost. The loss of this time-situational relation of the modal was illustrated as follows (ex. (13) above is repeated here as (31)):

---

[35] For the temporal relations and the distinction between Speech Time S, Event Time E and Reference Time R, cf. Reichenbach (1947); here I use the version outlined by Vikner (1985), who extended the number of time relations in the sense that there is no direct relation between S and E, which must always be mediated by R (cf. also Klein 1994, Giorgi and Pianesi 1997, Demirdache & Uribe-Etxebarria 2000); since it is not possible to visualise these relations unambiguously on a time axis, this indirectness is expressed by •; in embedded contexts with no direct link to S, the first time relation is linked to the time-relational situation of a matrix clause, cf. Enç (1987). The underline between S, R and E represents the temporal ordering; the comma indicates coincidence or inclusion (simultaneity). Subscript M refers to the matrix=modal verb, whereas subscript E refers to the embedded infinitive.

(31) Hans muss gestern gearbeitet haben.
H. must-3sg yesterday worked have
'H. must have worked yesterday.'
a. #S,R_M • R_M,E_M | Anchor= $E_M\_R_E$ • $E_E\_R_E$ with E_E/R_E_S (gestern)
b. #S,R_M • R_M,E_M | Anchor= E_M,R_E • $E_E\_R_E$ with E_E/R_E_S (gestern)
c. S,R_M • R_M,~~E_M | Anchor= E_M~~,R_E • $E_E\_R_E$ with E_E/R_E_S (gestern)
d. S,R_M | Anchor= R_M,R_E • $E_E\_R_E$ with E_E/R_E_S (gestern)
(cf. Remberger 2010: 16, ex. (10))

This example clearly has an epistemic interpretation.[36] The adverbial *gestern* (E_E/R_E_S) is incompatible with a posteriority (31a, $E_M\_R_E$) or a simultaneous (31b, E_M,R_E) reading of the first time-situational relation T1 of the embedded proposition (which is anchored to the event time of the matrix E_M). That is why this example can only have an epistemic (31c) reading (but see fn. 36). I assumed that in the case of an epistemic interpretation the complex biclausal construction gets reanalysed in order to be interpretable: The second time-situational relation of the modal cannot be morphologically expressed in the epistemic reading. This leads to the deletion of the event situation and T2, i.e. the relation between the reference situation and the event situation, of the modal (31d), which is possible because the relations involved are unmarked (simultaneity, see R_M,E_M and E_M,R_E). As a consequence, T1 of the embedded proposition is directly anchored to T1 of the matrix (R_M,R_E), allowing the evaluation of the modal at the speech situation S (S,R_M, but see further below the different behaviour of WANT). Thus, whereas root modals are evaluated at the situation provided by tense (Hacquard 2010 among others), i.e. the reference situation R, epistemic modals are evaluated at the speech situation S. Furthermore, the modal base of root modals is usually anchored to the external argument of the modalised clause (but see Hackl 1998), whereas the epistemic interpretation is given by the anchoring of the modal base to the speaker. So, for (31), the epistemic modal base compared to which the modal relation of necessity is evaluated is anchored not to the subject *Hans*, but to the speaker. Interestingly, this shift of the anchor does not happen in the reportative use of WANT, since the modal base remains anchored to the sentient subject.[37]

As discussed in Remberger (2011: 19), the shift to an epistemic interpretation requires two properties in the semantic time-situational structure of the

---

[36] The time-situational relational structure in (31a) and (31b) is nearly always incompatible with the adverb *gestern*; however, an interpretation is not completely out and therefore these examples are marked with "#" (for a possible example, see Remberger 2011, fn. 23).
[37] This would also be true for other propositional attitude verbs, like THINK or BELIEVE, where the attitude holder of the modal is lexically conditioned by the external theta role of the verb.

construction: 1) there is no modal event time, and 2), the first time-situational relation "of the modalised proposition is always simultaneously anchored to the modal evaluation time" (or situation). Let us now turn to the reportative modal WANT. As we have seen in Sections 3 and 4, reportative WANT is not eventive and – like epistemic modals – it has no event situation. We can therefore assume a parallel development (cf. 32):

(32) Hans   will   gestern   gearbeitet   haben.
      H.   wants   yesterday   worked   have
      'H. claims to have worked yesterday.'
      a. #S,R_M • R_M,E_M | Anchor= $E_M\_R_E$ • $E_E\_R_E$ with E_E/R_E_S (gestern)
      b. #S,R_M • R_M,E_M | Anchor= E_M,R_E • $E_E\_R_E$ with E_E/R_E_S (gestern)
      c. S,R_M • R_M,~~E_M | Anchor= E_M~~,R_E • $E_E\_R_E$ with E_E/R_E_S (gestern)
      d. S,R_M | Anchor= R_M,R_E • $E_E\_R_E$ with E_E/R_E_S (gestern)
      (cf. Remberger 2010: 30, ex. (45))

The interpretations in (32a) and (32b) are incompatible with the adverbial *gestern*. In (32c), the modal event time is deleted, giving rise to (32d). The loss of the interpretation of the second time-situational relation for the modal verb WANT with an evidential interpretation is not only mirrored in the impossibility for the verbal form to appear in complex tenses, but also in its interpretation: With the loss of the modal event situation, the eventiveness of WANT disappears (as there is no event to which to refer), which is one of the properties of the evidential interpretation, as described in Section 4 (following Bary and Maier 2021). WANT becomes "a grammatical marker insofar as it does not project a fully specifiable temporal structure anymore (with no proper event situation, but still a reference situation for which the evidential modal is evaluated)" (Remberger 2010: 176). The difference is that although the modal could in principle be evaluated at speech time, it is still anchored to the subject in Spec, TP. Therefore, the modal is not evaluated at S (as it would be the case with MUST), but at R_M.

Let us now return to the discussion of conversational backgrounds or modal bases: For deontic MUST and CAN, the modal base is usually circumstantial. For the "higher" interpretation of the modals MUST and CAN, the modal base is epistemic and anchored to the speaker. For deontic WANT we have a bouletic conversational background, anchored to the subject of the modal, functioning as an ordering source. However, we have already seen that there is also a non-empty modal base relevant to WANT, namely a doxastic modal base, which is again anchored to the subject (cf. Section 3.1). In the reportative interpretation of WANT, the conversational background is one of reported speech (as assumed e.g. in Quer 1998: 116), i.e. a particular instance of evidentiality, which is still anchored to the subject (and not to the speaker). Note that the epistemic (or realistic) modal base anchored to the speaker is different, since the speaker can both challenge (33) the content of the embedded proposition as well as confirm it (34):[38]

(33) Hans will gestern gearbeitet haben und das glaube
 H. wants yesterday worked have and this believe
 ich auch.
 I also
 'H. claims to have worked yesterday and I believe that, too.'

(34) Hans will gestern gearbeitet haben, aber das glaube
 H. wants yesterday worked have and this believe
 ich nicht.
 I not
 'H. claims to have worked yesterday, but I don't believe it.'

The example in (34) would not be interpretable with an epistemic modal (cf. also Remberger 2011: 29, ex. (38) vs. (39)). The doxastic conversational background and the epistemic modal base are thus differently anchored.

My claim is now that the intermediate step between the bouletic conversational background (volitional modality) and the reportative conversational background (evidentiality) is the doxastic conversational background (of belief or thought) already present in the root interpretation of WANT (all of them anchored to the subject x_{subj}). I propose the following grammaticalisation path (CB = Conversational Background):

(35) Grammaticalisation path
 $CB_{bouletic}(x_{subj}), CB_{doxastic}(x_{subj}) > CB_{doxastic}(x_{subj}) > CB_{doxastic}(x_{subj}), CB_{reportedSpeech}(x_{subj})$

Let us assume that the syntax of volitional modality is also more complex, and additionally contains doxastic modality, although there is no position for it in Cinque's

---

[38] Of course, reportatively marked utterances are pragmatically interpreted as if the speaker was not committed to the content. However, this is due to a conversational implicature since German does not need to obligatorily mark evidentiality by grammatical means; so if there is a reportative marking it must pragmatically mean something according to the Gricean maxims.

(1999) work.[39] I propose to combine both types of conversational background, the bouletic and the doxastic conversational background, in the syntactic position of Mod$_{volitional}$: WANT as a verb with a proper argument structure (a sentient external argument, and a complement proposition) is merged within the VP, climbing to T° which hosts T2 (for the sake of simplicity, we abstract away from German V2 and V-final syntax and represent the structures in a way that is compatible with Kayne's 1992 antisymmetry account). On its way up, it passes the specifier of the complex Mod$_{volitional}$ and Mod$_{doxastic}$ positions (cf. Figure 1).[40]

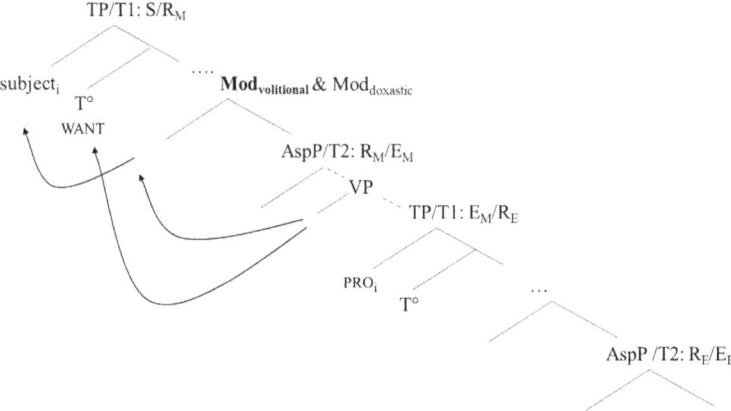

Figure 1: Volitional WANT.

In the reanalysis of WANT as a reportative modal, we have seen that there is no AspP/T2: R$_M$/E$_M$. The intermediate step in the reanalysis is then the deletion of T2, and with this the event time of the matrix (i.e. the modal). The reference time of the propositional event is now directly anchored to the reference time of the modal, i.e. the modal's evaluation time (R$_M$/R$_E$). Mod$_{volitional}$ is also deleted, such that only Mod$_{doxastic}$ remains. It might also be that Mod$_{doxastic}$ is first foregrounded and Mod$_{volitional}$ backgrounded, becoming a secondary ordering source (cf. Figure 2).

---

39 Note that in Cinque (1999) modal relations (like necessity and possibility) and conversational backgrounds (such as epistemic, evidential etc.) are equally syntactic positions. The notion of "bouletic" is taken as equivalent to Cinque's "volitional" and "reportative" is a particular instance of Cinque's "evidential".

40 And later also the Specifier of Mod$_{necessity}$, the modal relation, in Kratzer's terms, which is above Mod$_{volitional}$ but below T; note that the modal relation of necessity is still present in the reportative interpretation of WANT, although it is now evaluated with respect to another conversational background;

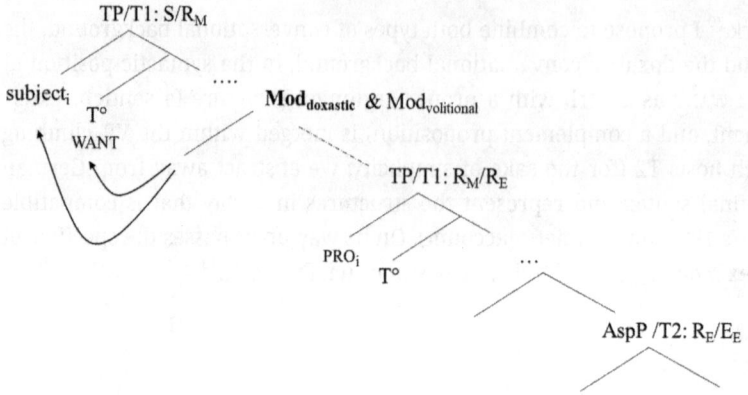

Figure 2: The intermediate step.

At the level of interpretation, the change could be sketched as follows:

(36) Reversal of the ordering:
$Mod_{volitional}$ & $Mod_{doxastic}$: 'what the subject x prefers following her belief worlds'
$Mod_{doxastic}$ & $Mod_{volitional}$: 'what the subject x believes following her preferred worlds'

The backgrounding and subsequent deletion of $Mod_{volitional}$ can also be explained by the deletion of T2 as follows: The modal reference situation and the propositional reference situation are simultaneous (R_M,R_E); volitional WANT, however, obeys a non-anteriority requirement. However, what is encoded in the propositional content of the reanalysed construction is clearly anterior to this simultaneously interpreted reference situation (E_E,R_E). The volitional interpretation/bouletic conversational background therefore vanishes and the doxastic modal base remains: An anterior event situation is necessarily true with respect of what the subject x believes and this belief is interpreted as exteriorised in the reportative reading.

This leads to a further interpretative change: There is no longer an appropriate control position for PRO, which means that it is re-interpreted as a trace. The subject now originates in Spec, VP via Spec, TP of the former embedded, and now evidentially marked clause. However, it is moved to a higher position where it serves as an anchor for the evaluation of reportative evidentiality at the reference time of the modal. I assume that this higher position emerges as a fusion of T1 (of the modal) with $Mood_{evidential}$ (which is above T) (and maybe also $Mod_{necessity}$, which is below T) (cf. Figure 3).

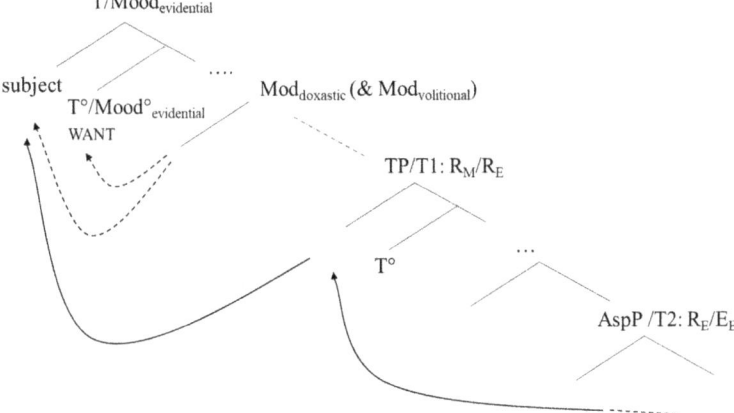

Figure 3: Reportative WANT.

The doxastic modal base may be maintained: The reportative evidentiality anchored to the subject should also be anchored to the subject's beliefs – or former preferred beliefs (otherwise she would be lying). As beliefs can also be seen as internalised speech (internalised propositions), the step from what the subject wanted considering her beliefs to what the subject does in fact believe (maybe still considering her wishes[41]) might go into the right direction.

The reanalysis of the biclausal structure into a monoclausal structure and the cancellation of the volitional event also explain the pragmatic changes: The embedded proposition, which represented the content of the main volitional verb, is promoted to at-issue status. The initial backgrounding first and later removal of the bouletic modal base, which goes hand in hand with the cancellation of the volitional event, causes the doxastic modal base to take over; however, since there still is a subject-argument that serves as an anchor for the evaluation time of the modal, the anchor of the modal base cannot shift to the speaker. The fact that in addition to the epistemic state of the speaker ('what the speaker knows') there is a doxastic state of an argument of the main clause ('what the subject believes') may also explain why the effect of a proposition marked by reportative evidentiality arises ('what the subject says'). The proposition in the scope of WANT, in the reportative construction, is now at-issue. The newly created saying component is neither eventive nor at-issue, but is backgrounded to a second dimension, which is not-at-issue. However, the unusual aspect of WANT-constructions of this type is that

---

[41] 'What the subjects x says following her belief worlds (which follow her preferred worlds)'

the subject – either as an external argument of the proposition or as an anchor for the modal base of the saying report – is stable. I summarise these steps as follows:

(37) Pragmaticalisation path: From WANT to THINK to SAY
    a. At-issue: want(x,p) $CB_{bouletic}(x_{subject})$, $CB_{doxastic}(x_{subject})$
        Non-at-issue: p
    b. believe(x,p) $CB_{doxastic}(x_{subject})$, $CB_{bouletic}(x_{subject})$
    c. At-issue: p(with x subject of p) $CB_{reportedSpeech}(x_{subject})$
        Non-at-issue: say(x,p)

Note that the development described in (36) and (37) finds an interesting parallel in Culy (1994), quoted by Speas (2004: 261), for logophoric predicates: Culy (1994: 1062) shows that in the languages that he investigates complements of speech predicates are more common contexts for logophoric pronouns (i.e. logophoric pronouns referring to the subject of the predicate) than thought predicates, which are more common contexts than epistemic predicates, which again are more common contexts for logophorics than predicates of direct perception:[42]

(38) logophoric predicate hierarchy: speech >> thought >> knowledge >> direct perception

It could be stated that this hierarchy is partially mirrored in the development of WANT from a volitional to a reportative modal, with the subject of the modalised proposition in coreference with the anchor of modal evaluation. However, this parallel, along with a possible connection between logophoric pronouns and the subjects of WANT-predicates, requires further study.

6 Conclusion: To WANT, to THINK, to SAY

In this paper, I claimed that the development of WANT in German from a volitional modal verb to a reportative modal is multidimensional and requires discussion at all grammatical levels, including pragmatics. I first discussed – albeit not in detail – the properties of some propositional attitude verbs like THINK and BELIEVE, SAY and WANT (Section 2). I then described the main grammatical properties of volitional and reportative WANT-constructions in German, at the level of both seman-

---

[42] Logophoric pronouns appear in reportative contexts, like indirect speech or indirect thought, "transmitting words or thoughts" of participants other than the speaker (cf. also Reuland 2017: 4).

tics and morphosyntax (Section 3). In Section 4, particular attention was paid to two dimensions of pragmatics, at-issueness and eventiveness, as exemplified by Bary and Maier (2021) for saying reports. I applied the tests that they developed to the reportative modal WANT. Reportative WANT in German clearly encodes a not-at-issue and non-eventive reportative component. Finally, in Section 5, I sketched a grammaticalisation (35) and pragmaticalisation (37) path for reportative WANT. The most important finding was that in WANT-constructions a doxastic conversational background is present, connected to volitional modality (sitting in the appropriate functional category). This doxastic conversational background then takes over and leads, finally, to a reportative evidential interpretation.

References

Bary, Corien & Emar Maier. 2021. The landscape of speech reporting. *Semantics & Pragmatics* 14(8). 1–54. (DOI: https://doi.org/10.3765/sp.14.8)

Brasoveanu, Adrian & Donka Farkas. 2007. Say reports, assertion events and meaning dimensions. In Gabriela Alboiu, Andrei A. Avram, Larisa Avram & Daniela Isac (eds.), *Pitar Moş: A Building with a View. Papers in Honour of Alexandra Cornilescu*, 175–196. Bucharest: Editura Universităţii din Bucureşti.

Cappelen, Herman & Ernest Lepore. 2012. Quotation. In Edward N. Zalta (ed.), *The Stanford Encyclopedia of Philosophy* (Spring 2012 Edition), cf. also http://plato.stanford.edu/archives/spr2012/entries/quotation/ [25.9.12].

Cinque, Guglielmo. 1999. *Adverbs and functional heads*. Oxford: Oxford University Press.

Comrie, Bernd. 1985. *Tense*. Cambridge: Cambridge University Press.

Cruschina, Silvio. 2011. Tra dire e pensare: Casi di grammaticalizzazione in italiano e in siciliano. *La Lingua Italiana: Storia, Strutture, Testi* 7. 105–125.

Cruschina, Silvio & Eva-Maria Remberger. 2008. Hearsay and reported speech. Evidentiality in Romance. In Paola Benincà, Federico Damonte & Nicoletta Penello (eds.), *Selected Proceedings of the 34th Incontro di Grammatica Generativa*, 95–116. Padova: Unipress [Special issue]. *Rivista di Grammatica Generativa* 33.

Culy, Christopher. 1994. Aspects of logophoric marking. *Linguistics* 32. 1055–1094.

Demirdache, Hamida & Myriam Uribe-Etxebarria. 2000. The primitives of temporal relations. In Roger Martin, David Michaels & Juan Uriagereka (eds.), *Step by step*, 157–186. Cambridge, MA: MIT Press.

Enç, Mürvet. 1987. Anchoring conditions for tense. *Linguistic Inquiry* 18. 633–657.

Etxepare, Ricardo. 2008. On quotative constructions in Iberian Spanish. In Ritva Laury (ed.), *Crosslinguistic studies of clause combining*: The multifunctionality of conjunctions, 35–77. Amsterdam & Philadelphia: Benjamins.

Etxepare, Ricardo. 2010. From hearsay evidentiality to samesaying relations. *Lingua* 120. 604–627.

Farkas, Donka F. 1992. On the semantics of subjunctive complements. In Paul Hirschbühler & E. F. K. Koerner (eds.), *Romance languages and modern linguistic theory*, 69–104. Amsterdam & Philadelphia: Benjamins.

Faller, Martina. 2002. *Semantics and pragmatics of evidentials in Cuzco Quechua*. Stanford: Standford dissertation.
Fintel, Kai von. 1999. NPI-licensing, Strawson-entailment, and context dependency. *Journal of Semantics* 16. 97–148.
Giannakidou, Anastasia. 2009. The dependency of the subjunctive revisited: Temporal semantics and polarity. *Lingua* 119(12). 1883–1908.
Giorgi, Alessandra & Fabio Pianesi. *Tense and aspect. From semantics to morphosyntax.* New York & Oxford: Oxford University Press.
Hackl, Martin. 1998. On the Semantics of "Ability Attributions". Unpublished manuscript. MIT [http://web.mit.edu/hackl/www/papers/files/AbilityAttributions.pdf <10.01.2022>]
Hacquard, Valentine. 2006. *Aspects of modality.* Cambridge, MA, PhD thesis.
Hacquard, Valentine. 2010. On the event relativity of modal auxiliaries. *Natural Language Semantics* 18. 79–114.
Heim. Irene. 1992. Presupposition projection and the semantics of attitude verbs. *Journal of Semantics* 9. 183–221.
Hill, Virginia. 2007. Romanian adverbs and the pragmatic field. *The Linguistic Review* 24. 61–86.
Jakobson, Roman. 1971. Shifters, verbal categories, and the Russian verb. In Roman Jakobson, *Selected Writings, II: Word and language*, 130–147. Den Haag: Mouton.
Kayne, Richard. 1994. *The Antisymmetry of Syntax.* Cambridge, MA: MIT Press.
Kaltenböck, Gunther, Bernd Heine & Tania Kuteva. 2011. On thetical grammar. *Studies in Language* 35(4). 852–897.
Keizer, Evelien. 2009. The interpersonal level in English: reported speech. *Linguistics* 47(4). 845–866. [Special issue *Interpersonal grammar: a cross-linguistic perspective*, edited by Evelien Keizer & Miriam Van Staden].
Klein, Wolfgang. 1994. *Time in Language.* London: Routledge.
Kratzer, Angelika. 1981. The notional category of modality. In Hans J. Eikmeyer & Hannes Rieser (eds.), *Words, worlds, and contexts: new approaches in word semantics*, 38–74. Berlin: De Gruyter.
Kratzer, Angelika. 1991. Modality. In Arnim von Stechow & Dieter Wunderlich (eds.), *Semantics: An international handbook of contemporary research*, 639–650. Berlin: De Gruyter.
Kratzer, Angelika. 2016. Evidential moods in attitude and speech reports. Slides for a talk at UConn, see also https://works.bepress.com/angelika_kratzer/10/ [17.12.2021].
Kratzer, Angelika. 2021. Situations in natural language semantics. In Edward N. Zalta (ed.), *The Stanford Encyclopedia of Philosophy* (Winter 2021 Edition), see also https://plato.stanford.edu/archives/win2021/entries/situations-semantics/ [6. 12. 2021].
Kratzer, Angelika. 2022. Attitude ascriptions and speech reports. In Daniel Altshuler (ed.), *Linguistics meets philosophy*, 17–50. Cambridge: Cambridge University Press.
Lobina, David (reply to Uli Sauerland). 2020. Inner speech and memory. *Inference* 5(3). [DOI: 10.37282/991819.20.68]
Maier, Emar. 2020. Quotes as complements: a Kratzerian approach. In Rajesh Bhatt, Ilaria Frana & Paola Menéndez-Benito (eds.), *Making worlds accessible. Essays in honor of Angelika Kratzer*, 91–98.
Mortara Garavelli, Bice. 1995). Il discorso riportato. In Lorenzo Renzi, Giampaolo Salvi & Anna Cardinaletti (eds.), *Grande grammatica italiana di consultazione*, 429–470. Vol. III. Bologna: Il Mulino.
Murray, Sarah E. 2017. *The semantics of evidentials.* Oxford: Oxford University Press.
Quer, Josep. 1998. *Mood at the interface.* The Hague: Holland Academic Graphics.
Reichenbach, Hans. 1947. *Elements of symbolic logic.* New York: MacMillan.

Remberger, Eva-Maria. 2010. The evidential shift of WANT. In Tyler Peterson, Uli Sauerland (eds.), *Evidence from evidentials*. Vancouver, Canada: *UBC Working Papers in Linguistics* 25. 161–182.

Remberger, Eva-Maria. 2011. Tense and volitionality. In Renate Musan & Monika Rathert (eds.), *Tense across languages*, 9–35. Tübingen: De Gruyter.

Remberger, Eva-Maria. 2013. Deontic existentials. In Delia Bentley, Francesco Ciconte & Silvio Cruschina (eds.), *Existential constructions in crosslinguistic perspective* [Special issue]. *Italian Journal of Linguistics / Rivista di Linguistica* 25(1). 75–106.

Reuland, Eric. 2017. Logophoricity. In Martin Everaert & Henk C. van Riemsdijk (eds.), *The Wiley Blackwell companion to syntax*, 1–20. Hoboken / New Jersey: Wiley Blackwell.

Sauerland, Uli & Artemis Alexiadou. 2020. Generative grammar. A meaning first approach. *Frontiers in Psychology* 11.

Sauerland, Uli (reply by David Lobina). 2020. Inner speech and memory. *Inference* 5(3). [DOI: 10.37282/991819.20.68]

Schlenker, Philipp. 2004. Context of Thought and Context of Utterance: A Note on Free Indirect Discourse and the Historical Present. *Mind & Language* 19(3). 279–304.

Speas, Margaret. 2004. Evidentiality, logophoricity and the syntactic representation of pragmatic features. *Lingua* 114, 255–276.

Speas, Margaret. 2010. Evidentials as generalized functional heads. In Virginia Hill & Anna Maria Di Sciullo (eds.), *Edges, heads, and projections: Interface properties*. Amsterdam & Philadelphia: Benjamins.

Speas, Penny & Carol L. Tenny (2003). Configurational properties of point of view roles. In Anna Maria Di Sciullo (ed.), *Asymmetry in grammar*, 315–344. Amsterdam: John Benjamins.

Verplaetse, Heide. 2003. What you and I want. A functional approach to verb complementation of modal WANT TO. In Roberta Facchinetti, Manfred Krug & Frank Palmer (eds.), *Modality in contemporary English*, 151–189. Berlin: Mouton de Gruyter.

Vikner, Sten. 1985. Reichenbach revisited: One, two, or three temporal relations? *Acta Linguistica Hafniensia* 19. 81–89.

White, Aaron S., Valentine Hacquard & Jeffrey Lidz. 2018. Semantic information and the syntax of propositional attitude verbs. *Cognitive Science. A Multidisciplinary Journal* 42, 416–456.

Willett, Thomas. 1988. A crosslinguistic survey of the grammaticisation of evidentiality. *Studies in Language* 12(1). 51–97.

Zucchi, Sandro. 2015. Events and situations. *Annual Review of Linguistics* 1. 85–106.

Karolina Grzech
4 Reporting speech and thought in Upper Napo Kichwa

Abstract: This chapter is a corpus-based analysis of reported speech and though in Upper Napo Kichwa (Quechuan, Ecuador). It focuses on clausal complements of two verbs: *ni-* 'say' and *iya-* 'think', discussing their morphosyntactic properties, and analysing the patterns of reporting speech and thought in relation to the complex systems of epistemic marking attested in the language. The chapter shows that Upper Napo Kichwa epistemic enclitics, including cognates of evidentials in other Quechuan varieties, play an important role in Upper Napo Kichwa reportative constructions, as they allow speakers to accurately and precisely attribute and convey multiple perspectives involved in reporting speech and thought.

1 Introduction

This chapter focuses on reported speech and thought in Upper Napo Kichwa (henceforth UNK), a Quechuan languages spoken in the Ecuadorian Amazon. It describes the most prominent linguistic structures used to express reported speech and thought in the language, and explores how these interact with epistemic/evidential marking, in particular with the direct evidential/epistemic authority marker =*mi*.

The aims outlined above might seem counterintuitive. Quechuan languages are widely known to exhibit an evidential paradigm including direct, inferential/conjectural and reportative evidentials. Why, then, discuss reported speech and thought in relation to the direct evidential, rather than the reportative? The reason is that UNK, unlike most Quechuan languages (cf. e.g. Weber 1986; Floyd 1997;

Acknowledgements: I would like to thank Stef Spronck and Daniela Casartelli, Silvio Cruschina and Pekka Posio for organising a series of workshops and data sessions that led to the creation of this paper. The data on which this research is based were collected with the support of ELDP, which I gratefully acknowledge (grant IDs: IPF0301 and IPF0301). I am also grateful to all the speakers of Upper Napo Kichwa who took me in and worked with me during my visits in Ecuador, in particular to the core members of the documentation team: Wilma Aguinda, Nilo Andy, Jacobo Chimbo and Edwin Shiguango, and well as to Lidia Chimbo and her family.

https://doi.org/10.1515/9783111065830-004

Faller 2002), does not exhibit a reportative evidential.[1] Rather, the speakers of UNK introduce reported information with periphrastic constructions, often involving =*mi*, the cognate of the direct evidential.

It is well-established that, cross-linguistically, reporting involves managing perspectives of multiple discourse participants. Less is known, however, about how specific grammatical elements contribute to this management, especially if they are mainly used for functions other than reporting. The Upper Napo Kichwa epistemic marker =*mi* has many discursive functions, but across these, its core semantics is to strengthen the stance of the speaker, signaling that he/she knows more than the addressee. Speech and thought reports, in which it also occurs, are an exception: here, the marker introduces the perspective of reported speaker or thinker. The aim of this chapter is to establish how the use of =*mi* in reports, apparently at odds with the marker's other discursive uses, can be reconciled with them.

Examples (1) and (2) below illustrate how reported speech in UNK compares to reported speech in other Quechuan languages:

(1) Cuzco Quechua
kutin=**si**   huk   {forastero}   Pinchimuro   ayllu-manta   ch'in
time=**REP**   one   forastero   Pinchimuro   village-ABL   quiet
{pajonal}[2]-kuna-pi   puri-sha-sqa.
pajonal-PL-LOC   walk-PROG-PST
'One time a *forastero* from Pinchimuro was walking through quiet *pajonales*.
                                    (Condori Mamani et al. 1996: 39; adapted from Faller 2002: 189)

(2) Upper Napo Kichwa
shu   rukumama   (…)   ishki   churi-ra   chari-shka   **ni-n**,
one   grandmother   two   son-ACC   have-ANT   **say-3**
shuj=ka   Duciru   shuk   Kuyllur   ni-shka-ra
one=TOP   Duciru   one   Kuyllur   say-RESULT-ACC
'[They say] A grandmother had two sons, one called Duciru, the other one (called) Kuyllur.' [ta_07062013_01 289–292]

Both (1) and (2) are excerpts from folktales. In (1), from Cuzco Quechua, reported information is introduced with =*si*: the reportative evidential. In UNK, shown in (2),

---

[1] UNK corpus (see Section 2) contains no instances of the reportative evidential. In several other varieties, the marker is attested, but not used as a reportative. This is the case e.g. for Imbabura Quechua, where =*shi* has 'largely lost its reportative use' (Cole 1982: 14) and become a speculative marker, akin to the English 'I wonder'.

[2] Following Nikolaeva (2014), words in the regional lingua franca (Spanish) are enclosed in {}.

hearsay is indicated by the verb *nin* 'say' (say-3), but no evidential/epistemic marker is present. However, speakers of UNK can also introduce reports with other structures, as shown in (3) and (4):

(3) (")Marcos   shamu-shka=mi(")   ni-sha=mi   rima-nun.
     Marcos   come-ANT =EP.AUTH1   say-COR=EP.AUTH1   talk-3PL
     'They say *Marcos has come back*.'/ 'They say (that) Marcos has come back.'
     [el_18092014_01 059]

(4) "Imashti=mi"   ni-sha   iya-ka-ni   (. . .)
     what=EP.AUTH1   say-COR   think-PST-1
     '"What is it" I thought.' [ev_15052013_03 062]

In (3), the reported content is a complement of the main verb of speech, *rima-* 'to talk'. *ni-sha* (say-COR) is a subordinate verb, occurring alongside the main verb with near-identical semantics. This suggests that *nisha* is semantically redundant and functions as a complementiser. Example (4) shows an analogous example of reported thought, expressed as a complement of *iya-* 'to think', and also followed by *nisha*.

In both (3) and (4), speakers present the reported information with the enclitic =*mi*, although in (3) it attaches to both the reported utterance and the complementiser, and in (4) – only to the content of the reported thought. Does the use of =*mi* in such contexts encode claims to authority by the current speaker? Should =*mi* be analysed as part of the reporting clause, or the main speech event? If, like in (3), the marker occurs in both clauses, how should each instance be interpreted? Do the reported speech/throught contexts call for a special interpretation of the marker? Is =*mi* used differently with reported speech, where the original utterance could have been witnessed, and in reported though, where the current speaker reports on an unexpressed mental process? This chapter explores the above questions. Through doing this, it contributes to a bigger research agenda: understanding how epistemic marking enhances effective communication.

2 Language, data, and method

Upper Napo Kichwa (ISO 693–3: quw) is a Quechuan language spoken in the Napo province of the Ecuadorian Amazonian region, along the upper course of the river Napo, a tributary of the Amazon. The most influential classification of Quechuan languages (Torero 1964) situates UNK and other Amazonian varieties in the QIIB branch of the family. Like other Quechuan languages, UNK is agglutinative and has relatively complex verbal morphology. Also typically of the family, it is head-final and exhibits Nominative-Accusative alignment. The default word order is SOV, but in the author's experience, SVO is also increasingly accepted, possibly due to the influence from Spanish.

Reported speech and thought in UNK is a broad and under-studied topic. Consequently, the study presented here is exploratory: it focuses on reported speech and thought constructions like those shown in (3) and (4) above: composed of the reporting and matrix clause, and such that the matrix clause contains verbs of speech and thinking. The full diversity of constructions which can be used to introduce reported speech and thought in UNK is a matter for further research. The corpus has not been mined systematically for a more diverse range of constructions which are cross-linguistically attested to introduce reports (cf. Spronck & Nikitina 2019 for an overview), such as reports introduced with other types of verbs (cf. English *go, be like*), or instances of reports only introduced by a specific intonation/prosodic patterns, in which the matrix clause is absent altogether (cf. e.g. Estellés-Arguedas 2015; de la Mora Gutiérrez 2018). The analysis presented here focuses on reportative constructions involving two verbs: *ni-* 'to say' and *iya-*, roughly translatable as 'to think.' They are good proxies for preliminary analysis of how reported speech and thought is expressed in UNK: *ni-* is the most frequent speech verb in the corpus (cf. Grzech, under review), and *iya-* designates thinking, as well as other mental processes, e.g. remembering or being aware of certain facts (see Section 5.2).

The analysis consisted of several steps. Firstly, an 11-hour sub-corpus of UNK communicative events (Grzech 2020a),[3] was mined for the instances of *ni-* and *iya-* using the ELAN software (2021). Secondly, a representative sample of the tokens was selected for further analysis. Thirdly, these tokens were reviewed manually, so as to select only those which introduced complements of reported speech and thought, given that only propositional complements can index the perspective of a given origo. It has to be stated, however, that in Upper Napo Kichwa (UNK), like in other varieties of Ecuadorian Quechua, clitics can function as copulas (Muysken 2010), and so speech/thought complements consisting of NPs with a copula are analysed as existential predicates.

Once the relevant tokens were selected, they were analysed in terms of morphosyntax (form of the matrix and reporting clause, position of the speech/thought

---

[3] The documentation of UNK is a result of a collaborative effort with a team of native-speaker researchers who recorded, transcribed and translated the data. Each transcription and translation in the 11-hour sub-corpus used for this study was revised and discussed with a native speaker to ensure that that the transcription and translation are accurate, and gain a better understanding of the data. The research was funded by (ELDP) Grant ID IGS0166.

verb with respect to the reported content etc.) and their co-occurrence with epistemic marking (see Section 5). Finally, the semantics and pragmatics of UNK reports were analysed, with special attention to the interplay between speech and thought reports and epistemic marking (see Section 6). The latter step of the analysis was based on corpus data, but complemented with insights into communicative use of UNK which the author gained during fieldwork, and with data from elicitation sessions, not included in the 11-hour sub-corpus.

3 Relevant notions

This section clarifies the most important notions used in the analysis presented in the remainder of the chapter.

3.1 Reported speech and thought

In line with the rest of the present volume, in this chapter *reported speech and thought* refers to both direct and indirect reports of speech and thought. At the same time, the chapter distinguishes between direct and indirect reports, based on how the clause expressing the current speech event relates to the clause containing the report (cf. Spronck & Casartelli 2020). Direct reports are those reconstructed in their (approximately) original form, while indirect reports become grammatically embedded in the clause expressing the current speech event (cf. Adelaar 1990). Thus, direct reports can be seen as depictions of the reported speech/thought events, and indirect reports – as their descriptions (Clark & Gerrig 1990).

It follows that direct reports include two perspectives, and thus have two deictic centres: the current speaker and the reported speaker/thinker. Conversely, in indirect reports these perspectives become conflated, and the current speaker is the only deictic centre that remains: only his/her perspective is relevant (cf. Steever 2002). The fact that direct reports have two deictic centres, and indirect reports have just one, brings about possible structural differences between these two types of reports. In direct reports, the reported speech/thought event and the current speech event can be constructed as structurally and semantically independent from one another. In indirect reports, on the other hand, the clause denoting current speech event and the clause denoting the reported speech/thought event are co-dependent. How this dependence is realised structurally varies across languages (cf. e.g. contributions to this volume and to Güldemann &

von Roncador 2002): linguistic resources used to this end include anaphoric linkage, TAM dependencies between the clauses, use of complementisers etc.

It should be kept in mind that, although direct and indirect speech could be perceived as polar opposites, they should rather be conceptualised as two ends of a continuum including a larger number of possible construction types (cf. e.g. Klamer 2002).

3.2 Evidentiality and epistemic authority

Evidentiality encodes the speaker's 'source of evidence' for a statement (e.g. Aikhenvald 2004), or 'mode of access' to it (cf. Cornillie 2009). The sources of information/modes of access can be either direct or indirect. Direct access means that the speaker witnessed the event. Indirect access – that he/she obtained information about the event through reasoning, observation of the event's results, or through verbal reports (cf. e.g. Willett 1988; Aikhenvald 2004).

Table 1: Taxonomy of sources of evidence (adapted from Willett 1988; Aikhenvald 2004).

Direct / Attested		Visual	
		Auditory	
		Other sensory	
Indirect	Reported	Hearsay	Second-hand
			Third-hand
		Folklore	
	Inferred	Results (inference)	
		Reasoning (conjecture)	

All of the possible sources of information/modes of access shown in Table 1 specify the relationship between the origo (the person to which the evidential is anchored, cf. Garrett 2001) and the described event.

Since this chapter is concerned with reporting, the evidential category of reports is particularly relevant here. Reported evidence can mean utterances of specific speakers, as well as hearsay, where the specific source is unknown or irrelevant. Evidential markers also frequently occur e.g. in myths and legends (see e.g. contributions to Chafe & Nichols 1986, among many others), and folklore can be treated as a separate source of reported information (cf. Kittilä 2020). A related source, not shown in Table 1, is general knowledge, shared among the speaker community and often acquired through verbal reports (Hintz & Hintz 2017; Kittilä 2019).

All these possible sources of reported information are relevant here because they allow a fine-grained classification of the different types of speech reports encountered in the UNK data. However, they have limited applicability to reported thought. In evidential literature, the internal states and thoughts of the origo are considered a direct source of information, and can be reported by the speaker with a direct evidential. However, thoughts of others can only be accessed through inference, if at all. In fact, the author is not aware of any systematic study of evidential marking of reported thought.

As already mentioned, UNK does not exhibit a reportative evidential. Rather, reports are introduced by verbs of speech or thinking, and both of these can additionally be marked with =*mi*: a cognate of direct evidential in other Quechuan varieties. In UNK, using =*mi* does not necessarily mean that the speaker witnessed the described event. Rather, the marker encodes *epistemic authority/primacy*:[4] the speaker's conviction of having the primary right to assess a certain state of affairs, or to inform others about it (Heritage & Raymond 2005: 16; Stivers 2011: 13). Epistemic authority is relative: the same speaker might be entitled to it only in certain situations. For example, the author of this paper could assume having epistemic authority when talking about Kichwa folktales with linguists working on other languages, but would lose epistemic authority when discussing the same topic with a member of the Upper Napo Kichwa community.

Direct access to given information might seem like a prerequisite for claiming epistemic authority, but this does not have to be the case. In languages with epistemic authority marking, it is frequently pragmatically exploited (cf. e.g. Gipper 2015; Grzech 2016). That is, speakers assume a specific epistemic stance even in the absence of a factual basis for it, so as to achieve a certain communicative goal, or project a certain self-image (cf. Mushin 2001).

---

[4] I treat *epistemic primacy* and *epistemic authority* as synonyms for the sake of simplicity, but different researchers use these terms with slightly different meanings (cf. García-Ramón 2018; Grzech 2021).

4 Evidentiality and reporting in Quechuan languages

The previous section provided the necessary context for discussing the evidential system(s) of the Quechuan language family. Although some Quechuan languages have richer evidential paradigms (cf. Hintz & Hintz 2017; Grzech 2020b), in most varieties there are three evidential markers: the direct, the conjectural/inferential and the reportative.

The morphosyntactic properties of Quechuan evidentials are similar across the family. The markers occur on phrasal heads from different lexical categories (in UNK: verbs, nominals, adverbs, see Grzech 2016). In UNK, I refer to them as clitics, but in Quechuan literature they are often referred to as affixes (Grzech 2016: chap. 3 for discussion).[5] Across the Quechuan family, evidentials are not restricted to occurring with a particular tense or aspect, although in some varieties they can only occur in main clauses (cf. Lefebvre & Muysken 1988; Sánchez 2010). Quechuan evidentials can be used in declarative and interrogative clauses, but not in syntactic imperatives, in line with a strong cross-linguistic tendency for epistemic expressions to be excluded from imperatives (Boye 2012: 201).

The canonical Quechuan evidential paradigm is illustrated by Cuzco Quechua data in (5):

(5) a. Direct/Best possible grounds *-mi*
 para-sha-n-**mi**
 rain-PROG-3-**BPG**
 'It is raining.' [speaker sees that it's raining]
 b. Inferential/conjectural *-chá*
 para-sha-n-**chá**
 rain-PROG-3-**INFR**
 'It is raining.' [speaker conjectures that it's raining]
 c. Reportative *-si*
 para-sha-n-**si**
 rain-PROG-3-**REP**
 'It is raining.' [speaker was told that it's raining] (adapted from Faller 2002: 122)

---

5 In the text, I consistently use the = to introduce the Quechuan evidentials. In examples from languages other than UNK, I use either '-' or '=' depending on the convention used by a given source.

In Cuzco Quechua, the direct evidential =*mi* indicates not only direct access to events, but also 'best possible grounds' (see Faller 2002): that the presented information comes from the most direct source possible, and that the speaker is convinced about its accuracy. For example, the speaker could use =*mi* with the statement 'giraffes live in Africa' even if he/she has never seen a giraffe. The speaker could felicitously use =*mi* after hearing about giraffes from a trustworthy source (e.g. a teacher), as long as the existence of giraffes is not at odds with the speaker's general world-knowledge and beliefs.

If 'best possible grounds' (henceforth BPG) can include information based on verbal reports, it follows that in Cuzco Quechua information based on reportative evidence can be marked by both the direct =*mi* and the reportative =*si*. However, whereas =*mi* conveys that the speaker believes to have the BPG for the proposition, the use of =*si* indicates that that "the speaker presents the embedded proposition for consideration..." rather than asserting it (Faller 2002: 23). When both interlocutors are aware that the speaker has sufficient evidence to use =*mi*, but s/he uses =*si* instead, the marker implicates a low degree of certainty (Faller 2002: 195; see also Faller 2019b).

Moreover, the Cuzco Quechua =*si* is not felicitous in all reportative contexts. It cannot be used if the reported statement was originally uttered by the current addressee (Faller 2002: 191–2). Consider the contrast between (6a) and (6b):

(6) Cuzco Quechua
    a. papa-ta-**si**   apa-mu-wa-na-yki   ka-rqa-n
       potato-ACC-REP take-CIS-1.OBJ-NMLZ-2 be-PST-3.SBJ
       'You told me that you were going to bring me potatoes.'/ 'It is said that you were going to bring me potatoes.'
    b. papa-ta   apa-mu-sa-yki   ni-spa   ni-wa-rqa-nki
       potato-ACC take-CIS-FUT-2.SBJ say-NMLZ say-1.OBJ-PST-2.SBJ
       'You said 'I will bring you potatoes.''

                                                (adapted from Faller 2002: 191–2)

Example (6a) is an indirect report, marked with =*si*, and (6b) is a direct report, involving a periphrastic construction with the verb *ni-* 'to say.' Only (6b) could felicitously be used to complain to the addressee if they did not deliver on their promise.

In UNK, the distinction between the direct and the reportative evidential markers is not relevant, as the latter marker is not attested. At the same time, the use of the UNK =*mi* is not restricted to statements based on any particular type of evidence. Rather, it is felicitous when the speaker believes to know more, and in more depth, than their interlocutors (see Section 3.2). Such belief can hold irrespective of the type of evidence for a statement. Consider:

(7) *Ukuma   tiaj   chundzulligunandi   shamukpi,*
    uku-ma   tia-k   chundzulli-guna-ndi shamu-kpi,
    inside-DAT   be-AG.NMLZ   intestines-PL-INCL come-SWREF
    yapami   ismun.[6]
    yapa=**mi**   ismu-n
    much=**EP.AUTH1** rot-3
    '[if one] brings [the kill from the hunt] with the intestines, it will rot quickly'
    [KICHB07AGOPEDROCHIMBO1 446]

The occurrence =*mi* in (7), extracted from a life story interview, is in line with the marker's analysis as a direct evidential: the speaker participated in many hunting expeditions and saw for himself what happens if one does not separate the intestines from the meat. However, UNK =*mi* also occurs in conjectural statements. Consider (8), from a retelling of the *Pear Story* (Chafe 1980):

(8) *Chi   rumira   paynami   churasha,   chapanushka   chibi...*
    chi   rumi-ta   payguna=**mi**   chura-sha   chapa-nu-shka chi-pi
    D.DEM   stone-ACC 3PL=**EP.AUTH1** put-COR   wait-3PL-ANT   D.DEM-LOC
    'They have placed this stone...they've waited [having put it there]'
    [el_25092014_03 048]

The speaker watched the protagonist crush his bicycle into a rock, and conjectured that other characters from the story (three boys) placed the rock on the road, even though this was not shown in the film. Because of the context in which it was uttered, (8) cannot be based on any prior evidence. In Quechuan languages in which =*mi* functions as direct evidential, an example akin to (8) would receive inferential/conjectural marking (cf. e.g. Floyd 1997; Faller 2002).

The UNK=*mi* can also be used in statements based on verbal reports, as in (2) and (3) above, and reported thought, as in (4) above, although it is not obligatory in either of these cases.

---

[6] In what follows, I include the original text without morphemic breaks when the allophones differ substantially from the underlying forms. In examples with complex meaning I also include free translation in Spanish provided by the native speakers of UNK, so as to give readers additional insight into the speakers' interpretation of the data.

5 Reporting speech and though in Upper Napo Kichwa

This study focuses on reports of speech and thought involving the verbs *ni-* 'to say' and *iya-* 'to think'. The verb 'to say' is extremely prominent in the analysed data: an 11-hour corpus of audiovisual recordings of naturalistic speech contain 2489 tokens of the root *ni-*, used as a main verb, a subordinate verb, or nominalised (cf. Grzech, under review). *iya-* is roughly 13 times less frequent: 191 tokens of the root were attested in the data.[7] Over half the tokens (n=108) were occurrences of the de-verbal noun *iyay*, meaning 'idea' or 'awareness,' and only 26 instances of the root were associated with clausal complements of reported thought. Because of this discrepancy between the attested numbers of tokens of the two verbs, and the large number of the tokens of *ni-*, this paper analyses all the attested tokens of the verb *iya-*, but only a selected sample of the tokens of *ni-*, described in more detail in Section 5.1.

Verbs of speech and thinking differ from other complement-taking predicated in UNK. Consider (9) and (10), showing the use of complement-taking verbs *yacha-* 'known/learn' and *muna-* 'want', respectively:

(9) Abigail yacha-n killka-shka-ra riku-**na-ra**
    Abigail learn-3 letter-RESULT-ACC see-**INF-ACC**
    'Abigail learns to read [lit. to see that what has been written].'
    [el_310502013_1 470]

(10) sacha aycha-ra miku-**na-ra** muna-ni
     jungle meat-ACC eat-**INF-ACC** want-1
     'I want to eat game meat.' [elicited]

In both cases, the complementation strategy consists of nominalising the verb with the infinitive/object nominalisation marker *-na*. The nominalised complements are also marked with the accusative *-ta*, used (among its other functions) to mark direct objects of transitive verbs.

In contrast to the above, the clausal complements of verbs of speech and thinking, including *ni-* 'say' and *iya-* 'think', are not nominalised. Also, unlike the

---

7 These numbers include all the tokens which could be unambiguously classified as the roots of either 'to say' or 'to think', with the exception of false starts i.e. cases like *ñuka ni. . .ñuka nini* 'I sa. . .. I say' were counted as one token). For *ni-* 'to say', the alternative spelling *ñi-* was also included in the search.

complements of other UNK complement-taking predicates, they optionally involve a complementiser (*nisha*, say-COR[8]).

(11) *Asnashka nin, waysakuinta asnakpi*
asna-shka **ni-n** waysa-kwinta asna-kpi
smell-ANT **say-3** ilex.guyusa-SEMBL smell-SWREF
"waysa yuramashka" nisha ninushka (...)
waysa yura=mi a-shka **ni-sha ni-nushka**
ilex.guayusa tree=EP.AUTH1 be-ANT **say-COR say-3PL.ANT**
'[The story] says [that the woman] smelled [the leaf], as [it] smelled like guayusa, they told [her] "it was the guayusa tree."' [ta_07062013_01 193]

In (11), extracted from a traditional narrative, the root *ni-* 'to say' occurs three times. At its first occurrence (*nin*), it introduces hearsay information, expressed by a finite verb (*asna-shka*, smell-ANT, note that UNK anterior tense bears no overt person marking in 3SG). The second and third occurrences of *ni-* both introduce the same information: reported speech of the story's characters, rendered through a finite clause. Given its semantic redundancy, the form *nisha* (say-COR) can be analysed as a complementiser (see Section 5.1).

Examples in (12) shows different complementation strategies compatible with *iya-* 'to think':

(12) a. ñuka=ga saki-ni=mi **iya-ngui?**
1SG=TOP leave-1=EP.AUTH1 **think-2**
'[Do/so] you think I stopped [drinking guayusa]?'
[in_25052013_2_03 041]
b. '*Washa shamuw wawawna imara minunawnga?*'
washa shamu-u wawa-guna ima-ta miku-nunga
after come-PROG child-PL what-ACC eat-3PL.FUT
nisha iyarini ñuka.
ni-sha iya-ri-ni ñuka
say-SWREF think-ANTIC-1 1SG
'"What are the children who come after [us] going to eat?", I think [to myself sometimes].' [KICHB07AGOPEDROCHIMBO1 400]

---

[8] The verbal suffix *-sha* indicates that the action denoted by its host is performed by the subject of the main verb. It is often used in subordinate clauses expressing simultaneity or manner (cf. Grzech 2016: 125–129). The suffix *-sha* is in complementary distribution with *-kpi*, indicating that the actions denoted by the subordinate and the main verbs are performed by different subjects.

In (12a), the verb *iya-* takes a finite clause as its complement. This also occurs in (12b), but in this case the clausal complement is followed by *nisha* (say-COR), which, like in (11), functions as a complementiser.

The examples above demonstrate that reported speech and thought complements stand out from other types of clausal complements in UNK. This section discusses their morphosyntactic properties, focusing on the form of the reporting clause and the matrix clause, their possible ordering with respect to one another, and the complementation strategies attested in the corpus.

5.1 Reported speech

The analysed part of the corpus contained almost 2500 tokens of the root *ni-* 'to say.' Therefore, as mentioned above, the analysis of morphosyntactic properties of reported speech in UNK developed below is based on a representative sample of the data. The detailed analysis of this sample with respect to all the verbs of speech is presented elsewhere (Grzech, under review). Here, I focus exclusively on the analysis of the forms of *ni-* , and their use in reporting constructions. The overview of the sample is given in Table 2.

Table 2: The sub-corpus for analysis of forms of *ni-* 'say'.

	ev_24052013_01	ta_07060213_01	TOTAL
Duration	2 min 38 sec	15 min 48 sec	18 min 20 sec
Transcription units	59	399	458
Speaking participants	2 (F, 45 y/o; F, ca. 30 y/o)	2 (M, ca. 75 y/o; M 27 y/o)	4 (2M, 2F, ages 27-75)
Genre	Spontaneous conversation	Interview/narrative	Conversation, interview, narrative
Tokens of *ni-*	8	128	136

The sample comprises two recordings and contains over 18 minutes of natural discourse. The recording ev_24052013_01 was selected as one of the few examples of completely spontaneous conversations in the corpus. It revolves around information obtained from a third party, which makes it particularly suitable for the analysis of reported speech. The recording ta_07062013_01 comes from an interview in which an older speaker is recounting myths always are traditional to a younger one. This recording permits an insight into how, in the absence of a reportative evidential, Upper Napo Kichwa speakers express reported and hearsay content, ubiquitous in traditional narratives. In the two analysed recordings, *ni*-based forms occurred roughly once every 8 seconds, i.e. twice as frequently as in the whole corpus. At the same time, the uses of *ni-* in the sample are representative of those attested in the reminder of the corpus.

The sample contains 136 tokens of the verb *ni-* 'to say', of which 96 are unambiguously associated with clausal reportative complements. Of those 96, 72 (ca. 76%) were constructions involving a single token of *ni-*, while the remaining 24 tokens occurred in 13 constructions involving multiple verbs of speech. These multi-verb constructions could be further classified into two groups: (1) those containing only tokens of *ni-* (n = 8, 2–4 tokens per construction); (2) those containing both *ni-* and other verbs of speech (n = 5, 2–3 tokens of verbs of speech per construction). The examples presented below illustrate this structural diversity and showcase the key morphosyntactic properties of reported speech constructions attested in the corpus.

(13) "Siku=chu   ima=ra=y"   ni-shka-wa
     CA.agouti=Q/NEG what=INTER=EMPH.INTER   say-ANT-INSTR
     "ukian   ukian" kallpa-n **ni-n=mi**   **ni-n**.
     ONO   ONO   run-3   **say-3=EP.AUTH** **say-3**
     'With [him having] said "[Are] you an agouti or what?", she runs [shouting] "ukian ukian", [the story] says.' [ta_07062013_01 258]

Example (13) is a good illustration of the variety of strategies which can be used in UNK to introduce reported content. It contains three instances of reported speech, each introduced differently, and with a reportative complement of a different type. The first instance is an utterance of a known reported speaker: one of the protagonists of the story, asking the other one, who is behaving strangely, if she is an animal (*sikuchu imaray* 'are you an agouti or what'). Prosodically, this reported utterance is fully integrated with the matrix clause: it is uttered with the same tempo, pitch and tone of voice. However, the reported utterance is interrogative, as evident from the use of three interrogative enclitics, =*chu*, =*ra* (=*ta*), and =*y*, while the rest of the clause is syntactically declarative. This suggests that the reported utterance preserves the syntactic form of the original, interrogative utterance, and is thus more akin to a depiction than a description (see Section 3.1), and, consequently, a quotation rather than an indirect report. It is also an example of the use of clitics as copulas (mentioned above, cf. Muysken 2010), given that it is interpreted as a finite clause in the absence of a finite verb. Finally, the report is followed by a single instance of nominalised *ni-* 'say' (*ni-shka-wa*, say-ANT-INSTR, 'with [him] having said'), functioning as a subordinator introducing an event concomitant to that encoded by the main verb, *kallpan* 'run-3'.

The second report in (13) is the onomatopoeia *ukian ukian*, representing the cry of the Central American agouti. This animal cry is not marked morphosyntactically in any way, is not introduced by any verb of speech, and does not convey propositional content, so it is outside of the main focus of this chapter. However, it does contribute important information about the possible range of structures introducing reports in UNK. The speaker utters the onomatopoeia representing the animal cry it in a different pitch, and the sound-symbolic nature of the cry leads to its interpretation as a quotative: it is more a representation than a report. I discussed examples of sound-symbolic reportative complements with several native speakers and, interestingly from the point of view of the current chapter, they explicitly rejected the use of epistemic clitics in reports of this type. In Section 6, I will propose that this is related to the fact that sound-symbolic complements cannot be analysed as conveying any particular perspective.

The third reportative construction attested in (13) is the utterance-final *ninmi nin*. This two-verb construction does not refer to an utterance of any specific speaker, but rather marks the whole clause as hearsay. Syntactically, it is redundant: the utterance has another finite verb, *kallpan* (run-3), describing the action of the subject of the matrix clause. Semantically, it can only be interpreted as scoping over the whole complex clause, since all of its content belongs to the narrative.

The repetition of *nin* is most likely due to the fact that the current speaker is reporting content which was previously reported to them as hearsay. A native speaker consultant suggested, when discussing a similar example, that the number of adjacent repetitions of *ni-* is indexical of the 'degrees of separation' between the current speaker and the hearsay content. In the analysed sample – and the entire corpus – the most complex example of this kind consists of 4 adjacent repetitions of *ni-*based verb forms:

(14) churi-guna   shamu-j-kuna,   "mama ima=ra=y   kay=ga
      son-PL   come-AG.NMLZ-PL   mom   what=INT=EMPH   P.DEM=TOP
      shina   awa-manda   shamu-nga,   ñuka miku-y=lla   asna-nga"
      like.this   high-ABL   come-FUT   1SG   eat-OBJ.NMLZ=LIM   smell-FUT
      ni-sha=mi   ni-nun   ni-n=mi   ni-n
      say-COR=EP.AUTH   say-3PL   say-1=EP.AUTH1   say-3
      'The sons have come, [saying] "mom, what would this thing be that comes from above. . . it smells just like my food" they said, the story goes.'
      [ta_07062013_01 311–312]

Example (14) comes from a traditional narrative, in which a jaguar-mother is hiding a human in the attic, and the jaguar-sons discover that because of spit dripping from the ceiling. The excerpt reports the utterance of one of the sons, which can be analysed as a quotation due to a clear presence of a separate deictic centre: the reported utterance is cast in 1st singular, in contrast to the reporting clause, cast in 3rd person plural.

Each of the four repetitions of *ni-* which follow the quoted utterance has a specific function. As mentioned above, the form *nisha* (say-COR) can function as a complementiser. In the sample, it occurs with reported utterances which can be attributed to a known source, either a specific person, as in (14), or loosely defined, by identifiable, like 'our ancestors'. The following verb, *ninun* (say-3PL), inflected for 3PL subject, directly indexes the original speakers of the quoted utterance: the jaguar-sons. The two final forms of *nin* (say-3) seems to function analogously to (13), indexing that the speaker heard the story as hearsay and that already then it was reported as such.

Example (15) features *ni-* co-occurring with a different verb of speech to introduce a speech report. It comes from the same story as (14):

(15) Ni-kpi, "Mana illa-n=mi, yanga=mi shutu-n"
 say-SWREF NEG lack-3=EP.AUTH1 in.vain=EP.AUTH1 drop-3
 ni-sha rima-n ni-n mama, umachi-sha.
 say-COR talk-3 say-3 mother lie-COR
 'So (lit. [this] being said), saying "No, there is nobody, it just drops like this" the mother talks, the story goes, lying.' [ta_07062013_01 313–315]

In (15), both tokens of *ni-* seem to be functional expressions, while *rima-* ('to talk') functions as a lexical verb. As in previous examples, *nisha* functions as a complementiser introducing a speech report, and *nin* could be analysed as a marker of hearsay. This verb form occurs 74 times in the sample, and in 68 'of those cases, it cannot be linked to a specific speaker. Examples (14) and (15) are the exceptions to this rule, where *nin* could be interpreted in connection to the speech of specific reported speakers, but the pattern in the data nonetheless suggests that it is at least on its way to grammaticalising into a hearsay marker.

Example (15), as well as (2) above, also shows that *nin* does not necessarily occur as a clause-final element, even if the whole clause can be understood as hearsay. The examples above suggest that the position of the complementiser or verb of speech after quoted utterances is more rigid. What the examples above do not show is that one quoted utterance can be felicitously divided into constituents, each followed by the complementiser *nisha*:

(16) "masha" **ni-sha** "chikta-ra chaki-chi-y-ri" **ni-sha,**
son-in-law say-COR river.section-ACC dry-CAUS-2.IMP-COV say-COR
kallpintiru shina=llara.... chi rima-shka shuk masha-ra,
woodpecker SEMBL=ID.REF D.DEM talk-ANT one son-in-law-ACC
shuk... "ambi-ngak" **ni-sha rima-nushka,**[9]
one cure-PURP say-COR talk-3PL.ANT

'That same way, the woodpecker said to a son-in-law...one...saying "son in law", saying "dry the river section up for me", saying "to throw *barbasco*[10] [lit. to cure]" he talked." [ta_07062013_01 266–268]

In (16), like in (15) above, the forms of *ni-* co-occur with the lexical verb *rima-* 'to talk' to introduce reported content. At this stage of research, it is not clear why, in some cases, reported speech complements are presented as a continuous clause, followed by a single complementiser, and in others they are broken up into constituents, but both strategies are frequent in the corpus.

The discussion and examples above have shown that UNK reported speech can be marked in a variety of ways, and that while *ni-* 'to say' is the most frequent verb introducing it, it is not the only one. However, it is only this verb that grammaticalises into markers related to introducing reported content, as shown by its two forms: *nisha* (say-COR), functioning as a complementiser, and *ni-n* (say-3) functioning as a hearsay marker. We have also seen that, when the reported content is a specific utterance, verbs of speech and complementiser always follow the reported content, which can either be continuous, or divided into constituents, each followed by the complementiser *nisha*. This ordering is less rigid for hearsay content, where *nin* most often occurs at the end of the clause, but is also attested in other positions. In the sample, all of the reported speakers/sources of hearsay were cast in 3rd person – either plural or singular. However, in the corpus, reported speech also occurs with 1st and 2nd person. In case of 2nd person, instances of reported speech are cast almost exclusively as questions or requests for confirmation of what had been said.

A key aspect of UNK reported speech which was shown in examples across this section, but not discussed so far, is the use of epistemic clitics with reportative complements. In example (13), we have seen that these clitics can function as copulas, giving rise to interpreting the constituents on which they occur as finite clauses even in the absence of a finite verb. This is shown again in (17):

---

9 It is not clear why this verb is inflected for 3PL subject, it most likely is a speech error, with the correct form being *rimashka* (talk-ANT), indexing 3SG subject.
10 Throwing *barbasco* in the section of a river is a traditional form of fishing. The plant stuns the fish and they float up to the surface.

(17) shina   puklla-j-kuna=**mi**   ni-n=**dá**
     like.this play-AG.NMLZ-PL=**EP.AUTH1** say-3=**EP.AUTH2**
     '(the story) says they used to play like this' [ta_07062013_01 375]

The past habitual construction involving a complementiser, used together with the epistemic authority marker =*mi*, receives a clausal interpretation. Another important property of epistemic clitics, shown in (17) and relevant to how they are used with reports, is that they index the perspectives of different discourse participants.

In (17), an excerpt from a traditional narrative, this is evident through the use of =*mi* and =*tá*. The first of these markers encodes epistemic authority which is exclusive to the origo, and is often used with information unknown or unexpected to the hearer. Conversely, =*tá* encodes that the information is to some extent known to the hearer, but it is the speaker who has epistemic authority. It can only be used with information which has already been introduced into discourse and is expected by the hearer (cf. Grzech 2020b). In (17), =*mi* attaches to the content of the story, while the hearsay marker *nin* acts as host for =*tá*. This is in line with the speech situation: the speaker is telling the story to a younger member of the same speech community. Therefore, =*mi* could be analysed as indexing the current speaker's specific re-telling of the myth, and =*tá* – as indicating that, from the perspective of the current speaker, the story is not completely new to the addressee. The co-occurrence of the two markers opens questions about their relationship to one another, such as whether =*mi* can be analysed as embedding under =*tá*. I come back to this issue in Section 6, where the role of epistemic marking in indexing different perspectives in UNK reported speech and thought is discussed in more detail.

5.2 Reported thought

As mentioned at the outset of this section, the 11h corpus of UNK contains 191 tokens of the verbal root *iya*-. It translates loosely as 'to think', but other translations are possible, such as 'to be aware of'. *iya*- can also be nominalised. Over half of the tokens of *iya*- in the corpus is the de-verbal noun *iyay* (n=108). It frequently occurs in the construction *iyay tian* (think-OBJ.NMLZ exist-3), which translates as 'I am aware (of something)/I have an idea (about something)', and in some contexts can mean remembering. The same construction, preceded by the negative particle *mana* (i.e. *mana iyay tian*) is used to express lack of knowledge. Only 23 instances of the root *iya*- in the corpus (ca. 12.5%) were unambiguously associated with clausal complements of reported thought. This means that the generalisations which can be drawn from the data on reported thought in UNK are less robust than those related to reported speech, but it also gives an insight into the extent to which reported thought constructions are used in UNK.

However, even this limited number of examples sheds light on the different possible ways of expressing reported thought in the language. Complements of reported thought are either introduced by a single verb of thinking (n=9), or by a verb of thinking and a form of the verb *ni-* (n=14). Let us first discuss reported thought complements introduced solely by the verb of thinking. In only 2 out of 9 cases, the verb *iya-* follows its complement, like in (18):

(18)   [payguna]   ñukanchi   runa   tunu   miku-na-ra
       3PL   1PL   Kichwa.person   custom eat-OBJ.NMZL-ACC
       iya-ri-nawka   (. . .)
       think-ANTIC-3PL.PROG
       '[They] thought about eating our Kichwa way (. . .).'

Note that in this case the complement of reported thought is expressed through a nominalised clause, reminiscent of the complementation strategies used for complement-taking predicates which are not verbs of speech and thought. This was discussed at the outset of Section 5, and shown in examples (9) and (10). In the sample, this is the only thought complement expressed this way. Consider the other case of the verb of thinking following its complement:

(19)   waysa=ga   ñuka=ga saki-ni=mi   **iya-ngui**, waysa-ra
       ilex.guayusa=TOP 1SG=TOP   leave-1=EP.AUTH1 **think-2**   ilex.guayusa-ACC
       mana   ansa   saki-ni=chu,   tukuy tuta   {domingo}
       NEG   much   leave-1=Q/NEG all   night Sunday
       tuta-ndi-ma   upi-sha
       night-INCL-DAT drink-COR
       'guayusa is good. . .me, you think I stopped [drinking it], I do not leave guayusa, every night, also on the Sundays, [I am] drinking [it]' [in_25052013_2_03 041]

In (19), the verb *iya-* takes a finite clause as its complement. The speaker, an elderly woman, reports the alleged thoughts of her interlocutor, a younger member of the speech community. She assumes that he thought she had stopped drinking guayusa (*ilex guayusa*) tea, the preparation of which requires getting up before dawn. Note that the reported thought is cast in 1st person, which indicates lack of deictic shift – the whole utterance, including reported thought, is cast from the perspective of the current speaker. Example (19) is a marked context of reported thought, since it involves reporting the thoughts of the addressee. I will come back to this issue in Section 6.

Apart from the two examples above, in all other thought reports introduced by a single verb of thinking (n=7), the verb preceded the reported content:

(20) **iya-ri-shka-nchi**   kay-ta   kanguna-ma   tuku-chi-sha
      think-ANTIC-ANT-1PL   P.DEM-ACC   2PL-DAT   end-CAUS-COR
      ku-ngaj   (...)
      give-PURP
      'We have thought to finish this [the community house] to give it to you'
      [ev_04102013_05 008]

(21) Nakpiga   ñukanchi...   ñuka   iyarini...   ñukanchi
      shinakpiga   ñukanchi   ñuka   **iya-ri-ni.**   ñukanchi
      therefore   1PL   1SG   **think-ANTIC-1** 1PL
      rukuwnara   iyarinanchi...
      ruku-guna-ra   iyari-na   a-nchi...
      old-PL-ACC   think-OBJ.NMLZ   COP-1PL
      'So we...I think we have to think about our ancestors...'
      [KICHB07AGOPEDROCHIMBO1 550–551]

Note that, again, the types of complement clauses differ. In (20), uttered by a politician at an opening of a community house, the complement of the verb of thinking is a purpose clause. In (21), the complement is a finite clause expressing obligation. These are not isolated cases: each of these types of complement occurred 3 times in the dataset.

It is also not incidental that, in the two reports in (20) and (21), the reported thinker is the current speaker, as in (21), or a collective including the current speaker, as in (20). In fact, 1st person reported thinkers jointly amount to over 65% of reported thinkers in the data (n=15), with 1st person singular occurring 13 times, and 1st – 2 times. There was one instance of reported thought where the identity of the thinker was unclear, 3 instances of 2SG, a further 3 of 3PL, and 1 of 3SG reported thinkers. Who the reported thinker was did not seem to affect the syntactic form of the reported thought construction, or the type of the reported thought complement.

As mentioned above, the majority of reported thought complements in the sample (n=14, over 60%) are introduced by constructions involving two verbs: *iya-* and a form of *ni-*, specifically either *nisha* (say-COR, n=12) or *nishka* (say-ANT, n=2). In these constructions, the verb of thinking can either precede (n=4) or follow (n=10) the reported thought complement, but the form of *ni-* always follows it. These configurations are shown in (22) and (23) below:

(22) Kay-ta,   ñuka   mana   api-ya-n   **ni-sha**   **iya-j**   **a-ni**.
     P.DEM-ACC 1SG   NEG   soft-VRBLZ-3   say-COR   think-AG.NMLZ   AUX-1
     'This [the heart of palm], I used to think it didn't soften.'
     [in_20092013_03 365]

(23) Ñukanchi   **iya-ka-nchi=ma**   {Nuevo Paraíso}   tuku-kpi=ga,
     1PL   think-PST-1PL=EP.AUTH3   New Paradise   become-SWREF=TOP
     llaki-ra   mana   chari-nga   ra-u-nchi   **ni-sha**.
     trouble-ACC   NEG   have-FUT   AUX-PROG-1PL   say-COR
     'We thought that [with the community] becoming [called] New Paradise, we will not have problems [in it].' [KICHB07AGOPEDROCHIMBO1 300]

In case of reported thought introduced by two-verb constructions, all but one reported thought complements were finite clauses. The one exception was a purpose clause, analogous to the one in example (20).

In sum, the data show that in terms of their morphosyntactic properties, the reported thought constructions in UNK are far from uniform. Reported thought complements can be finite clauses or subordinate clauses (adverbial clauses of purpose or simultaneity), but they can also be nominalised, like complements of other complement-taking-predicates in the language. Reported thought complements can be introduced by just the verb of thinking, either preceding or following the complement, or the verb of thinking and a non-finite form of the verb *ni-* 'to say', which always follows the reported thought complement.

The majority of reported thought constructions attested in the corpus were reporting prior thoughts of the current speaker. Therefore, whether they should be analysed as indirect reports or quotations is difficult to evaluate. The clearest indicator of deictic shift is whether or not the matrix and reported clause have the same subject person, and if the current speaker and the reported thinker are the same person, this cannot be evaluated. Some insight is delivered by the few cases where the reported thinker is someone else than the current speaker. Such an example was given in (19) above, where no deictic shift occurred. Consider also (24) below, where the reported thinker is a third person (3SG):

(24) shamu-k,   chi   pay-wa-j=mi   **ni-sha=chu**
     come-AG.NMLZ   D.DEM   3SG-INS-BEN=EP.AUTH1   say-COR=Q/NEG
     iya-n   imachari
     think-3   or.what
     '[she] comes [and] thinks that is hers, or what' [in_01082013_02 059]

In (24) the speaker talks about a neighbour who steals from the speaker's field. The alleged reported thought of the neighbour is cast in third person, and thus – like the reported thought complement in (19) – it cannot be interpreted as a quotation.

Lack of deictic shift in the reported thought complement points to the presence of just one deictic centre – the current speaker. However, note that the clause contains several epistemic enclitics: =*mi*, =*chu* and =*chari*. The enclitic =*chari*, roughly indicating doubt or lack of epistemic authority (cf. Grzech 2016: 383) occurs here as part of a highly lexicalised expression *imachari*, but the role of =*mi* and =*chu* warrants a more detailed explanation. The enclitic =*mi* delimits the boundary of what was supposedly thought by the neighbour, while the negation/question marker =*chu* attaches to the complementiser, possibly indicating a rhetorical question asked by the current speaker with respect to the thoughts of the neighbour. Thus, each of the two enclitics seems to be anchored to a separate deictic centre, indicating the need to look closely at epistemic marking in reportative complements to understand their discourse functions and their role in the assignment of different discourse perspectives. Section 6 is dedicated to exploring these issues in more detail.

5.3 Reported speech and thought in UNK: a summary

Despite their superficial similarity, upon a closer examination, the UNK reports of speech and thought exhibit substantial differences. The most striking of those is perhaps their frequency, with reported speech being very prominent in the corpus, and reported thought only used marginally.

The two types of constructions also differ in terms of their morphosyntax. Reported speech complements always precede the verb of speech and the complementiser. In case of reported thought, the complement can either precede or follow the verb, although the ordering of the complement and the complementiser is more fixed: the complementiser always follows the complement. Complements of reported speech were attested to be introduced by up to four verbs of speech, while in case of reported thought the most complex construction consists of one verb of thinking and the complementiser. Furthermore, while clausal complements of reported speech are always finite, complements of reported thought can take a variety of syntactic forms: finite clauses, adverbial clauses, or nominalised clauses. While reported speech is used mostly to report the utterances of others, reported thought seems to be used mostly to report previous thoughts of the current speaker. Deictic shift occurs in some complements of reported speech, which can be analysed as quotations, but is absent from the instances of reported thought attested in the corpus.

What reported speech and thought constructions have in common is the optionality of the complementiser, and the fact that they can co-occur with different epistemic clitics. The patterns of this co-occurrence, as well as a more function-oriented perspective on reported speech and thought in UNK, is discussed in the next section.

6 Epistemic marking and perspective

Across this chapter, I have suggested that epistemic clitics play a role in UNK reported speech and thought constructions through indicating the different perspectives present in such context. In the current section, I examine this claim in more detail, focusing on the analysis of epistemically-marked reports of speech and thought. Apart from =*mi*, discussed at length in Section 3.2, other epistemic clitics featuring in the data are: =*mari*, indicating that the hearer should be aware of something but acts as if they are not (cf. Grzech 2021); =*ma* the semantics of which is similar to =*mi*, =*tá*, indicating shared access to information within the epistemic authority of the speaker, =*cha* and =*chari*, signalling the speaker's lack of epistemic authority, the question/negation marker =*chu*, and the topic marker =*ga*.[11]

In the chapter, I have analysed 85 reported speech constructions, involving 96 instances of *ni-*. Out of those 85, 42 (ca. 49%) were epistemically marked, meaning that epistemic clitics occurred either on the reported speech complement, or on at least one of the verbs of speech involved in the reported speech construction. For reported thought constructions, this proportion was lower, with ca. 39% (n=9) of the 23 analysed constructions being epistemically marked. In both reported speech and thought it was more common for epistemic clitics to occur on the speech/thought complements than on the verbs introducing them. In reported speech, clitics occurred on 33 complements vs. 19 speech verbs/speech verb series.

The speech complements were only marked with clitics indicating epistemic authority: =*mi* (n=27), =*ma* (n=2) or the proclitic *m=* (n=4), which can be interpreted as either of the latter. The enclitics =*mi* and =*ma* were also the most frequent on the verbs of speech introducing the reports, with 6 occurrences each. In only 10 (under 12%) reported speech constructions both the complement and the series of verbs of speech were marked.

---

[11] I include the topicality marker =*ga* as an epistemic enclitic, despite lack of clarity with respect to its potentially epistemic semantics, given that it occurs in complementary distribution with other epistemic markers.

For reported thought, epistemic marking occurred on 9 complements and only 3 verbs introducing them. On the complements, =*mi* was the most frequent (n=5), =*chu* occurred twice, there was one instance of =*ga* and one occurrence of both =*mi* and =*chu* on two constituents of the same thought complement. The verbs of thought were marked with either =*cha*, =*chu* or =*ma*, with one occurrence each. In only 3 constructions did epistemic clitics occur both on the reported thought complement and the verb introducing it (ca. 13%).

In order to understand how epistemic markers, interact with speech and thought reports, it is useful to systematise the reportative constructions encountered in the corpus. Given that their morphosyntactic properties, described in Section 5, do not deliver any clear patterns, another possible approach is to look at them from the perspective of the grammatical person of the reported speaker/thinker. This is warranted by the observation that 1st, 2nd and 3rd person reports do not fulfil the same discourse function. The unmarked context for reporting is that of 3rd person, where the current speaker is conveying information obtained from others. If reports involve the current speech act participants, the picture becomes more complex.

Within the epistemically-marked reported thought constructions, in 6 out of 9 the reported thinker was either the current speaker (n=5), or a group involving the current speaker (n=1). Example (23) shows one such thought report. On the basis of the available examples, it seems that the discourse function of 1st person thought report is either to indicate the context or justification for the current utterance, or – more frequently – to indicate a previous mis-judgement of a certain situation, which the current speaker views differently. This is the case in (23). The speaker reports his group's prior expectation that the new community will have no problems, in the context of discussing its current troubles. A similar situation obtains for epistemically unmarked (22), where the speaker didn't expect the heart of palm to be boiled soft, and was proven wrong. Thus, the indication of mis-judgement does not seem to depend on whether epistemic clitics are used or not. Rather, they seem to be used to strengthen the message that the reported thinker – the former self of the current speaker – has been proven wrong. Although the sample of reported speech constructions analysed for this chapter does not include 1st person reports, they are attested in the corpus, and they play a similar discourse role, indicating that the current speaker has had a change of mind. Compare (25) and (26), both from outside the sample analysed throughout the chapter:

(25) panda-ri-nchi, 'lluki-wa=**mi**' iya-ka-ni ñuka
 mistake-ANTIC-1PL left-INS =**EP.AUTH1** think-PST-1 1SG
 'we were mistaken, I thought "[it was] with the left"' [el_03102014_01 062]

(26) Muyu-ra   piti-u-n..... ima... coco.... Mana, coco=**mi**
      fruit-ACC cut-PROG-3   what   coconut   NEG   coconut=**EP.AUTH1**
      ni-ni...   coco=**chá**...
      say-1   coconut=**NO.EP.AUTH**
      'He is cutting [harvesting] fruit...what... [It's a] coconut...no, I said coconut, [is it a] coconut?' [el_24092014_03 003–5]

Both examples come from video-based elicitations. In (25) the speaker was asked to guess the result of a three-shell game shown in the video without the final reveal. He uttered (25) upon seeing the reveal, marking his prior thought with =*mi*. Given that at the moment of speech he already knew that his previous thought was wrong, the use of epistemic authority marking in this context only makes sense if we treat =*mi* as anchored to the reported thinker, treating him as a different discourse participant than the current speaker, despite them both being the same person.

A similar observation can be made for (26), which is an example of reported speech. Here, the dissociation of the two perspectives is even more explicit. The speaker is narrating the 'Pear Story' video (Chafe 1980), but as soon as he mentions coconut, he realises that what the farmer is cutting is a different fruit. He signals this by repeating his prior utterance as a quote marked with =*mi*, and immediately afterward issues a corrective utterance with =*cha*, signaling a change of perspective: his current speaking self sees reality differently than his former speaking self from seconds ago, and now he is not sure anymore whether the fruit is a coconut. In sum, in the context of 1st person reports of both speech and thought, the use of epistemic clitics helps the current speaker delimit two different discourse situations, in which, despite being the same person, the reported speaker/thinker and the current speaker are conceptualised as separate discourse participants with different pools of knowledge. Spronck & Nikitina (2019: 133) observe that reported speech typically involves suspension of belief with regard to the reported proposition, but that this is not the case for 1st person reports. The UNK data suggests differently, showing that this distancing also occurs in case of 1st person speech and thought reports.

Second person reports are a marked context for both reported speech and thought, since they involve either repeating our interlocutor's words to them, or assuming we have access to their thought processes. In the UNK culture, as in many other cultures around the world, there is a strong constraint on such discourse moves, and statements about the actions of one's interlocutor are usually cast as questions or requests for confirmation, unless they are a marked speech act: a warning or an accusation. Speaking about internal states of one's interlocutor is not attested in the data, and not judged as felicitous. Although 2SG reports were not found in the analysed sample of reported speech, they are attested in the corpus: they tend to be requests for confirmation, or links to prior discourse by the interlocutor, and optionally receive epistemic marking. As for reported thought, there were two instances of it in a 2nd person context in the analysed data. One was given in (19). The other one, shown in (27), comes from the same speaker as (19):

(27) mana ni-ni chi-ta-ra,[12] mana kuya-k-kuna=mari,
NEG say-1 P.DEM-ACC-ACC NEG gift-AG.NMLZ-PL=EP.AUTH4
ñawpa=ga ima kuya-k-kuna=mi **ni-sha=cha**
before=TOP what gift-AG.NMLZ=EP.AUTH1 **say-COR=NO.EP.AUTH**
iya-nguichi, shina shina=lla upi-u-shka=ma,
think-2PL SEMBL SEMBL=LIM drink-PROG-ANT=EP.AUTH3
'I am not saying this, they used not to give [presents], in the old times, do you think they used to give [presents], they drank just like this [at weddings]' [in_25052013_2_03 041]

This example is a response to a question by the interviewer about whether in the old times people used to give presents at weddings. The speaker in (27) uses a variety of epistemic clitics. First she explicitly rejects having mentioned gifts, and uses =mari to signal that the hearer should be aware that there was no such custom. She then reports the hearer's false belief regarding the gifts, marking the content of reported thought with =mi, indexing speaker-exclusive epistemic authority, anchored to the reported thinker, and the complementiser with =cha, indexing lack of epistemic authority. The marker =cha seems to be anchored to the current speaker, and could be an attenuating device, to make pointing out that the hearer was mistaken less face-threatening. After that the speaker reports the true state of affairs (*they drank just like this*), marked with =ma, indexing epistemic authority of the current speaker. In this case, just like in (19), 2nd person reported thought construction is used to signal the hearer's alleged mistaken belief, and, like in 1st person reports discussed above, epistemic clitics delimit and differentiate the perspectives of the different discourse participants.

In 3rd person contexts, which are the default context for reports, epistemic markers are used to similar ends. While all the epistemically-marked speech reports in the sample are cast in 3rd person, the analysed data contain only one instance of reported thought in 3rd person, given in example (24) in Section 5.2. In that example, reported thought attributed to 3rd person was not an actual thought, but the current speaker's interpretation of that person's actions. Epistemically-marked reported speech constructions cast in 3rd person were also given above,

---

12 The function of what seems to be double accusative marking here still requires more analysis.

in examples (13), (14) and (17) in Section 5.1. In all these examples, epistemic clitics occur on the verbs introducing the reported content. A possible interpretation of such use of epistemic markers is that the current speaker wants to draw the hearer's attention to the actual act of speaking/telling, and put it forward as e.g. unexpected, novel, or surprising (use of =mi in (13) and (14)), or as expected, or already mentioned in prior discourse (allophone of =tá in (17)).

When occurring on the content of reported speech complements cast in 3rd person, epistemic clitics seems to delimit the perspectives of reported speakers/ characters in stories, or the different units of a story. In general, the use of =mi and other markers indexing epistemic authority in reportative contexts seems to indicate that the reported information is not to be considered within the epistemic domain of the current speaker. The markers are used to explicitly defer the epistemic authority over the reported information to the original speaker or thinker. The mere fact that a given piece of information is cast as a report already indexes that it originated with someone else than the current speaker, but the occurrence of epistemic marking explicitly encodes the change of perspective, possibly making it more salient for the addressee of the reporting utterance. This epistemic practice also showcases the narrator's skills in manipulating the perspectives of the different protagonists.

The observation about epistemic marking as linked directly to a certain perspective is supported by the patterns of its occurrence in the data, which I discuss using =mi as an example. If =mi is a marker of perspective of a given origo, we could expect that it would not occur in contexts in which the perspective of the reported speaker is irrelevant or non-existent. One such example would be when the quoted utterance is non-propositional, like (13) above or (28) below:

(28) unkulu   mana=chu   kapari-n   sacha-y   kapari-n
     bird.type   NEG=Q/NEG shout-3   jungle-LOC   shout-3
     chi-manda=mi...   unn   unn **ni-n**   mana=chu!
     P.DEM-ABL=EP.AUTH1   IDEO   IDEO say-3   NEG=Q/NEG
     'The *unkulu* bird, isn't it, [it] shouts in the jungle. So it says/shouts *unnn unnn*, doesn't it?' [ta_07062013_01 353–355]

In (28) the reported speech complement is the sound of the *unkulu*, followed by *nin* (say-3), which in this example functions as the main verb. The cited ideophone does not convey a proposition – it merely mimics a birdsong. I discussed examples like (28) with several native speakers and they explicitly rejected the use of =mi on reportative complements of this type. Nature and animal sounds are not propositional; They cannot be analysed as conveying a perspective. Thus, the rejection of =*mi* in contexts like (28) is consistent with its analysis as a marker indexing a specific epistemic perspective.

Furthermore, if the perspective encoded by =*mi* is epistemic, it should be related to 'knowing how the world is', and proving a specific evaluation of the state of the world. For this reason, epistemic marking is not compatible with imperatives, where the relevant type of authority is not epistemic, but deontic: rather than describing how the world is, imperatives specify how it ought to be (cf. Stevanovic & Peräkylä 2012: 298). In line with cross-linguistic tendencies for epistemic markers, =*mi* cannot occur in syntactic imperatives (Grzech 2016: 346) outside of reportative context, and the data show that it preserves this property when used in reports:

(29) kuna upi-na-ra   kuya-wa-ychi   **ni-n**,   yarka-n=mi
     now   drink-INF-ACC   give-1OBJ-2PL.IMP   **say-3** be.hungry-3=EP.AUTH1
     ni-n
     say-3
     "'Now give me a drink", [he] says, "I'm thirsty/hungry", [he] says.'" [in_07072013_01 408]

In (29), the reported utterance is distributed across two speech complements. The first one includes a morphologically imperative form of the verb *kuya*- 'to gift', while the second part of the same report is cast in the declarative. Only the second complement clause is marked with =*mi*. Several other examples in the corpus confirm this pattern, indicating that =*mi*, as a marker indicating epistemic perspective, is incompatible with imperatives, within or without reportative contexts.

This observation is important because it bears on the interpretation of =*mi*, as well as of other epistemic markers, in the context of reported speech and thought. Although UNK epistemic clitics have been discussed throughout the chapter, I have not yet explicitly addressed the issue of their scope. In line with the observations made by Faller (2019) for Cuzco Quechua, I analysed UNK epistemic markers as having different scope properties in terms of their association with focus (cf. e.g. Muysken 1995) and their evidential/epistemic value. While their focus-related scope is determined by their position in the clause, their epistemic value always scopes over the whole clause. It follows that the epistemic perspective indexed by a given marker holds for the whole clause in which it occurs, and this is in fact what we can see in the data, where different clitics can occur in adjacent clauses to index the perspectives of different discourse participants.

What is less clear is the relation of epistemic clitics to the verbs of speech. Embedding tests for =*mi* deliver mixed results, showing that it scopes over negation, but that it can be semantically embedded under verbs of speech and thinking (cf. Grzech 2016: 356–364). Further research is needed to spell out how this relates to its interpretation as a marker of perspective in reportative contexts. What also warrants further research is the relationship between epistemic marking and the quoting vs. reporting distinction. Given that I analyse UNK epistemic markers as indexing different perspectives, it follows that the reportative constructions in which they occur should be analysed as quotatives – as a distinct perspective is related to the presence of a separate deictic centre. However, in line with Boye (2012: 32), true quotatives scope over illocutions and imperatives, while reportatives scope over propositions, and do not scope over imperatives. According to these criteria, reportative UNK constructions which use epistemic clitics should be analysed as reportative, rather than as quotative.

This discrepancy gives rise to several broader, and perhaps more philosophical questions. What does it mean to attribute a perspective to another person? When we report the speech and thoughts of others, are we really reporting their utterances and thoughts, or barely our own interpretation of those, based on other people's actions, much like what we do when, while telling a story, we attribute dialogue to characters to portray them in a certain way (cf. Couper-Kuhlen & Selting 2017 online chapter E). The latter is suggested by several examples given across this chapter, where attribution of thoughts was an output of certain perceived actions or communicative moves of the reported thinker.

Although on the basis of the analysed sample it can be observed that reported speech and thought in UNK have some distinct morphosyntactic properties, they also share many similarities, i.e. the possibility of taking finite clauses as complements, and the optional use of the complementiser *nisha*. Therefore, it is possible that the UNK distinction between reported speech or thought is not rigid, and not necessarily based on whether the current speaker is actually reporting a prior utterance or thought. Rather, whether speakers choose to convey a given piece of information as reported speech or thought could depend on whether they feel in a position to accurately portray the mental processes of the reported speaker or thinker (cf. Vries 1990). The optional use of complementiser forms and epistemic enclitics aids the current speaker in this portrayal, delimiting the content of the reported utterances and explicitly separating the mental process of the current speaker from those of the reported speaker or thinker.

7 Conclusions

Throughout this paper, I have described and analysed the different aspects of reported speech and thought constructions in UNK. I have focused on clausal complements of two verbs: *ni-* 'to say' and *iya-* 'to think', and have shown that, although reported speech and thought constructions attested in the language differ in terms of morphosyntax, they also exhibit certain important similarities. I have also analysed the interaction of reported speech and thought with epistemic markers, showing that they play a role in indexing the perspectives of different discourse participants in reportative contexts, and thus contribute to reducing the current speaker's responsibility for the content of the report.

Reducing the responsibility or commitment of the current speaker for the content of the reported speech/thought is a well-attested feature of speech and thought reports. As stated by Goffman (1981), reported speech is an 'unserious' speech act, in that it does not necessarily reflect the proposition to which the current speaker is willing to commit, as would be the case with declaratives which do not contain reported speech or thought. This also obtains for the UNK data – when introducing reported speech or thought, the current speaker uses epistemic enclitics to delimit the utterance/thought of others and separate it from their own perspective. Thus, the use of clitics anchored to the reported speaker/thinker allows the current speaker (who might, but does not need to, be the same person) to reduce their own commitment to or involvement in what is being said. This is in line with cross-linguistic properties of reported speech and thought as a strategy for attenuation (cf. Albelda 2020) or reducing commitment of the speaker of the matrix clause (Krifka 2013; 2014).

Epistemic marking attested in UNK gives speakers a rich set of possibilities related to indicating and reducing commitment, and navigating multiple perspectives, which is particularly relevant in the context of reported speech and thought. The co-existence of multiple perspectives is salient in Amazonian discourse (Uzendoski & Calapucha-Tapuy 2014) as well as in the verbal artistry of the Andes (Emlen et al. 2019). Stenzel & Franchetto (2017: 4) observe it in Amazonian oral literature. In line with the above, in many Amazonian cultures, there is a cultural requirement of 'precision in telling how one knows things' (Aikhenvald 2012: chap. 9). In this chapter, I have shown that the use of epistemic markers in speech and thought reports is a complex communicative resources which allows speakers of Upper Napo Kichwa to achieve such precision.

Abbreviations

1	1st person
2	2nd person
3	3rd person
ABL	ablative
ACC	accusative
AG	agentive
ANT	anterior
ANTIC	anticausative

AUX	auxiliary
BEN	benefactive
BPG	best possible grounds
CAUS	causative
CIS	cislocative
COR	co-reference
COV	coverb
D	distal
DAT	dativ
DEM	demonstrative
DIM	diminutive
EMPH	emphatic
EP.AUTH1	epistemic authority exclusive to the speaker
EP.AUTH2	shared access, epistemic authority of the speaker
EP.AUTH3	epistemic authority similar to EP.AUTH1
EP.AUTH4	epistemic authority of the speaker and the addressee, with addressee behaving as if unaware of having it
EPEN	epenthetic
FUT	future
GEN	genitive
IDEO	ideophone
ID.REF	identity of reference
IMP	imperative
INCL	inclusive
INF	infinitive
INS	instrumental
INT	interrogative
LOC	locative
NEG	negative
NMLZ	nominaliser
NO.EP.AUTH	lack of epistemic authority
OBJ	object
P	proximal
PART	particle
PL	plural
PROG	progressive
PST	past
PURP	purpose
Q	question
REP	reportative
RESULT	resultative
SBJ	subject
SEMBL	semblative
SG	singular
SWREF	switch-reference
TOP	topic
VRBLZ	verbaliser.

References

Adelaar, William F.H. 1990. The role of quotations in Andean discourse. In Harm Pinkster & Inge Genee (eds.), *Unity in Diversity*, 1–12. Berlin/Boston: De Gruyter. https://doi.org/10.1515/9783110847420.1.

Aikhenvald, Alexandra Y. 2004. *Evidentiality*. Oxford: Oxford University Press.

Aikhenvald, Alexandra Y. 2012. *Languages of the Amazon*. 1st edn. Oxford /New York: Oxford University Press.

Albelda Marco, Marta. 2020. On the Mitigating Function of the Spanish Evidential se ve que. *Corpus Pragmatics* 4(1). 83–106. https://doi.org/10.1007/s41701-019-00067-8.

Boye, Kasper. 2012. *Epistemic Meaning, A Crosslinguistic and Functional-Cognitive Study*. Berlin/Boston: De Gruyter Mouton.

Chafe, Wallace L. 1980. *The Pear Stories: Cognitive, Cultural and Linguistic Aspects of Narrative Production*. Norwood, N.J: Ablex.

Chafe, Wallace L. & Johanna Nichols. 1986. *Evidentiality: the linguistic coding of epistemology*. Norwood, NJ: Ablex.

Clark, Herbert H. & Richard J. Gerrig. 1990. Quotations as Demonstrations. *Language* 66(4). 764–805. https://doi.org/10.2307/414729.

Cole, Peter. 1982. *Imbabura Quechua: A Descriptive Grammar*. Edited by Bernard Comrie, Norval Smith & Anna de Haas. (Lingua Descriptive Studies Vol. 5). Amsterdam: North-Holland.

Condori Mamani, Gregorio, Paul H. Gelles & Eulogio Nishiyama. 1996. *Andean Lives: Gregorio Condori Mamani and Asunta Quispe Huaman: Gregorio Condori Mamani and Asunta Quispe Huamán*. Edited by Ricardo Valderrama Fernández & Carmen Escalante Gutiérrez. Translated by Gabriela Martínez Escobar. Austin: University of Texas Press.

Cornillie, Bert. 2009. Evidentiality and epistemic modality: On the close relationship between two different categories. *Functions of Language* 16(1). 44–62. https://doi.org/10.1075/fol.16.1.04cor.

Couper-Kuhlen, Elizabeth & Margret Selting. 2017. *Interactional Linguistics: An Introduction to Language in Social Interaction*. Cambridge: Cambridge University Press.

Emlen, Nick, Matt Coler & Edwin Banegas-Flores. 2019. Blackmail, fortunetellers, and mistaken identities: How thought experiments and narrative analyses clarify Aymara evidential/epistemic marking. Presentation given at the 52nd Annual Meeting of Societas Linguistica Europea, Leipzig. OSF: https://osf.io/87s3h/#! (10 October, 2022).

Estellés-Arguedas, Maria. 2015. Expressing evidentiality through prosody? Prosodic voicing in reported speech in Spanish colloquial conversations. *Journal of Pragmatics* 85. 138–154. https://doi.org/10.1016/j.pragma.2015.04.012.

Faller, Martina T. 2002. *Semantics and Pragmatics of Evidentials in Cuzco Quechua*. Stanford University. PhD Thesis.

Floyd, Rick. 1997. *La estructura categorial de los evidenciales en el quechua wanka* (Serie Lingüística Peruana 44). Lima: SIL International.

García-Ramón, Amparo. 2018. Indexing epistemic incongruence: uy as a formal sign of disagreement in agreement sequences in Spanish. *Journal of Pragmatics* 131. 1–17. https://doi.org/10.1016/j.pragma.2018.04.011.

Garrett, Edward. 2001. *Evidentiality and Assertion in Tibetan*. Los Angeles: University of California. https://www.academia.edu/4701945/Evidentiality_and_Assertion_in_Tibetan. (24 April, 2016).

Gipper, Sonja. 2015. (Inter)subjectivity in interaction: Investigating (inter)subjective meanings in Yurakaré conversational data. *STUF – Language Typology and Universals* 68(2). 211–232. https://doi.org/10.1515/stuf-2015-0011.

Goffman, Erving. 1981. *Forms of talk* (University of Pennsylvania Publications in Conduct and Communication). Philadelphia: University of Pennsylvania Press.

Grzech, Karolina. 2016. *Discourse enclitics in Tena Kichwa: A corpus-based account of information structure and epistemic meaning*. SOAS, University of London. PhD Thesis. https://eprints.soas.ac.uk/24336/ (15 March, 2022).

Grzech, Karolina. 2020a. *Upper Napo Kichwa: a documentation of linguistic and cultural practices*. London: SOAS. Http://hdl.handle.net/2196/00-0000-0000-000C-F5FB-A. SOAS, University of London, Endangered Languages Archive. (15 December, 2020).

Grzech, Karolina. 2020b. Managing Common Ground with epistemic marking: 'Evidential' markers in Upper Napo Kichwa and their functions in interaction. *Journal of Pragmatics* 168. 81–97. https://doi.org/10.1016/j.pragma.2020.05.013.

Grzech, Karolina. 2021. Using discourse markers to negotiate epistemic stance: A view from situated language use. *Journal of Pragmatics* 177. 208–223. https://doi.org/10.1016/j.pragma.2021.02.003.

Grzech, Karolina. Under review. Reports, quotations and extended reported speech in Upper Napo Kichwa. In Stef Spronck & Daniela Casartelli (eds.), *Reported speech – New data studies*. Berlin: Language Science Press.

Güldemann, Tom & Manfred von Roncador (eds.). 2002. *Reported Discourse : A meeting ground for different linguistic domains*. Amsterdam: John Benjamins.

Heritage, John & Geoffrey Raymond. 2005. The Terms of Agreement: Indexing Epistemic Authority and Subordination in Talk-in-Interaction. *Social Psychology Quarterly* 68(1). 15–38.

Hintz, Daniel J. & Diane M. Hintz. 2017. The evidential category of mutual knowledge in Quechua. *Lingua* (Essays on Evidentiality) 186–187. 88–109. https://doi.org/10.1016/j.lingua.2014.07.014.

Kittilä, Seppo. 2019. General knowledge as an evidential category. *Linguistics* 57(6). 1271–1304. https://doi.org/10.1515/ling-2019-0027.

Kittilä, Seppo. 2020. Folklore as an evidential category. *Folia Lingüística* 54(3). 697–721. https://doi.org/10.1515/flin-2020-2051.

Klamer, Marian A.F. 2002. 'Report' constructions in Kambera (Austronesian). In Tom Güldemann & Manfred von Roncador (eds.), *Reported Discourse: A meeting ground for different linguistic domains*, 323–340. (Typological Studies in Language, vol. 52). Amsterdam: John Benjamins. https://doi.org/10.1075/tsl.52.20kla.

Krifka, Manfred. 2013. Embedding Speech Acts: Why, and How. Department of Philosophy, University of Wellington, Victoria, NZ. http://amor.cms.hu-berlin.de/~h2816i3x/Talks/EmbeddingSpeechActs_Wellington.pdf. (25 April, 2016).

Krifka, Manfred. 2014. Embedding Illocutionary Acts. In Thomas Roeper & Margaret Speas (eds.), *Recursion: Complexity in Cognition*, 59–88. Cham: Springer International Publishing.

Lefebvre, Claire & Pieter Muysken. 1988. *Mixed categories: nominalizations in Quechua*. Leiden: Kluwer Academic Publishers.

Mora Gutiérrez, Juliana de la. 2018. Las citas directas en el habla de la Ciudad de México. *Anuario de Letras. Lingüística y Filología* 6(2). 145–171.

Mushin, Ilana. 2001. *Evidentiality and epistemological stance: narrative retelling*. (Pragmatics & Beyond new ser. 87). Amsterdam /Philadelphia: John Benjamins.

Muysken, Pieter. 2010. The Copula in Ecuadorian Quechua. In Eithne B. Carlin & Simon van de Kerke (eds.), *Linguistics and Archaeology in the Americas*, 191–206. Leiden: BRILL. https://doi.org/10.1163/9789047427087_011.

Nikolaeva, Irina. 2014. *A Grammar of Tundra Nenets*. Berlin: Mouton De Gruyter.

Sánchez, Liliana. 2010. *The Morphology and Syntax of Topic and Focus: Minimalist Inquiries in the Quechua Periphery*. Amsterdam/Philadeplhia: John Benjamins.

Spronck, Stef & Daniela Casartelli. 2020. Reported speech: A typological questionnaire.
Spronck, Stef & Tatiana Nikitina. 2019. Reported speech forms a dedicated syntactic domain. *Linguistic Typology* 23(1). 119-159. https://doi.org/10.1515/lingty-2019-0005.
Steever, Sanford B. 2002. Direct and indirect discourse in Tamil. In Tom Güldemann & Manfred von Roncador (eds.), *Reported Discourse: A meeting ground for different linguistic domains*, 91-108. (Typological Studies in Language, vol. 52). Amsterdam: John Benjamins. https://doi.org/10.1075/tsl.52.07ste.
Stenzel, Kristine & Bruna Franchetto. 2017. Amazonian Narrative Verbal Arts And Typological Gems. In Kristine Stenzel & Bruna Franchetto (eds.), *On this and other worlds: Voices from Amazonia*, 1-19. Berlin: Language Science Press. https://doi.org/10.5281/ZENODO.1008775.
Stevanovic, Melisa & Anssi Peräkylä. 2012. Deontic Authority in Interaction: The Right to Announce, Propose, and Decide. *Research on Language & Social Interaction* 45(3). 297-321. https://doi.org/10.1080/08351813.2012.699260.
Stivers, Tanya, Lorenza Mondada & Jakob Steensig. 2011. Knowledge, morality and affiliation in social interaction. In Tanya Stivers, Lorenza Mondada & Jakob Steensig (eds.), *The Morality of Knowledge in Conversation*, 3-24. Cambridge: Cambridge University Press. http://ebooks.cambridge.org/ref/id/CBO9780511921674A012. (24 April, 2016).
Torero, Alfredo. 1964. Los dialectos quechuas. *Anales Científicos de la Universidad Nacional Agraria, Lima* 446-78.
Uzendoski, Michael & Edith Felicia Calapucha-Tapuy. 2014. *The ecology of the spoken word: Amazonian storytelling and shamanism among the Napo Runa*. Champaign, IL: University of Illinois Press.
Vries, Lourens J. de. 1990. Some remarks on direct quotation in Kombai. In Harm Pinkster & Inge Genee (eds.), *Unity in Diversity: Papers Presented to Simon C. Dik on his 50th Birthday*, 291-309. Berlin / New York: Mouton de Gruyter.
Weber, David. 1986. Information perspective, profile, and patterns in Quechua. In Wallace Chafe & Johanna Nichols (eds.), *Evidentiality: the linguistic coding of epistemology*, 137-55. Norwood, NJ: Ablex.
Willett, Thomas. 1988. A Cross-Linguistic Survey of the Grammaticization of Evidentiality. *Studies in Language* 12(1). 51-97.

Malte Rosemeyer & Pekka Posio

5 On the emergence of quotative *bueno* in Spanish: A dialectal view

Abstract: The Spanish discourse marker *bueno*, literally 'good', is a notoriously polyfunctional item that has been argued to serve several seemingly divergent functions, ranging from the expression of agreement to the expression of disagreement. It has also been observed that, as *bueno* frequently occurs at the beginning of reported speech, it may be grammaticalizing into a quotative marker, perhaps replacing other, more canonical markers like the verb *decir* 'say'. In this paper we adopt a cross-dialectal view to the use of *bueno* as a discourse marker, mapping it with the expression of reported discourse (a notion subsuming both reported speech and thought) in a multi-dialect corpus of spoken Spanish. Our analysis provides quantitative and qualitative evidence for the assumption that *bueno* is grammaticalizing into a marker of reported discourse. We also show that reported speech and reported thought are not routinely distinguished from each other in Spanish: rather, reported thought is conceptualized as reported speech, recurring to the metaphor of thinking as speaking. Nevertheless, we find evidence for the assumption that in those dialects in which the use of *bueno* is particularly productive, some speakers seem to routinely associate the use of *bueno* with reported thought rather than speech.

1 Introduction

In Spanish, the polyfunctional discourse marker *bueno*, grammaticalized from the adjective 'good', has several functions that range from the expression of agreement or disagreement to turn organization in conversation. For instance, *bueno* is frequently used at the beginning of a turn, as in example (1), taken from the PRESEEA corpus consisting of semi-structured sociolinguistic interviews.[1] Here, the use of *bueno* serves an intersubjective function that can be described as attenuation (the speaker I does not want to fully subscribe to the statement that she had a bad time with her first child). The closest equivalent of this use of *bueno* in English would be *well*. At the same time, the first occurrence of *bueno* can be considered to serve a turn-taking function (see Section 2).

---

[1] The PRESEEA corpus will be introduced in Section 3.

https://doi.org/10.1515/9783111065830-005

(1) [I and E are talking about I's children. I explains that she is enjoying the time with her second child more than she did with her first time.]

E: *con la primera lo pasaste peo:r ¿no?*
I: **bueno** *yo soy muy tranquila pero y tampoco lo pasé mal lo que pasa que* **bueno** *pues la inexperiencia te hace: ir aprendiendo en el día a día y en el. . . la hora a hora y en el minuto a minuto ¿no?*

E: 'with the first one you had a worse time, right?'
I: '**BUENO**, I am very calm and I did not really have a bad time, it's rather that **BUENO** the lack of experience makes you learn every day and. . . from hour to hour and from minute to minute, right?'
(ALCA_M22_028)[2]

As observed by Borreguero Zuloaga (2017), *bueno* also occurs with certain regularity in sequences of direct reported speech (see example (2)).

(2) *y yo decía* **pues bueno**-- *me decía la gente* → / *ya te enterarás de cómo es ¿no? y yo decía* **bueno** *ya me enteraré*

'and I said "okay **BUENO**". . . people would say to me "eventually you will find out how it is", right? and I said "**BUENO** yes, I will find out"'
Borreguero Zuloaga (2017: 70, mark-up in the original, translation ours)

On the basis of an interactional analysis of *bueno* and other discourse markers in Peninsular Spanish, Borreguero Zuloaga (2017) claims that one of the functions of these discourse markers is to signal transition to reported speech. In other words, the use of *bueno* in examples such as (2) does not necessarily reflect an actual earlier use of *bueno* that is being reported by the speaker, replicating its original function, but rather serves to mark the segment as reported speech. Borreguero Zuloaga's (2017) analysis furthermore implies that this new function of *bueno* has arisen over time on the basis of the original interactional functions of *bueno* in discourse, in line with recent proposals such as Detges and Waltereit (2011), who argue that turn-taking mechanisms in interaction can lead to grammaticalization processes.

---

2 The examples follow the transcription conventions of the PRESEEA corpus; however, in the interest of perspicuity, they have been simplified with regard to the marking of overlapping turns. 'E' refers to the interviewer and 'I' to the informant. The sign: has been adopted to mark lengthening of the previous vowel and . . . is used instead of the tag *vacilación* 'hesitation'. A single (/) and double (//) slash refer to shorter and longer pauses, respectively. Since our analysis is not morphosyntactic but pragmatic, we do not provide glosses but a translation as close to the original as possible, leaving the discourse marker BUENO untranslated.

In this paper, we aim at testing two hypotheses, based on Borreguero Zuloaga's observations from Peninsular Spanish: (1) *bueno* has developed new functions as marker of reported speech and discourse polyphony based on its earlier dialogical discourse marker uses and (2) these functions arise in those dialects with highest overall frequency of *bueno* as a discourse marker. In addition, we aim at teasing out any eventual differences in the use of *bueno* associated with reported speech (RS) and reported thought (RT). Since the distinction between RS and RT is not usually made in previous literature, we use the term reported discourse (RD) to subsume both. Due to the difficulty of tracing changes in the pragmatic functions of linguistic elements typically associated to spoken language in diachrony (see Rosemeyer 2019a), we adopt a cross-dialectal perspective. Standard theories of grammaticalization (e.g., Hopper and Traugott 2003) assume a correlation between the acquisition of new functions by a linguistic element and its usage frequency, such that an expansion of the functional domain of the element is usually accompanied by a general increase in its usage frequency. If *bueno* has indeed acquired the new function of marking polyphony, we should be able to document a cross-dialectal correlation between the proportion of discourse-marker uses of *bueno* (relative to lexical uses as an adjective) and the likelihood that speakers use *bueno* at the beginning of RD.

This chapter is structured as follows: in Section 2 we present an overview of the functions of *bueno* in addition to the "new" quotative function discussed here, in the light of both previous studies and a scrutiny of our data, which is presented in Section 3. Section 4 focuses on the qualitative analysis of *bueno* in RD in the data, and Section 5 presents a qualitative analysis of the quotative contexts across dialects displaying different usage patterns. Our findings are summarized in the concluding Section 6.

2 *Bueno* between argumentative, metadiscursive and polyphonic functions

There is a considerable body of research on discourse particles in Spanish (see, e.g., Martín Zorraquino and Portolés 1999; Briz, Pons, and Portolés 2008; López Serena and Borreguero Zuloaga 2010, to name but a few). As pointed out by Martín Zorraquino and Portolés (1999), the discourse particle *bueno* is extremely versatile and can express several pragmatic functions. The main functions identified in previous studies are the following:
i. expression of agreement with the interlocutor, possibly with hedges or modifications of the propositional content being agreed with;
ii. expression of disagreement with the interlocutor while protecting the positive face of the speaker through mitigation;

iii. metadiscursive uses, e.g., beginning, ending or changing a conversational topic (Martín Zorraquino and Portolés 1999); reformulation of previous speech (Pons 2003), presenting what is being said as continuation of previous topic (Briz, Pons, and Portolés 2008).

It should be noted that these classifications are based on the uses of *bueno* in spontaneous conversations, while our data consist of sociolinguistic interviews (see Section 3), where it is difficult to find clear instances of agreement and disagreement with the interlocutor due to the asymmetric roles of interviewer and informant. However, our data present several contexts of question-answer turn pairs where the first member projects an affirmative or a negative answer: *bueno* typically occurs in the second members of these adjacency pairs when the answer is not simply affirmative or negative but, rather, presents a modification or elaboration of the projected response. This is illustrated by examples (3) and (4). In (3), the speaker affirms the assumption expressed by the interviewer but also modifies it: she had to quit studies for various reasons, not only family-related ones, as implied by the interviewer. In (4), the informant begins both of her turns by *bueno*: the first is a negative answer to the interviewer's question, providing an explanation of why she does not like participating in manifestations, and the second one is an evasive answer that can be interpreted as neither affirmative nor negative.

(3) **positive answer with a modification of the presupposition of the question**

I: [. . .] *yo podía haber sido un buen estudiante lo que pasa es que lo dejé / lo tuve que dejar*
E: *por problemas familiares ¿no?*
I: ***bueno** sí // problemas familiares problemas económicos // ahí ayudó: / todo un poquito*

I: '[. . .] I could have been a good student but I quit / I had to quit'
E: 'due to family problems, right?'
I: '**BUENO** yes // family problems economic problems // everything summed up there a little bit'
(MALA_H11_114)

(4) **negative answer with an explanation / evasive answer**

E: *señora G. / y ¿le gusta ir para las marchas y eso? ¿o no? /*
I: ***bueno** no me gusta ir porque como me duelen las piernas / no puedo caminar mucho /*

E: *¿y tocar cacerola? //*
I: ***bueno** / en vez en cuando //*

E: 'Ms G. / and do you like to go to the marches and all that? or don't you?'
I: '**BUENO** I don't like to go because my feet hurt / I can't walk much /'
E: 'and bang the pots? //'
I: '**BUENO** / from time to time //'
(CARA_M32_067)

In the type of question-answer pairs represented by our data, *bueno* signals that the answer is not just positive or negative – in which case the speakers tend to use the polarity items *sí* 'yes' and *no* 'no' – but rather adds an explanation or a modification of the presupposition included in the question.

As for the metadiscursive function, our data present several examples of contexts where *bueno* is not a reaction to something said by the interlocutor but rather serves topic management functions. The *bueno* in the last line of example (5), may serve simultaneously as a marker of acceptance of the answer 'it's a friendship' given by the informant and a marker of closing this topic and moving to the next one (the informant's children).[3]

(5) **metadiscursive marker (=non-preferred change of topic; acknowledgement: closing one conversational topic and moving to the next one)**

E: *eh / ¿eres casada actualmente? /*
I: *no / estoy separada del papá del niño //*
E: *eeh / ¿estás con otro muchacho?*
I: *mmm*
E: *bueno no / no*
I: *no / no / no // no / no vamos a / no vamos a / a mentir // no / no es una relación*
E: *ya*
I: *es una amistad*
E: *una amistad //* ***bueno*** */ mmm // me dijiste que tienes dos niños*

E: 'eh / are you married at the moment? /'
I: 'no / I'm separated from the father of the child //'
E: 'eeh / are you with another guy?'
I: 'mmm'

---

[3] The first occurrence of *bueno,* produced by the interviewer in the fifth line, can be understood as a mitigation marker, as she seems to start an apology for having asked a potentially face-threatening question.

E: 'BUENO no / no'
I: 'no / no / no // let's not / let's not / lie // no / it's not a relationship'
E: 'ok'
I: 'it's a friendship'
E: 'a friendship // BUENO / mmm // you told me you have two children'
(LHAB_M21_019)

The fourth function of *bueno*, namely marking a sequence of speech as reported, was identified by Borreguero Zuloaga (2017), who examines the occurrence of several discourse particles in stretches of reported speech in spoken, colloquial Spanish. Her conclusion is that *bueno* has acquired a new discourse function as a marker of reported speech and discourse polyphony along with other markers such as prosodic cues and quotative uses of the verb *decir* 'say' (see Posio and Pešková 2020). Although Borreguero Zuloaga (2017: 81) does not systematically distinguish between reported speech (RS) and reported thought (RT), she remarks that *bueno* and other discourse markers with quotative functions may introduce the voice of another person as well as the speaker themselves or their thoughts (cf. Benavent Payá 2015 on the quotative uses of *decir* 'say').

Bueno is not the only quotative marker in Spanish. Typically, reported speech is introduced using verbal markers such as *digo* 'I say' and nominal markers such as the *y* 'and' + PRO(NOUN) construction (e.g., *y yo* 'and I') (cf. Posio and Pešková 2020). Although *bueno* often co-occurs with these other quotative markers, this is not always the case (Borreguero Zuloaga 2017). As we will show in Section 5, the quotative function of *bueno* presents different degrees of detachment from its other discourse functions, and that the quotative function emerges in those dialects displaying the most extensive use of *bueno* for other functions.

3 Data

Our data come from the PRESEEA corpus of spoken Spanish (PRESEEA 2014) and include the subcorpora currently available from nine countries (Chile, Guatemala, Colombia, Cuba, Mexico, Peru, Spain, Uruguay, and Venezuela). Table 1 lists the number of interviews, total number of words (including tags and metadata), and places and years of recordings by country.

As already mentioned in Section 2, the type of discourse represented by these data is semi-structured sociolinguistic interview. Consequently, each conversation

Table 1: Summary statistics of the PRESEAA corpus.

Country	n of interviews	n of words	Place of recording	Date of recording
Chile	18	235,069	Santiago de Chile	2007–2009
Guatemala	18	152,611	Guatemala	2003–2005
Colombia	71	615,407	Barranquilla, Cali, Medellín, Pereira	2001–2019
Cuba	17	161,535	La Habana	2010–2011
Mexico	70	919,240	Guadalajara, Mexicali, México D.F., Monterrey	2001–2018
Peru	18	177,004	Lima	2009–2010
Spain	88	916,331	Alcalá de Henares, Granada, Madrid, Málaga, Valencia	1988–2011
Uruguay	18	168,424	Montevideo	2007–2010
Venezuela	18	218,462	Caracas	2004–2008
Total	336	3,564,083		

has at least two participants with highly asymmetric discourse roles, as the interviewer is expected to ask questions and the informant is expected to answer them. Discourse phenomena like agreement and disagreement, and to a certain extent also turn management, are thus underrepresented in our data. However, the interviews offer plenty of examples of narratives where the informants tell the interviewers about their experiences, leading to occurrences of reported discourse (RD).

For our quantitative analysis, we extracted all instances of *bueno* (n = 12,625), as well as all instances of RD (n = 12,143) from the data. The extraction of RD was based on the coding with the tag *cita* 'quote' that was included in the corpus by the transcribers. Although the description of the corpus does not specify whether the code *cita* is applied to both RS and RT, it is evident from the examples that both types are included, and we will therefore use the hyperonym RD for all sequences marked as *cita*. This procedure thus allowed us to not only analyze the usage frequency of *bueno* in the interviews, but also the number of utterances that represent RD. Once these two data sets were extracted, all subsequent data annotation was carried out manually, starting with the separation of the discourse marker uses ($n = 11,443$) and the adjectival[4] uses ($n = 1,182$) of the word.

In the following quantitative analysis (Section 4), we analyze the contextual variation in the use of *bueno* on the level of the individual interviews. For instance, we first measure the normalized usage frequency of *bueno* in each interview and then group these results by country. The advantage of this analytical procedure is that it allows for capturing idiosyncratic variation displayed in each interview, which in turn reflects the speakers' individual usage patterns and preferences. We are thus able to gauge with much higher precision the range of variation when considering cross-dialectal differences in the usage of *bueno* than if we were relying on normalized frequencies on country level alone.

4 Cross-dialectal differences in the use of *bueno*

This section presents a quantitative analysis of cross-dialectal differences in the use of *bueno* in our data. First, we analyze overall cross-dialectal differences in the usage frequency and productivity of *bueno* (4.1). In Section 4.2, we test the hypothesis that quotative uses emerge most often in those dialects with highest overall frequency of *bueno* marker by inspection of the correlation between the usage frequencies of *bueno* in RD contexts and its overall usage frequencies. In Section 4.3, we test the hypothesis that this change leads to a lower usage of quotative markers such as *digo* 'I say'. Sections 4.2 and 4.3 employ both descriptive statistical methods and inferential statistical methods from variationist sociolinguistics, in particular linear mixed-effects regression models, in order to test for statistical significance. The results from these analyses are discussed in Section 4.4.

The analyses presented in this section are based on two crucial premises. First, we assume that cross-linguistic and cross-dialectal differences can be used as synchronic evidence for the existence of historical processes of linguistic change, common in typological approaches to the study of language (see, e.g., Croft 2016). The simplest case of such an approach is to analyze the use of an element in various languages or dialects in terms of distributional features. When significant differences regarding the use of that element in the distinct languages or dialects are found, a conceptual space (Croft 2016: 591–592) is posited for this range of functions. From this conceptual space, a historical change in terms of the relative succession of these

---

4 Note that *bueno* is the masculine singular form of the adjective: thus, the frequency of the adjective *bueno* in our data does not reflect the overall frequency of the lexeme, but only the frequency of this particular form.

functions can be inferred. To give an example from Romance, Carlier, De Mulder and Lamiroy (2012: 288–290) order Modern Spanish, Italian and French in terms of the degree of grammaticalization of verbal mood and, specifically, the productivity of the subjunctive mood. Such an approach can thus be used to infer a historical change when there is no access to real-time historical data. This is particularly useful for the description of linguistic change in elements such as discourse markers because discourse markers typically grammaticalize in interaction (cf. Heine 2013) and historical data usually lacks the richness required in order to conduct longitudinal diachronic analyses that model changes in interactional routines (Rosemeyer 2019a). As was shown in Rosemeyer (2019b), even when historical texts approximate spoken interaction in narrated discourse, this representation of spoken interaction is influenced by textual models imposed by genre. This typically leads to biases in terms of the represented discourse functions. In addition, the present case is even more complex, as a diachronic analysis of the usage of *bueno* in historical written texts would have to trace the development of reported speech markers within narrated discourse, in itself reported speech. In the light of these methodological obstacles, it seems to us that the hypothesis of an emergence of quotative functions of *bueno* is extremely difficult to prove in a longitudinal analysis.

Second, the analyses in this section employ the usage frequency of *bueno* as a crucial predictor of the assumed historical change towards polyphonic functions. This premise rests on a solid basis of historical evidence for a correlation between changes in usage frequency and grammatical change. Grammaticalization processes are usually accompanied by an increase in the usage frequency of the grammaticalizing element, reflecting the acquisition of new functions of the element. In particular, the "repetition of forms may lead to their 'liberation', or 'emancipation' (Haiman 1994), from their earlier discourse contexts and to increased freedom to associate with a wider variety of other forms" (Hopper and Traugott 2003: 127; cf. also Bybee and Torres Cacoullos 2009). For instance, Hopper and Traugott (2003: 194–196) explain the grammaticalization of Akkadian *enma*, a marker possibly derived from a verb of saying, towards a quotative discourse marker as the result of the frequent and conventionalized co-occurrence of *enma* with reported speech. A similar process appears to have taken place for the verb *decir* 'to say' in Peninsular Spanish (cf. Posio and Pešková 2020).

4.1 Usage frequency and productivity of bueno as a discourse marker

Figure 1 visualizes the usage frequency of *bueno* as a discourse marker (*n* = 11,443), both relative to the usage frequency of *bueno* in general (= including discourse both discourse marker uses and adjectival uses; n = 1,182, left plot) and in absolute usage frequency (right plot), by country.[5] We take the relative frequency of *bueno* as a discourse marker to be indicative of its degree of grammaticalization and consequently, its productivity: the higher the usage frequency of *bueno* as a discourse marker relative to adverbial uses in a specific dialect or idiolect, the more likelier speakers are to assign the new grammatical meaning to that element (see, e.g., Hay 2001). While the results differ slightly in terms of the relative order of the dialects, they suggest that the discourse marker use of *bueno* is most productive in (1) Venezuelan, Peruvian, Cuban, European and possibly, Uruguayan Spanish and least productive in (2) Guatemalan, Colombian, Mexican, and Chilean Spanish.

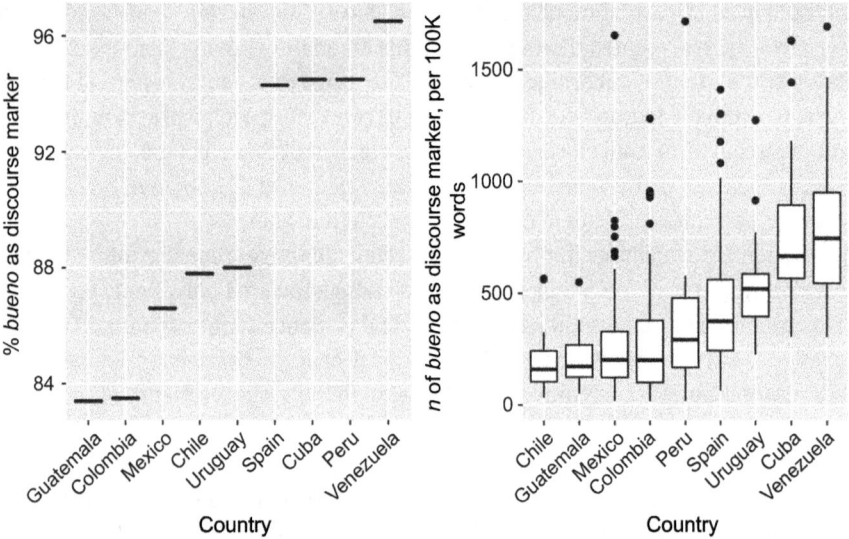

Figure 1: Usage frequency of *bueno* as a discourse marker relative to overall usage frequency of *bueno* (including adverbial uses), by country
Left plot: Mean percentage of the usage of *bueno* as a discourse marker by country
Right plot: Normalized usage frequency of *bueno* as a discourse marker, grouped by interview and country.

Having assessed the usage frequency of *bueno* as a discourse marker relative to the usage frequency of *bueno* as an adjective in Figure 1, we continued to eliminate the adjectival uses of *bueno* from the data, leaving us with a final dataset of n = 11,443

---

5 All plots were created in R (R Core Development Team 2021), using the ggplot2 package (Wickham 2016).

occurrences of *bueno* as a discourse marker. In the remainder of this paper, we will use the term *bueno* to refer exclusively to the discourse marker uses.

As was discussed at the beginning of Section 4, we assume that a greater productivity is mirrored in the freedom to be combined with a wider variety of other forms. This effect is well-known in grammaticalization studies, where it was observed that grammaticalization leads to an increase in the type frequency of grammaticalizing elements. For instance, Bybee (2003) analyzes the grammaticalization of the Old English verb *cunnan* 'to know', leading to Modern English *can*. She finds that initial modal uses of *cunnan* were restricted to a limited set of complement verbs (most importantly, communication verbs). The modal meaning was then gradually transferred to uses of *cunnan* with other complement verbs by virtue of an actualization process. Consequently, the high grammatical productivity of Modern English *can* can be measured in terms of its high type frequency, i.e. its freedom to combine with virtually all types of complement verbs.

In this paper, we assume that the productivity of discourse markers such as *bueno* can be measured in very much the same way. *Bueno* frequently co-occurs with prefaces such as *ah* 'ah'. Prefaces are formally defined in Conversation Analysis as elements than occur in turn-initial position and that are "followed by additional elements within the same intonation contour" (Heritage 1998: 292), meaning that no prosodic break between the preface and *bueno* may occur. Table 2 provides an inventory of the prefaces preceding *bueno* in our data.[6]

Table 2: Preface types occurring before *bueno* in the PRESEEA data, sorted by usage frequency.

Preface	Translation	Frequency
y	'and'	1,129
ah	'ah'	339
ee(h)(m)	'eh'	210
pues/pos	'then/well'	182
entonces	'then'	100
porque	'because'	90
este	'eh'	80
mm	'mm'	78

---

6 Note that the term "preface" in Conversation Analysis is defined in terms of its function in discourse (indeed, just like the term "discourse marker"). As a result, the prefaces listed in Table 2 belong to very different morphosyntactic categories (conjunctions, interjections, adverbs etc.). As correctly noted by one of the anonymous reviewers, a previous classification of these prefaces could offer a more accurate picture of the combination possibilities of *bueno*. Since this approach transcends the scope of the present paper, we leave this analysis to future research.

Table 2 (continued)

Preface	Translation	Frequency
ya	'okay'	40
aha/aja	'aha'	16
ay	'oh'	14
así	'so'	12
aunque	'although'	9
ahor(it)a	'now'	8
además	'also'	7
hm	'hm'	7
uhm	'uhm'	7
hh	'hh'	5
okay	'okay'	4
oh/oy	'oh'	2
uy	'uh'	1
bah	'bah'	1

These preface-*bueno* combinations have specific interactional functions, which cannot be described in detail here. As a case in point, however, consider example (6), in which the informant, who is a schoolteacher, has just told the interviewer that the kids call her by her first name (anonymized as X in the transcript). In the first line of the transcript, E asks I for confirmation. I repeats her assertion in the next line and gives an example from everyday life in order to give greater credibility to her claim. In the last line, E uses the assertion *sí* 'yes' to signal that she believes I now. E then goes on to introduce a new topic, namely the question whether they should finish the interview. This topic change is signaled by the sequence *y bueno*. Arguably, the discourse function of *y bueno* in this context cannot be derived in terms of its compositional meaning ('and' + 'well'); rather, it appears that *y bueno* has conventionalized the function of topic transition.

(6) E: *te llaman X / ni señorita ni profesora*
I: *nada no / X / el otro día precisamente ayer o antesdeayer encontré a uno pero muy mayor... que ya está en carrera y todo "hola X"*
E: *sí... y bueno // pue:::s yo creo que más o menos / no sé ya ha terminado*

E: 'everybody calls you X / neither madam nor professor'
I: 'no no / [only] X / the other day, yesterday or the day before yesterday, to be precise, I met one who was already old... he was already on the street and [says] "Hi X"'
E: 'yes, and BUENO // so... I think that was it more or less / it's over, I think'
(ALCA_M23_10)

Crucially for our purposes, it seems plausible to assume that the creation of conventionalized preface-*bueno* sequences is only possible in a situation in which *bueno* is already a grammaticalized discourse marker. Consequently, we would expect *bueno* to occur more frequently with prefaces in those dialects where it has a high usage frequency. The results from Figure 2, which visualizes the mean percentage of preface usage before *bueno* by interview and country, demonstrates that this prediction is mostly borne out by our data. In particular, four of the five dialects in which the use of *bueno* was shown to be most productive also show the highest rates of mean preface usage (Peru, Spain, Uruguay, Cuba). However, Venezuela is a notable exception, as mean preface usage is lowest in this dialect despite the high frequency of *bueno*. Despite this exception, the positive correlation between the usage frequency of *bueno* and mean rate of preface usage reaches high statistical significance.[7]

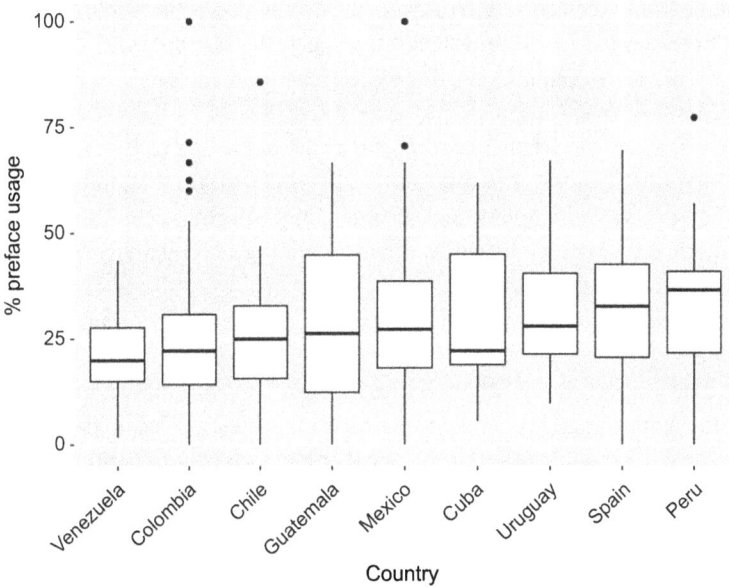

Figure 2: Mean percentage of preface usage before *bueno*, by interview and country.

---

7 Since the data violated the assumption of normality, a U-test was computed (Gries 2009: 209-210). The U-test showed that the positive correlation between the usage frequency of *bueno* and mean rate of preface usage is significant (W= 2770.5, $p_{\text{two-tailed}}$<.001). Here and in the remaining statistical analyses, we assumed a significance threshold of p <.05.

4.2 Usage frequency of bueno in reported discourse (RD)

Having established the overall distinction between dialects with more vs. less productive use of *bueno* as a discourse marker, we can now examine the hypothesis that quotative uses are more likely to emerge in those dialects with highest overall frequency of *bueno* as a discourse particle. We predict that the more frequently *bueno* is used in a specific interview and a specific dialect, the more likely it is to be found in the beginning of a stretch of RD. Such a correlation might be indicative of a grammaticalization of *bueno* towards a quotative marker (cf. Van Olmen and Tantucci 2022:171 for a similar hypothesis concerning English *look*).

We calculated the usage frequency of *bueno* at the beginning of RD contexts (i.e., as the first element of the stretch of RD, eventually preceded only by one of the prefaces listed in Section 4.1) relative to the overall number of RD contexts, which, as described in Section 3, was obtained by extracting all instances of the *cita* 'quote' tags from the data. In the process of this analysis, we realized that the tag *cita* had not been used in 62 interviews that nevertheless contained reported speech. Consequently, we eliminated these files from our analysis, leading to a total of *n* = 274 interviews.

Figure 3 visualizes the frequency of *bueno* at the beginning of RD relative to all occurrences of RD, by interview and country. It demonstrates that, in line with our expectations, *bueno* is relatively more frequent at the beginning of RD contexts in those dialects that were identified as displaying a high productivity of *bueno* (i.e., Uruguay, Spain, Cuba, and Venezuela).

In order to assess the statistical significance of this finding, we calculated a linear mixed-effects regression model predicting the usage frequency of *bueno* in RD relative to all occurrences of RD from the independent variables summarized in Table 3. Most importantly, we included the usage frequency of *bueno* per file as a predictor to test the hypothesis that the speakers who show a particularly productive use of *bueno* are more likely to use *bueno* at the beginning of RD, as well. We also included a number of sociolinguistic variables in order to control for social characteristics of the speakers. Testing such sociolinguistic predictors is a standard approach in variationist sociolinguistics (see, e.g., Tagliamonte 2012) and did not reflect any hypotheses on our part. As random effects, we included the variables COUNTRY (the dialect in question), and YEAR (the year of recording of the interview), thus also controlling for this variation. The model was calculated in R (R Core Development Team 2021) using the lmer (Bates et al. 2015) and lmerTest (Kuznetsova, Brockhoff, and Rune 2017) packages.

Table 4 summarizes the results from the regression model. As predicted, the model found a statistically significant positive correlation between (a) the usage frequency of *bueno* in RD relative to all occurrences of RD and (b) the overall, i.e.

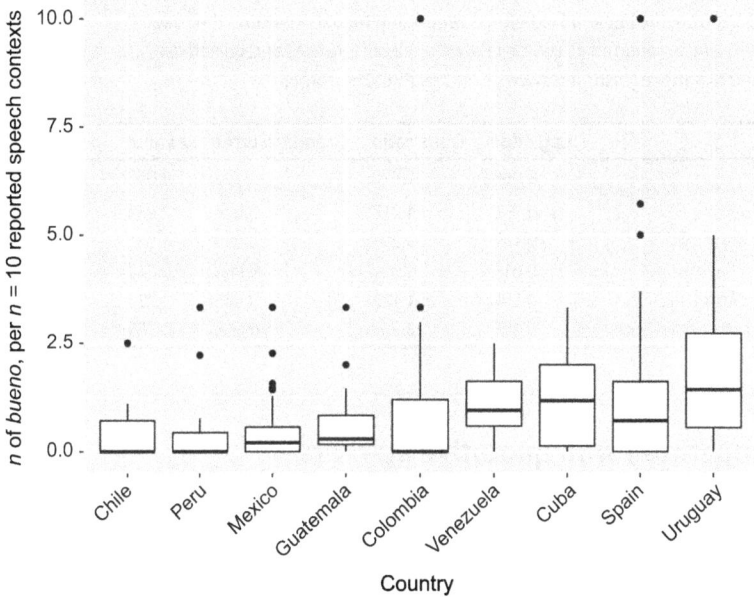

Figure 3: Frequency of *bueno* at the beginning of RD relative to all occurrences of reported speech, by interview and country.

Table 3: Operationalization of predictor variables for the linear mixed-effects regression model predicting the usage frequency of *bueno* in RD relative to all occurrences of RD.

Variable	Description
BUENO_FREQUENCY	Usage frequency of *bueno* per 100,000 words in the file, z-standardized
PERCENT_SEX_FEMININE	Percent of speakers of feminine sex per file, z-standardized
MEAN_AGE	Mean age of speakers per file, z-standardized
PERCENT_EDUCATION_HIGH	Percent of speakers with university education per file, z-standardized
PERCENT_SPEAKER_INTERVIEWER	Percent of turns attributed to the interviewer per file, z-standardized

RD-independent, usage frequency of *bueno* in the interviews. While none of the social variables were shown to correlate significantly with the usage frequency of *bueno* in RD relative to all occurrences of RD, the model found marginally statistically significant effects for the variables PERCENT_SEX_FEMININE and PERCENT_EDUCATION_HIGH.

Table 4: Results from the linear mixed-effects regression model predicting the usage frequency of *bueno* in reported discourse relative to all occurrences of reported discourse in *n* = 274 sociolinguistic interviews from the PRESEEA corpus.

Variable	Log odds	Odds ratio	Standard error	z value	p value
(Intercept)	0.068	1.070	0.102	0.662	0.508
BUENO_FREQUENCY	0.197	1.217	0.066	2.964	0.003
PERCENT_SEX_FEMININE	−0.116	0.891	0.060	−1.94	0.052
MEAN_AGE	0.013	1.014	0.063	0.214	0.830
PERCENT_EDUCATION_HIGH	0.114	1.120	0.065	1.756	0.079
PERCENT_SPEAKER_INTERVIEWER	−0.065	0.937	0.068	−0.955	0.340

4.3 Competition with quotative markers

Although the results from Section 4.2 correspond to expectations, it might be argued that the positive correlation between the probability of usage of *bueno* at the beginning of RD contexts and the overall usage frequency of *bueno* is a simple frequency effect, i.e., the higher probability of usage of *bueno* at the beginning of RD contexts for interviews in which *bueno* is used particularly productively is not higher **than would be expected** on the basis of the simple fact that *bueno* is generally more productive in those dialects. Consequently, in order to demonstrate that high-frequency *bueno* is indeed more likely to develop into a quotative marker than low-frequency *bueno*, additional analyses are necessary.

One further possibility to assess the relevance of the grammaticalization hypothesis is to analyze to what extent *bueno* competes with other quotative expressions such as the verb *decir* 'to say'. In Borreguero Zuloaga's (2017) view, the existence of instances of RD not introduced by *decir* or other quotative markers, but rather *bueno* alone, would be an indicator that *bueno* has undergone the grammaticalization process towards expression of polyphonic functions. This proposal leads to the prediction that dialects in which the use of *bueno* is particularly productive should demonstrate lower rates of overt quotative expressions before *bueno*.

Consequently, we restricted our dataset to all tokens of *bueno* in RD (*n* = 905) and established a new variable QUOTATIVE, which described the type of immediately preceding quotative marker. Table 5 describes the operationalization of this variable.

It is crucial to note that the coding of QUOTATIVE only refers to the immediately preceding quotative marker. In fact, we did not find a single clear-cut case in which *bueno* is used at the **beginning** of a stretch of RD without being preceded by a quotative marker in the extended context. Rather, tokens annotated as QUOTATIVE =

Table 5: Operationalization of the variable QUOTATIVE describing the type of quotative marker preceding *bueno* in RD.

Level	Description
say	immediately preceding *verbum dicendi* such as *digo* 'I say' or *dije* 'I said'
think	immediately preceding *verbum cogitandi* such as *pienso* 'I think'
noun	immediately preceding pronoun or noun referring to the speaker of the RD, such as *yo* 'I', *mi tía* 'my aunt'
adverbial	immediately preceding adverbial expression such as *total* 'in sum', *así como* 'as well as', *entonces* 'then'
none	no immediately preceding quotative marker

'none' are typically structured as the example in (7), where we have annotated the turns in the stretch of RD by indentation:

(7) *y me **dijo** / no pues es que no piense [. . .] se pone a trabajar y todo / y ya viene y ya se ha olvidado de la novia*
 */ le **dije** no apá es que / yo estaba ya muy enamorado*
 */yo **dije** no / no apá no / no puedo hacer eso / yo la quiero mucho a ella / ¡ah! / **bueno** haga lo que a usted le provoque*

'and he **said** to me "no well you don't think [. . .] you will start working and everything / and then you come and you'll have forgotten about the girlfriend"
 / I **said** to him "no dad it's like" / I was very much in love
 /I **said** "no / no dad no / I can't do that / I love her very much" /
 "ah! / BUENO you do whatever you want"' (MEDE_H31_002)

We find that in the first three stretches of RD in (5), the verb *decir* 'to say' is used as a quotative. In the last reported turn, attributed to the speaker's interlocutor, *bueno* is used without a preceding quotative marker. However, the characterization of the turn as RD is clearly projected by the use of the previous quotative markers, and possibly also by specific intonational features (which are not reflected in the corpus).

A very similar discourse configuration is typical of the usage of (pro)nominal quotative markers, as evinced in the last line of example (8). The use of the communication verb *pregunté* 'I asked' activates the quotative frame in which *y yo* 'and I' receives a quotative interpretation. Note that the stretch of RD consists solely of *ah bueno* which might be interpreted here as an expression of disbelief (cf. English *and I was like "okay"*). This example also illustrates a case where it is difficult to say whether the RD is intended to represent reported speech or reported thought.

(8)   entonces le **pregunté** "seño no me ha dicho nada de B"
               "no: no a él le ha ido bien ta ta/ni desordenado ni nada/bien bien que le ha ido"
                     y yo "ah bueno"
       'then I **asked** him "sir you haven't said to me anything about B"
               "no, no he's been good, ok? / not disoriented or anything / all good, all good he's been"
                     and I "ah BUENO"'
       (BARR_H23_015)

These considerations give rise to an alternative hypothesis regarding the use of quotative expressions. In particular, examples such as (7) and (8) might not be indicative of a change of *bueno* (or *y yo*, for that matter) towards the expression of polyphony, but rather a process by which the scope of quotative verbs has extended, such that these quotative verbs can project over longer stretches of discourse through the activation of a **quotative frame** in which the subsequent turns are also interpreted as RD.

Indeed, in line with studies on the grammaticalization of quotative markers (see the beginning of Section 4), the assumed change of *bueno* towards the expression of polyphony would lead us to expect not a decrease in the overall usage frequency of quotative markers such as *digo* 'I say', but rather the inverse effect. Thus, we would predict an increased strength of collocation between such quotative markers and *bueno*, in the sense that the usage of *bueno* becomes more frequent after quotative markers than would be expected on the basis of the usage frequency of *bueno* alone. In line with usage-based approaches to the description of language, such a routinization process should be mirrored in an increased, i.e., conventionalized, syntagmatic association between the quotative marker and *bueno*, leading to the creation of a prefab (see, e.g., Bybee 2006: 713).[8] In particular, we would predict a decrease in the frequency of prosodic boundaries between the quotative marker and *bueno*. Crucially, the routinization of the association between quotative markers and *bueno* would result in an increased predictability of *bueno* from quotative marker usage (i.e., upon hearing a quotative marker, the hearer will

---

[8] Bybee (2010: 35) defines prefabs (=prefabricated expression) as "any conventionalized multi-word expression" that results from the historical process of "chunking". A prefab such as Engl. *pull strings* differs from its compositional counterpart *pull strings* in that its form is immutable (e.g., saying I pulled a string does not lead to the meaning 'to secretly use the influence you have over important people in order to get something or to help someone' (https://dictionary.cambridge.org/de/worterbuch/englisch/pull-strings, accessed 7 July 2021), suggesting a holistic representation of the prefab in the language user's mind. Likewise, the meaning of the prefab is stored holistically, and is consequently not established compositionally (i.e., by combining the meaning of *pull* and the meaning of *strings*), due to a historical conventionalization process.

be more likely to predict the use of *bueno* as the next word uttered by the speaker). This higher predictability of *bueno* in sequences marked as RD might lead to a higher-based reanalysis (see Detges and Waltereit 2002; Eckardt 2009; Rosemeyer and Grossman 2017), such that *bueno* comes to be associated with RD irrespectively of the usage of a previous quotative marker. Only such a change would enable an eventual omission of other quotative markers with *bueno*.

Essentially, the scenario sketched above is not so much a contradiction to the negative correlation between quotative marker usage and usage frequency of *bueno* in RD, but rather a more detailed description of the change that might lead to the existence of such a negative correlation. In other words, if this latter scenario were found to be consistent with the data, it would suggest that although there is no conclusive evidence for the assumption that *bueno* is starting to replace quotative markers, such a change might well be incipient.

Figure 4 visualizes the mean percentage of quotative marker usage before *bueno*, by country, in RD (*n* = 905). It demonstrates that the use of quotative markers before *bueno* is more likely in those dialects in which the usage of *bueno* is particularly frequent and productive (especially Spain and Cuba).

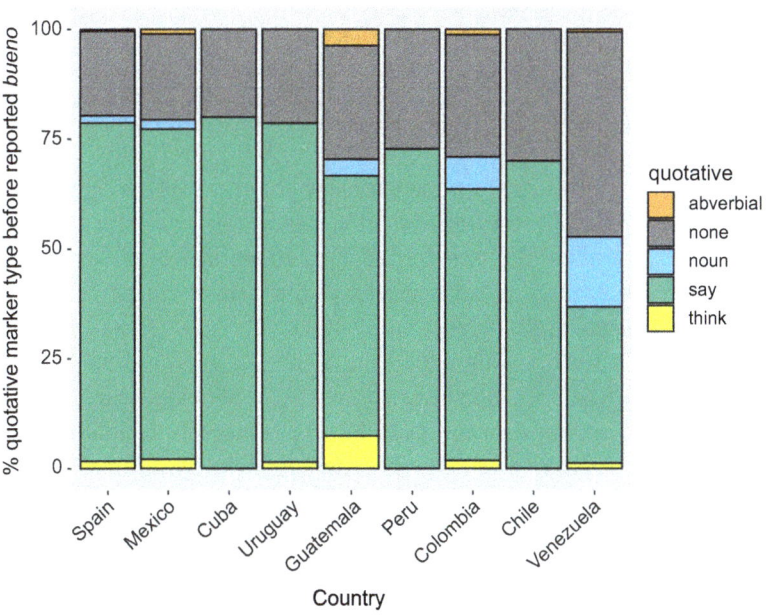

Figure 4: Mean percentage of quotative marker usage before *bueno*, by country.

However, this generalization appears to be rather weak, given that not only the Venezuelan, but also the Mexican and, to a smaller extent, Peruvian data do not seem to conform to the interpretation. In order to tackle this question, we again calculated a linear mixed-effects regression model to confirm the significance of these findings. This regression model predicts the mean percentage of quotative marker usage in each interview from the predictors already used in the previous regression model, summarized again in Table 6. It thus tests the hypothesis that speakers who show a particularly productive use of *bueno* are more likely to introduce *bueno* with a quotative marker. In keeping with standard sociolinguistic practices, we again tested for various social variables (sex, age, education, role in the conversation).

Table 6: Operationalization of predictor variables for the linear mixed-effects regression model predicting percentage of quotative marker usage in RD introduced by *bueno* in the PRESEEA corpus.

Variable	Description
BUENO_REPORTED_FREQUENCY	Log-transformed usage frequency of reported *bueno* per file, normalized by words per file, z-standardized
PERCENT_SEX_FEMININE	Percent of speakers of feminine sex per file, z-standardized
MEAN_AGE	Mean age of speakers per file, z-standardized
PERCENT_EDUCATION_HIGH	Percent of speakers with university education per file, z-standardized
PERCENT_SPEAKER_INTERVIEWER	Percent of turns attributed to the interviewer per file, z-standardized

As random effects, we again included the variables COUNTRY (the dialect in question), and YEAR (the year of recording of the interview), thus controlling for this variation. Crucially, we also included a third random effect, namely REPORTED_FREQUENCY, which represents the mean normalized and z-standardized usage frequency of all occurrences of RD (irrespectively of whether *bueno* is used in these stretches of reported speech) within a file. This random effect was nested within the random effects for COUNTRY and YEAR, in order to rule out the possibility that a higher frequency of quotative expressions is simply due more frequent RD and/or differences in the rigor of coding for RD in the different interviews.[9] Table 7 reports the results from the regression analysis.

---

[9] See Gries (2015) for a description of the relevance of using nested random effect structures and instructions for their implementation.

Table 7: Results from the linear mixed-effects regression model predicting the percentage of quotative marker usage in RD introduced by *bueno* in the PRESEEA corpus.

Variable	Log odds	Odds ratio	Standard error	z value	p value
(Intercept)	0.129	1.137	0.142	0.907	0.365
BUENO_REPORTED_FREQUENCY	0.095	1.100	0.032	2.938	0.003
PERCENT_SEX_FEMININE	−0.089	0.915	0.066	−1.358	0.174
MEAN_AGE	0.118	1.125	0.066	1.796	0.073
PERCENT_EDUCATION_HIGH	0.016	1.016	0.064	0.243	0.808
PERCENT_SPEAKER_INTERVIEWER	0.075	1.078	0.077	0.98	0.327

Table 7 demonstrates a significant positive correlation between the usage frequency of *bueno* in RD and the mean percentage of quotative marker use. This effect is visualized in Figure 5, demonstrating that quotative marker usage before *bueno* is more likely for interviews that display a particularly high usage frequency of reported *bueno*.

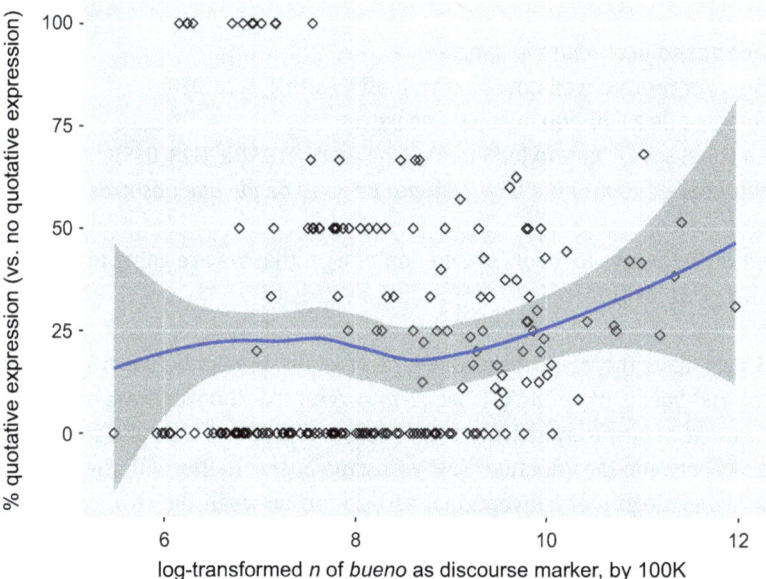

Figure 5: Correlation between between the usage frequency of *bueno* in RD contexts and the mean percentage of quotative marker use.

These results contradict Borreguero Zuloaga's (2017) assumption of a negative correlation between quotative marker usage and usage frequency of *bueno* in RD.

Rather, we find the inverse effect, in that probability of quotative marker usage before *bueno* in RD increases the more *bueno* is used in RD.

However, our finding is consistent with the alternative scenario proposed above, namely, an increased routinized association between quotative markers and the usage of *bueno* in RD, which is likewise indicative of the historical change of *bueno* towards the expression of polyphony. As was suggested above, such a scenario can be tested by exploring the degree to which quotative markers and *bueno* have become a prefab. In order to do so, we analyzed the correlation between the frequency with which speakers insert a prosodic break between immediately preceding quotative markers and reported *bueno* in our data. Given that quotatives based on *verbi dicendi* such as *decir* 'to say' constitute by far the most frequent group of quotative expressions in our data (n = 595 of 905, see also Section 5 below), we restricted our analysis to contexts in which reported *bueno* is immediately preceded by such a speech act verb.

The PRESEEA distinguishes between three types of prosodic breaks, i.e. none (9a), weak (9b) and strong (9c) prosodic breaks. A weak prosodic break is conceptualized as a short pause, a strong prosodic break as a longer pause.[10]

(9) a. *dice **bueno** pues ahora lo apagaré*
'(s/he) says "BUENO well now I'll turn it off"' (GRAN_M23_010)
b. *entonces dice: / **bueno** mijo pero no vayas*
'then (s/he) says / "BUENO kid but don't go there"' (BARR_H23_015)
c. *entonces mi esposa me dice // **bueno** no se te olvide que nosotros vamos a jugar* [. . .]
'then my wife says to me // "BUENO don't forget that we are going to play. . ."' (CARA_H21_013)

Figure 6 visualizes the mean percentage of prosodic breaks between quotative 'say' verbs and *bueno,* by country. It seems to suggest that indeed, those dialects in which the usage of *bueno* is particularly frequent and productive display fewer prosodic breaks between the quotative 'say' verbs and *bueno,* in line with the assumption of a higher degree of conventional association between the two expression types.

---

10 See https://preseea.linguas.net/Portals/0/Metodologia/Marcas_etiquetas_minimas_obligatorias_1_2.pdf (p. 7, accessed 11 February 2021).

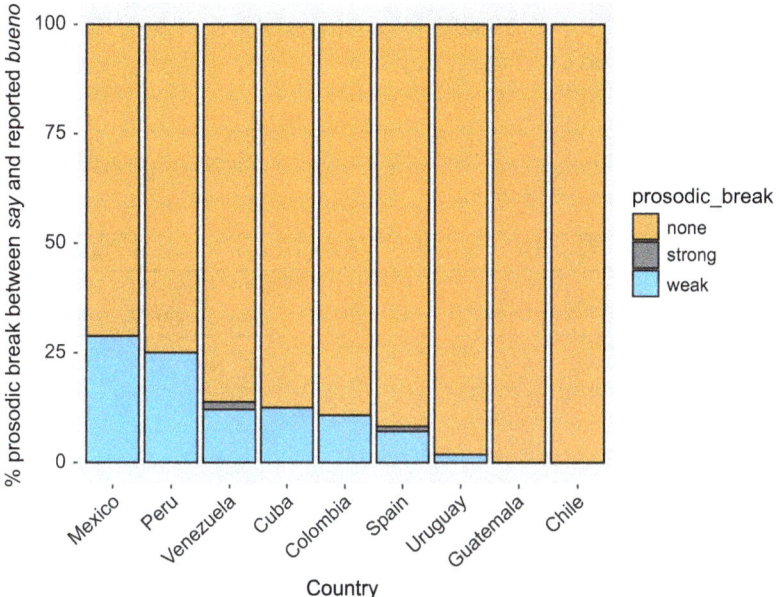

Figure 6: Mean percentage of prosodic breaks between quotative 'say' verbs and bueno, by country.

However, once again, several dialects in Figure 6 do not seem to conform to this proposed pattern. Contrary to expectations, Mexican Spanish shows the highest mean frequency of prosodic breaks, whereas Chile and Guatemala have the lowest mean frequency of prosodic breaks. This might be due to relative differences in sample size, as indicated in Table 8. If we consider only those dialects with a minimum usage frequency of reported *bueno* following a quotative 'say' expression of $n = 50$, a much clearer picture emerges, where Uruguay and Spain show low rates of prosodic breaks between *bueno* and the 'say' quotative, whereas Mexico, Venezuela and Colombia show relatively high rates of prosodic breaks.

Table 8: Usage frequency of reported *bueno* following a quotative 'say' expression.

Spain	Mexico	Colombia	Venezuela	Uruguay	Cuba	Guatemala	Peru	Chile
182	142	102	58	54	16	16	16	7

This interpretation is backed by a simple linear mixed-effects regression model predicting the mean percentage of prosodic breaks between *bueno* and quotative 'say' in the interviews from the usage frequency of *bueno* in RD introduced by quotative 'say', controlling for YEAR and COUNTRY as random effects. The model, summarized in Table 9, calculates a significant positive correlation between the mean percentage of prosodic breaks between *bueno* and quotative 'say' and the usage frequency of *bueno* in RD introduced by quotative 'say'.

Table 9: Results from the linear mixed-effects regression model predicting the mean percentage of prosodic breaks between *bueno* and quotative 'say' in the interviews from the usage frequency of *bueno* in RD introduced by quotative 'say'.

Variable	Log odds	Odds ratio	Standard error	z value	p value
(Intercept)	−0.350	0.704	0.105	−3.348	0.001
Bueno_reported_frequency	0.053	1.055	0.013	4.165	0.000

Figure 7 visualizes this positive correlation.

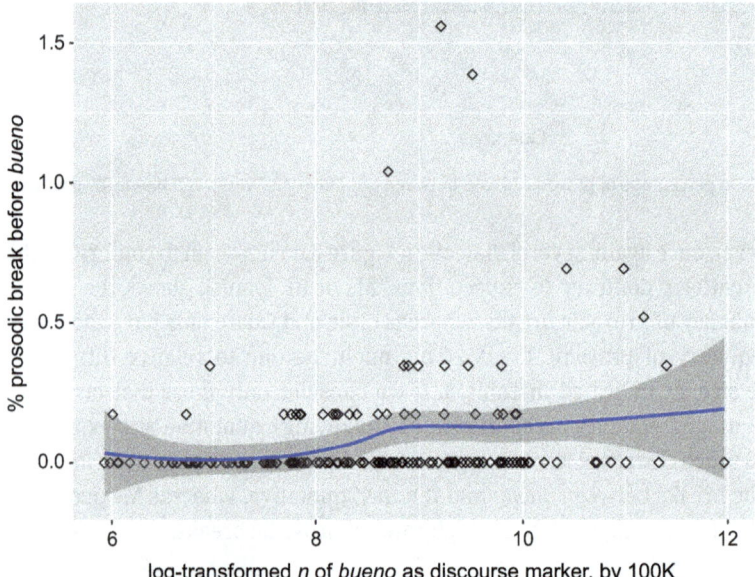

Figure 7: Correlation between the mean percentage of prosodic breaks between *bueno* and quotative 'say', and the usage frequency of reported *bueno* in the interviews.

4.4 Discussion

In summary, our quantitative analysis of the usage of *bueno* in the PRESEEA supports the hypothesis based on Borreguero Zuloaga (2017) that *bueno* is evolving towards a quotative marker used to express polyphony in discourse. In concrete, we have shown that (a) *bueno* is more likely to be used in RD contexts in those interviews that show a particularly productive and frequent usage of *bueno*, indicating that higher productivity of *bueno* in general can lead to a more frequent usage of *bueno* in RD, and (b) that this change seems to be bound to a routinization of the collocation between *bueno* and preceding quotative markers (especially quotative *decir* 'say'), as mirrored in a decreasing frequency of prosodic breaks between *bueno* and *decir*. Although we did not find evidence for the assumption that *bueno* has started to replace other quotative expressions in those dialects in which it is particularly productive and hence grammaticalized, our findings are consistent with proposals of mechanisms of grammaticalization based on the notion of hearer-based reanalysis. Consequently, our analysis suggests that while *bueno* has not developed into a quotative marker itself even in those dialects in which it is most productive, it may do so in the future.

5 *Bueno* in reported speech and thought

In this section, we examine the eventual distinctions between reported speech (RS) and reported thought (RT) in our data, focusing especially on those contexts where *bueno* occurs as part of the stretch of reported discourse (RD).

A simple quantitative examination of the lexical items most frequently used to introduce RD reveals a strong predominance of the verb *decir* 'say', while *pensar* 'think' is marginal in this function. The verb *decir* precedes the sequence of reported discourse in 6,450 of the 12,143 occurrences of the tag *cita* 'quote' in the totality of our data consisting of all occurrences of the tag, i.e., over half of the instances of RD are introduced using this verb. The verb *pensar* occurs only 27 times before RD. This comparison confirms Posio and Pešková's (2020) observation that *decir* has clearly specialized in the quotative function while other communicative verbs are marginal in the quotative function. It also shows that RT is very rarely distinguished from RS by the choice of the verb in the quotative expression. Indeed, speakers recur to the verb *decir* in contexts that are clearly instances of RT, as in example (10). In this example, the speaker does not refer to any actual dialogue but rather describes what he is thinking at the moment or in general (i.e., the quotative is not episodic but generic; see Posio and Pešková (2020) for a discussion of the two types).

(10) ahora lo pienso y **digo** qué bárbaro
'now I think about it and **I say** "how amazing"'
(GUAD_H22_002)

Since the same lexical verb can be used to introduce both RS and RT, let us now turn into a qualitative scrutiny of the data in order to examine whether other usage patterns distinguishing between reported speech and thought emerge, focusing on those dialects where *bueno* is most frequently associated with RD.

The qualitative analysis of these data lends further support to our hypothesis that quotative *bueno* does not necessarily display any of the other discourse functions of *bueno* such as expressing agreement, disagreement or mitigation (see Section 2), but can rather just mark the beginning of the reported sequence. This can be observed in examples (11) and (12) from the Uruguayan data – one of the dialects with most frequent and productive use of *bueno*. We find frequent use of the quotative *bueno* in combination with *decir* 'say' in contexts that clearly pertain to RS, i.e., stretches of dialogue that the speaker presents as episodic, having occurred and being anchored in a point in time. Such a case of RS is found in example (11), where the speaker attributes the words to a third person (medical personnel in a hospital). There is nothing in the context supporting an interpretation of *bueno* (in this particular example) as serving other discourse marker functions in addition to marking the sequence as RS.

(11) [. . .] *sentía dolor muy fuerte en el pecho y. . . ta fui al médico y **me dijeron bueno** / andá a hacerte una placa / y ahí fue que descubrieron eso* / [. . .]
'[. . .] I felt a very strong pain in my chest and. . . so I went to the doctor and **they said to me** "BUENO / go and let them do an X-ray" / and it was there they noticed that / [. . .]'
(MONV_H11_035)

The same combination of *decir* and *bueno* also occurs before RT, i.e., stretches of dialogue that the speaker presents as inner speech or something that they or anyone in their position might say or think in a given scenario that are not episodic (anchored to a specific point in time and space) but rather generic or irrealis (see Posio and Pešková 2020). A clear example of reported thought is given in (12), where the interviewer asks if the informant has ever experienced a near-death experience – an essential part of the classic Labovian sociolinguistic interview.

(12) [. . .] *y ¿te ha pasado alguna vez de tener. . . / aparte de esta operación ¿no. . . peligro de muerte? De que **vos decís bueno**. . . me me muero o sea. . .*
'[. . .] and has it happened to you some time that you'd have. . . / in addition to that surgery, like. . . danger of death? Like **you say** "BUENO. . . I, I'm going to die" like. . .'
(MONV_H11_035)

As can be observed in examples (11) and (12), the Uruguayan data does not present any formal differences in the marking of RS and RT. However, looking at other dialects with frequent and productive *bueno* usage, the Cuban data seems to show some evidence to the effect that speakers may formally distinguish between RT and RS. An analysis of the Cuban interviews suggests that the quotative *bueno* typically occurs in sequences intended to represent what the speaker (or anyone, typically expressed as a generic *tú* 'you') may think or say (to themselves) in a given scenario, with no reference to actual dialogue. This is illustrated by example (13) where the speaker describes the old times and introduces what we interpret as RT, with no reference to actual, episodic, dialogue.

(13) [. . .] *tocaban grupos musicales en la playa / eeh / aquí en el malecón / o sea / que había una diversidad / para tú poder escoger / una salida tuya un fin de semana para desconectar que era inmensa / tú podías darte el lujo de* **decir** *"bueno / voy aquí" / los cines / la ciudad estaba llena de cines / de películas de estreno* [. . .]
'[. . .] there were bands playing on the beach / eeh / here on the pier / like / there was diversity / for you to choose / where you want to go out on a weekend to disconnect that was immense / you had the luxury of **saying** "BUENO / I'm going here" / the movies / the city was full of movie theaters / movie premieres [. . .]'
(LHAB_H22_049)

Example (14) from the Cuban data illustrates a complex stretch of RD where the quotative verb *decir* is used in the beginning, in combination with *bueno* (lines a, b) while *bueno* alone functions as a quotative marker once the frame of reported discourse has been established (line e). In this example, the speaker is explaining why she decided to quit her job as an informatician. Our interpretation is that the example contains both RT (the speaker saying – to herself – that she must change jobs: lines a, b, e) and RS by the speaker herself and two other persons (lines c, d, f). Interestingly, *bueno* only occurs here in those instances of RD that seem to be construed as RT (lines a, b, e) but not in RS (lines a, b, e). This interpretation is supported by the fact that in the former cases there is no recipient (i.e., the speaker does not direct her words to anyone in particular) while in the latter cases the recipient is marked (*a mi hermana* 'to my sister', *me* 'to me') which construes a reference to an actual dialogue rather than thought or 'inner speech' without an external recipient.

(14) [. . .] *por un tiempo fui la informática como un año y pico dos años / hasta que llegaron. . . muchachos recién graduados los pusieron ahí y llegamos a ser como once personas. . . pero. . .eh //*

[a] *dije "**bueno** voy a cambiar ya porque"*
además que ahí trabajaba mucho mucho mucho mucho y con la universidad no me daba casi tiempo / y hacía lo que me tocaba y lo que no me tocaba bueno llegué hasta hacer nómina y todo... eh
[b] *dije "**bueno** me voy a cambiar"*
[c] **le dije a mi hermana** un día *"oye eeh averíguame mmh algún trabajo que haya por allá [...]" /[...] y entonces*
[d] **Adriana me dijo** *"no ahí está hay una plaza componedor... pero tienes que aprender un programa hay que no sé que"* //
[e] *"**bueno** yo voy a ir a probar"* // vine / acababan de inaugurar la editorial //
[f] **Aidé habló conmigo me dijo** *"¡no! Para que empieces" no sé que [...]*

'[...] for some time I was the informatician like a year and a bit two years / until there arrived... some recently graduated guys they were placed there and we went up to like 11 people... but... eh //
[a] I said "BUENO I will change [job] already because"
in addition to working a lot a lot a lot there and with the university I had hardly any time / and I was doing my duties and other stuff well I started receiving a salary and everything. eh
[b] I said "BUENO I will change"
[c] **I said to my sister** one day "listen eeh find me mmh a job that's available there [...]" and then
[d] **Adriana said to me** "no there's a place for a technician... but you have to learn a program you have to I don't know what" //
[e] "BUENO I'm going to try" // I came / they had just opened the agency //
[f] **Aidé talked with me she said to me** "no! why would you start" I don't know what [...]'
(LHAB_M12_043)

Example (14) also illustrates the distribution of *bueno* and other quotative markers already discussed in Section 4.3: in longer stretches of RD, *decir* occurs in the beginning either alone or with other markers, while *bueno* and other markers alone function as quotatives only after the quotative frame has been established by the use of *decir*.

Contrasting with the Uruguayan and Cuban examples discussed above, in the varieties with least occurrences of *bueno* in RD, not only is *bueno* less frequently used but it also seems to convey other discourse marker functions in addition to marking a stretch of dialogue as RD. Rather, it seems to maintain the 'original' discourse marker function, for instance, marking a dispreferred turn in a conversation. This is exemplified by (15) from the Guatemalan data. This excerpt is part of a lengthy monologue where the informant refers to a situation where his father was offering money to his son, which caused him to feel both upset and ashamed and to respond '*bueno* then I'll just leave'.

(15) [...] *le dio diez pesos y yo pues dije yo ganas de //* **"*dáselos nene*" *le dije* //** *me dieron ganas de decirle así pero bueno* / [teeth-sucking sound] / *aquel es un niño veá / me enojó mucho y // y / con él me dio vergüenza /* **"*bueno entonces ya me voy*" *le dije yo***
'he gave him ten pesos and I said wanted to [say] **"give them to him kid" I said to him** // I wanted to say that to him but well [teeth-sucking sound] / it is a child, look / I became very angry and // and / I was ashamed for him / **"BUENO then I'll go already" I said to him**'
[...](GUAT_H11_011)

Since the speaker in example (14) is reproducing a conflictive situation where *bueno* may have been used as a discourse marker to signal, e.g., the unexpectedness of the verbal reaction or used as a hedge, it can be interpreted as being part of the RS. Thus, this example differs from (11)–(14), where the presence of *bueno* is not motivated by contextual clues from the original discourse context where the stretch of RD is nested.

Although examples like (13) and (14) do suggest that local discourse patterns distinguishing between RS and RT emerge in dialects with most productive usage of *bueno*, it is difficult to say to what extent such patterns are generalized or, rather, depend on the local discourse context – or even reflect the idiolectal preferences of individual speakers. Thus, regarding the eventual distinction between RS and RT, the main finding of our analysis is that the two are generally not distinguished in Spanish but, rather, RT is represented similarly to RS. In other words, thinking – an invisible, mental activity – is metaphorically represented as speaking when reported to an interlocutor.

6 Discussion and conclusions

This paper has examined the emergence of the polyphonic functions of the discourse particle *bueno* across dialects of Spanish, testing the hypothesis that *bueno* and other discourse particles frequently occur in the beginning of reported discourse, that *bueno* may grammaticalize into a marker of polyphony and that it may even replace quotative markers such as *decir* 'say'.

A quantitative analysis of our data identified dialects with very productive use of *bueno* (i.e., our Venezuelan, Peruvian, Cuban, Uruguayan and European samples) and another group of dialects with less productive use of *bueno* (i.e., our Mexican, Guatemalan, Colombian, and Chilean samples). All dialects of the first group except Venezuela also showed frequent combination of *bueno* with other discourse particles as prefaces. As expected, the dialects with most frequent and productive uses of *bueno* were also the ones with most frequent use of *bueno* at the beginning of reported discourse. In order to exclude the possibility that this finding is due to a simple frequency effect, we moved on to assess the degree to which *bueno* has started competing with quotative markers in dialects in which it is particularly productive. Contrary to expectations, in these dialects reported *bueno* is more likely to co-occur with quotative markers (again, with the exception of Venezuela). Finally, we identified a positive correlation between the appearance of prosodic breaks between the quotative verb *decir* and the quotative marker *bueno*, and the usage frequency of the quotative *bueno*. We interpreted these findings in line with a scenario in which the grammaticalization of *bueno* towards expression of a quotative function is due to a hearer-based reanalysis on the basis of the frequent collocation of *bueno* with quotative markers. Thus, while we did not find direct evidence of *bueno* replacing other quotative markers (as predicted by Borreguero Zuloaga 2017), the creation of *decir* + *bueno* prefabs might lead to a situation in which the use of *decir* is no longer necessary in order to mark reported discourse.

A more detailed qualitative analysis provided further evidence for this proposal by analyzing the use of reported *bueno* in two dialects in which *bueno* is particularly productive, namely Uruguayan and Cuban Spanish. Thus, it was shown that in *decir* + *bueno* collocations from these dialects, *bueno* no longer necessarily displays any of the interactional functions typical for *bueno* in direct, non-reported, discourse, suggesting that *bueno* is indeed conventionally used to (co-)mark RD.

Our analysis also shows that reported speech and reported thought are not routinely distinguished by speakers of Spanish: the use of mental verbs to introduce reported discourse is marginal, and typically thoughts are reported as if they were spoken words, i.e., using the verb *decir* 'say' and, occasionally, the quotative *bueno*. However, inspection of the Cuban data suggested that in dialects in which *bueno* is particularly productive, *decir* + *bueno* collocations might even be recruited as markers of reported thought. Such uses of *bueno* can be characterized as even more innovative, as the function of reporting thought is even more dissociated from the original interactional functions of *bueno* (cf. also Rosemeyer and Sansiñena 2019 for a similar approach to *que* 'that'-prefaces in Spanish). In particular, when using *bueno* in a stretch of RT, it is highly unlikely that the speaker has indeed mentally uttered the word *bueno* in the situation they are describing. However, since operationalizing the distinction between reported speech and reported thought for a quantitative analysis seems extremely difficult due to non-distinct marking of the two types of reported discourse, this observation is based only on qualitative scrutiny of the data. Subsequent quantitative corroboration of these tendencies seems necessary, an issue we leave to future research.

References

Bates, Douglas, Martin Maechler, Ben Bolker & Steve Walker. 2015. Fitting linear mixed-effects models using lme4. *Journal of Statistical Software* 67(1). 1–48.
Benavent Payá, Elisa. 2015. *Decir y discurso directo en los relatos de la conversación coloquial.* València: Universitat de València.
Borreguero Zuloaga, Margarita. 2017. Los relatos coloquiales: partículas discursivas y polifonía. *Pragmalingüística* 25. 62–88.
Briz, Antonio, Salvador Pons & José Portolés (eds.). 2008. *Diccionario de partículas discursivas del español.* www.dpde.es (accessed 21 September 2020).
Bybee, Joan L. 2003. Mechanisms of change in grammaticization: the role of frequency. In Richard Janda & Brian Joseph (eds.), *The Handbook of Historical Linguistics*, 624–647. Oxford: Blackwell.
Bybee, Joan L. 2006. From usage to grammar: the mind's response to repetition. *Language* 82(4). 711–733.
Bybee, Joan L. 2010. *Language, Usage, and Cognition*. Cambridge & New York: Cambridge University Press.
Bybee, Joan L. & Rena Torres Cacoullos. 2009. The role of prefabs in grammaticization: how the particular and the general interact in language change. In Roberta Corrigan, Edith A. Moravcsik, Hamid Ouali & Kathleen M. Wheatley (eds.), *Formulaic Language, Volume I: Distribution and Historical Change*, 187–217. Amsterdam & Philadelphia: Benjamins.
Carlier, Anne, Walter De Mulder & Béatrice Lamiroy. 2012. Introduction: The pace of grammaticalization in a typological perspective. *Folia Linguistica* 46(2). 287–301 [Special issue *The Pace of Grammaticalization in a Typological Perspective*, edited by Anne Carlier, Walter De Mulder & Béatrice Lamiroy].
Croft, William. 2016. Typology and the Future of Cognitive Linguistics. *Cognitive Linguistics* 27(4). 587–602.
Detges, Ulrich & Richard Waltereit. 2002. Grammaticalization vs. reanalysis: a semantic-pragmatic account of functional change in grammar. *Zeitschrift für Sprachwissenschaft* 21(2). 151–195.
Detges, Ulrich & Richard Waltereit. 2011. Turn-taking as a trigger for language change. In Sara Dessì Schmid, Ulrich Detges, Paul Gévaudan, Wiltrud Mihatsch & Richard Waltereit (eds.), *Rahmen des Sprechens. Beiträge zur Valenztheorie, Varietätenlinguistik, Kreolistik, Kognitiver und Historischer Semantik. Peter Koch zum 60. Geburtstag*, 175–190. Tübingen: Narr.
Eckardt, Regine. 2009. APO: Avoid Pragmatic Overload. In May-Britt Mosegaard Hansen & Jaqueline Visconti (eds.), *Current Trends in Diachronic Semantics and Pragmatics*, 21–41. Bingley: Emerald.
Gries, Stefan Th. 2009. *Quantitative Corpus Linguistics with R. A Practical Introduction*. New York & London: Routledge.
Gries, Stefan Th. 2015. The most under-used statistical method in corpus linguistics: Multi-level (and mixed-effects) models. *Corpora* 10(1). 95–125.
Hay, Jennifer. 2001. Lexical frequency in morphology: Is everything relative? *Linguistics* 39. 1041–1070.

Heine, Bert. 2013. On discourse markers: Grammaticalization, pragmaticalization, or something else? *Linguistics* 51(6). 1205–1247.

Heritage, John. 1984. A change-of-state token and aspects of its sequential placement. In J. Maxwell Atkinson & John Heritage (eds.), *Structures of Social Action: Studies in Conversation Analysis*, 299–345. Cambridge: Cambridge University Press.

Heritage, John. 1998. *Oh*-prefaced responses to inquiry. *Language in Society* 27. 291–334.

Hopper, Paul J. & Elizabeth C. Traugott. 2003. *Grammaticalization*. 2nd edn. Cambridge: Cambridge University Press.

Kuznetsova, Alexandra, Per B. Brockhoff & Rube H. B. Christensen. 2017. lmerTest Package: Tests in Linear Mixed Effects Models. *Journal of Statistical Software* 82(13). 1–26.

López Serena, Araceli & Margarita Borreguero Zuloaga. 2010. Los marcadores del discurso y la variación lengua hablada vs. lengua escrita. In Óscar Loureda & Esperanza Acín Villa (eds.), *Los estudios sobre marcadores del discurso en español, hoy*, 415–495. Madrid: Arco Libros.

Martín Zorraquino, María & José Portolés. 1999. Los marcadores del discurso. In Ignacio Bosque & Violeta Demonte (eds.), *Gramática descriptiva de la lengua Española*, 4051–4213. Madrid: Espasa Calpe.

PRESEEA. 2014. *Corpus del Proyecto para el estudio sociolingüístico del español de España y de América*. Alcalá de Henares: Universidad de Alcalá. http://preseea.linguas.net (accessed 9 September 2020).

Pons, Salvador. 2003. From agreement to stressing and hedging: Spanish *bueno* and *claro*. In Gudrun Held (ed.), *Partikeln und Höflickeit*, 219–236. Frankfurt am Main: Peter Lang.

Posio, Pekka & Andrea Pešková. 2020. Construccionalización de los introductores cuotativos con el verbo *decir* en español peninsular y argentino. *Spanish in Context* 17(3). 391–414.

R Development Core Team. 2021. *R: A language and environment for statistical computing*. R Foundation for Statistical Computing, Vienna, Austria. http://www.R-project.org (accessed 9 February 2021).

Rosemeyer, Malte. 2019a. Actual and apparent change in Brazilian Portuguese *wh*-interrogatives. *Language Variation and Change* 31(2). 165–191.

Rosemeyer, Malte. 2019b. Brazilian Portuguese *in-situ wh*-interrogatives between rhetoric and change. *Glossa* 4(1). 1–29.

Rosemeyer, Malte & Eitan Grossman. 2017. The road to auxiliariness revisited: the grammaticalization of FINISH anteriors in Spanish. *Diachronica* 34(4). 516–558.

Rosemeyer, Malte & María Sol Sansiñena. 2019. The discourse functions of insubordination in Spanish *wh*-interrogatives. *Papers of the Linguistic Society of Belgium* 13. https://sites.uclouvain.be/bkl-cbl/en/journals/pap (accessed 3 March 2021).

Tagliamonte, Sali. 2012. *Variationist Sociolinguistics. Change, Observation, Interpretation*. Malden, MA: Wiley-Blackwell.

Van Olmen, Daniël & Vittorio Tantucci. 2022. Getting attention in different languages: A usage-based approach to parenthetical look in Chinese, Dutch, English, and Italian. *Intercultural Pragmatics* 19(2). 141–181.

Wickham, Harald. 2016. *ggplot2: Elegant Graphics for Data Analysis*. New York: Springer.

Part II: **Pathways from saying to thinking**

Sophia Fiedler
6 Thinking out loud? *Je me suis dit* 'I said to myself' and *j'étais là* 'I was there' in French talk-in-interaction

Abstract: In this article, I investigate two, so far little studied, constructions from oral French that introduce direct reported thought: *je me suis dit* 'I said to myself' and *j'étais là* 'I was there'. Whereas many studies target direct reported speech, research on direct reported thought remains sparse. Direct reported speech has been shown to allow speakers to display their affective stance during storytellings. I argue that in French talk-in-interaction, speakers can also use direct reported thought to take a stance. Drawing on Conversation Analysis and Interactional Linguistics, I analyzed 10h47min of video recordings of coffee breaks among students. The sequential analysis encompasses speech as well as the speakers' bodily conduct including gaze, gesture, posture, and facial expressions. I show that *j'étais là* is used to take an affective stance in the ongoing talk, while being reenacted verbally, prosodically and bodily. In contrast, *je me suis dit* is used to take a rational stance by making publicly available a conclusion or decision that accounts for previous actions. This rational stance is *not* accompanied by a bodily reenactment.

I thereby demonstrate that *je me suis dit* and *j'étais là*, when introducing direct reported thought, carry out distinct actions in talk-in-interaction. This result complements the growing body of research on a grammar-body-interface, and addresses a multimodal bifurcation in the rather novel research topic of direct reported thought.

1 Introduction

The French complement-taking predicate *penser* '(to) think' semantically designates the process of inner speech. In my data, however, the past forms of *penser*, *j'ai pensé/je pensais* 'I thought / I have thought', are not used to introduce direct reported thought but for other actions, such as displaying a change in epistemic state (Jefferson 2004a). Instead, speakers resort to other lexical resources. In this

---

Acknowledgements: This study was carried out with the support of the Swiss National Science Foundation, grant no. 100012_178819. I thank Simona Pekarek Doehler and two anonymous reviewers for their comments on an earlier version of this paper. All remaining errors are mine.

https://doi.org/10.1515/9783111065830-006

paper I present two, so far little studied, constructions from oral French that are used to quote thought in naturally-occurring conversation: *je me suis dit* 'I said to myself' and *j'étais là* 'I was there' (Dostie 2020; Secova 2015). Both forms are used in tellings to project reported thought from a past event, as the following two examples illustrate:

(1) LAU: pis j'ai attendu pis **je me suis dit** bon ben: je verrai,
            so I waited and I said to myself good well I'll see
            (Pauscaf 10, 19min30)

(2) ELI: et je suis relevée j'ai vu <u>tout</u> noir **j'étais là** ((imitates her frozen body
            posture during 1.1s))
            and I came up again and I saw all black I was there ((posture))
            (Pauscaf 20, 32min10)

Direct reported thought (DRT), together with direct reported speech (DRS), are powerful resources for speakers in everyday conversation to make co-participants "directly experience" the depicted events (Clark and Gerring 1990). Especially storytellings (Jefferson 1978; Stivers 2008) are laced with reported speech and thought, which are often delivered with expressive prosody, facial expressions, and gestures.

To mark DRT and DRS, speakers can – but need not – use quotative constructions. Research on English has shown that in addition to the standard quotatives, for instance constructions including *think* or *say*, speakers also use more colloquial forms such as *I was like* or *he goes* (Buchstaller 2001; Butters 1980; Fox Tree and Tomlinson, Jr. 2007; Romaine and Lange 1991; Schourup 1982; Streeck 2002 on English *like* and German *so*; Underhill 1988).

I argue that, although similar in their role as quotatives, *je me suis dit* 'I said to myself' and *j'étais là* 'I was there' carry out distinct actions. *Je me suis dit* accounts for a change in the course of action at the end of a reported rationalization process (Jefferson 2004a; Bangerter et al. 2011). Similar to what Golato (2002) describes for self-quotation to report past decisions, reported thought introduced by *je me suis dit* allows the speaker to make publicly available why a course of action, that has been previously described, was initiated or modified. Speakers mobilize fewer multimodal resources to deliver this conclusive thought. *J'étais là* is – within the reported situation – responsive to prior reported events or talk. What is reported is reenacted with multiple resources (see Dostie 2020; Secova 2015 for similar findings) as a spontaneous and *ad hoc* delivery of an affective stance towards preceding events. The main analytic concern of this article is how the respective actions manifest in interaction. The bodily conduct of the speaker (fewer vs. more resources) is crucial for the analysis of *je me suis dit* + DRT and *j'étais là* + DRT as two functionally distributed items carrying out different actions in everyday talk: taking an affective or a rational stance.

In the following, I show that *j'étais là* and *je me suis dit* both introduce reported thought while carrying out different actions. The speaker's more pronounced embodied conduct when using *j'étais là* is crucial for how these different actions come to be designed and understood as distinct.

2 Background

During tellings, speakers enhance "direct experience" for recipients by resorting to multiple resources. One of these resources is what Yule and Mathis (1992) describe as staging. It "organizes the various elements of the speaker's contribution into background and foreground positions" (Yule and Mathis 1992: 199).[1] An event can be placed into the foreground through a dramatization of reported events. The authors observe that this dramatization is done by means of a shift from a description or reporting with verbs like *ask* or *say* in the past tense to *be like* in the present tense (Yule and Mathis 1992: 204). Not having access to video data, their study could only describe linguistic and prosodic features of reported speech and thought.

More recent research has shown that such dramatization-processes are often achieved through bodily enactment (Fox and Robles 2010; Sidnell 2006; Streeck 2002). Prosody (Couper-Kuhlen 1996), linguistic means (especially through the choice of vocabulary), facial expressions (Peräkylä and Ruusuvuori 2012), and gestures form a network of resources to report events, speech, and thought in a meaningful way. I show that the enquoting devices *je me suis dit* and *j'étais là*, because they introduce different actions in conversation, also come with different degrees of bodily enactment.

Research on English quotatives has evidenced a systematic relation between the quotative and the quoted material (Fox Tree and Tomlinson 2007; Streeck 2002). Fox Tree and Tomlinson (2007) show in their experimental study that English *like* (compared to *say*) can be used to quote a variety of material sources such as talk, bodily conduct or sounds (Fox Tree and Tomlinson 2007: 86; cf. also Sidnell 2006).

---

[1] The technique of foregrounding a topic through highly enacted direct reported speech has also been called *depiction* by Clark and Gerring (1990) or *reenactment* by Sidnell (2006). Both authors describe their respective concepts as having the interactional goal of making co-participants re-experience what happened.

According to their results, the greater flexibility of *like* lies in its prioritization of marking approximation instead of a faithful reproduction (Fox Tree and Tomlinson 2007: 86). Streeck (2002) goes one step further by claiming that English *like* and German *so* are "body quotatives" making a "'nonverbal behavior' salient" (Streeck 2002: 581). Both observations are in line with Buchstaller and van Alphen's (2012) claim that new quotatives (like *like* or [*to*] *go*) often have "non-reportative semantics" (Buchstaller and van Alphen 2012: xii) and express approximation instead of suggesting a faithful reproduction of prior talk. Similar results have been formulated by Dostie (2020) who argues that *j'étais là* cataphorically refers to the following quotation, which is characterized by a systematic bodily conduct of the speaker.

Sacks (1992a) points out that "[t]he sheer fact of doing quoting can be the expressing of a position" (Sacks 1992a: 309). His claim has been relevantly confirmed by Stivers (2008) and several others, who show that certain types of tellings, such as complaints, favor the use of DRS and DRT as a staging tool (Haakana 2007 on complaints; Holt 2000 also on amusing stories). Haakana (2007) explains that Finnish *minä/mä aattelin et* 'I thought that' is a tool for speakers to "[give] the current recipient access to what went on in the narrator's mind at the specific point of the narrated interaction" (Haakana 2007: 153). He describes how DRT that is introduced with this construction is used to evaluate reported events thus "[guiding] the recipient in evaluating the story-in-progress" (Haakana 2007: 153). In my data, especially the *j'étais là* 'I was there'-construction shows similar characteristics.[2] It is a means through which speakers take an affective stance towards prior talk or events.

Stance as a more general phenomenon can have several functions in everyday talk. According to Du Bois (2007), there are three frequent and easily distinguishable functions of stance: evaluation, positioning, and alignment (Du Bois 2007: 144). For each of these functions, as he points out, speakers need some point of reference towards which the stance can be taken, for instance, a prior turn. *Affective* stance, which has been the focus of a growing body of research, shares this feature (Goodwin, Cekaite, and Goodwin 2012; Ochs 1996; Selting 2012). Being defined by Ochs (1996: 410) as referring to "a mood, attitude, feeling, and disposition, as well as degrees of emotional intensity vis-à-vis some focus of concern", it is the

---

2 Similar to what Haakana (2007) points out concerning Finnish *mina/mä attelin*, I also have examples where speakers leave open whether what is quoted has been said or not. I agree with Haakana's analysis that, especially in complaint stories, this ambiguity can be used "to the speaker's benefit: to give or imply a picture of the situation in which the speaker possibly resisted the antagonist by criticising him or her" (2007: 175). A further discussion of the matter lies, unfortunately, beyond the scope of this paper.

speaker's perceivable emotional attitude towards something specific that characterizes affective stance as an action. At the same time, to become interactionally relevant and visible to others, (affective) stance also needs to be "made publicly accessible" (Sorjonen and Peräkylä 2012: 5) by speakers. I observe, in line with Du Bois (2007) and many others, that participants display their affective stance by means of bodily and prosodic resources (e.g., Couper-Kuhlen 2012; Goodwin 2007; Goodwin, Cekaite, and Goodwin 2012; Haddington 2006; Kaukomaa, Peräkylä, and Ruusuvuori 2015; Streeck 2002).

These bodily features occur, however, *only* with *j'étais là*, not with *je me suis dit*. Indeed, as my analysis will show, *affective* stancetaking does not play a role when speakers introduce their reported thoughts with *je me suis dit*. Instead, speakers use this quotative to make publicly available an explanation or description that accounts for past actions of the speaker. The format [*je me suis dit* + DRT] allows the speaker to display a *rational* stance towards a certain matter instead of an *affective* one. This is why I call the sequences containing *je me suis dit* rationalizations: Speakers *describe* and do not depict the relevant scene (for a discussion see Clark and Gerring 1990).

Several features characterize this description which allows speakers to take a rational stance: They are "formed from articulated symbol systems, such as the discrete words and sentences of language" (Clark and Gerring 1990: 767) instead of "dense, or nonarticulated" (Clark and Gerring 1990: 767) ones, such as gestures or sounds; they are uttered with little emotional involvement; and they project a similarly non-affective reaction from the recipient. The sharing of an affective stance makes co-participants' reactions highly relevant, which has been evidenced particularly for storytellings (Stivers 2008; Voutilainen et al. 2014).

I show in my analyses that, after *j'étais là*, affiliative responses[3] are usually delivered and if not, pursued by the speaker. With *je me suis dit*, recipients respond accordingly with much less or no emotional involvement, for instance by displaying understanding or confirming the speaker's rational stance. This short juxtaposition of affective and rational stance clarified that even though *j'étais là* and *je me suis dit* both introduce DRT, they carry out different kind of actions: They allow speakers to either take an affective or a rational stance.

In the following, I will first illustrate the methodology of Conversation Analysis and Interactional Linguistics. The qualitative analyses of six examples, three with *je me suis dit* and 3 with *j'étais là* will illustrate my initial claim of those constructions implementing different actions through DRT.

---

3 Concerning the concept of *affiliation*, I follow Steensig (2013: 1) who defines it in terms of: "Display empathy; Match, support, and endorse stance; Cooperate with action preference".

3 Methodology and data

In what follows, I investigate the *interactional* use of *je me suis dit* 'I said to myself' and *j'étais là* 'I was there'. To do so, I use the methodology of Conversation Analysis (CA) (Sacks 1992a, 1992b; Sacks, Schegloff, and Jefferson 1974) and Interactional Linguistics (IL) (Couper-Kuhlen and Selting 2018). Taking an emic, data-driven perspective, my analyses are based on the sequentiality of turns-at-talk.

In everyday talk, interlocutors try to build actions in mutually recognizable ways; speakers design their turns to achieve that goal in order to be understood by others. They use specific grammatical formats to shape their turns accordingly. A verb like *dire* 'to say', for example, or any other transitive verb, is expected to have a direct object which can be a noun or a complement clause. One central idea in CA and IL is to not separate this grammatical projection from the real-time machinery of conversation "because grammatical accounts are intercalated with accounts of interactional trajectory, of the texture of activity, of the shape of sequences and the emergent upshot of the interactional episode" (Schegloff, Ochs and Thompson 1996: 21). Auer (2003) takes up on this interplay of temporality, grammar, and action in spontaneous talk and suggests in his (2003) seminal paper that grammar provides speakers with "sedimented and shared ways of organising projection in interaction" (Auer 2003: 1).

Je me suis dit and *j'étais là* both project reported thought while carrying out different actions. Grammatically, they are also distinctive. There is grammatical projection in the case of *je me suis dit* where the verb asks for a direct object. When this direct object takes the format of a clausal direct object (the complement clause), it can be syntactically even more bound to the matrix clause with the use of the complementizer *que* 'that'.[4] *J'étais là* cannot have a complementizer as it is already syntactically complete as [predicate + local/temporal adverbial]-construction. The data show that *là* 'there' has here lost its semantics of referring to a specific location or moment. The *là* 'there', one might argue, projects a specification, which is delivered as direct reported thought. Both forms are thus in need of a second "component", be it a complement clause or a specification.

Projection also involves bodily conduct. As recent research on multimodality has shown, not only words but also body movements can be projected with linguistic devices (Keevallik 2018; Streeck 2002). Relevant to this study are therefore multimodal aspects of interaction such as gaze, facial expressions, gestures or posture which have been shown to be crucial in social interaction (Goodwin 1979,

---

[4] I have, however, only 3 cases out of 45 where the complement clause is introduced with the complementizer.

1981; Kendon 2004 on gesture; Mondada 2014 on movement in space; Rossano 2012, 2013; Streeck 2014 on gaze; Maschler et al. 2020; Pekarek Doehler 2019 on the interrelation of grammar and multimodality). The analysis of multimodal conduct allows me to understand sequences where (re)enactment plays an important role.

I analyzed one corpus comprising 30 videotaped everyday conversations between students. It contains two parts, Pauscaf 1, recorded in 2013, and parts of Pauscaf 2, recorded in 2019. Both data sets were recorded in a university cafeteria in the French-speaking part of Switzerland. In the 10h47min of data, groups of 2 to 4 participants are recorded during their regular coffee breaks, totaling 33 males and 37 females (total: 70). Before the recording, all participants provided an informed consent for data collection and publication. The detailed explanation of data use did not reveal the specific purpose of interactional linguistic studies, thus keeping conversations as natural as possible. All recordings were transcribed according to the conversation analytic conventions elaborated by Jefferson (2004b). Additional embodied conduct was annotated following Mondada's (2018) conventions for multimodal transcription.

In the 10h47min of data I identified 47 instances of *je me suis dit* 'I said to myself' and 58 of *j'étais là* 'I was there'.

All occurrences were sequentially analyzed and coded with respect to syntactical, interactional, and multimodal features: presence or absence of the complementizer, sequential position, position in the turn, and the presence or absence of bodily conduct in the turn in which the notable construction occurs.

The analyses revealed that *je me suis dit* and *j'étais là* occur frequently in tellings. While *j'étais là* is responsive to a prior event, *je me suis dit* is not. Within the reported scene, *je me suis dit* does not introduce a response to a previously reported action but rather a conclusive thought presented as the logical consequence from what has been described. This matches the observation that *je me suis dit* introduces direct reported thought from monological situations while *j'étais là* is part of a reported dialogue.

On a morphological level the two forms are composed as follows

(3) je   me   suis   dit
    1SG.NOM   1SG.REFL   be.1SG.PR   say.PST.PTCP
    'I said to myself'

(4) j'   étais   là
    1SG.NOM   be.1SG.IPFV   DEICT
    'I was there'

(3) is the first person analytic past of the reflexive form of *dire* 'to say' and semantically conveys a monologic, reflective speech event. By introducing thoughts with *je me suis dit* speakers make this past interior speech publicly available to their current interlocutor(s). In my data, what follows *je me suis dit* remains mostly prosodically flat, is delivered under one intonation contour with the construction itself, and without or with only little bodily enactment.

(4) is the first person imperfective form of *être* 'to be' combined with a deictic particle that usually refers to a location or moment. The interactional dimension of responsiveness is somehow reflected through the deictic particle. The data shows that speakers enact their state at a specific point (in time or space) that is deictically referred to with *là* 'there' for the co-participant to literally "see" it in the ongoing conversations. The construction thus invites co-participants to experience the reported situation with the speaker.

Based on the sequential analysis of 47 occurrences of *je me suis dit*, I identified 29 instances where speakers use the construction as a means to make available a rationalization process which can consist of a train of thought (assumptions, assertions, rhetorical questions) concerning the past, present, or even future with regards to the speech event (n=17), or decisions that had been taken in the past (n=12). In 14 cases, *je me suis dit* introduces an assessment that accounts for another reported action. The 5 remaining cases are either interrupted or reformulated during the reported thought.

Concerning the 58 occurrences of *j'étais là*, 53 introduce reported thought or speech. Of the remaining 4 cases, 2 are followed by a description of what the speaker did, and 2 have the literal meaning of being at a certain place.

The following sequential and multimodal analyses will illustrate that (i) *j'étais là* and *je me suis dit* project reported thought but that (ii) they project different actions, and (iii) that those actions are characterized by a diverging multimodal conduct of the speaker.

4 Analyses

4.1 *Je me suis dit* ('I said to myself'): making publicly available a rational stance

This section examines the use of *je me suis dit* 'I said to myself' in everyday talk. The quoting device introduces reported thought that makes publicly available why a course of action was initiated or modified. The construction allows speakers to share decisions or conclusions, which are reported as rational trains of thought for recipients to comprehend. The rational stancetaking is accompanied by little bodily conduct.

In excerpt 1, Cédric tells Camille how he has been shopping alone with his mother. While she was looking for something else, he spotted a package of cookies, so-called *mendiants*. Cédric knows that Camille likes them, which made him buy a package for her.

Excerpt 1: mendiants (Pauscaf 07, 00min59s)
```
01   CED:    j'ai fait les courses seul avec ma mère,
             I was shopping alone with my mother
02           et pis du coup elle elle voulait acheter un truc,
             and then PART she she wanted to buy something
03           pis [j'ai vu ç-]
             then I saw th-
04   CAM:        [hmhm,    ]
05   CED:    pis je me souve↑nais ↓bien que tu m'avais parlé de
             then I remembered well that you had talked to me about
             mendiants, (.)
             mendiants
06           j'ai donc bien pensé,=
             so I thought well
07           =parce que j'ai vu les mendiants je me suis dit, %(0.4)
             because I saw the mendiants I said to myself
     ced                                                     %extends r
                                                             hand->1.09
08           +mendiants,
             mendiants
     cam     +gz at CED-->1.13
09           cam%ille,%$
             camille
     ced             $turns head&gz right-->1.10
     ced        %points with index finger tw front%
10           (0.2)%(0.5)%$
     ced                -->$gz at CAM->1.17
     ced          %nods,purses lips%
11   CAM:    ouais °d'accord°.=
             yeah okay
12   CED:    =ça va [°bien $ensem$ble.°]
             that goes well together
13   CAM:           [t'as $fait $      ] +le bon lien.
                     you made the right connection
     cam                                 -->+
     ced                  -->$gz left$gz at CAM------------>>
14   CED:    °hm.°
```

Je me suis dit introduces Cédric's sudden rationalization from the past. The storytelling in lines 01 to 03 forms the background for it by describing the circumstances in which the rationalization occurred. First, Cédric describes the situation in which he was when had the idea of buying *mendiants* for Camille (lines 01 to 03): He has been shopping with his mother. After a continuer (Schegloff 1982) from Camille at line 04, he adds the motivation behind him buying the biscuits. After a cut-off at line 03, where he is about to describe his next action (of having seen something), he restarts his turn and says that he remembered Camille telling him about *mendiants* (line 05). This is followed by a positive assessment of his thoughts (line 06) and an account for line 07. Cédric's account, which is introduced with *parce que* 'because' (line 07), replaces his cut-off from line 03, only that this time he rewords it explicitly as an explanation. His account comprises the description of seeing the biscuits and then relating them (line 08) to Camille (line 09). While doing so, he extends his right hand – just after *je me suis dit* – towards Camille and points in her direction while saying her name (line 09). Seeing the biscuits is presented as the triggering event for him buying them. That Camille and the biscuits "go well together" is first bodily displayed during the pause, when Cédric nods and purses his lips, thus confirming his, already positively assessed, conclusion (line 10).

Camille shifts her gaze at Cédric after the short pause following *je me suis dit*, which enables her to observe her friend's bodily conduct. Cedric, who turned his head and gaze right at line 09, gazes back at Camille at the end of the pause thus projecting the end of his turn (Kendon 1973; Streeck 2014) and mobilizing her response (Stivers and Rossano 2010). She confirms the conclusion that Cédric has reached by aligning with his prior turn (line 11). Cédric then extends his turn confirming verbally his conclusive rational stance from lines 08 and 09.

Excerpt 1 illustrated that *je me suis dit* is used to introduce talk that is presented to the recipient as an actual past train of thought. Through the format of direct reported thought, Cédric makes his purported inner monologue and thus his rational stance available to Camille. Publicly displaying the reflection process that led the speaker to a specific conclusion – which potentially also affects the recipient – makes the co-participant's reaction conditionally relevant (Sacks, Schegloff, and Jefferson 1974). The speaker invites the recipient to follow the different rational steps during the reflection process. What is introduced with *je me suis dit* is only minimally enacted.

The next excerpt shows a conversation between two friends, Elinda and Ekti. They talk about a situation Elinda found herself in because she tried to help a friend by setting him up with a girl. Elinda's telling is, contrary to the previous example, emotionally charged because the friend was not amused about her helping even though he had asked explicitly for her help in the first place. Despite a higher degree of affectivity in the telling, the turn initiated with *je me suis dit* is only moderately reenacted on a prosodic and bodily level.

Excerpt 2: bon c'est bon / okay that's it (Pauscaf 20, 11min28s)

```
01   ELI:    >je voulais< essayer de: (0.3)$(0.5)
             I        wanted to try to:
     eli                                    $gz at EKT-->l.02
02           et pi au final+ j'étais là$+ %ouais %bon::,
             and then in the end I was like yeah okay
     eli                            -->$gz left-->l.03
     eli                                    %lifts eyebrows%
     ekt                    -->+gz at her cup +gz at ELI-->l.05
03           $écoute euh:: va chier quoi.
              listen uh:: piss off PART
     eli     ->$gz at EKT-->l.06
04           enf[+in: tu me saoules et   ] pi euh:,$
             PART    you are annoying and then uh:
     eli                                     -->$gz down-->l.06
05   EKT:    [+non mais c'est clair.]
              no but of course
     ekt     -->+gz at her cake-->l.13
06   ELI:    °mrm° (0.2) $°nt°
     eli                 -->$gz alternately down&at EKT->l.09
07           [limite ça me prenait] même trop de temps&
             like   it almost took me too much time
08   EKT:    [mais j'pense,       ]
             but I think
09   ELI:    &de faire ce genre de trucs,$
             to do such kind of things
     eli                           -->$gz down-->l.10
10           pis je me suis dit euh::,$
             then I said to myself uh::
     eli                           -->$gz at EKT-->l.12
11           %bon c'est bon [hein,%$
             okay that's it PART
     eli     %shakes head 'no'------>%
12   EKT:                   [.HH  $]
     eli                         -->$gz down-->l.13
13           +à mon avis %$je pense qu'i- il te kiffait beaucoup,
              in my opinion I think h- he was really into you
             ->+gz at ELI-->>
     eli                 %lifts fork with cake, eats cake,chews-->>
     eli              -->$
```

At line 02, Elinda introduces reported thought (or speech, see footnote 3) with *j'étais là* 'I was there'. She reports what she had imagined saying to her friend: that he should "piss off" (line 03). She then reformulates line 03 by downgrading its intensity (line 04). Elinda's first strong display of affective (negative) stance (on stancetaking cf. Englebretson 2007) from line 03 is responded to by Ekti with an affiliative reaction (line 5) – in overlap with Elinda's second negative assessment. Elinda then initiates, after a short pause and a click (line 06), an account for her being annoyed: The matchmaking also "took her too much time" (lines 07 and 09). At line 10, she utters her rational stance towards the described circumstances: she told herself that she was done with it.

Her conclusive rational stance is formatted as direct reported thought, addressed to herself in the past situation and stands in contrast to the emotionally charged telling preceding *je me suis dit*. What Elinda tells herself, *c'est bon* 'that's it' (line 11), is presented as a consequence resulting from the circumstances that she described in lines 01 to 09. The interjection *bon* 'okay' (line 11) between the quotative *je me suis dit* and the direct reported thought marks a break between her account of why she will stop helping her friend (lines 07 and 09) and her final decision that she makes publicly available through reported thought (line 11). In contrast to the emotional reported thought in lines 02 to 04, the account in lines 07 to 11 allows Elinda to share her rationalization for not helping her friend anymore. Just after *je me suis dit* Elinda gazes at her interlocutor thus inviting her co-participant's reaction (Kendon 1973; Streeck 2014). By starting to eat her cake just after Ekti has taken the floor, Elinda also momentarily disengages from further talk. Ekti has already tried to take the turn at line 08 but without success. At line 12, in overlap with Elinda's turn-ending, Ekti projects with her audible inhale her upcoming turn. Introduced with *à mon avis je pense* 'in my opinion I think', she prospectively mitigates her turn-to-come. She then delivers herself an explanation for Elinda's friend's behavior.

Once again, what is introduced by *je me suis dit* is barely reenacted. There is neither a change in voice quality nor a strong bodily expression of Elinda's stance even though she reports an emotional story. She only shakes her head slightly from left to right (line 11) thus emphasizing her stopping the matchmaking activity. Note also that Ekti's affiliation already comes in right after Elinda's display of a strong affective stance, which was introduced with *j'étais là* 'I was there' (line 02). From line 03, Elinda's talk is a more rational explanation of her stance, which she concludes with *je me suis dit*. Sequentially speaking, there is no need for more affiliation.

The last excerpt illustrates that *je me suis dit* 'I said to myself' can also introduce thought related to the ongoing conversation thus referring to a very recent thought. Liv and Oréane discuss whether the books in the cafeteria they are having their coffee in are fake or not.

Excerpt 3: une feinte / a fake (Pauscaf 19, 15min22s)
```
01          (1.0)
02   ORE:   tu crois qu'c'est des ↑vrais livres,+=
            do you think that these are real books
     liv                                   +turns head l,gz at
                                            bookshelves-->1.07
03          =ou dedans c'est de c'est des pages [blanches?   ]
            or inside it's th it's white pages
04   LIV:                                       [°<<creaky>uh>]
                                                               uh
05          non c'est des vrais livres, $(.)
            no these are real books
     ore                              -->$gz at LIV-->1.08
06          j'ai regardé.
            I took a look
07   ORE:   ((chuckles, (0.6)+(1.1)))
     liv                  -->+turns head,gz to ORE-->1.08
08   LIV:   °hi°+ £j'me suis $dit aussi£ y a une $fein+te.
            I also said to myself   this is a fake
     liv      -->+gz into space-------------------->+turns head&
                                                     gz r->1.10
     ore                   -->$turns head r,
                              gz at bookshelves------>$gz at LIV->1.09
09          (0.3)$(0.7)
     ore         -->$turns head r,gz at bookshelves-->1.12
10   ORE:   mais %ceux-là c'est des%+ feintes?
            but they there it's fakes?
     ore          %points 2x w head tw books%
     liv                                  -->+gz at ORE-->1.11
11          (0.2)+(1.0)
     liv         -->+gz tw books at her left->1.14
12   LIV:   ça j'sais pas$ °par contre°.
            that I don't know though
          ore             -->$shifts head tw LIV-->>
```

Oréane initiates the sequence by asking whether Liv thinks (literally 'believes') that the books on the shelves on her left are real books or only have blank pages in them (lines 02 and 03). At the end of line 02, Liv turns her head right to look at the same books and then confirms her friend's initial supposition that the books are real. The turn-initial *non* 'no' also displays the turn's responsiveness to line 03, thus rejecting Oréane's second assumption. Liv then delivers an account for her non-mitigated response: She took a look herself to verify whether the books were real (line 06). This account in turn-extension may have been triggered by Oréane's preceding shifting her gaze to her co-participant (Stivers and Rossano 2010) just after Liv's response (line 05). During the subsequent pause at line 07, Oréane chuckles and Liv shifts her gaze from the bookshelves to Oréane. As the latter does not project her taking the floor, Liv extends her turn again at line 08. Her short laughter displays alignment with her co-participant's chuckles (line 07). *Je me suis dit aussi* 'I also said to myself' then introduces an account for line 06, which provoked her friend's amusement, thus referring back to Oréane's initial question from lines 02 and 03.

In this example, *je me suis dit* occurs in post-gap turn-extension (Schegloff 2016; Stoenica and Pekarek Doehler 2020). With Liv's response at line 5, the question-answer sequence could be closed. That Liv extends her turn a second time may indicate that she understood her friend's chuckles not as a closing-implicative assessment (Schegloff and Sacks 1973 on closings in general) but as a mocking of her having actually verified if the books were real. Liv's turn, which is initiated with a soft laughter, aligns with the co-participant's chuckles. *Je me suis dit aussi* 'I also said to myself' initiates a conclusive rational stance while referring to the shared thought Liv and Oréane had: that the books were fake.

Similar to the preceding examples, the reported thought makes a past rational stance publicly available, displaying the reasons behind an action. In this case the reported thought is not reenacted at all. Prosodically it is pronounced under one intonation contour with *je me suis dit* and attached without pause. That there is neither a pause after the quotative (as in ex. 1) nor a disruptive item like *euh* 'uh' or *mais* 'but' (as in ex. 2) demonstrates that line 08 is delivered as one unit which does not foreground or background one part of the complex clause.

In the preceding analyses I have shown that *je me suis dit* introduces reported thought; it allows speakers to share a past train of thoughts with their interlocutors during the ongoing conversation. Speakers thus make publicly available their rational stance that provides an explanation for a reported action, decision or for a change of course of action in the past. Interactionally speaking, the pattern [*je me suis dit* + reported thought] initiates turn-closure. This means that speakers use the pattern towards the end of a multi-unit turn, after describing – often in great detail – the circumstances or events that led to their final rational stance. Delivering a personal reflection at the end of a multi-unit turn invites the co-participant to react to the shared train of thought. The reported thought is neither prosodically nor bodily reenacted. If gestures are used, they are gestures of "*ceiving* or *caption*" (Streeck 2009: 9, original emphasis), which Streeck describes as "a bodily form of conceiving, i.e. of conceptually structuring content to be articulated in speech" (Streeck 2009: 9). They are used "whenever speakers, without attending to the process and without wishing to depict anything, use their hands to give form to – i.e. construe – content" (Streeck 2009: 9). This specific multimodal configuration of reported thought introduced with *je me suis dit* matches the speakers' display of a rational stance, which does not need dramatization or staging (see §2 *supra*).

This multimodal configuration contrasts with the affective stance that speakers convey with the pattern [*j'étais là* + reported thought], and which is also expressed bodily, for instance through facial expressions (Kaukomaa et al. 2015; Peräkylä and Ruusuvuori 2012; Ruusuvuori and Peräkylä 2009). In the next chapter, I analyze the quotative *j'étais là* 'I was there', which, in contrast to *je me suis dit*, projects bodily and prosodically reenacted thought in emotionally charged contexts.

4.2 *J'étais là* ('I was there'): displaying an affective stance

The following section describes the quotative *j'étais là* 'I was there', which introduces reported thought that is reenacted through notable bodily conduct. Speakers use the construction to display their affective stance, thus inviting their co-participants to affiliate with their telling during which they mostly take a negative stance or complain (Couper-Kuhlen 2012).

Mathilde reports how her mother is always too critical towards changes in society, or innovation – here concerning the women's strike, which Mathilde participated in.

Excerpt 4: grève des femmes / women's strike (Pauscaf_02_17, 08min29s)
```
01    MAT:    +c'est $comme %la grève des% femmes,§
              it's like the women's strike
      mat               $gz at FRA-->1.06
      mat                      %points tw FRA with
                               1 index finger%
      fra     +gz at MAT-->1.03
      fra                              §grabs his bottle->1.03
02            elle est là genre^euh ouais mais ça sert à %↑rien:%,
              she is there like uh yeah but that's useless
      mat                                            %head fw%
03            vous allez rien chan§◊↑ger:,+
              you are not going to change anything
      fra                    -->§opens bottle-->1.10
      fra                       ◊nods slowly-->1.06
      mat                       +closes eyes-->1.05
04    FRA:    [mhm,    ]
05    MAT:    [j'tais là] ↓bon %super,+
              I was there well super
      mat                      %lifts r h, drops it on table->1.06
      fra                          -->+gz at MAT-->1.11
```

```
06          si tout le monde% <<laughing>pense comME TOI◊ c'est$
            if everyone thinks like you do it's
     mat                   -->%
     mat                                            -->$gz down
                                                    -->1.10
     fra                                                  -->◊
07          CLAIR qu'on va rien chang°er°.>
            clear that we're not going to change anything
08          [.hh     ]
09   FRA:   [ouais.=]
            yeah
10   MAT:   =cet$ esprit de: défai↑tiste ça m'énerve.§
            this defeatist attitude it gets on my nerves
     mat    -->$
     mat                                                  -->§
11          (0.4)+(0.6)
     fra                -->+
```

Mathilde has already given one example of her mother's attitude prior to this extract. At line 01, she gives a second example. While gazing at Frank, she briefly points towards him when referring to the crucial event: the women's strike. At line 02, Mathilde introduces her mother's reported speech with *elle est là genre* 'she is there like'. The quotative *elle est là* 'she is there' in combination with *genre* 'like' projects an approximation of the original speech. Note that Mathilde switches to (historical) present tense thus staging the reported talk as a foreground event (Yule and Mathis 1992). Her using the second person plural pronoun *vous* demonstrates a change in footing (Goffman 1981) thus indicating that Mathilde is enacting her mother. The mother's generalizing negative assessment is enacted with a change in voice quality and an exaggerated stress on *rien* 'nothing', and the second syllable of *changer* 'to change' as well as a head movement forward (lines 04 and 05).

Mathilde's mimicking activity displays her negative stance towards her mother's assessment. At line 05, after a nod and a continuer from Frank (lines 03–06), Mathilde verbally elaborates on her negative stance. Introduced with a morpho-phonologically reduced form of *j'étais là*, Mathilde comments on her mother's assessment by reporting her own past thought, starting with a response cry. *Bon super* 'well super' (line 05) ironically assesses the mother's stance positively. The configuration of [*j'étais là* + response cry] comes very close to what Fox and Robles (2010) describe concerning the format [*it's like* + enactment], often with response cries: It is used "to enact thoughts, feelings and attitudes which are internal and affect-laden assessments of a prior utterance or event" (Fox and Robles 2010: 715). Mathilde's in fact negative stance is further enhanced by her bodily conduct: She drops her hand on the table as if to express hopelessness towards the mother's reactionary stance. Mathilde extends her turn at line 06 with an account, which is still directed to her mother.

Mathilde's gaze down in line 06 and 07 can be understood as part of the reenactment (cf. Sidnell 2006). When recounting her dispreferred response to the mother's stance, she gazes down – a conduct that has been proven to co-occur with dispreferred responses (Kendrick and Holler 2017). She closes the turn with an assessment (Goodwin and Goodwin 1992) that is produced with final falling intonation. Her gaze at Frank at the end of her strong stancetaking actively mobilizes Frank's response (Stivers and Rossano 2010), which follows after the pause (not in transcript).

In contrast to *je me suis dit*, the turn-constructional unit introduced with *j'étais là* is responsive to a prior action, here the mother's reported turn (on enacted dialogues consisting of multiple turns or sequences see Arita [2018]). French *j'étais là* also makes past thoughts available to the co-participant in the ongoing conversation. Instead of a rationalization, which is introduced with *je me suis dit*, speakers use *j'étais là* to display their strong affective stance thus inviting the recipient, through the activation of numerous, also bodily, resources to affiliate. The semantics of *j'étais là* emphasizes this difference in action-projection: The verb *être* 'to be' and the deictic particle *là* do not foreshadow, grammatically speaking, further talk because they form a grammatically complete clause. Neither does their semantics indicate the upcoming formulation of a thought. Instead, the verb *être* projects, together with the deictic particle *là*, in this specific sequential context of a telling, an (emotional or physical) state of the speaker at a specific time or place. This state is made accessible to the co-participant by the means of various (bodily) resources for depiction.

The above is further confirmed by the fact that, when the co-participant's stance towards the speaker's telling is not clearly displayed, speakers extend their tellings, thus pursuing a reaction. In the following excerpt, Frank describes how he tried to study at the university library. A fellow student who was sitting next to him behaved in a way so that Frank could not concentrate at all: Not only did his neighbor's elbow always reach into Frank's half of the table but he also made a lot of noise while constantly opening and closing his highlighters.

Excerpt 5: son coude / his elbow (Pauscaf_02_17, 10min32s)
```
01    FRA:    mais il était comme ça.
              but he was like that
02            (0.5)
03    FRA:    pour écri- fin pour faire ses stabilos,
              to wri-  well to do his highlighters
```

```
04            parqu'c'était même pas genre écri:↑re,
              because it wasn't even like writing
05            c'était st- st- c'était ses stabi%los (qu-) ses
              it was st st it was his highlighters that his
     fra                                          %enacts opening and closing
                                                      of highlighter-->l.14
06            stabilos c'était tout l'temps genre:
              highlighters it was every time like
07            ah il prend son jaune,
              oh he takes the yellow one
08            il ouvre le cla- le cla↑pet le: capuchon
              he opens the ca the closing flap the cap
09            °le capuchon,°
               the cap
10            i::l fait sa phrase,
              he does his sentence
11            il re::£ferme£,
              he closes it again
12            .hh hh.
13            après il prend l'autre pis il les ouvrait tout l'temps,
              then he takes the other one then he opens them all the time
14            donc ça faisait clic clic clic §clic.%
              so it made click click click click
     fra                                       -->%moves l elbow left->1.17
     mat                                       §leans fw,head down,moves left
                                                     hands tw mouth-->1.17
15            pis il [avait son cou$de] comme ça.
              then he had his elbow like that
     fra                      $gz at MAT-->1.20
16   MAT:            [h↑IN          ]
17   FRA:     pis deux§ trois fois j'ai %tapé son ↑coude,
              then two three times I tapped his elbow
     mat           -->§
     fra                              -->%taps in the air w r elbow-->1.18
18            pis %j'tais là mais mec,+
              then I was there but man
     fra       -->%moves both elbows back to middle-->1.19
     mat                         +gz at FRA-->1.19
19            t'%as ta place là à: droite donc^eu:h,+
              you have your space there on the right so uh
     fra      ->%reaches hand wide to right-->1.21
     mat                                       -->+gz at her cookie->1.20
20            limite:^euh si on est tro:p^$euh coin↑ce$ coin↑ce+ ben:,
              if uh       if we are too         squeeze  squeeze well
     fra                              -->$gz down---->$gz at MAT-->1.23
     mat                                                   -->+gz at
                                                              FRA -->1.25
```

```
21            (0.5)%(0.7)
     fra        -->%depicts moving something to the right with both
                    hands-->1.22
22   FRA:     dér↑ive.*%
              move
     fra             *smiles-->1.23
     fra        -->%both hands on table-->1.25
23            (1.4)*§(0.2)$
     fra        -->*
     fra             -->$gz at his bottle-->1.25
     mat          §shakes with laughter-->1.24
24   MAT:     £HH.£§
     mat        -->§
25   FRA:     et pi:%::s fi$nalement il s'est ca$ssé °au bout d'un mo+ment°
              and then in the end he took off after a while
     fra        -->%reaches his bottle with 1 hand,holds it-->1.35
     fra             -->$gz at MAT----------->$
     mat                                                         -->+
26            donc^euh tant mieux.
              so uh all the better
27            (1.2)
((8 lines omitted))
36   MAT:     mais ouais mais t'aurais d- t'aurais dû dire quelque chose,
              but yeah but you should have s you should have said something
37            (1.5)
38   FRA:     [ouais. ]
              yeah
39   MAT:     [t'aurais] dû dire excuse-↑moi: tes stabi↑lo:s tu peux faire
              you should have said sorry your highlighters can you make
40            moins d'bruit?
              less noise
41            (0.5)
42   FRA:     ouais.
              yeah
```

The excerpt begins with Frank reenacting the student's body posture with his elbows extended left and right thus depicting that the fellow student occupied too much space (line 01). Between lines 03 and 14 Frank first describes, then reenacts (lines 05–14) that the student also had highlighters in different colors, which he constantly opened and closed. He resumes the enacted scene with *donc* 'so', a repetition of the noise, and the gestures of the opening and closing of the highlighters (line 14).

During the last *click*, Frank already extends his left elbow to the side. This gesture is then verbalized in line 15 in which he repeats his complaint from line

01 about the fellow student's elbow position. Frank's repeated complaint is coupled with a gaze towards Mathilde, who is orienting towards Frank's story as amusing with an intense, bodily displayed laughter at lines 14 to 16.

Frank's reformulation (line 15) closes the side sequence (Jefferson 1972) about the highlighters and reinitiates the telling from line 01. He continues reenacting the scene by gesturing with his right elbow as if he was tapping someone next to him while recounting what happened (line 17–18). At line 18, introduced with a morpho-phonologically reduced form of *j'étais là*, he utters what he thought in that very moment of the described situation. That he did not say it out loud becomes clear through Mathilde's comment at lines 36 and 39. What he reports is initiated with *mais* 'but', here functioning as a discourse marker indicating a disruption between two parts of an utterance (Anscombre and Ducrot 1977). Reaching out his right hand, he points towards the spot where the fellow student sat (line 19) while reenacting how he pointed out to the fellow student that he has his place on the right side.

Frank's deictic gestures to his left and right demonstrate his changing between the roles of the fellow student and himself in the reenacted scene. In the lines depicting the body movements of the fellow student with *il était comme ça* 'he was like that' and *il avait son coude comme ça* 'he had his elbows like that' (lines 01 and 05), Frank reaches his elbow towards the left. In those lines where he reenacts himself he points towards his right to show (in the reenacted situation) the fellow student his place (lines 19–21, lines 21–22). He also uses his right hand to tap the fellow student's elbow (line 17).

These deictic gestures provide multimodal evidence for Frank being involved in a reenactment. It also emphasizes line 18 being responsive to some prior action in the sense that in the reported turn the speaker also bodily refers to his imaginary antagonist. Interestingly, Frank's bodily reenactment is not designed for his co-participant as a "listener". Instead, he keeps all spatial coordinates of his reenactment as they apparently were, thus demonstrating that he is really involved in his reenacting: When he wants his (imagined) neighbor to move, he points to the right (where the fellow student originally sat) while the fellow student's elbow is reaching to the left (FRA was sitting at his left). The situation is thus not adapted like a "play" with the two interactants sitting next to each other but is rather reenacted with the original spatial configuration.[5] This could underpin the argument that, during a

---

[5] This is not entirely in line with Clark and Gerring's (1990) description of depictions of another person's actions. According to the authors "the demonstrator usually takes that person's role, and the recipients experience them as if they were observing that person" (Clark and Gerring 1990: 768). The fact that Frank depicts the scene with the two participants (himself and the fellow

telling, speakers try to make the co-participant experience the reenacted situation from an omniscient perspective, not from an observing one.

Just after the vocative *mais mec* 'but man', Mathilde starts gazing at Frank. After a brief gaze at her cookie at lines 19 and 20 she reestablishes mutual gaze in line 20 just before Frank's turn-closure in line 22. He completes his clause first in an embodied manner (Keevallik 2018) and then, at line 22 verbally with *dérive* 'move' – an imperative directed to the fellow student. After a 1.6 second pause, Mathilde responds with laughter only, even though the turn-final falling intonation at line 23 and Frank's gaze shift from Mathilde to his bottle indicate his moving towards turn-closure thus leaving the floor for his co-participant to self-select (Auer 2021; Sidnell 2006). After Mathilde's short laughter, Frank extends his turn thus continuing his telling. He adds that finally the fellow student left. After another short side sequence Mathilde finally reacts, but in a disaffiliative way. By telling Frank that he should have said something (lines 36–40), she displays her understanding of Frank's stance introduced with *j'étais là* as something that has never been said, thus treating it as reported thought.

This excerpt illustrates that the speaker's bodily conduct contributes in a meaningful way to the reenactment in order to depict a reported situation. It became particularly clear that the speaker does not adapt to the co-participant's perspective but invites her to change footing in order to experience the speaker's situation from an omniscient perspective.

Excerpt 5 also evidenced that recipients may orient to *j'étais là* as quoting thought instead of speech. The fact that Mathilde could infer that Frank's reaction towards the fellow student's behavior remained unspoken shows that recipients constitute meaning based on sequential, bodily, and linguistic information emerging through turns-at-talk.

In the next excerpt, *j'étais là* reports a thought that is displayed as having just occurred a few seconds before, during the preceding turn (lines 07–12). Excerpt 6 also illustrates that the reported negative stance can be delicate to utter in the original situation. Two friends, Elinda and Ekti, are talking about people who feel insecure about their sexual orientation. Ekti is very skeptical towards the phenomenon while Elinda tries to find an explanation for it. During her explaining she takes more and more the side of people who are not sure about their sexual orientation until gliding into a joking-activity where she makes Ekti believe that Elinda herself has always known that she loves women.

---

student) not turning towards each other while speaking but away may demand more effort from the recipient in order to being able to re-experience the speaker's situation.

Excerpt 6: peur / fear (Pauscaf 20, 40min45s)

```
01    ELI:    $moi j'ai toujours su§ ce que j'aimais^hein,
              I have always known what I loved huh
      eli                    §turns head left-->1.02
      ekt     $gz at ELI-->1.07
02            °mais§ b(h)on.°%
              but yeah
      eli       -->§head turned tw EKT-->>
      ekt                      %stops manipulating packaging,freezes
                               her hand and arm movements-->1.07
03            ah(h)↑↑AN,
              ((laughter))
04            +£je me suis jamais posée de question^hein,£=
              I have never questioned myself huh
      eli     +gz at EKT-->1.10
05    EKT:    =*que [t' ◊aimais quoi.*◊]
               that you loved what
      ekt     *moves head straight-->1.06
06    ELI:          [les ◊femmes bien *◊] sûr.
                     women of course
      eli                  ◊opens eyes,lifts eyebrows◊
      ekt                              -->*
07            >non je plais(h)an$te.<%
              no I'm joking
      ekt                 $closes eyes-->1.09
      ekt                             -->%
08            [.hih    *↑HIN,                      ]
              ((laughter))
09    EKT:    [.h non s *j'ai eu peur$ là,$>j'tais là<*]
               no s   I got scared there I was there
      ekt              *puts packaging on the table----->*
      ekt                           -->$gz at
                                    ELI->$gz down-->1.10
10            qu'est-ce qu'elle me $di(h)i(h)i(h)t,+ .HH$
              what is she telling me
      ekt                   -->$gz at ELI---------->$gz down->1.13
      eli                                                -->+
11            (0.2)%(0.2)
      ekt          %wipes twice over table with r hand-->1.13
12    EKT:    [(c'est clair)        ]
               it's clear
13    ELI:    [£tu sais$ que je suis] en couple% avec $un homme?£ °hi^hi°=
               you know that I'm in a relationship with a man
      ekt                                         -->%
      ekt                                                -->$gz at ELI-->1.14
```

```
14    EKT:    =mais non mais p't-être qu't'étais $bi,
              but no but maybe you were bi
      ekt                                    -->$
15            chais [pas moi. par ton ]&
              I dunno       because of your
16    ELI:          [non c'était- NON.]
                    no that was no
```

Prior to this extract, Elinda says that many people have a phase of insecurity concerning their sexual orientation. At line 01, she emphasizes that she has always known what she loved, thus inferring that she had not had this phase. During this turn, she turns her head left, which can be interpreted as a signal of discomfort (cf. Pekarek Doehler 2019 for a similar observation and Rossano 2012 on gaze aversion in dispreferred responses). At line 02, Elinda projects with *mais bon* 'but yeah' and her turning of the head back towards Ekti a potential closure. Ekti only reacts bodily: She stops manipulating the packaging of her cake and freezes her arm and hand movements thus conveying augmented attention and the suspension of any further action (line 2).

Elinda then extends her turn: first with a short, high-pitched laughter (line 03), then by reformulating line 01 by saying that she had never questioned herself about her sexuality (line 04). During this turn, Elinda gazes at Ekti. The repetition is immediately followed by Ekti's question for more information, which evidences her being now insecure about Elinda's sexual orientation herself. Ekti's question is accompanied by her moving her head upright, which signals her increased attention. In overlap with Ekti's question, Elinda already specifies what she loves: "women of course" (line 06). At the same time, she lifts her eyebrows, opens her eyes wide, and smiles. At line 07, Elinda then reveals her making fun of Ekti. In overlap with Elinda's laughter, Ekti informs her friend that she "got scared" thus inferring a negative – or at least skeptical – stance towards homosexuality. Ekti also expresses her relief bodily: She releases the tension in her torso and arms and drops the packaging that she was holding in her hands during Elinda's turn.

With *j'étais là*, Ekti reports what she had thought during the prior turn while depicting her stance first embodiedly (lines 02, 05 and 09). Her negative stance is then displayed verbally through a rhetorical direct question during which Ekti gazes down (lines 09 and 10). Through this negative stance, which is verbally and bodily displayed, she conveys that her thought, if she had said it and if Elinda actually had been lesbian, would have been a potentially face-threatening act (Brown and Levinson 1987). However, as Elinda reveals her joking-activity and both participants laugh, the situation remains non-problematic. Elinda's rhetorical question at line 13 and her vehement reaction to Ekti's assumption of her being maybe bisexual (lines 14–15) clarifies the improbability of her loving women.

The three excerpts show that *j'étais là* introduces DRT to display a strong affective stance. Analyses of the sequentiality of turns-at-talk and the participants' multimodal conduct demonstrated the following: (i) Turns introduced with *j'étais là* are responsive to a preceding action, (ii) *j'étais là* projects an affective stance, which is delivered as a package of bodily and prosodically reenacted DRT, and (iii) the affective stancetaking is enacted as spontaneous, emotional, and non-hedged reaction to the beforehand described situation, thus giving the co-participant the possibility to re-experience the reenacted situation. Excerpt six is slightly different because the reported thought introduced with *j'étais là* conveys even more: As the rhetorical question concerns a present party (Elinda) and her previous actions, the affective stancetaking indicates that the discovered matter – if it had been true – would have led to consequences for their mutual trust and friendship.

5 Conclusion

Direct reported thought has remained fairly understudied in contrast to reported speech (but see Jefferson 2004a). In this article, I have presented two, so far unanalyzed quotatives in French everyday talk that speakers use to report thought. Drawing on Conversation Analysis and Interactional Linguistics, I have scrutinized their interactional functioning, demonstrating that *je me suis dit* 'I said to myself' and *j'étais là* 'I was there' are used to construct different actions in conversation. I identified *je me suis dit* and *j'étais là* to be distributed accordingly and to have different functions in talk-in-interaction.

Je me suis dit 'I said to myself' occurs during explanations or tellings about a logical and consequential train of thought that reveals the rationalization behind a decision or change in a course of action and allows speakers to account for this change. It displays the purported conclusive thought as a rational stancetaking that is displayed as neutral and not affect-laden. The telling that makes available how the speaker came to this decision or conclusion allows the co-participant to comprehend this train of thought. There is a significant absence of embodied conduct, which conveys the descriptive nature of the rational stance.

J'étais là 'I was there' often occurs in emotionally charged tellings. The construction depicts *ad hoc* reactions to a preceding stretch of talk or behavior. The construction allows speakers to display their expressive, affective reaction to a preceding action. It is thus a strong tool to simplify understanding, or even to enable it, "by an emotional experience of interpersonal involvement" (Tannen 2007: 46). Crucial to the present study is that with *j'étais là* speakers activate numerous resources, prosody, gesture, facial expressions, and gaze, thus augmenting their chances to achieve this "interpersonal involvement". Of course, the bodily and prosodic enactment is not part of the past thought but belongs to the reporting in the here-and-now of the ongoing conversation as a staging tool. This bodily enactment to achieve affective involvement has not been observed with *je me suis dit*, where rational stancetaking is the main activity.

The analysis revealed that, similar to direct reported speech, direct reported thought can be used by speakers to take an affective or rational stance in interaction. In French, the actions of affective and rational stancetaking are tied to grammatical and bodily features. In my data, speakers resort to a specific linguistic device, *j'étais là*, to take an affective stance, and only when doing so do they activate multimodal resources. When taking a rational stance, they activate fewer multimodal resources and resort to *je me suis dit*. This result, that multimodal resources can be a decisive analytical factor when delimiting and describing actions, is in line with what has been demonstrated by a growing body of research on the grammar-body interface in everyday talk (Pekarek Doehler 2019; Stoenica and Pekarek Doehler 2020; Streeck 2002). Most importantly, Goodwin's extensive work underpins this interwovenness of embodied practices and the organization of everyday talk (Goodwin 1981, 2007). Goodwin convincingly argues that participants design, carry out, and coordinate actions not only by the means of linguistic resources but also through posture, gesture, and gaze which "mutually elaborate each other to create a whole that is both greater than, and different from, any of its constituent parts" (Streeck, Goodwin, and LeBaron 2011: 2).

With its multimodal approach to interaction, this study also extends the understanding of the interactional use of reenactments (Sidnell 2006; Thompson and Suzuki 2014) to the more specific domain of direct reported thought.

Appendix

Transcription conventions for verbal conduct following Jefferson (2004b)

[	start of overlap
]	end of overlap
=	latching (no pause, no overlap)
(.)	micro-pause, less than 0.2 seconds
(0.7)	measured pause in seconds and tenths of seconds

wo-	truncated word
wo:rd	syllable lengthening
?	rising final intonation
.	falling final intonation
,	continuing intonation
word	accentuation
°word°	softer than surrounding speech
WORD	louder than surrounding speech
↑word	marked high rise in pitch (refers to the next syllable)
↓word	marked fall in pitch (refers to the next syllable)
.h	in-breath
h.	out-breath
((laughter))	transcriber's comment
£word£	smiling voice
w(h)ord	speech with in- or out-breaths from laughter
<<laughing> word>	paralinguistic feature with a reach

Transcription conventions for embodied conduct following Mondada (2018)

+ +	Indicates start and end of gaze of speaker A.
§ §	Indicates start and end of gestures (e.g., pointing) or posture of speaker A.
◊ ◊	Indicates start and end of head movement (e.g., nodding) of speaker A.
$ $	Indicates start and end of gaze of speaker B.
% %	Indicates start and end of gesture or posture of speaker B.
* *	Indicates start and end of a head movement of speaker B.
+---->l.05	Continuation of the described embodied conduct until line 05 of transcript.
------>+	End of the described embodied conduct.
+----->>	Continuation of the described embodied conduct until end of excerpt.
#1	Reference to the figure depicting the embodied conduct

Abbreviations

AUX	Auxiliary
DEICT	Deictic
IPFV	Imperfective

PRS	Present tense
PTCP	Past Participle
REFL	Reflexive
SG	Singular

References

Anscombre, Jean-Claude & Oswald Ducrot. 1977. Deux *mais* en français? *Lingua* 43. 23–40. https://doi.org/10.1016/0024-3841(77)90046-8

Arita, Yuki. 2018. Enactment in Japanese talk-in-interaction: Interrelationship between there-and-then and here-and-now sequential organizations. *Journal of Pragmatics* 123. 78–101. https://doi.org/10.1016/j.pragma.2017.10.016

Auer, Peter. 2003. Projection in interaction and projection in grammar. *InLiSt* 33. 1–43.

Auer, Peter. 2017. Gaze, addressee selection and turn-taking in three-party interaction. *InLiSt* 60. 1–32.

Auer, Peter. 2021. Turn-allocation and gaze: A multimodal revision of the "current-speaker-selects-next" rule of the turn-taking system of conversation analysis. *Discourse Studies* 23. 117–40.

Bangerter, Adrian, Eric Mayor & Simona Pekarek Doehler. 2011. Reported speech in conversational storytelling during nursing shift handover meetings. *Discourse Processes* 48(3). 183–214. https://doi.org/10.1080/0163853X.2010.519765

Brown, Penelope & Stephen C. Levinson. 1987. *Politeness: Some universals of language usage*. Cambridge: Cambridge University Press.

Buchstaller, Isabelle. 2001. *He goes* and *I'm like*: The new quotatives re-visited. Paper presented at New Ways of Analyzing Variation 30 (NWAVE), North Carolina State University, Raleigh, North Carolina, 11–14 October 2001.

Buchstaller, Isabelle & Ingrid van Alphen. 2012. Introductory remarks on new and old quotatives. In Ingrid van Alphen & Isabelle Buchstaller (eds.), *Quotatives: Cross-linguistic and Cross-disciplinary Perspectives*, XI–XXX. Amsterdam & Philadelphia: John Benjamins.

Butters, Ronald R. 1980. Narrative go 'say'. *American Speech* 55(4). 304–307.

Clark, Herbert H. & Richard J. Gerring. 1990. Quotations as demonstrations. *Language* 66(4). 764–805.

Couper-Kuhlen, Elizabeth. 1996. The prosody of repetition: on quoting and mimicry. In Elizabeth Couper-Kuhlen & Margret Selting (eds.), *Prosody in conversation. Interactional Studies*, 366–405. Cambridge: Cambridge University Press.

Couper-Kuhlen, Elizabeth. 2012. On affectivity and preference in responses to rejection. *Text & Talk* 32(4). 453–475. https://doi.org/10.1515/text-2012-0022

Couper-Kuhlen, Elizabeth & Margret Selting. 2018. *Interactional Linguistics*. Cambridge: Cambridge University Press.

Deppermann, Arnulf. 2015. Wissen im Gespräch: Voraussetzungen und Produkt, Gegenstand und Ressource. *InLiSt* 57. 1–31.

Dingemanse, Mark. 2020. Between sound and speech: Liminal signs in interaction. *Research on Language and Social Interaction* 53(1). 188–196. https://doi.org/10.1080/08351813.2020.1712967

Dostie, Gaétane. 2020. Deixis à l'imaginaire et périphrases en *être* et *faire* préfaçant une scène recréée (*j'étais comme, t'es là, j'ai fait. . .*). In Federica Diémoz, Gaétane Dostie, Pascale Hadermann & Florence Lefeuvre (eds.), *Le français innovant*, 83–106. Bern: Peter Lang.

Du Bois, John W. 2007. The stance triangle. In Robert Englebretson (ed.), *Stancetaking in discourse: Subjectivity, evaluation, interaction*, 139-182. Amsterdam & Philadelphia: John Benjamins.
Englebretson, Robert (ed.). 2007. *Stancetaking in discourse: Subjectivity, evaluation, interaction*. Amsterdam & Philadelphia: John Benjamins.
Fox, Barbara A. & Jessica Robles. 2010. It's like *mmm*: Enactments with *it's like*. *Discourse Studies* 12. 715-738.
Fox Tree, Jean E. & John M. Tomlinson, Jr. 2007. The rise of *like* in spontaneous quotations. *Discourse Processes* 45(1). 85-102. https://doi.org/10.1080/01638530701739280
Goffman, Erving. 1981. *Forms of talk*. Philadelphia: University of Pennsylvania Press.
Golato, A. 2002. Self-quotation in German. Reporting on past decisions. In Tom Güldemann & Manfred von Roncador (eds.), *Reported Discourse: A meeting ground for different linguistic domains*, 49-70. Amsterdam/Philadelphia: John Benjamins.
Goodwin, Charles. 1979. The interactive construction of a sentence in natural conversation. In George Psathas (ed.), *Everyday language: Studies in ethnomethodology*, 97-121. New York: Irvington Publishers.
Goodwin, Charles. 1981. *Conversational organization: Interaction between speakers and hearers*. New York: Academic Press.
Goodwin, Charles. 2007. Participation, stance and affect in the organization of activities. *Discourse & Society* 18(1). 53-73.
Goodwin, Charles & Marjorie H. Goodwin. 1992. Assessments and the construction of context. In Alessandro Duranti & Charles Goodwin (eds.), *Rethinking context: Language as an interactive phenomenon*, 147-192. Cambridge: Cambridge University Press.
Goodwin, Marjorie H. 1980. Processes of mutual monitoring implicated in the production of description sequences. *Sociological Inquiry* 50. 303-317.
Goodwin, Marjorie H., Asta Cekaite & Charles Goodwin. 2012. Emotion as stance. In Marja-Leena Sorjonen & Anssi Peräkylä (eds.), *Emotion in Interaction*, 16-41. Oxford: Oxford University Press.
Goodwin, Marjorie H. & Charles Goodwin. 2001. Emotion within situated activity. In Alessandro Duranti (ed.), *Linguistic anthropology: A reader*, 239-257. Malden, MA, Oxford: Blackwell.
Haakana, Markku. 2007. Reported thought in complaint stories. In Rebecca Clift & Elizabeth Holt (eds.), *Reporting talk. Reported speech in interaction*, 150-178. Cambridge: Cambridge University Press.
Haddington, Pentti. 2006. The organization of gaze and assessments as resources for stance taking. *Text & Talk* 26(3). 281-328. https://doi.org/10.1515/TEXT.2006.012
Holt, Elizabeth. 2000. Reporting and reacting: Concurrent responses to reported speech. *Research on Language and Social Interaction* 33(4), 425-454. https://doi.org/10.1207/S15327973RLSI3304_04
Jefferson, Gail. 1972. Side sequences. In David Sudnow (ed.), *Studies in social interaction*, 295-338. New York: The Free Press.
Jefferson, Gail. 1978. Sequential aspects of storytelling in conversation. In Jim N. Schenkein (ed.), *Studies in the organization of conversational interaction*, 213-248. Academic Press: New York.
Jefferson, Gail. 2004a. "At first I thought": A normalizing device for extraordinary events. In Gene H. Lerner (ed.), *Conversation analysis. Studies from the first generation*, 131-167. Amsterdam & Philadelphia: John Benjamins.
Jefferson, Gail. 2004b. Glossary of transcript symbols with an introduction. In Gene H. Lerner (ed.), *Conversation analysis: Studies from the first generation*, 13-31. Amsterdam & Philadelphia: John Benjamins. https://doi.org/10.1075/pbns.125

Kaukomaa, Timo, Anssi Peräkylä & Johanna Ruusuvuori. 2015. How listeners use facial expression to shift the emotional stance of the speaker's utterance. *Research on Language and Social Interaction* 48. 319–341.

Keevallik, Leelo. 2018. What does embodied interaction tell us about grammar? *Research on Language and Social Interaction* 51(1). 1–21.

Kendon, Adam. 1973. The role of visible behavior in the organization of social interaction. In Mario von Cranach & Ian Vine (eds.), *Social communication and movement: Studies of interaction and expression in man and chimpanzee*, 29–74. New York: Academic Press.

Kendon, Adam. 2004. *Gesture. Visible action as utterance*. Cambridge: Cambridge University Press.

Kendrick, Kobin H. & Judith Holler. 2017. Gaze direction signals response preference in conversation. *Research on Language and Social Interaction* 50(1). 12–32. https://doi.org/10.1080/08351813.2017.1262120

Maschler, Yael, Simona Pekarek Doehler, Jan Lindström & Leelo Keevallik (eds.). 2020. *Emergent syntax for conversation: Clausal patterns and the organization of action*. Amsterdam & Philadelphia: John Benjamins.

Mondada, Lorenza. 2014. Bodies in action: Multimodal analysis of walking and talking. *Language and Dialogue* 4. 357–403.

Mondada, Lorenza. 2018. *Conventions for multimodal transcription*. https://franzoesistik.philhist.unibas.ch/fileadmin/user_upload/franzoesistik/home/Personen/Mondada/Unterordner/Mondada_conv_multimodality.pdf (accessed 31 January 2021).

Ochs, Elinor. 1996. Linguistic resources for socializing humanity. In John J. Gumperz & Stephen C. Levinson (eds.), *Rethinking linguistic relativity*, 407–437. Cambridge: Cambridge University Press.

Pekarek Doehler, Simona. 2019. At the interface of grammar and the body: *Chais pas* ("dunno") as a resource for dealing with lack of recipient response. *Research on Language and Social Interaction* 52(4). 365–387. https://doi.org/10.1080/08351813.2019.1657276

Peräkylä, Anssi & Johanna Ruusuvuori. 2012. Facial expression and interactional regulation of emotion. In Marja-Leena Sorjonen & Anssi Peräkylä (eds.), *Emotion in interaction*, 64–91. Oxford: Oxford University Press.

Romaine, Suzanne & Deborah Lange. 1991. The use of *like* as a marker of reported speech and thought: A case of grammaticalization in progress. *American Speech* 66(3). 227–279.

Rossano, Federico. 2012. *Gaze behavior in face-to-face interaction*. Nijmegen, Netherlands: Max Planck Institute for Psycholinguistics dissertation.

Rossano, Federico. 2013. Gaze in conversation. In Jack Sidnell & Tanya Stivers (eds.), *The handbook of Conversation Analysis*, 308–329. Malden & Oxford: Blackwell.

Ruusuvuori, Johanna & Anssi Peräkylä. 2009. Facial and verbal expressions in assessing stories and topics. *Research on Language and Social Interaction* 42. 377–394.

Sacks, Harvey. 1992a. Lectures on conversation, Vol. II. Oxford: Blackwell.

Sacks, Harvey. 1992b. Lectures on conversation, Vol. I. Oxford: Blackwell.

Sacks, Harvey, Emanuel A. Schegloff & Gail Jefferson. 1974. A simplest systematics for the organization of turn-taking for conversation. *Language* 59(4). 696–735.

Schegloff, Emanuel A. 1982. Discourse as an interactional achievement: Some uses of 'uh huh' and other things that come between sentences. In Deborah Tannen (ed.), *Analyzing discourse: Text and talk*, 71–93. Georgetown University Roundtable on languages and linguistics. Washington, D.C.: Georgetown University Press.

Schegloff, Emanuel A. 2016. Increments. In Jeffrey D. Robinson (ed.), *Accountability in social interaction*, 239–263. Oxford & New York: Oxford University Press.

Schegloff, Emanuel A., Elinor Ochs & Sandra A. Thompson. 1996. Introduction: Interaction and grammar. In Elinor Ochs, Emanuel A. Schegloff & Sandra A. Thompson (eds.), *Interaction and grammar*, 1–51. Cambridge: Cambridge University Press.

Schegloff, Emanuel A. & Harvey Sacks. 1973. Opening up closings. *Semiotica* 8. 289–327.

Schourup, Lawrence C. 1982. Common discourse particles in English conversation. *Working Papers in Linguistics* 28. Columbus, OH: Ohio State University.

Secova, Maria. 2015. Discours direct chez les jeunes : nouvelles structures, nouvelles fonctions. *Langage et société* 151. 131–151.

Selting, Margret. 2012. Complaint stories and subsequent complaint stories with affect displays. *Journal of Pragmatics* 44(4). 387–415.

Sidnell, Jack. 2006. Coordinating gesture, talk, and gaze in reenactments. *Research on Language and Social Interaction* 39(4). 377–409. https://doi.org/10.1207/s15327973rlsi3904

Sorjonen, Marja-Leena & Anssi Peräkylä. 2012. Introduction: Emotion in interaction. In Marja-Leena Sorjonen & Anssi Peräkylä (eds.), *Emotion in interaction*, 3–15. Oxford: Oxford University Press.

Stivers, Tanya. 2008. Stance, alignment, and affiliation during storytelling: When nodding is a token of affiliation. *Research on Language and Social Interaction* 41(1). 31–57. https://doi.org/10.1080/08351810701691123

Stivers, Tanya & Federico Rossano. 2010. Mobilizing response. *Research on Language and Social Interaction* 43(1). 3–31.

Stoenica, Ioana-Maria & Simona Pekarek Doehler. 2020. Relative-clause increments and the management of reference. A multimodal analysis of French talk-in-interaction. In Yael Maschler, Simona Pekarek Doehler, Jan Lindström & Leelo Keevallik (eds.), *Emergent syntax for conversation: Clausal patterns and the organization of action*, 303–330. Amsterdam & Philadelphia: John Benjamins. https://doi.org/10.1075/slsi.32.11sto

Streeck, Jürgen. 2002. Grammars, words, and embodied meanings: On the uses and evolution of *so* and *like*. *Journal of Communication* 52(3). 581–596. https://doi.org/10.1111/j.1460-2466.2002.tb02563.x

Streeck, Jürgen. 2009. *Gesturecraft: The manu-facture of meaning*. Amsterdam & Philadelphia: John Benjamins.

Streeck, Jürgen. 2014. Mutual gaze and recognition: Revisiting Kendon's 'Gaze direction in two-person interaction'. In Mandana Seyfeddinipur & Marianne Gullberg (eds.), *From gesture in conversation to gesture as visible utterance: Essays in honor of Adam Kendon*, 35–55. Amsterdam: John Benjamins.

Streeck, Jürgen, Charles Goodwin & Curtis LeBaron. 2011. Embodied interaction in the material world: An introduction. In Jürgen Streeck, Charles Goodwin & Curtis LeBaron (eds.), *Embodied interaction. Language and body in the material world*, 1–28. Cambridge: Cambridge University Press.

Tannen, Deborah. 2007 [1989]. *Talking voices*. 2nd edn. Cambridge: Cambridge University Press.

Thompson, Sandra A. & Ryoko Suzuki. 2014. Reenactments in conversation: Gaze and recipiency. *Discourse Studies* 16. 816–46.

Underhill, Robert. 1988. *Like* is, like, focus. *American Speech* 63(3). 234–246.

Voutilainen, Liisa, Pentti Henttonen, Mikko Kahri, Maari Kivioja, Niklas Ravaja, Mikko Sams & Anssi Peräkylä. 2014. Affective stance, ambivalence, and psychophysiological responses during conversational storytelling. *Journal of Pragmatics* 68. 1–24.

Yule, George & Terrie Mathis. 1992. The role of staging and constructed dialogue in establishing speaker's topic. *Linguistics* 30. 199–215.

Denys Teptiuk

7 Self-quotations of speech and thought, and how to distinguish them

Abstract: In this paper, I investigate the ambiguity between reported speech and reported thought in quotations and self-quotations appearing in non-standard written speech. I primarily target six Finno-Ugric languages: Hungarian, Estonian, Finnish, Erzya, Udmurt, Komi. In addition, I look at Russian as the main contact language for Eastern Finno-Ugric languages spoken in Russia, and at English for comparison. Four types of quotative indexes (QIs) where such ambiguity is expected are investigated: (i) QIs with generic speech verbs, (ii) QIs with equational verbs, (iii) non-clausal QI with (self-)quotative particles, and (iv) QIs with ellipsis of the speech/mental verbs.

The results show that the ambiguity between speech and thought appears more frequently in self-quotations, although it can often be resolved by considering the context, and using such characteristics as addressivity of speech and egocentricity of thought and pragmatics of concrete situation as cues. Reported speech is usually directed at the interlocutors present in the reported situation and causes their (verbal) reaction, while reported thought is egocentric, i.e. directed at the reporters themselves. Since thoughts are available to the reporters but not interlocutors, there are also more cases of reported thoughts in self-quotations than in quotations. In turn, quotations in colloquial speech represent someone else's speech and only rarely thoughts. Reported thought of others is often hypothetical and presents the reporter's assumption about the reported speaker's mental processes.

> "Language, when it *means*, is somebody talking to somebody else,
> even when that someone else is one's own inner addressee."
> (Holquist 1981a: xxi; original emphasis)

Acknowledgements: This work was supported by the Estonian Research Council grants PRG927 and PRG1290. I am grateful to the participants and organizers of the workshop "The grammar of thinking: Comparing reported thought and reported speech across languages" for their fruitful comments and suggestions to the first version of this paper, which aided me enormously in reporting this study. I want to thank Denys Savchenko for his help with the figures used in this paper, the reviewers and editors of this special issue, and Gerson Klumpp, Elena Markus, Iuliia Zubova for their constructive comments on an earlier version of this paper, which helped me improve its quality. The responsibility for all remaining shortcomings is entirely mine.

https://doi.org/10.1515/9783111065830-007

1 Introduction

Self-quotations as a type of reported speech and thought have received relatively less attention in previous studies compared to cases where reporters attribute speech and thought to some other speakers than themselves. Syntactically they are often equivalent to reports of others, for which I will use the label *quotation* here.[1]

(1)   English (etTenTen15)
   a.   **He said** "Girls! Find a position as full professor before I retire or you will suffer!" [quotation]
   b.   **I said** "Please don't touch me. I don't know you." [self-quotation]

Most so-far described languages use the same markers for quotations and self-quotations, e.g. *say* in (1). However, there are also languages with dedicated self-quotative markers not used outside self-quoting contexts. Such markers are typologically quite rare and are found in a couple of languages outside of Europe (see e.g. Teptiuk 2021: 216, and references therein). Among European languages, dedicated self-quotative markers are used in two Uralic languages Komi and Udmurt (Permic branch), discussed in this paper.

Even though self-quotations are usually quite similar to quotations in the choice of quotative indexes (QIs), i.e. linguistic expressions introducing reported speech (Güldemann 2008: 1), they differ in the source of the report. Only in self-quotations is the reporter also the author of the reported speech. This characteristic also partially holds for reported thought. In the real world, thoughts usually remain covert from the audience. Available by default to their authors only, thoughts can only be reported if the reporter is their author (see Section 2 for a broader discussion). Because of their author property, self-quotations and reported thought share a common semantic basis, which I explore here.

According to Vygotsky ([1934] 1986: 30), thoughts can be realized as either voiced egocentric speech or soundless inner speech. The possibility for the opposite ways of realization in terms of verbalization makes the distinction between voiced and soundless speech quite vague in certain contexts. This seems to be the case in self-quotations among QIs that introduce both reported speech (RS) and reported thought (RT). For instance, what is known as "new quotative constructions", e.g. *be like* in English (2), is a type of such QIs (for more details, see e.g. Romaine and

---

[1] In the examples, I mark the boundaries of quotations with an underline and self-quotations with a double underline, marked in English texts directly or in the translations of examples (see e.g. examples 2 and 3).

Lange 1991; Buchstaller 2001, among others). The same holds for non-clausal use of quotative particles, e.g. the self-quotative particle *miśa* in Komi-Zyrian (cf. Teptiuk 2019: §2.6.2.2; Teptiuk 2021; also see Section 4.3).

(2) English (enTenTen15)
 I was like *"I'm to[o] busy looking at everything and gawking at the buildings and sites that I didn't want to talk."*

(3) Komi-Zyrian (KoZSmC)
 (Tenyd pö kolö setćö munny.)
 Me öd, ***miśa,*** veśig samoďejaťeľnöj koncertyn šoća
 1SG PTCL QUOT.SELF even amateur concert:INE rarely
 petködći. Kyďźi, ***miśa,*** scena vylas
 go.out:PST.1SG how QUOT.SELF stage upon.3SG
 vorsny kuta?
 play:INF start:PRS.1SG
 '(You need to go there.) But I was going rarely even to the amateur concerts. How will I start playing on stage?'

My observations show that strategies leading to the ambiguity between the representation of speech and thought are characterized by un(der)specification of the event behind report. Instead of describing the event, like the QI with the verb *say* (1) does, the constructions in (2) and (3) indicate the presence of report but say nothing about the event behind it. According to Güldemann's morphosyntactic classification of QIs, such markers are *quote-oriented* (Güldemann 2008: 118–124; Güldemann 2012: 119–120). Among quote-oriented QIs, there are more complex structures, additionally specifying the event behind the report, e.g. *he said like*: {report}. Thus, only those quote-oriented QIs formed by originally non-reportative elements or having non-clausal structures are expected to cause ambiguity in the presentation of RS and RT unless they are conventionally restricted to the introduction of only one type of report.

The ambiguity between the representation of speech and thought can be observed among two more types of QIs. One of them is the *participant-oriented* QIs, as in (4). Such QIs exclusively encode the speaker and/or the addressee of the quote (see Güldemann 2012). Among participant-oriented QIs, those mentioning only the original speaker are relevant, since adding the addressee would necessarily point to the speech situation, e.g. *én meg* **neki** 'and I **to him/her** [said/*thought]'. Such strategies are often turn-taking, i.e. signaling exchanges between the listener and speaker roles, but can also connect to the previous discourse by presenting the reporter's unverbalized reaction, as in (4).

(4) Hungarian (Teptiuk 2019: 218, translation adjusted; original source: nlcafe.hu)
    én   meg,   hogy   mivaaaaaaaaaan?
    1SG   also   COMP   what:be.PRS.3SG
    '**And I was like** whaaaaaaaaaat?'

The other type of QI is observed among the languages that use the same speech verb to introduce RS and RT (see Chappell 2008 on Sinitic; Matić and Pakendorf 2013 on languages of Siberia; McGregor 1994, 2014, Rumsey 1990 and Spronck 2016, 2017 on Australian languages). For instance, the self-quotative *mondok* 'I say' in Hungarian can also introduce the reporter's thoughts.

(5) Hungarian (MNSz)
    (*Mikor a strandot kerestem, akkor láttam a faluban egy fából készült útjelzőt, hogy aszongya "Robinson 3 km."*)
    *No,   **mondok**,   biztos   ez   a   kemping   neve,*
    PTCL   say.PRS.1SG   certainly   DEM.P   DEF   camping   name:3SG
    vagy   mi.
    or   what
    '(When I was looking for the beach, I saw a sign made of wood in the village, which said "Robinson 3 km.") Well, **I say** [to myself], this is certainly the name of the camping site, or what.'

The first aim of this study is to provide a micro-typology of QIs that are ambiguous concerning representations of speech vs. representations of thought. As discussed above, these constructions are all characterized by event-un(der)specification. I check four possible scenarios characterized by event-un(der)specification for their use with RS and RT. First, I investigate constructions with generic speech verbs that can also introduce RT, as in (5). Second, constructions with an equational verb and etymologically non-reportative quotative markers, as in (2), are analyzed. Third, I check the non-clausal use of (self-)quotative particles, as in (3). And finally, turn-taking constructions with ellipsis of the speech/mental verb, as in (4), are investigated.

For this, I primarily target 6 Finno-Ugric (FU) languages representing 3 linguistic areas: Northeastern Europe (Finnish, Estonian), Central Europe (Hungary), and Russia (Erzya, Komi and Udmurt). In addition, I look at Russian as the main contact language for Eastern FU languages and at English for a broader comparison (see Table 1). The possibility for such ambiguity among these constructions was touched upon in previous studies (see overviews in Teptiuk 2019 for 5 FU languages and Russian; Teptiuk 2020 for Erzya; Romaine and Lange 1991, Buchstaller 2001 for *be like* in English). This study investigates whether the ambiguity between

RS and RT is observed regularly when these strategies are used. In all languages, these constructions are not limited to representations of the reporter's own RS and RT and can be used with someone else's discourse. Thus, one parameter to be included in the investigation is their appearance in both self-quotations and quotations.

Table 1: Constructions with event-underspecification.

(i) Generic speech verbs:	Hungarian (Ugric, FU), Erzya (Mordvin, FU)
(ii) Equational verb + etymologically non-reportative quotative particle:	Finnish, Estonian (both Finnic, FU), English (Germanic, IE)
(iii) Non-clausal (self-)quotative particles:	Komi, Udmurt (both Permic, FU), Russian (Slavic, IE)
(iv) Turn-taking construction with ellipsis of the speech/mental verb:	Hungarian (Ugric, FU), Russian (Slavic, IE)

The second aim of this study is to check whether the ambiguity between RS and RT arises more frequently in self-quotative or in quotative contexts. The third aim is to outline how the ambiguity between RS and RT can be resolved. The considerations behind the second and the third aim are presented in detail in Section 2, where the characteristics of RS and RT, and contextual cues setting apart these two types of report are discussed. The remainder of the paper is organized as follows. Section 3 describes the methodology and data. The results are presented in Section 4 and summarized in Section 5. Possibilities for further research on reported thought and self-quotations are also briefly discussed at the end of the paper.

2 Reported speech and reported thought: context and internal characteristics

Although the strategies outlined in Section 1 leave the event un(der)specified and may cause ambiguity between RS and RT, RS and RT can be identified based on the contextual and internal characteristics thereof. If we come back to example (2) and investigate the context, we realize that despite the ambiguity present at first glance, the example contains RS. In (6), representing an extended version of (2), the self-quotation is part of the reproduced dialogue and forms a coherent 'question-answer' set. Hence, we end up with a rather predictable speech situation.

(6) English (enTenTen15: English Web 2015)
she kept asking <u>"why are you not talking to me? are you mad?"</u> ***I was like*** <u>"I'm to[o] busy looking at everything and gawking at the buildings and sites that I didn't want to talk."</u>

What characterizes RS is its *addressivity*, i.e. the quality of being directed at someone, and its dialogic nature (see Bakhtin [1979] 1986: 95). Both ideas come back to Bakhtin (1986). However, here I use the adjective *dialogic* in its quite canonic meaning, i.e. as such that appears in the form of dialogue, and not in more conceptualized Bakhtinian way where "[a] word, discourse, language or culture undergoes 'dialogization' when it becomes relativized, de-privileged, aware of competing definitions for the same thing" (Holquist 1981b: 427). Nonetheless, I adopt Bakhtin's idea that all utterances imply the presence of an addressee (Bakhtin 1986: 95–100). For instance, RT in (5) partly repeated here as (7) is also dialogic. What sets RS apart in (6) and RT in (7), is the addressee.

(7) Hungarian (MNSz)
No,	**mondok,**	biztos	ez	a	kemping	neve,
PTCL	say:PRS.1SG	certainly	DEM.P	DEF	camping	name:3SG

vagy mi.
or what
'Well, **I say** [to myself], <u>this is certainly the name of the camping site, or what.</u>'

In a RS situation, the addressee is necessarily different from the original speaker. In Figure 1, this is illustrated with the male character speaking to a female interlocutor, which is reproduced later as RS. In an RT situation, the original speaker and the original addressee coincide (see Figure 2). In Figure 2, I illustrate this with the male speaker situated in front of the mirror. His thoughts depicted by thought bubbles are reproduced in the mirror as speech directed towards himself. Thus, the internal dialogue is happening inside his head, which is reproduced later as RT.

Vygotsky (1986: 26, 28), following Piaget ([1923] 1959), refers to this internal dialogue as *egocentric*, primarily discussing *egocentric speech* that among smaller children further develops into *egocentric thought*, or among adults is simultaneously realized as either *voiced egocentric speech* or *soundless inner speech* (Vygotsky 1986: 30). Between these subcategories, egocentric thought and soundless[2] inner speech probably best correspond to the content of RT. However, it is not always possible to know if reported egocentric speech/thought was previously voiced (referred by

---

2 I use the adjectives *soundless* and *unverbalized* interchangeably.

Figure 1: RS situation: Reported speaker: {Reported speech} → Addressee.

Figure 2: RT situation: Reported speaker: {Reported thought} → Reported speaker.

Goffman 1981a as *self-talk*) or remained soundless unless it is explicitly pointed out in the context. Therefore, to lower the level of speculation around this question, I would not distinguish egocentric speech from egocentric thought and will discuss their reports under the cover term reported thought.

In practice, someone else's thoughts remain covert unless they become somehow accessible to the audience. Speakers access others' thoughts mainly via previous verbalization of these thoughts by their author (see Schlenker 2004: 290–291 for a similar argumentation).³ For instance, in (8), Alfie first said to the newspaper what he thought, and the fact that he told them was reported by a third party.

(8) *Alfie told the newspaper that **he thought** "it would be good to have a baby."* (enTenTen15)

Alternatively, RT can be (i) a result of the inference, i.e. the reporter's speculation over what others might have thought based on their actions or regular behavior,⁴ or (ii) fictional. In situation (i), the evidential source of RT changes from reported (8) to inferential.⁵ Situation (ii) is often found in fiction where the author verbalizes the characters' thoughts and, in this way, makes their "inner world" accessible to the reader (see e.g. Goffman 1981a: 83). In the self-quoting context, the reporter as the author of RT has access to their own thoughts by default.

In the presentation of the results in Section 4, I will focus on self-quotations because I hypothesize that due to the availability of the reporter's thoughts to themselves, we find cases of RT represented more in self-quotations than in quotations. In contrast, I expect to find mainly cases of RS in quotations, while RT will be presented quite rarely and probably be part of the fictional rather than factual representations of someone else's thoughts. Hence, considering a larger number of RT presentations expected in self-quotations, the number of ambiguous cases shall also be larger. At the same time, cases considered initially ambiguous in quotations shall be mainly resolved as presentations of RS.

As for the means of disambiguation, I hypothesize that in efficient communication differences between RS and RT could be possible to guess from the context or features peculiar to RS and RT. Thus, RS shall be originally directed at the interlocutor, as e.g. in (6), or shall cause some reaction to its content by the addressee(s). In contrast, RT shall be egocentric, either voiced or soundless inner speech, as in

---

3 Body language and facial expressions can also be used to communicate someone's thoughts, in a way similar to the processes happening around inferred thoughts that are shortly mentioned after the example 8 and in footnote 4.
4 One could consider situations when the speaker predicts another's thoughts ("I will go now and ask him for money") based on their actions (verbalized or not) as in (i).
(i) [A child approaching his father to ask for money with pleading facial expression:]
"Dad? I just need..."
"Don't even think about asking for money, Glen. I've told you already – no more." (Source: https://www.englishclub.com/ref/esl/Conversational_Phrases/D/don_t_even_think_about_4132.php, accessed 15 December 2020; the preceding description added).
5 See Cornillie (2020) for the opposite scenario where inference is based on reported information.

(7). Being egocentric, RT will cause no reaction of the potential interlocutor, or the potential interlocutor will not be present in the reported situation at all.[6]

3 Methodology and data

To test the hypotheses, I conducted a pilot corpus-based study and used data from social network sites (SNS) as a database. For all languages, I used social media corpora available online (see Table 2). The corpora of the Eastern FU languages Erzya, Komi and Udmurt are a part of the Corpora of Uralic Volga-Kama languages.[7] The Finnish Internet communications database (Fin. *Internet-keskusteluaineistoja*) is accessible via the platform Korp;[8] the English and Estonian corpora via Sketch Engine.[9]

Table 2: The corpora used in the study.

Finnish	Internet communications corpus (IKA), 6.95 billion words
Estonian	etTenTen13, 270 million words
English	enTenTen15, 13 billion words
Udmurt	Press and blog subcorpus of the Udmurt corpus, 7 million words; Udmurt social media corpus (UdSmC), 2.66 million words
Komi-Zyrian	Komi-Zyrian social media corpus (KoZSmC), 1.85 million words
Russian	Russian National Corpus, electronic communications (RNC), 1.3 million words
Hungarian	Hungarian National Corpus, personal subcorpus (MNSz), 18.6 million words
Erzya	Erzya social media corpus (ESmC), 830 thousand words, and Blog subcorpus of the main corpus (EC), 138 thousand words

The following principles govern my choice of data. First, I look into QIs that have the potential to occur in non-standard varieties (consider e.g. *be like* in English). Second, I investigate the appearance of RS and RT in colloquial conversations. The

---

[6] Interestingly, similar criteria were chosen to distinguish between RS and RT among ambiguous reports in the Bible (Niehoff 1992: 582): "[a]n obvious formal indication of such self-reflective speech [alias: egocentric speech] may be the complete lack of any response to the utterance of someone who is presented as actually addressing others."
[7] http://volgakama.web-corpora.net/index_en.html (accessed 15 December 2020); the platform currently contains the corpora of 5 FU languages: Erzya, Komi-Zyrian, Meadow Mari, Moksha and Udmurt.
[8] https://korp.csc.fi (accessed 15 December 2020).
[9] https://www.sketchengine.eu/ (accessed 15 December 2020).

reason for this is that I would like to avoid data from sources that systematically depict someone's fictional thoughts (e.g. prose) or render someone's speech into thoughts (e.g. journalist texts).[10] Only in the Udmurt case do I make an exception and turn to the use of the Press subcorpus[11] as one of the sources that contain a larger number of examples with the dialectal self-quotative particle *pöj*,[12] which is not present in the literary standard and rarely appears on SNS. The data in the Press subcorpus differ a bit from regular journalist texts. The speech of the interviewed speakers is presented directly without rendering it into the literary standard (cf. the presence of strictly dialectal *pöj*) and stylistic transformations of someone's speech into thought are usually avoided. Therefore, I include the material from this subcorpus even though it does not belong to the SNS genre. For the rest of the languages, data derive from SNS and are not restricted to any subgenre and topic of conversation. The third and final remark about the choice of the data is based on my own previous experience with using SNS as a database. Specifically, despite different orthographic symbols, unstandardized shortenings, emoticons, etc., the language on SNS can be considered a written approximation of spoken language, combining the features of colloquial speech and standard writing within one text.

Since the study is preliminary, I investigated a limited number of examples for every strategy. If the number of examples did not exceed the 400 occurrences in the corpora, they were all examined. In other cases, the number of samples was limited with the following considerations. If one strategy has multiple ways of realization (e.g. *be + like* or *be + all* in English), the number of samples was limited to 100 for each combination. If it had only one form of realization (e.g. *erre* 'upon this' + Speaker in Hungarian), up to 1000 samples were investigated when available. The exact numbers of strategies investigated for each type of construction with the size of samples for the respective strategy are provided in Section 4.

In addition to the online corpora, some Estonian, Russian and Hungarian strategies were investigated using the Google search engine when the corpora did not provide sufficient data. The query for a strategy was placed in quotation marks

---

10 Consider the title of an article on CNN (https://money.cnn.com/2016/10/16/media/donald-trump-snl/; accessed 15 December 2020): "Donald Trump **thinks** SNL is rigging the election and should be canceled." If we browse the article, we find that what Trump "thinks" in the title is actually what he had said/tweeted: "And **he said** [on Twitter] that SNL was trying to rig the election against him."
11 The Press subcorpus is the biggest part (91%) of the Udmurt corpus (http://web-corpora.net/UdmurtCorpus/search/, accessed 15 December 2020), containing newspaper texts written between 2007 and 2015. The total size of the Udmurt Corpus is 7.3 million tokens.
12 *Pöj* is one of the markers that appears on its own and causes ambiguity between RS and RT (see Teptiuk 2019: 121–122). It also belongs to the category of dedicated self-quotative particles, which are typologically quite rare.

and was made in two variants: for self-quotations (containing the 1st person singular forms: verb forms or pronouns) and quotations (the 3rd person singular forms: verb forms or pronouns). I checked the first 10 search pages (ca. 100 unique query matches) since these results tend to contain the best hits with respect to the strategy. I excluded hits that did not fall under the category of SNS and did not include such data into the analysis.

During the corpus and Google searches, I excluded constructions that would contain elements specifying the event behind a report, e.g. speech/mental verbs and nouns encoding speech and mental processes, since such elements would indicate the type of report. For the same reason, QIs with the mention of addressees were also excluded.

The analysis consisted of three stages concentrating on: (i) the basic quantitative difference between the presentation of RS and RT in self-quotations; (ii) a comparison of quantitative differences between quotations and self-quotations; (iii) the means of disambiguation where report can be interpreted without the context as either RS or RT. To determine the basic quantitative difference, I counted cases of RS and RT with the cross-linguistic types of QIs outlined in the introduction. If such a type can potentially lead to the same ambiguity in quotations, I contrasted the number of RS and RT encountered in self-quotations with that found in quotations. Since this study is just the first attempt to count differences in the appearance of RS and RT in colloquial speech, I will not attempt statistical analyses here and will only provide descriptive statistics in terms of simple counts. Nonetheless, I hope that this study will establish a solid basis for further quantitative research on the tendencies outlined below.

For each case of RS and RT I assigned a label specifying the factors which led me to the interpretation of a concrete case as either RS or RT. Since this study is exploratory and mainly intends to verify the hypotheses specified above, the labels assigned are rather impressionistic and would require further elaboration in the future. Nonetheless, they are kept short (e.g. "context (dialogue between 2 speakers)", "content (reference to addressee)", etc.) and are intended to grasp the most important cue that motivated me to choose one interpretation over another. I will discuss these labels in Section 4 and assign them to the examples presented henceforth. Thoroughly ambiguous cases for which I could not choose one interpretation over the other were also expected and received their own label during the analysis. Such cases were excluded from the analysis in this paper because they would require a closer examination beyond this study. However, I come back to discuss these in Section 5 and explore them for generating hypotheses for future studies.

All examples are provided in their original form, meaning that neither spelling mistakes nor punctuation errors were corrected, together with translations and glosses. Russian examples are presented in transliteration without the original text in Cyrillic. Examples from Erzya, Komi and Udmurt are presented in transcription. Functional words borrowed from Russian are also transcribed.

4 Results: QIs and ambiguity between RS and RT in self-quoting contexts

4.1 Generic speech verbs

The first strategy discussed here is the use of generic speech verbs that, in addition to their original function of delivering the *verbalized* content, can also introduce not-necessarily-verbalized egocentric speech. Such generic speech verbs appear in two languages of the sample: Erzya (*meŕiń* 'I said') and Hungarian (*mondok/ mondom* 'I say/I say it').[13] Even though one can find dedicated mental verbs (Hungarian *gondol*, Erzya *arśems*, both 'think') used for the presentation of RT in both languages,[14] generic speech verbs can also introduce RT. It is worth mentioning that the situation in these languages is a bit different compared to some languages (e.g. Australian) where the meaning of both speech and thought are encoded within one verb (see Section 1). These speech verbs in Erzya and Hungarian encode RT less systematically and such use depends on the speaker's choice among the set of QIs available for these purposes.

The Hungarian forms are in the present tense. However, when used with report, they refer to past events in the historical present (past-tense reference with non-past morphology). There are also cases when these forms introduce the current speaker's stance with illocutionary reinforcement, similarly to Eng. *I am telling you* (see Teptiuk 2021). Since the content of stance belongs to the current and not to the reported speech situation, I do not include such cases into the quantitative results presented below. As for the present tense form *meŕan* 'I say' in Erzya, it only intro-

---

13 The variant *mondok* represents the indefinite conjugation form in contrast to the definite conjugation in *mondom*. Functionally, these markers are interchangeable; stylistically, they are not: *mondom* is common to Standard Hungarian; *mondok* pertains to vernacular speech and is often stigmatized as incorrect by language purists. Partially, this is reflected in the number of respective occurrences in the corpora, which is higher for *mondom* (see Teptiuk 2021).
14 This is, probably, one of the reasons why this function of the verbs has not been discussed much before, although it is familiar to native speakers (cf. Kubinyi, Suranyi, p.c. for Hungarian; Aasmäe, p.c. for Erzya).

duces the current speaker's stance or RS, but not RT (218 examples checked in ESmC and EC). Therefore, this form is not included in the results either.

In both quotations and self-quotations, the difference between speech and thought can be emphasized by mentioning the addressee(s). In the case of RS, the addressee will be someone other than the original speaker; in the case of RT, the addressee is the original speaker themselves (9)–(10). Hence, when RT is introduced, the reflexive pronoun can be used (Px-s highlighted), pointing to the egocentricity of the report (see Section 1).

(9) Erzya (personal knowledge)
   a. *meŕiń eśkan / esťeń* 'I said by **my**self / to **my**self' [self-quotation]
   b. *meŕś eśkanzo* '(s)he said by **her-/him**self' [quotation]

(10) Hungarian (personal knowledge)
   a. *mondok / mondom magamban* 'I say / say (it) to **my**self (lit. inside **my**self)' [self-quotation]
   b. *mondja magában* '(s)he says (it) to themselves (lit. inside self)' [quotation]

Mentioning the addressee is not necessary for the presentation of RT in self-quotations. In quotations, however, the RT reading can only be achieved when the addressee is specified in the QI. Henceforth I will only focus on those cases where the speech verb is the sole element of the QI. Moreover, I will not compare the use of these speech verbs in quotations and in self-quotations since there is no evidence that these verbs on their own can introduce RT in quotations.

Among 2000 examples of *mondok/mondom*, a limited number of cases (46) were encountered where these verbs were used on their own (see Table 3). A similar situation is found in Erzya with 12 examples out of 98 occurrences of the verb in the corpora. In both languages, we find more cases of RS introduced by these verbs. Only *mondok* in Hungarian shows a different pattern: 9 cases of RS vs. 13 cases of RT.

Table 3: Generic speech verbs in self-quotations (Hungarian and Erzya).

	Speech	Thought
Hugarian:		
mondok	9	13
mondom	19	5
Erzya *meŕiń*	11	1

In general, RS situations are easy to distinguish from RT. Most typically, RS is originally directed at interlocutor(s), as in (11a), or is a response to the utterance produced by interlocutor(s), as in (11b). Instead of strictly propositional, RS can also consist of illocutionary content directed at other speakers. By *illocutionary content* I mean discourse that has illocutionary force, realized as assertions, questions or commands directed at interlocutors. For instance, the question in (11a) triggers the interlocutor's answer. In (11b), the reporter responds to the interlocutor's command.

(11) RS: context (dialogue) + content (illocutionary)
   a. Hungarian (MNSz)
      Te, **mondok**, *van ennek gyereke? Nem*
      2SG say:PRS.1SG be.PRS.3SG DEM.P.DAT child:3SG NEG
      tom, igy a fonokom.
      know.PRS.1SG.DEF so DEF boss:1SG
      'Hey, **I say**, <u>does this one have kids</u>? **My boss was like** <u>I don't know.</u>'
   b. Erzya (ESmC)
      Meŕiť: *"Śormadt...",* **Meŕiń:** *"A karman..."*
      say:PST:2SG write:IMP.2SG say:PST:1SG NEG start:PRS.1SG
      '**You said:** <u>"You write..."</u>, **I said:** <u>"I won't..."</u>'

In addition, context can be a reliable index pointing at the speech situation, as in (12). The reporter mentions that the interlocutor has audibly perceived what was said.

(12) Erzya (ESmC), RS: context (addressee's perception)
   (... *son čaťmońeź učoś, jovtan a jovtan meźejak ťenze. Eźiń jovta.*)
   Meŕiń *anśak, kije iľazo sa, mon ťese*
   say:PST:1SG only who NEG.OPT.3SG come.CN 1SG here
   araśan (...) **Babam kunsolimim.**
   NEG.EXIST:1SG grandma:1SG listen:PST:3SG.OC.1SG
   '(... she looked at me silently: will I tell her something or not. I didn't tell.) **I** just **said**, <u>nobody shall come, I'm not here</u> (...) **My grandma listened to me.**'

Another use of RS is possible for Hungarian *mondok/mondom*. Specifically, these markers frame the repetition of a part of the reporter's previous utterance. The repetition usually happens right away and verbatim, emphasizing a part of the reporter's previous discourse. Since such a reduced report was previously uttered/written, it is interpreted as RS and not RT. The index for that is the context.

(13) Hungarian (MNSz), RS: context (previously mentioned parts)
      (*Nem egymást kéne ütni,*)
      van   ellenség   elég.   Ellenség,   **mondom**,
      be.PRS3SG   enemy   enough   enemy   say:PRS.1SG.DEF
      és   nem   ellenfél.
      and   NEG   opponent
      '(No need to hit one another,) there are enough **enemies**. Enemies, **I say**, and not opponents.'

In contrast to RS, Hungarian RT framed by self-quotative *mondok/mondom* requires a slightly more elaborated study of the context, in which there is typically no interlocutor (14). Therefore, what is uttered or remains unverbalized is the discourse directed at the reporter themselves, labeled here as RT (see Section 1).

(14) Hungarian (MNSz), RT: context (no interlocutor)
      (. . . *eppen gondolkodom, hol alszom, mikor trappolast hallok: ket ember szalad, eltunik egy sikatorban, par meterrel lemaradva harom katona utanuk, sisak, melleny, puska, ahogy kell.*)
      No,   **mondok**,   megis   keresek   valami   fedett   helyet.
      PTCL   say:PRS.1SG   anyway   search:PRS.1SG some   covered   place:ACC
      '(. . . I'm just thinking about where I will sleep when I hear marching: two people running, disappearing in an alley, three meters behind them three soldiers, helmets, vests, rifles, as they should be.) Well, **I said** [to myself], I'm looking for some shelter anyway.'

RT introduced by *meŕiń* appears quite rarely in contemporary Erzya. I have found only one case with the quotative *meŕiń* (15), which could qualify for the interpretation of the reported content as RT rather than RS.[15] My observations show that Erzya speakers nowadays turn to the use of the mental verb *aŕsems* 'think' to report what they or other speakers (might have) thought. Alternatively, the strategy *meŕiń esťeń* 'I said to myself', appearing in three cases in the corpora, can be used.

The bare use of the verb with RT in first-person reports (singular or plural) is also reported in Aasmäe (2012: 66) and the Dialect Dictionary of Mordvin languages (see

---

[15] In Teptiuk (2020: 55), I have reported two cases of RT framed by *meŕiń* in ESmC and EC. A closer investigation of these examples, however, shows that there is no ground to assume that the second case represents RT and not RS. Hence, I would like to correct my previous report here.

the entry "m̌eŕems").[16] Besides the presentation of RT, the speech verb may acquire the additional connotation of mistaken belief and is interpreted here as 'I supposed so (but it turned out to be different)' rather than more neutral 'I thought' (cf. Aasmäe 2012: 66). Such a connotation can be observed in (15), which I suggest interpreting as an RT-situation. Furthermore, the context of (15) does not show that some speech situation has previously taken place (in contrast to Hungarian cases as in example 13), and most likely the reporter only quotes their thoughts which were not uttered previously.

(15)   Erzya (EC), context: (mistaken belief + no interlocutor)
       (Ńeť valtne śe morostońť. Meŕťado, avoľ isťa? Śeste beŕańste sodasink čačoma keľeńek.)

Mon,	ono,	natoj	alamńeďe	mańaviń,
1SG	PTCL.DEM.D	even	a.bit.DIM:ABL	be.mistaken:PST:1SG

       meŕiń, pokščiś ušodovś morosto.
       say:PST:1SG holiday:DEF start:PST:3SG song:ELA
       (Avoľ. Vaśńa uľńesť kortamot, meźeś tuś melezeńek, – avoľ kuvakat.)
       '(These words are from this song. You'll say, it's not true? Then you know your native tongue badly.) You see, even I was mistaken a bit, **I said** (to myself), <u>the holiday started with a song</u>. (No. First there were some conversations that we liked, – they were not long.)'

To sum up, the ambiguity between RS and RT is not that prominent among the speech verbs of the languages in the sample. However, the Hungarian cases show that despite the variety of functions associated primarily with RS we find cases where speech verbs in self-quotations can introduce RT. As was hypothesized in Section 1, RS is distinct from RT that appears as egocentric in contexts where interlocutors are not present. Unfortunately, the situation in Erzya does not allow drawing similar conclusions, and – based on the corpora – such cases are not very frequent in contemporary non-standard written speech.

4.2 QIs with equational verbs

The second strategy involves the use of equational verbs together with originally non-reportative markers (also labeled as *new (innovative) quotatives*, see Buchstaller and Van Alphen 2012), and was observed in three languages of the sample: English,

---

[16] Available online: https://www.mv.helsinki.fi/home/rueter/PaasonenMW.shtml?fbclid=IwAR3pWc-TUWgvO2186JMTft_jf%205SWmin9aY7O4A0RRoVN-U6P17VnkQxoe2hc (accessed 15 December 2020).

Finnish and Estonian. In all three languages, a type of quote-oriented QI comprises the combination of the 'be'-verb with similative markers or quantifiers; in Finnish and Estonian, manner demonstratives and epistemically neutral complementizers ('that') are also used (see Table 4). The 'be'-verb in such QIs is typically in the past tense. However, present tense forms are also used to refer to past events (e.g. *I'm like what is going on here?*). For reasons of space, only past tense forms are considered here; possible differences between present and past tense of equational verbs in QIs shall be confronted in the future. The figures for Estonian in Table 4 indicate the total number of occurrences of the strategy in the corpora and found using Google search, excluding repetitions. In English and Finnish, these constructions are limited in number in the corpora (although they are also used in non-reportative contexts); hence, 100 samples per strategy were investigated out of principle.

As Table 4 shows, the number of RS and RT is equal in Estonian, and only the strategy *olin nagu* 'I was like' is used slightly more with RT than with RS. It also appears to be one of the most frequently used quotative strategies with an equa-

Table 4: QIs with equational verbs in self-quotations.

	Speech	Thought
English:		
I was like	38	55
I was all	39	43
Total:	77	98
Finnish:		
olin + niinku 'like'	3	12
olin + tyyliin 'like'	3	0
olin + vaan 'just'	10	14
olin + aivan 'totally'	1	4
olin + ihan 'totally'	15	52
olin + silleen 'thus'	10	17
olin + et 'that'	20	52
Total:	62	151
Estonian:		
olin + nagu 'like' (56)	22	34
olin + a la 'like' (1)	0	1
olin + mingi 'something' (17)	14	3
olin + nii 'so' (4)	2	2
olin + niimoodi 'so' (1)	0	1
olin + lihtsalt 'simply' (6)	4	2
olin + täiega 'completely' (2)	0	2
olin + et 'that' (11)	7	4
Total:	49	49

tional verb. In Finnish and English, these strategies are found in more cases introducing RT than RS. A minor exception in Finnish is the strategy with the similative *tyyliin* 'in the style, like', for which there are three cases of RS vs. zero cases of RT. However, a brief check with Google search confirms that this difference is only accidental in the corpora, and one can observe this strategy introducing egocentric speech in contexts where no interlocutor is present (16).

(16) Finnish (saysite.fi),[17] RT: context (no interlocutor)
(*Motifene dual nimistä tulehduskipulääkettä tuli myös syötyä vajaa kuuri. Oli pakko lopetttaa* [sic!] *kuuri kesken kun ripuloi verta oli muuten vitun kuumottaa ja*)
olin   tyyliin   et   nyt   delaan   ku   tulee
be:PST:3SG   like   COMP   now   die:PRS.1SG   when   come:PRS.3SG
jo   perseestäki   verta.
already   ass:ELA:ADD   blood:PAR
'(An anti-inflammatory painkiller called Motifene dual was also given after a short course of treatment. I had to stop the course during the diarrhea[,] by the way it was fucking burning and) **I was like** <u>now I will die since the blood comes even from my ass.</u>'

As for the means of how to distinguish RS from RT, we find similarities with the previously discussed cases in Hungarian and Erzya. I will use English to illustrate some of the peculiarities of RS (17) and RT (18) which are also relevant for Finnish and Estonian. RS is characterized by its illocutionary content directed at others (17a), or by usually causing some reaction of interlocutors (17b).

English (enTenTen15)
(17) RS: (a) content (illocutionary, directed at other speakers); (b) context (dialogue between two speakers, interlocutor's reaction)
   a. *But when we got back for rehearsal **I was like** <u>"Guys, this is so great. Look, we're all back together."</u>*
   b. *I saw him in the hallway the other day before I'd had my coffee and **he was all** <u>"HEY BEEJ HOW ARE WE TODAY?!?"</u> and **I was all** <u>"Fuck off"</u> and **he was all** <u>"HAHAHAAA You ARE SOOO FUNNY!"</u> and **I was all** <u>"No, really. Fuck off."</u>*

---

17 https://saysite.fi/viestiketju/huolestuttaa-vaehaen.509/page-10 (accessed 15 December 2020).

The vocative ("guys") and imperative ("look") expressions in (17a) indicate that the report was originally directed at other speakers present in the reported situation. Therefore, the report is interpreted as RS and not RT. In (17b), we find the interlocutor's reaction to the reporter's cue "fuck off". If this cue was not followed by any reaction as in the hypothetical example (17b'), the cue "fuck off" could also be perceived as the reporter's unverbalized thoughts. However, in (17b), the dialogue continues and contains the interlocutor's response to the reporter's utterance ("HAHAHAHAAA You ARE SOOO FUNNY!"). Hence, the interlocutor's verbal reaction[18] shows that both parts of the reporter's discourse were utterances and not unverbalized thoughts.

(17) b'. *I saw him in the hallway the other day before I'd had my coffee and* **he was all** *"HEY BEEJ HOW ARE WE TODAY?!?"* and **I was all** *"Fuck off"*

The same characteristics are also relevant for RT but realized differently than in RS. In (18a), the question marks comprising the reported content depict the reporter's surprise. This type of discourse is not directed at others and the reporter merely demonstrates their non-verbal egocentric reaction to the described circumstances. Such illocutionary signs[19] are used to demonstrate the reporter's emotional state rather than depict verbalized thoughts. In (18b), the reporter presents their thoughts about a story they were reading in the context where no interlocutor appears.

English (enTenTen15)
(18) RT: content: reporter's emotions (a); context (egocentric, no interlocutor) (b);
   a. *Yeah I saw "deliberating"* **I was like** *"?????????????"*
   b. *I read it and* **I was like** *"This is like my life story!"*

Furthermore, in some cases the reporter may use different QIs to differentiate RT from RS appearing within one situation, as in (19). Note that the content of RT also differs from the content of RS: the former depicts the reporter's emotions (compare

---

18 The interlocutor's reaction does not have to be necessarily verbal and can be any type of action, as in (a) and (b) here:

(a) *Trapper came back and was still trying to talk about sexual things.* **I was like** *"Just get me the fuck out of here"* **and he slapped my face.**
(b) *he was saying "I want you to put it together" [next dooor neighbors house]-* **I was like** *"Fuck"* **and he was giving me the look** *and I said "Whatever"* (enTenTen15).

As noted by Goffman (1981b: 38), "the very structure of a social contact can involve physical as opposed to verbal (or gestural) moves", realized as nonlinguistic responses (also see Bakhtin 1986: 69–70).
19 In addition to question marks, netspeak expressions like *wtf, lol,* etc. can demonstrate the reporter's emotions, surprise, or disagreement.

with 18a and partially 20) while the latter is illocutionary (*katotaan* 'let's see') and hence is directed at other speakers (compare with 17).

(19) Finnish (IKA), different QIs; RT: content (reporter's emotions) + RS: content (illocutionary)
(*Sit tä 1 sano mul et jos mä en alota 2 kans ni alotaks mä 1 kans.*)
olin **niinku et** voi herran jumala ja **sanoin**
be:PST:1SG like COMP INTERJ lord:GEN god and say:PST:1SG
et katotaan nyt et se 2 saa
COMP see:PASS.PRS now COMP DEM two can.PRS.3SG
itte kysyy...
self ask.INF
'(this 1st one says to me that if I don't start with the 2nd one, then would I start with the 1st one.) **I was like** oh my God and **I said** let's see now, the 2nd one can ask herself...'

In addition, referential shift excluding the potential addressee from the report situation (20) can characterize RT. Thus, instead of directly addressing a speaker present in the reported situation (e.g. '**Are you** lying to me or **are you** joking with that woman?'), the reporter only silently discusses that speaker. Also consider the content of RT where the reporter is accusing the speaker of lying. Thus, instead of doing it directly, the reporter chooses to keep accusations to themselves.[20]

(20) Finnish (IKA), RT: content (referential shift: 2SG>3SG; accusation)
(*Mun kundikaveri sano et sil o yx systeri ja kolme broidia sit se kuitenki kerran ku me oltiin ostarilla sano ihan selvästi tosta vaan yhelle muijalle et niit on VIIS sisarusta!!!!!!!!*)
Siis **mä olin niinku et** mitäHHH!!! Siis
then 1SG be:PST:1SG like COMP what then
valehteleekse niinku mulle vai heittikse vaan
lie:PRS.3SG:Q.3SG like 1SG.ALL or throw:PST.3SG:Q.3SG just

---

[20] A somewhat similar implication is also found in the study on RT in the Bible: "[i]f a speaker can be shown to refer to personal matters, which are known to the speaker and which the speaker would logically wish to keep private, it is to be suspected that he or she is not really communicating but talking to himself or herself" (Niehoff 1992: 582). Also see Buchstaller (2013: 8) for a similar example in colloquial English.

7 Self-quotations of speech and thought, and how to distinguish them — 191

>   jotain   läppää   sille   muijalle?????
>   some   joke:PAR DEM.ALL   woman:ALL
>   '(My boyfriend says that <u>he has one sister and 3 brothers</u>, then once when we were shopping he clearly just tells one woman that <u>he has FIVE siblings</u>!!!!!!!!)
>   Then **I was like** <u>whatTTT!!! Is he lying to me or is he joking with that woman?????</u>'

The constructions with an equational verb are not restricted to self-quotations. However, if the numbers of RT in quotations and self-quotations are compared, we find that in self-quotations they are significantly higher (see Table 5). In quotations, these constructions are used mainly with RS and only rarely with RT.

Table 5: QIs with an equational verb: self-quotations vs. quotations.

	Self-quotation		Quotation[21]	
	RS	RT	RS	RT
Finnish	62	151	118	5
Estonian	49	49	11	0
English	77	98	68	2

If we look into rare cases of RT in quotations, framed by these constructions, we find that RT represents the reporter's assumption about the reported speaker's thoughts, and not their factual thoughts. Consider these examples from English (21) and Finnish (22).

RT in quotations
(21)   English (enTenTen15)
       ***I think** at this time, **the director was like** "I have to fill HOW many more minutes? Screw it, it's dancing time!"*

(22)   Finnish (IKA)
       (16. Varmaankin happopäissään se sit kelas ettei pidä olla öisin liian pimeetä, jottaei vois lukee sarjiksii ja sit se loi kuun auringon heijastuspinnaksi ja muutaman muun auringon lisää.)
       17. Sit   **Se**   **kelas**,   et   kyl   nyt   kelpoo
           then   DEM   think:PST.3SG   COMP   PTCL   now   be.enough:PRS.3SG
           lukee   sariiksii
           read.INF   comics:PL.PAR

---

21 As with self-quotations, for each strategy 100 samples were investigated out of principle.

18. Ja   sit   **oli**   vaan   et   tää   on   jees!
    and   then   be:PRS.3SG   just   COMP   DEM   be.PRS.3SG   INTERJ
    '(16. Probably being completely on acid He then thought that it shouldn't be that dark at night, so that one could read comics and He created the moon as a reflecting surface of the sun and a few more suns.) 17. Then **He thought** well now one can read comics. 18. And **He was like** that's alright!'

In (21), the reporter right away indicates that the report is only their speculation about the director's thoughts.[22] In (22), the reporter presents an alternative plot for the Genesis creation narrative. Since the narrative involves only one character (the Christian God) and there are no interlocutors, the part in (22) framed with *oli vaan et* is a hypothetical thought attributed to that God. Note also that the hypothetical discourse presented in the context is RT framed by the mental verb *kelata* 'think'. This can serve as an additional argument for the interpretation of (22) as a RT situation, and not a RS situation.

To sum up, the strategies with equational verbs are used either more with RT than with RS or almost equally in self-quotations. In contrast, in quotative contexts, RS is prevalent, and RT appears only as hypothetical, i.e. the reporter speculates about the reported speaker's potential thoughts in the circumstances described. Such cases come close to *fictive interaction*, as discussed in Pascual (2006, 2014), Pascual and Sandler (2016), among others. Although fictive interaction acquires a non-token interpretation (cf. Pascual and Sandler 2016: 10), unlike the cases discussed here, they can be considered neighboring phenomena and share a few functions. Pascual (2006: 255) specifies that fictive interactions serve to enact internal dialogues, views and beliefs, and attitudes and behaviors. Such cases "open up a mental space in which a verbal interaction takes place, typically not constituting a report of an actual one" (Pascual 2006: 261). In the same vein, hypothetical RT is meant to demonstrate a mental space of the reported speaker to the audience, although it does not constitute an actual report and remains only a speculation on behalf of the reporter.

4.3 Non-clausal use of (self-)quotative particles

The third strategy involves (self-)quotative particles when they are not accompanied by any other element that could occur in a QI, i.e. NPs encoding speaker(s)/addressee(s) and verbs describing the event behind the report, cf. (3). Such uses

---

[22] For a similar case discussed previously in the literature, see Pascual (2014: 127).

can be observed in three languages in the sample: Komi, Udmurt, and Russian.[23] In Komi and Udmurt, there are dedicated markers that are not used in other contexts besides self-quotative ones.[24] In Russian, which lacks dedicated self-quotative markers, the quotative particles *mol, deskat'* and the new quotative *tipa* 'like' can also introduce the reporter's (previous or hypothetical) speech and thought in addition to their primary use with quotations and reported evidence (see Teptiuk 2019: 92–101). Table 6 presents the number of occurrences of non-clausal (self-)quotative particles in self-quotations of speech and thought. Here, I list the total number of occurrences checked. For Russian, the first figure next to the quotative marker depicts the occurrences in the corpus, while the latter indicates the occurrences checked via Google Search.

Table 6: Non-clausal (self-)quotative particles in self-quotations.

	Speech	Thought
Russian:		
mol (309 + 100)	2	3
deskat' (42 + 100)	2	2
tipa (351 + 100)	3	3
Total:	7	8
Komi-Zyrian:		
miśa (257)	52	51
Udmurt:		
pöj (166)	48	55
mol (27)	0	1
t'ipa (198)	0	3
Total:	48	59

Interestingly, there are relatively few cases in Russian, where quotative particles used non-clausally introduce self-quotations. However, among these few examples, we still find more cases of RT than RS. In Komi-Zyrian, there are more cases of RS

---

23 In other languages of the sample, e.g. Erzya and Hungarian, quotative particles used as non-clausal QIs are also encountered (see Teptiuk 2019, 2020 for the most recent overviews). However, some markers like Erzya *kel'a* are not used with self-quotations in non-clausal QIs; others like Hungarian *aszongya* do not introduce self-quotations at all. Given that, quotative particles from these languages will not be considered in this subsection.
24 In quotations, these markers are substituted by proper quotative markers, autochthonous and replicated from Russian (in Udmurt). I will contrast the use of the self-quotative markers with quotative ones at the end of this subsection.

than RT, but the difference is insignificant, as in Russian. Thus, only in Udmurt is the difference between RS and RT more significant and slightly higher in favor of RT. To save space, I will not dwell on the peculiarities of RS since these show strong similarities to this category in other languages described in previous subsections. Instead, I will concentrate on RT.[25]

RT in self-quotations is often illocutionary in Russian. It is meant to be directed at other speakers but used in contexts where the reporter puts their actions into words but does not utter them (23).

(23) Russian (RNC), context (reported situation)
(*Tetečka sprašivaet "Javljaetsja li vaše rešenie svobodnym? Prošu otvetit' vas, ženix." Ženix vmesto otveta smotrit na menja.*)

| Ja | načinaju | dergat' | ego | za | rukav, | **tipa**, | «Ženix |
| 1SG | start:PRS.1SG | pull:INF | he.ACC | for | sleeve.ACC | like | groom |

| že — | èto | ty!» |
| PTCL | DEM.N | 2SG |

'(The woman asks <u>"Is this decision done on your own will? I ask you to answer, the groom."</u> Instead of answering, the groom looks at me.) I start pulling his [the groom's] sleeve **like** <u>"And the groom, that's you!"</u>'

The reported situation in (23) happens at a wedding ceremony. Upon the request to answer the marriage registry officer's question directed at the groom, he remains silent. In turn, the bride starts pulling the groom's sleeve. The report accompanying these movements, although it verbalizes them, demonstrates thoughts and not an utterance, because she is not supposed to speak in this situation.

In Udmurt, another peculiar case (24) is observed; here the reporter uses the 2nd singular forms, addressing herself. Formally, a split happens between the reporter as a speaker and as an addressee. This way the reporter also reflects on her future actions and motivates the refusal to visit her friend's place.

(24) Udmurt (UdSmC), RT: content (egocentric: reported speaker = addressee)
(*Dyšetskonze jylpumjasa no, aďďźiśkyny vuyliz, śoraz oťe val, kvarťira no, pe, visjalozy. Pumit lui.*)

| Nunally | byde | vožjaśkod, | **pöj**, | ešjosydlen |
| day:DAT | every | envy:PRS.2SG | QUOT.SELF | friend:PL:2SG:GEN |

---

[25] Cases in which Permic self-quotative particles frame the reporter's thoughts describing intentions and purpose of their actions will also be excluded for the reason of space. Readers interested in this use of self-quotative particles in Komi and Udmurt are referred to Teptiuk (2021).

kyšnoossyly.
wife:PL:3PL:DAT
(*Aćim ujjosy luškem bördiśko.*)
'(After graduating he came to visit me, invited me to his place, they will give him a flat, he said. I was against the invitation.) Then every day **you**₁ will envy **your**ₘᵧ friends' wives. (I am crying myself all night.)'

If we compare the use of Russian quotative particles in quotations and self-quotations, and Permic self-quotative with quotative particles, we again find that in self-quotations the cases of RT are prevalent, while in quotations they are rather marginal (see Table 7). For Komi, the self-quotative particle *miśa* was contrasted with the non-clausal use of quotative *pö*. For Udmurt, in addition to the autochthonous quotative particle *pe*, Russian quotative particles appearing in self-quotations (see Table 6) were also investigated. For autochthonous particles, 500 samples were checked. The number of replicated elements was lower; therefore, every occurrence in the corpora was investigated.

Table 7: Non-clausal (self-)quotative particles: self-quotations vs. quotations.

	Self-quotations		Quotations	
	RS	RT	RS	RT
Udmurt	48	59	35	1
Komi	52	51	42	0
Russian	7	8	74	17

Interestingly, we end up with 17 RT cases among quotations in Russian, compared to one in Udmurt and zero in Komi. However, if we take a closer look at the use of quotative particles with RT in quotations, we again observe cases where RT is only hypothetical. Consider (25) where the reporter assumes what the reported speaker might have thought about Dontsov, based on his facial expressions.

(25) Russian (RNC), RT: context (hypothesizing over someone else's thoughts)
... *a   na   Doncova   smotrel   s   krajnim   podozreniem*
and   on   PN:GEN   look:PST.M with extreme:INSTR   suspicion:INSTR
(***mol**, ne   kliničeskij   li   idiot   sidit   peredo   mnoj?*)
QUOT   NEG clinical   Q   idiot   sit:PRS.3SG in.front.of 1SG.INSTR
'... and he looked at Dontsov with extreme suspicion (**like/thinking**, isn't that a clinical idiot sitting in front of me?)'

To sum up, we find either a bigger or almost equal number of RT cases compared to RS in self-quotations introduced by non-clausal (self-)quotative particles. In contrast, RT in quotations typically represents the reporter's assumption about the reported speaker's thoughts and appears in fewer cases compared to RS.

4.4 Turn-taking QIs with ellipsis of the speech/mental verbs

The last strategy concerns turn-taking QIs with ellipsis of the speech and mental verbs (see Table 8). Two turn-taking strategies are observed in Hungarian. One comprises the proximal demonstrative *ez* in the sublative case (*erre* 'upon this') connecting to the preceding discourse, and the NP encoding the reported speaker. The demonstrative formation *erre* signals the reported speaker's reaction towards some speech or other non-verbal situation and initiates the turn. Another turn-taking strategy consists of the additive coordinating conjunction *meg* 'and' and the NP encoding the reported speaker. For the strategy *én meg* 'and I', a corpus search was initially carried out, but since the combination 'coordinating conjunction + 1SG' yielded many non-quotative uses, a Google search was used as an alternative tool where more manipulations with the query could be done, excluding non-quotative uses of the combination. In Russian, the construction consists of the NP encoding the reported speaker and the type demonstrative *takoj* 'such' that can change in number (*takie* 'such.PL') and gender (*takaja* 'such.F'), depending on the reported speaker's characteristics.[26] A Google search was also used as additional tool for the Ru. strategy *ja takoj/takaja* since the corpora did not yield enough relevant examples and the initial search results were poor for both combinations. Both types of constructions can accommodate speech and mental verbs and hence depict the reported speaker's speech or thought. Since there is ellipsis of the verb, one can expect general ambiguity between the types of report. However, as Table 8 shows, this is relevant only for Russian QIs.

Table 8: Turn-taking constructions with ellipsis of the speech/mental verbs in self-quotations.

	Speech	Thought
Hungarian:		
erre én 'upon this I' (1000)	27	0
én meg 'and I' (100 + 100)	10	0
Ru. *ja takoj* (18 + 100) / *takaja* (21 + 100)	3	9

---

26 For now, I have excluded plural forms because of a low expectation that such report would demonstrate collective thoughts of the group of people, including the reporter.

Based on the corpus investigation, the construction in Hungarian appears exclusively delivering the reporter's speech, while in Russian we observe the construction presenting the reporter's thoughts, cf. (29). Moreover, we find the presentation of RT more frequently than RS when this strategy is used. In a previous study (Teptiuk 2019), I reported a couple of cases for Hungarian from Google where the report introduced by these constructions is egocentric, as in (26). A more detailed investigation unveils that such cases are quite marginal and do not appear regularly in the corpora where these strategies mark speech turns made by different speakers (27).

Hungarian
(26) RT: egocentric (Teptiuk 2019: 216; adjusted)
      (*Sokat gondolkoztam, hiszen a szöveg nem úszott a dallal,*)
      erre   én   meg   "*basszus,   ezt   akkor   ki   kell*
      DEM.P.SBLT   1SG   also   fuck   DEM.P:ACC   then   PRE   must.PRS.3SG
      dobnom,   és   újrakezdenem   előről".
      throw.INF:1SG   and   start.again.INF:1SG   before:DELA
      '(I thought a lot, but the text did not flow together with the song,) **so I also [thought]** "damn, then I must throw this out and start afresh."' (phenomenon.hu)

(27) RS: context (dialogue)
      Erre   én,   hogy   *itt   a   pénz,   ő   meg,   hogy*   *ez   nem*
      DEM.P.SBLT   1SG   COMP   here   DEF   money   3SG   and   COMP   DEM.P   NEG
      ennyibe   kerül.
      so.much:ILL   cost.PRS.3SG
      '**Upon this I**: here's the money, **and (s)he**: that's not how much it costs' (blog.hu)

The Russian turn-taking QI introduces both RS (28) and RT (29). RS is directed at other speakers and appears as part of the reproduced dialogue. In turn, RT is egocentric. It can either contain the reporter's thoughts when no interlocutor is present, or its content signals that it was not meant to be perceived by other speakers, as in (29).

Russian
(28) RS: context (dialogue between two speakers) (ukrainer.net)[27]
      (*"Da, da, davajte my togda sjadem s planom xutora i zaplaniruem, gde u nas čto budet. Zaplaniruem territoriju."*)

---

[27] https://ukrainer.net/hutor-gojch-les-volky-y-katya/ (accessed 15 December 2020).

Ja   takaja: „*Super!   Davajte*".
1SG   such.F   super   PTCL.ADH
'("Yes, yes, let's sit then with the plan of the location and plan where we will place things. Plan the territory.") **I was like:** "Super! Let's do it."'

(29) RT: egocentric (content + context) (proekt.media)[28]

I	**on**	**takoj:**	*čej*	*rjukzak?*	*Ja*	*takoj*:	*nu*	*na**j.*	*Ja*
and	he	such	whose	rucksack	1SG	such	PTCL	fuck.it	1SG

ne	*znaju*	*čto*	*oni*[29]	*sdelajut,*	*esli*	*uznajut,*
NEG	know:PRS.1SG	COMP	3PL	PRF.do:PRS.3PL	if	PRF.know:PRS.3PL

čto	*èto*	*moj*	*rjukzak,*	*poètomu*	*ja*	*prosto*	*ležu.*
COMP	this.N	my	rucksack	therefore	1SG	simply	lie:PRS.1SG

'And **he's like**: whose rucksack is this? **I'm like**: well, fuck it. I don't know what they will do, if they find out that this is my rucksack, therefore I simply lie there [silently].'

When compared with quotations, the situation in Hungarian is not different (see Table 9). The constructions are used to frame the reported speaker's speech and not thoughts (see e.g. example 27). As for Russian quotations, we do not find cases of RT introduced by the turn-taking QI, in contrast to self-quotations (see Table 8).

Table 9: Turn-taking constructions with ellipsis of the speech/mental verbs: self-quotations vs. quotations.

	Self-quotations		Quotations	
	RS	RT	RS	RT
Hungarian	37	0	39	0
Russian	3	9	8	0

To sum up, turn-taking constructions behave differently in the languages considered here. In Hungarian, this construction presents RS and only marginally RT. This probably happens due to the turn-taking nature of these strategies and their further conventionalization as the construction used mainly in reproduced dialogues. In contrast, the turn-taking QI in Russian can appear in contexts where the report is

---

28 https://www.proekt.media/report/monolog-o-pytkah-belorussia/ (accessed 15 December 2020).
29 Compare with (20) from Finnish, where a similar type of referential shift ("I don't know what **they** will do") happens and the reported content remains unavailable to other participants of the reported situation.

egocentric or the reporter signals that their thoughts remained covert from interlocutors present in the reported situation.

5 Summary and discussion

To provide a general summary, I return to the hypotheses examined here. The first hypothesis stated that since only the reporter's own thoughts are directly available to them, we shall find more cases of RT in self-quotations than in quotations. Consequently, the ambiguity between RS and RT shall arise more regularly in self-quotations compared to quotations. In principle, this hypothesis was confirmed. In colloquial speech, we find that RT in self-quotations occurs either more often than RS or on a par with RS. Some strategies are used more often with RS, e.g. the turn-taking QIs in Hungarian. However, if we compare the total number of RT in quotations and self-quotations in colloquial speech independently of the specific strategy, we find that, in quotations, RS is mostly presented, while RT appears as the reporter's hypothetical assumption about the reported speaker's mental processes. This can be explained by the reporter's default lack of accessibility to others' thoughts. Interestingly, only a few cases where the reporter accessed someone else's thoughts via their previous report are observed in colloquial speech, similarly to example (8), repeated here as (30). Therefore, in general the reporter can only infer the thoughts of others based on their past, current and/or consequent actions. In addition, the reporter may choose to attribute some hypothetical thoughts to a concrete speaker if it is pragmatically suitable.

(30) **Alfie told the newspaper that he thought** "it would be good to have a baby."
 (enTenTen15).

The second hypothesis stated that differences between RS and RT could be possible to guess in efficient communication from the context or features unique to either RS or RT. The analysis shows that RS is usually directed at the interlocutors present in the reported situation. As directed at other speakers, RS is likely to contain illocutionary elements, e.g. vocative expressions, commands, or questions triggering answers. Such speech often causes the interlocutor's reaction to the content of RS: a verbal response or any other reaction signaling that the interlocutor somehow perceived the reporter's utterance. As for RT, it appears as egocentric verbalized or soundless speech that causes no reaction. Usually, this type of report appears in a context where no interlocutor is present; hence, it is automatically egocentric. Nevertheless, we do find some formally illocutionary elements in RT, e.g. interjections, self-address, (rhetorical) questions, but they fulfill a slightly different function and demonstrate the reporter's emotional state.[30] In addition, the contentious load of the reported content that could be perceived as offensive by potential interlocutor(s) can serve as a cue for RT. In my data, such cases coincide with RT situations where the reporter uses referential shift: the potential interlocutor, addressed in RS with 2SG forms (e.g. '[I said:] **you are** lying'), is talked about with the 3SG reference (e.g. '[I thought:] **he is** lying'). Referential shift signals that the report was not addressed to potential interlocutors and only depicts the reporter's unverbalized thoughts.

Although most frequently the ambiguity between RS and RT can be resolved, we still find a certain number of ambiguous cases, as in (31). Such cases are typically characterized by the illocutionary content as if directed at the other speakers present in the reported situation. However, the context does not confirm this reading and leaves such report without any reaction. Since the fact that no reaction was described in the context does not necessarily confirm that such a reaction did not take place, such cases were given the label "ambiguous" in my corpus.

(31) *Cassidy and I shared a bedroom, but had our own beds. When* **we** *came in* **I was like** *"Is this bed just for me? But it's so big?!" I guess I should get used to the fact that it's normal to have a big bed in America.* (enTenTen15)

In the future, it would be interesting to investigate such cases more thoroughly and check why speakers turn to QIs that intentionally leave an interpretation as either RS or RT pending. Another question may relate to the functions of such report. For instance, one might get a reading that the report in (31) demonstrates the reporter's surprise. Such a demonstration adds vividness and presents surprise in a more dramatic way than a mere description, e.g. *When we came in I was surprised by the size of my bed.* Research in this direction could add to the existing studies on fictive interaction and its functions in discourse (see Pascual 2006, 2014; Pascual and Sandler 2016, among others). In addition, one could also check whether there is a relationship between the polyfunctionality of QIs that can already introduce RS and RT, and other functional extensions in the quotative domain. For instance, could one use a QI, conventionally used with RS only, to present unverbalized surprise? Do functional extensions of QIs such as presentation of reason, purpose and

---

30 Similar types of content are also found in self-talk discussed by Goffman (1981a), for which he uses the term 'response cries'. Among response cries, one can find examples of interjections and other non-clausal emotive expressions.

intention (see e.g. Güldemann 2008: 425–436, 460–467) necessarily develop from the possibility of presenting RT, or could they also develop independently?[31]

Finally, one of the aims of this paper was also to determine the strategies leading to the ambiguity between self-quotations of speech and thought. Among them, the following can be outlined:

i. Generic speech verbs (Hungarian: confirmed; Erzya: only marginally);
ii. QIs with equational verbs (Finnish, Estonian, English: confirmed);
iii. Non-clausal use of quotative particles (Komi, Udmurt, Russian: confirmed);
iv. Turn-taking QIs with ellipsis of the speech/mental verb (Russian: confirmed; Hungarian: only marginally).

Interestingly, some constructions behave differently across languages. The speech verb is used with RT more frequently in Hungarian than in Erzya. As for turn-taking QIs, the Russian construction shows more regular use with RT in self-quotations, while the Hungarian construction almost exclusively introduces RS. Therefore, in my micro-typology, only QIs with equational verbs and a non-clausal use of quotative particles can be confirmed as constructions that frequently cause the ambiguity between RS and RT in self-quotations of both typologically similar and distinct languages.

If we compare the use of these strategies in quotations and self-quotations, we find that generic speech verbs in the languages of the sample show no evidence for their use with RT, unless reflexive pronouns are present in the QI to signal the egocentricity of the report. QIs with equational verbs and non-clausal quotative particles can introduce RT in quotations, albeit rarely; however, such RT is likely to be hypothetical and not based on previous reports by their original authors. As for turn-taking QIs, we observe the same difference between self-quotations and quotations in Russian, while the same type of QIs in Hungarian are mainly used in reproduced dialogues and signal a change in turns between the speakers.

As a final remark, it should be mentioned that although the constructions discussed here were meant to cover all possible scenarios leading to the ambiguity between RS and RT in colloquial speech, they cannot be considered an exhaustive list. For instance, one of the constructions not considered here due to reasons of limited space is the use of quotative verbs with originally non-reportative semantics, e.g. English *go*. An initial brief survey that could be expanded upon in the

---

31 I owe this idea to Michael Daniel (p.c.) and would like to thank him for the discussion on this topic during the online data workshop "The grammatical variation of reported speech across languages" (25 February 2021).

future shows that the quotative *go* can also present RT in self-quotations (32), but in quotations it seems to be limited to the presentation of RS.[32]

(32) English (enTenTen15)
    a. *The first time I ever heard the name "Google",* **I went** <u>*"WTF is that?"*</u>
    b. *When Barack Obama ran for president, he said* <u>*he would pull the troops out of Iraq – and send them to Afghanistan*</u>*, and* **I went** <u>*"What?"*</u>[33]

Hence, un(der)specification of the event in a QI and the polyfunctionality of some elements in the quotative domain often lead to the ambiguity between RS and RT. However, self-quotation has more chances to represent thought, leaving more grounds for flexibility. As a result, it might appear that the strategies so far considered limited to presentations of RS can show more variation in self-quotations.[34] Furthermore, additional functions of self-quotations as instruments demonstrating the reporter's emotions, surprise, etc. (see e.g. examples 18a, 19, 20, 31, 32) could be a promising direction for future research. I hope that this study will encourage new research on self-quotations and RT even in languages where dedicated self-quotative markers do not appear and the phenomenon of speech and/or thought reporting has already been described substantially.

List of abbreviations

ACC	accusative
ADD	additive
ADH	adhortative
ALL	allative
CN	connegative
COM	comitative
COMP	complementizer
D	distal
DAT	dative
DEF	definite
DELA	delative

---

32 100 random samples with QIs *I go/went* and *X goes* were checked in enTenTen15. In self-quotations, I found 11 cases of RS and 12 cases of RT. For quotations, only 5 cases of RS vs. 0 cases of RT can be reported so far.
33 Compare example (32) with example (18).
34 For instance, Pascual (2014: 128) reports a case in English where the speech verb *say* is used to present the reporter's thoughts.

DEM	demonstrative
ELA	elative
EXIST	existential
F	feminine
FU	Finno-Ugric
GEN	genitive
ILL	illative
IMP	imperative
INF	infinitive
INSTR	instrumental
INTERJ	interjection
N	neuter
NEG	negative
OC	objective conjugation
OPT	optative
P	proximal
PAR	partitive
PASS	passive
PL	plural
PN	proper noun
PRE	preverb
PRF	perfective
PRS	present
PST	past
PTCL	particle
PTCP	participle
Q	question particle
QI	quotative index
QUOT	quotative particle
QUOT.SELF	self-quotative particle
RS	reported speech
RT	reported thought
SBLT	sublative
SG	singular

References

Aasmäe, Niina. 2012. *Kortatano erźaks. Räägime ersa keelt* [Let's speak Erzya]. Tartu: Bookmill.
Bakhtin, Mikhail M. 1986 [1979]. The problem of speech genres. In Caryl Emerson & Michael Holquist (eds.), *Speech genres and other late essays*, 60–102. Austin: University of Texas Press.
Buchstaller, Isabelle. 2001. An alternative view of "like": Its grammaticalisation in conversational American English and beyond. *Edinburgh Working Papers in applied Linguistics* 11. 21–41.

Buchstaller, Isabelle. 2013. *Quotatives: New trends and sociolinguistic implications.* Blackwell: Wiley.
Buchstaller, Isabelle & Ingrid van Alphen. 2012. Introductory remarks on new and old quotatives. In Isabelle Buchstaller & Ingrid van Alphen (eds.), *Quotatives: Crosslinguistic and Cross-disciplinary Perspectives,* xii–xxx. Amsterdam: Benjamins.
Chappell, Hilary. 2008. Variation in the grammaticalization of complementizers from verba dicendi in Sinitic languages. *Linguistic Typology* 12. 45–98.
Cornillie, Bert. 2020. On inferential hearsay readings in European languages. Paper presented at the 53rd Annual Meeting of the Societas Linguistica Europaea, workshop "The grammar of thinking: Comparing reported thought and reported speech across languages", online, 26 August – 1 September 2020.
D'Arcy, Alexandra. 2012. The diachrony of quotation: evidence from New Zealand English. *Language Variation and Change* 24(3). 343–369.
Dialect Dictionary of Mordvin languages based on the Heikki Paasonen Materials. https://www.mv.helsinki.fi/home/rueter/PaasonenMW.shtml?fbclid=IwAR3pWcTUWgvO2186JMTft_jf5SWmin9aY7O4A0RRoVN-U6P17VnkQxoe2hc (accessed 15 December 2020).
Goffman, Erving. 1981a. Response Cries. In Erving Goffman & Dell Hymes (eds.), *Forms of talk,* 78–124. Philadelphia: University of Pennsylvania Press.
Goffman, Erving. 1981b. Replies and Responses. In Erving Goffman & Dell Hymes (eds.), *Forms of talk,* 5–78. Philadelphia: University of Pennsylvania Press.
Güldemann, Tom. 2008. *Quotative indexes in African languages: a synchronic and diachronic survey.* Berlin: Mouton de Gruyter.
Güldemann, Tom. 2012. Thetic speaker-instantiating quotative indexes as a crosslinguistic type. In Isabelle Buchstaller & Ingrid van Alphen (eds.), *Quotatives: Cross-linguistic and cross-disciplinary perspectives,* 117–142. Amsterdam: Benjamins.
Holquist, Michael. 1981a. Introduction. In Michael Holquist (ed.), *Bakhtin, Mikhail Mikhailovich. The Dialogic imagination,* xv–xxxiii. Austin: University of Texas Press.
Holquist, Michael. 1981b. Glossary. In Michael Hoquist (ed.), *Bakhtin, Mikhail Mikhailovich. The Dialogic imagination,* 423–435. Austin: University of Texas Press.
Matić, Dejan & Brigitte Pakendorf. 2013. Non-canonical SAY in Siberia. Areal and genealogical patterns. *Studies in Language* 37(2). 356–412.
McGregor, William B. 1994. The grammar of reported speech and thought in Gooniyandi. *Australian Journal of Linguistics* 14(1). 63–92.
McGregor, William B. 2014. The 'say, do' verb in Nyulnyul, Warrwa, and other Nyulnyulan languages is monosemic. In Klaus Robering (ed.), *Events, Arguments, and Aspects: Topics in the Semantics of Verbs,* 301–329. Amsterdam & Philadelphia: Benjamins.
Niehoff, Maren. 1992. Do biblical characters talk to themselves? Narrative modes of representing inner speech in early biblical fiction. *Journal of Biblical Literature* 111(4). 577–595.
Pascual, Esther. 2006. Fictive interaction within the sentence: A communicative type of fictivity in grammar. *Cognitive Linguistics* 17(2). 245–267.
Pascual, Esther. 2014. *Fictive interaction: The conversation frame in thought, language, and discourse.* Amsterdam & Philadelphia: John Benjamins.
Pascual, Esther & Sergeiy Sandler (eds.). 2016. *The Conversation Frame: Forms and functions of fictive interaction.* Amsterdam: Benjamins.
Piaget, Jean. 1959 [1923]. *The Language and Thought of the Child.* London: Routledge and Kegan Paul.
Romaine, Suzanne & Deborah Lange. 1991. The use of like as a marker of reported speech and thought: A case of grammaticalization in progress. *American Speech* 66(3). 227–279.

Rumsey, Alan. 1990. Wording, meaning and linguistic ideology. *American Anthropologist* 92(2). 346–361.

Schlenker, Philippe. 2004. Context of thought and context of utterance: A note on free indirect discourse and the historical present. *Mind & Language* 19(3). 279–304.

Spronck, Stef. 2016. Evidential fictive interaction (in Ungarinyin and Russian). In Esther Pascual & Sergeiy Sandler (eds.), *The Conversation Frame: Forms and functions of fictive interaction*, 255–277. Amsterdam & Philadelphia: Benjamins.

Spronck, Stef. 2017. Defenestration: deconstructing the frame-in relation in Ungarinyin. *Journal of Pragmatics* 114. 104–133.

Teptiuk, Denys. 2019. *Quotative Indexes in Finno-Ugric (Komi, Udmurt, Hungarian, Finnish and Estonian)*. Tartu: University of Tartu dissertation.

Teptiuk, Denys, 2020. Quotative indexes in Erzya: a typological overview. *Finnisch-Ugrische Mitteilungen* 44. 47–79.

Teptiuk, Denys, 2021. Self-quotative markers in Permic and Hungarian. *Linguistica Uralica* 57(3). 213–232.

Vygotsky, Lev. 1986 [1934]. *Thought and language*: *Revised edition*. Cambridge, MA: MIT Press.

List of data sources

EC = Main Corpus of Erzya of the Corpora of Uralic Volga-Kama languages, http://erzya.web-corpora.net/erzya_corpus/search

enTenTen15 = The English Web Corpus, accessed through https://www.sketchengine.eu/

ESmC = Erzya social media corpus of the Corpora of Uralic Volga-Kama languages, http://erzya.web-corpora.net/erzya_social_media/search

etTenTen13 = Estonian Web 2013, accessed through https://www.sketchengine.eu/

IKA = Internet-keskusteluaineistoja [Internet-communications database], https://korp.csc.fi/

KoZSmC = Komi-Zyrian Corpora, Social Media Corpus, http://komi-zyrian.web-corpora.net/index_en.html

MNSz = Magyar Nemzeti Szövegtár, személyes alkorpusz [Hungarian National Corpus, personal subcorpus], http://mnsz.nytud.hu

RNC = Russian National Corpus, Electronic communications, http://www.ruscorpora.ru/new/en/

Udmurt corpus, Blog & Press subcorpora, http://web-corpora.net/UdmurtCorpus

UdSmC = Udmurt Corpora, Social Media Corpus, http://udmurt.web-corpora.net/index_en.html

Nino Amiridze
8 When *saying* becomes *thinking*: A case of the Georgian autonomous quotative *metki*

Abstract: The paper discusses Georgian quotative markers that derive from a speech verb via grammaticalization and represent clitics. It deals with a specific use of one of the markers, which started getting employed as an unbound item as well, clause-initially. As the use further develops a meaning of *thinking*, while blocking its interpretation as *saying* in a part of the data, the work argues for this development to be considered as a case of constructional shift of the meaning rather than that of de-grammaticalization.

1 Introduction

In order to mark the reported speaker, Standard Georgian uses several reported speech markers, including the postverbal clitic =*metki* (1a). It is derived from the full clause *me vtkvi* 'I said' (1b) (see Shanidze (1973: 610) and Boeder (2002: 13), and marks firsthand information reporting quotations in the first person singular:

(1) Standard Georgian
   a. *c'avida=metki.*
       (s)he.left=QUOT
       'I said (s)he left.'

Acknowledgements: The work was done within the project FR-19-18557, supported by the Shota Rustaveli National Science Foundation of Georgia. For valuable comments and suggestions, I am very grateful to Zurab Baratashvili, Barbara Karlson, Stef Spronck, Manana Topadze Gäumann, Daniel Van Olmen and two anonymous reviewers. I take full responsibility for any possible mistakes and shortcomings.

https://doi.org/10.1515/9783111065830-008

b. *me vtkvi.*
   I.NARR[1] I.said.it
   'I said.'

Standard Georgian and its dialects illustrate different forms related to the postverbal =*metki*, starting from the form *me+vtkvi* (2a) consisting of the elements of the full clause fused as one item (cf. (2a) vs. (1b)), up to the most reduced form -*mei* (2c).

(2) Quotative markers in Georgian dialects
   a. Imeretian and Javakhian
      ak   ra   ginda=mevtkvi.
      Here what you.want=QUOT
      '"What do you want here?", I said.'
   b. Imeretian and Javakhian
      ak   ra   ginda=metkvi.
      Here what you.want=QUOT
      '"What do you want here?", I said.'
   c. Mtiulian
      gavak'eteb=mei.
      I.will.do.it=QUOT
      '"I will do it", I said.'
      (Adapted from Jorbenadze et al. (1988: 293))

These forms illustrate reduction of the initial fused form =*me+vtkvi* (2a), derived from the full clause *me vtkvi* 'I said' (1b):

(3) Full clause (Ex. 1b)   =QUOT (Ex. 2a)   =QUOT (Ex. 2b)
    me vtkvi.   >>   =*me+vtkvi*   >>   =*metkvi*
       =QUOT (Ex. 1a)   =QUOT (Ex. 2c)
    >> =*metki*   >>   =*mei*

Usually, these uses can imply both speech and thought. However, in the second half of the 20th century, an autonomous *metki* referring to thought (and not to speech) started getting used in Tbilisi Georgian. It acquired epistemic reading of speaker's reliability like 'I thought', 'I was sure' (4).

---

[1] The narrative case has also been referred to as ergative (ERG) in the literature (see Hewitt (1995a)). There has been some debate, whether Georgian is an ergative language or not (see Hewitt (1995b), Hewitt (1989), Harris (1985), Amiridze (2006)). In this paper, I will be using the term narrative instead of ergative to avoid the bias towards the ergative alignment type.

(4) metki   saxlši   damxvdeboda.
    QUOT   at.home   (s)he.would.wait.for.me
    'I thought/*said (s)he would wait for me at home.' [but (s)he did not]

Such an interpretation is partially caused by the presence of a verb form from the Conditional TAM paradigm (4); however, the expression of an unsuccessful expectation towards *metki* can be expressed also with the Present Indicative form (5).

(5) dzalian   ggavs,   metki šeni   da+a.
    very.much   she.resembles.you   QUOT   your   sister+is
    Lit.: she resembles you a lot, I though she is your sister
    'She resembles you a lot, I thought/*said (s)he was your sister.' [but (s)he apparently was not]

In some part of the collected data, the neutral thought reading is the only possible one, without a speech reading:

(6) A speaker reporting their state when searching for words why they felt happy
    metki   ra   mixaria   am   dilit[...]
    QUOT   what   I.am.glad.of.it   this   morning
    'I was thinking what I was glad of (/happy about) this morning[...]'

I will overview the literature on Georgian quotative markers and, based on data of modern spoken Georgian, I will try to explain how the quotative enclitic =*metki*, based on the verb of speech, got reanalyzed into an unbound quotative *metki* meaning thought, and how it fits within the grammaticalization theory.

In the following sections, I will briefly overview reported speech/thought and evidentiality marking in Georgian (section 2). Then I will deal with the meaning (section 3) and the morphological status of quotative markers (section 4). Sections 5 and 6 will respectively discuss diachronic and synchronic variation of both standard and non-standard uses of those markers. Section 7 gives a possible explanation for the non-standard, autonomous use of the quotative marker *metki* that seems to contradict the unidirectionality of grammaticalization. Section 8 concludes the paper.

2 Reported speech/thought and evidentiality in Georgian

In the linguistic literature, quotation has been regarded as one of the ways to express reported evidentiality. Depending on whether the information is acquired by witnessing it or by somebody's report, by inferring or assuming from visual or non-visual sources and depending on whether and how the types of sources are reflected in language, one can have different types of evidentiality systems (see Aikhenvald (2004: XIV)). Depending on the number of choices, there can be grammatical marking of distinction of up to five choices. The latter is exemplified by Tariana (Arawak), which grammatically distinguishes whether information is visual, non-visual sensory, inferred, assumed, or reported (Aikhenvald (2004: 1–3, 60)).

According to Aikhenvald (2004), in systems with two choices, to which Georgian can also be attributed, there is a grammatical distinction between encoding firsthand vs. non-firsthand information. The traditional grammar by Shanidze (1973), Hewitt (1995a) as well recent works by Boeder (2000), Ramat and Topadze (2007), Topadze Gäumann (2016) and Margiani et al. (2019) make it clear that Georgian can be viewed as a language having a two-way system, as it distinguishes between firsthand and non-firsthand information. Non-firsthand information is coded via the perfect, which has various other uses as well. In the absence of a proper grammatical tool that marks exclusively evidentiality, it is probably more accurate to consider the Georgian perfect as an evidentiality strategy, as done by Aikhenvald (2004: 113).

Apart from the perfect, Georgian uses quotative enclitics to mark the information source. They are used to report both speech and thought (see Dzidziguri (1969), Shanidze (1973), Boeder (2002)).

When reporting speech, in self-reports, the narrator refers to the information that they have already uttered before. In reporting others' speech, they refer to the information they heard being uttered by another person. In both cases the information referred to by the reported speech is based on non-visual (auditory) information and could qualify as a type of non-visual evidentiality.

By reporting thought, a narrator can either refer to their own thought process (in case of selfreports) or their own assumption of another person's thinking (in third-person reported thought). Those assumptions are usually based on visual information the narrator has access to and infers from (such as facial expressions, see, for instance, Buchstaller (2014)) but can come from non-visual information as well. Depending on the type of the information the narrator has for reported thought, one can categorize it as a type of evidentiality (inferential or non-visual).

The next section describes Georgian quotative markers in reported discourse that stand for both speech and thought.

3 The meaning of the quotative markers in Georgian

In Georgian there are two possibilities for reported discourse:[2] a direct (7) and an indirect one (8) (see Boeder (2002)).[3] Both imply the interaction of two clauses, where one clause represents a *quotative index* (QI), or "a segmentally discrete linguistic expression which is used by the reporter for the orientation of the audience to signal in his/her discourse the occurrence of an adjacent representation of reported discourse" (Güldemann (2008: 11)) and another clause is the reported discourse (RD) clause. The position of the QI with respect to the RD clause can be preposed (7a) or postposed (7b):

(7) a. Preposed quotative index
[*kal-ma   tkva*]QI: ['*ic'vimebs*']RD.
woman-NARR   she.said   it.will.rain
'The woman said: 'It will rain'.'
b. Postposed quotative index
['*mšia*']RD, – [*gaipikra   bavšv-ma*]QI.
I.am.hungry   (s)he.thought   child-NARR
"'I am hungry', – thought the child.'

In the reported indirect discourse though, the two components such as QI and RD clause, irrespective of their order (whether preposed QI (8a) or the postposed one (8b)), do not represent two independent clauses. Instead, they are each a part of a biclausal syntactic structure, where the QI represents the main clause and the RD

---

2 Instead of reported *speech*, I use reported *discourse*, as apart from verbs of speech, verbs referring to cognitive acts or states can also be involved. Güldemann (2008: 6) defines *reported discourse* as "the representation of a spoken or mental text from which the reporter distances him-/herself by indicating that it is produced by a source of consciousness in a pragmatic and deictic setting that is different from that of the immediate discourse." However, 'distancing' does not necessarily entail that the speaker of a reported utterance necessarily doubts the veracity of the quote.
3 The Kartvelian language family of four languages, to which Georgian belongs, distinguishes mainly between direct vs. indirect reported speech and thought. The only exception is its most archaic member, Svan, for which a three way distinction (direct vs. indirect vs. semi-indirect) has been reported (see Boeder (2002: 17–37)).

clause is the subordinate one, whatever the order of the clauses (see the preposed QI in (8a) and the postposed one in (8b)). Apart for the obvious differences in the use of quotation marks in the direct vs. indirect reported discourse, the latter involves an optional use of connectives (see the optional *rom* 'that' in (8a)) and the obligatory use of quotative markers (see the enclitic *=o* in (8)), not characteristic to the reported direct discourse (7):

(8)   a.   Preposed quotative index
         [*kal-ma*   *tkva*]QI,   [(*rom*)   *ic'vimebs=o*]RD.
         woman-NARR   she.said   that   it.will.rain=QUOT
         'The woman said (that) it would rain.'
  b.   Postposed quotative index
         [*mšia=o*]RD,   [*gaipikra*   *bavšv-ma*]QI.
         I.am.hungry=QUOT   (s)he.thought   child-NARR
         'The child thought [that] (s)he was hungry.'

The RD clauses in Georgian indirect reported discourse employ the following three quotative particles that may encliticize to different constituents of a clause: *=metki*, *=tko* and *=o*.

The quotative enclitic *=metki* is used when the information source is the 1st person singular (9); it is unambiguous as no QI is necessary.

(9)   [(*me*)   *vtkvi*]QI,   [(*rom*)   *tovda=metki*]RD.
      I.NARR   I.said   that   it.was.snowing=QUOT
      'I said (that) it was snowing.'

Although the verb form *vtkvi* is an Aorist Indicative form (1b), in modern Georgian the derived quotative enclitic *=metki* (1a) can be used with QIs that contain verb forms of other TAM paradigms as well, see (10a) and (10b):

(10)   Standard Georgian
    a.   Present Indicative
         [(*me*)   *vambob*]QI,   [*mivdivar=metki*]RD.
         I.NOM   I.am.saying   I.am.leaving=QUOT
         'I am saying [that] I am leaving.'
    b.   Future Indicative
         [(*me*)   *vit'q'vi*]QI,   [*c'aval=metki*]RD.
         I.NOM   I.will.say   I.will.be.leaving=QUOT
         'I will say [that] I will be leaving.'
         (Adapted from Dzidziguri (1969: 446))

When the information source is 1st person plural, the enclitic =o is used. However, the enclitic alone is not sufficient and requires a QI (here, čven vtkvit 'we said') identifying the source:

(11) [čven   vtkvit]QI, [tovda=o]RD.
      We.NARR   we.said   it.was.snowing=QUOT
      'We said it was snowing.'

If no QI is present, the enclitic =o can only refer to the 3rd person as an information source (12):

(12) tovda=o.
      it.was.snowing=QUOT
      '(S)he said it was snowing.'
      'They said it was snowing.'

The enclitic =o is used both in cases where the reported speaker is a specific person and where it is not (e.g., in hearsay). The types of the reported speaker do not have effect on the use of QUOT enclitics but rather the employed TAM paradigm has. Namely, the Perfect TAM paradigm is used for the non-specific speaker (13a), while the Aorist Indicative (or Simple Past) TAM paradigm is used for the specific one (13b).

(13) a. [ase utkvamt]QI, [c'vima-s cisart'q'ela   mohq'veba=o.]RD
          so   they.have.said rain-DAT rainbow.NOM it.will.follow.it=QUOT
          'They say that after the rain comes the rainbow.'
      b. [ase tkves]QI, [c'vima-s cisart'q'ela mohq'veba=o.]RD
          so   they.said   rain-DAT rainbow.NOM   it.will.follow.it=QUOT
          'They said that after the rain the rainbow will appear.'

The enclitic =o can also be used when the information source is the 2nd person singular or plural, provided that a respective QI is also present. Consider (14a) and (14b):

(14) a. [šen   tkvi]QI,   [tovda=o.]RD
          you.SG   you.SG.said it.was.snowing=QUOT
          'You(sg) said it was snowing.'
      b. [tkven   tkvit]QI,   [tovda=o.]RD
          You.PL   you.PL.said it.was.snowing=QUOT
          'You(PL) said it was snowing.'

To summarize in Table 1, the unambiguous =*metki* is used in case the information source is the 1st person singular, while the polyfunctional =*o* is used elsewhere. In case of the enclitic =*o*, if no QI is provided, the information source is by default the 3rd person (SG/PL) (see Example (12)). However, it can be used in cases where the information source is not the 3rd person, but a clarifying QI is strictly necessary (cf. (15a) vs. (11), (15b) vs. (14a), (15c) vs. (14b)):

(15) *tovda=o.*
      it.was.snowing=QUOT
      a. *'We said it was snowing.'
      b. *'You(sg) said it was snowing.'
      c. *'You(pl) said it was snowing.'

For standard Georgian, the enclitic =*tko* (16) does not have a place within this table. It is referred to as instructional in the literature (see Boeder (2002: 14)) and is used when the speaker is instructing the addressee to transmit the quote to somebody (see Topuria and Gigineishvili (1970: 161)):[4]

Table 1: The Georgian QUOT markers =*metki* and =*o*.

	Singular	Plural
1st person	=*metki* (Example (9))	=*o* (Example (11))
2nd person	=*o* (Example (14a))	=*o* (Example (14b))
3rd person	=*o* (Example (12))	=*o* (Example (12))

(16) Instructional =*tko*
      utxari   šen-s   da-s,   radio   gamotiše=tko.
      you.SG.tell.her your-DAT   sister-DAT   radio.NOM   you.SG.switch.it.off=QUOT
      'Tell your sister to switch the radio off.'

Note that the enclitics =*metki* and =*o* may imply both reported speech and thought (17). However, the latter interpretation requires the QI to be present (cf. (17a) vs. (18a) and (17b) vs. (18b)):

---

4 Compare, for instance, Imeretian (Jorbenadze (1989: 483)), Gurian (Jorbenadze et al. (1988: 199)), Rachan (Jorbenadze (1989: 437)), and Lechkhumian (Jorbenadze (1989: 510)) dialects of Georgian, where the QUOT marker =*tkva*, a variant of the standard Georgian QUOT marker =*tko*, is used when information source is 1st person, thus, as an equivalent of the standard Georgian =*metki*.

(17) a. *saxl-i   daic'va=metki.*
       house-NOM it.burnt.down=QUOT
       1. 'I said the house burnt down.'
       2. *'I thought the house burnt down.'
    b. *saxl-i   daic'va=o.*
       house-NOM it.burnt.down=QUOT
       1. '(S)he said the house burnt down.'
       2. *'(S)he thought the house burnt down.'

(18) a. [*vipikre*]QI, *saxl-i   daic'va=metki.*
       I.thought   house-NOM it.burnt.down=QUOT
       'I thought the house burnt down.'
    b. [*ipikra*]QI,   *saxl-i   daic'va=o.*
       (s)he.thought house-NOM it.burnt.down=QUOT
       '(S)he thought the house burnt down.'

Instructional =*tko* is different from the two quotation markers above by having a reported speech interpretation only (cf. (19a) vs. (19b)):

(19) *saxl-i   daic'va=tko.*
     house-NOM it.burnt.down=QUOT
     a. 'Tell him/her the house burnt down.' (QI not necessary)
     b. 'Let him know/*think the house burnt down.'

All of them are used as enclitics (section 4), though =*metki* can have an autonomous, unbound use as a clause-initial *metki* as well, to be discussed in section 6.

4 The placement and morphological status of the quotative markers

In Georgian, QUOT markers are postposed and encliticized as a non-autonomous unit exclusively to the head of a phrase (see also Shanidze (1973: 72) and cf. (20a) vs. (20b); (20a) vs. (20c) and (20a) vs. (20d)) and the rightmost suffix in word forms representing the head (cf. (21a) vs. (21b); (21a) vs. (21c), and (21a) vs. (21d)).

(20) a. *im   axal   saxl-ši-c*
       DIST.OBL new   house-in-ADD
       'in that new house too'
    b. *im   axal   saxl-ši-c=o*
       DIST.OBL new   house-in-ADD=QUOT
       'In that new house too, (s)he said.'
    c. **im=o   axal   saxl-ši-c*
       DIST.OBL=QUOT new   house-in-ADD
       'In that new house too, (s)he said.'
    d. **im   axal=o   saxl-ši-c*
       DIST.OBL new=QUOT   house-in-ADD
       'In that new house too, (s)he said.'

(21) a. *saxl-ši-c*
       house-in-ADD
       'in a/the house too'
    b. *saxl-ši-c=o*
       house-in-ADD=QUOT
       'In a/the house too, (s)he said.'
    c. **saxl=o-ši-c*
       house=QUOT-in-ADD
       'in a/the house too'
    d. **saxl-ši=o-c*
       house-in=QUOT-ADD
       'In a/the house too, (s)he said.'

They usually attach at the very end of a clause. If any other item gets cliticized by a QUOT marker within that clause, it is obligatory to have the same marker at the end of the clause as well. For instance, in (22a), the QUOT marker cliticizes the head (*mzareul-ma*) of the noun phrase (*am axalgazrda mzareul-ma*) representing the subject argument. The clause is grammatical if the end of the clause is cliticized as well (cf. (22b) vs. (22a)):

(22) a. *am   axalgazrda   mzareul-ma=o   dyes   k'inayam*
       PROX.OBL   young   cook-NARR=QUOT   today   almost
       gadac'va   is   axal-i   rest'oran-i-c=o.
       (s)he.burnt.it.down DIST.NOM   new-NOM   restaurant-NOM-ADD=QUOT
       'Today this young cook almost burnt down that new restaurant as well, (s)he said.'

b. *am   axalgazrda   mzareul-ma=o   dyes   k'inayam
   PROX.OBL   young   cook-NARR=QUOT   today   almost
   gadac'va   is   axal-i   rest'oran-i-c.
   (s)he.burnt.it.down   DIST.NOM   new-NOM   restaurant-NOM-ADD
   'Today this young cook almost burnt down that new restaurant as well, (s)he said.'

Below, when cliticized to the head of the verb phrase (that is the verb *gadac'va*), the clause is ungrammatical (23b), unless the same marker cliticizes to the final item of the clause as well (23a):[5]

(23) a. am   axalgazrda   mzareul-ma   dyes   k'inayam
        PROX.OBL   young   cook-NARR   today   almost
        gadac'va=o   is   axal-i   rest'oran-i-c=o.
        (s)he.burnt.it.down=QUOT   DIST.NOM   new-NOM   restaurant-NOM-ADD=QUOT
        'Today this young cook almost burnt down that new restaurant as well, (s)he said.'
     b. *am   axalgazrda   mzareul-ma   dyes   k'inayam
        PROX.OBL   young   cook-NARR   today   almost
        gadac'va=o   is   axal-i   rest'oran-i-c.
        (s)he.burnt.it.down=QUOT   DIST.NOM   new-NOM   restaurant-NOM-ADD
        'Today this young cook almost burnt down that new restaurant as well, (s)he said.'

Complex clauses require QUOT markers to be present at the very end of the second clause, whether it is the main (cf. (24b) vs. (24a)) or the subordinate one (cf. (25b) vs. (25a)). In case the preceding clause gets a QUOT marking, it is obligatory to give the second occurrence of the same marker at the end of the following clause as well, whether it is the main clause (cf. (24c) vs. (24d)) or the subordinate one (cf. (25c) vs. (25d)):

(24) a. roca   dac'er,   gamomigzavne!
        when   you.SG.will.write.it   you.SG.send.IMPER.it.to.me
        'When you write it, send it to me!'
     b. roca   dac'er,   gamomigzavne=o.
        when   you.SG.will.write.it   you.SG.send.IMPER.it.to.me=QUOT
        'When you write it, send it to me, (s)he said.'

---

5 Spoken language illustrates some variation. Namely, for some speakers, (23b) does not seem to be ungrammatical but rather a variant of (23a).

c. *roca   dac'er=o,   gamomigzavne=o.*
   when you.SG.will.write.it=QUOT you.SG.send.IMPER.it.to.me=QUOT
   'When you write it, send it to me, (s)he said.'

d. **roca   dac'er=o,   gamomigzavne*
   when you.SG.will.write.it=QUOT you.SG.send.IMPER.it.to.me
   'When you write it, send it to me, (s)he said.'

(25) a. *gamomigzavne,   roca   dac'er!*
        you.SG.send.IMPER.it.to.me when you.SG.will.write.it
        'Send it to me when you write it!'

   b. *gamomigzavne,   roca   dac'er=o.*
      you.SG.send.IMPER.it.to.me when you.SG.will.write.it=QUOT
      'Send it to me when you write it, (s)he said.'

   c. *gamomigzavne=o,   roca   dac'er=o.*
      you.SG.send.IMPER.it.to.me=QUOT when you.SG.will.write.it=QUOT
      'Send it to me when you write it, (s)he said.'

   d. **gamomigzavne=o,   roca   dac'er*
      you.SG.send.IMPER.it.to.me=QUOT when you.SG.will.write.it
      'Send it to me when you write it, (s)he said.'

The same is true for the other two QUOT markers. Namely, the following two examples illustrate that =*metki* (26) and =*tko* (27) get postposed and encliticized as a non-autonomous unit exclusively to the head of a phrase:

(26) a. *es   ʒvel-i   saxl-i-c*
        PROX.NOM   old-NOM house-NOM-ADD
        'this old house too'

   b. *es   ʒvel-i   saxl-i-c=metki*
      PROX.NOM   old-NOM house-NOM-ADD=QUOT
      'This old house too, I said.'

   c. **es=metki   ʒvel-i   saxl-i-c*
      PROX.NOM=QUOT old-NOM   house-NOM-ADD
      'This old house too, I said.'

   d. **es   ʒvel-i=metki   saxl-i-c*
      PROX.NOM   old-NOM=QUOT house-NOM-ADD
      'This old house too, I said.'

(27) a. mag⁶   nakiraveb-i   bin-is-tvis
   MED.OBL   rented-NOM   apartment-GEN-for
   'for that rented apartment'
b. mag   nakiraveb-i   bin-is-tvis=tko
   MED.OBL   rented-NOM   apartment-GEN-for=QUOT
   'For that rented apartment, tell him/her that.'
c. *mag=tko   nakiraveb-i   bin-is-tvis
   MED.OBL=QUOT   rented-NOM   apartment-GEN-for
   'For that rented apartment, tell him/her that.'
d. *mag   nakiraveb-i=tko   bin-is-tvis
   MED.OBL   rented-NOM=QUOT   apartment-GEN-for
   'for that rented apartment, tell him/her that.'

And just like the enclitic =o (21), =metki (28) and =tko (29) also are the rightmost among the items attached to the stem:

(28) a. bin-is-tvis
   apartment-GEN-for
   'for the apartment'
b. bin-is-tvis=metki
   apartment-GEN-for=QUOT
   'For the apartment, I said.'
c. *bin=metki-is-tvis
   apartment=QUOT-GEN-for
   'For the apartment, I said.'
d. *bin-is=metki-tvis
   apartment-GEN=QUOT-for
   'For the apartment, I said.'

(29) a. bin-is-tvis
   apartment-GEN-for
   'for the apartment'
b. bin-is-tvis=tko
   apartment-GEN-for=QUOT
   'For the apartment, tell him/her that.'

---

6 Georgian has a tripartite system of demonstrative pronouns: proximate-medial-distal.

c. *bin=tko-is-tvis
apartment=QUOT-GEN-for
'For the apartment, tell him/her that.'
d. *bin-is=tko-tvis
apartment-GEN=QUOT-for
'For the apartment, tell him/her that.'

Both =*metki* (30) and =*tko* (31) attach usually at the end of a clause, just like the clitic =*o* (22). If any other item gets cliticized by a QUOT marker within that clause, it is obligatory to have the same marker at the end of the clause as well:

(30) a. *am   axalgazrda   mzareul-ma=metki   dyes   k'inayam*
       PROX.OBL   young   cook-NARR=QUOT   today   almost
       gadac'va   is   axal-i   rest'oran-i-c=metki.
       (s)he.burnt.it.down DIST.NOM   new-NOM   restaurant-NOM-ADD=QUOT
       'This young cook almost burnt down today that new restaurant as well, I said.'
   b. **am   axalgazrda   mzareul-ma=metki   dyes   k'inayam*
       PROX.OBL   young   cook-NARR=QUOT   today   almost
       gadac'va   is   axal-i   rest'oran-i-c.
       (s)he.burnt.it.down DIST.NOM   new-NOM   restaurant-NOM-ADD
       'This young cook almost burnt down today that new restaurant as well, I said.'

(31) a. *am   axalgazrda   mzareul-ma   dyes   k'inayam*
       PROX.OBL   young   cook-NARR   today   almost
       gadac'va=tko   is   axal-i
       (s)he.burnt.it.down=QUOT   DIST.NOM   new-NOM
       rest'oran-i-c=tko.
       restaurant-NOM-ADD=QUOT
       'This young cook almost burnt down today that new restaurant as well, tell him/her that.'
   b. **am   axalgazrda   mzareul-ma=tko   dyes   k'inayam*
       PROX.OBL   young   cook-NARR=QUOT   today   almost
       gadac'va   is   axal-i   rest'oran-i-c.
       (s)he.burnt.it.down DIST.NOM   new-NOM   restaurant-NOM-ADD
       'This young cook almost burnt down today that new restaurant as well, tell him/her that.'

Like the enclitic =*o* (see (24) and (25)), =*metki* and =*tko* are also required to be present at the very end of the second clause, whether it is the main one (cf. (32b) vs. (32a)) or the subordinate one (cf. (32d) vs. (32c)).

(32) a. *roca   dac'er,   gamomigzavne!*
         when you.SG.will.write.it you.SG.send.IMPER.it.to.me
         'When you write it, send it to me!'
         (Repeated from (24a))
    b. *roca   dac'er,   gamomigzavne=metki.*
         when you.SG.will.write.it you.SG.send.IMPER.it.to.me=QUOT
         'When you write it, send it to me, I said.'
    c. *gamomigzavne,   roca   dac'er!*
         you.SG.send.IMPER.it.to.me when you.SG.will.write.it
         'Send it to me when you write it!'
         (Repeated from (25a))
    d. *gamomigzavne,   roca   dac'er=tko.*
         you.SG.send.IMPER.it.to.me when you.SG.will.write.it=QUOT
         'Send it to me when you write it, tell him/her that.'

In case the preceding clause gets a QUOT marking, it is obligatory to have the second occurrence of the same marker at the end of the following clause as well, whether it is the subordinate clause (cf. (33a) vs. (33b)) or the main one (cf. (33c) vs. (33d)):[7]

(33) a. *roca   dac'er=metki,   gamomigzavne=metki.*
         when you.SG.will.write.it=QUOT you.SG.send.IMPER.it.to.me=QUOT
         'When you write it, send it to me, I said.'
    b. **roca   dac'er=metki,   gamomigzavne.*
         when you.SG.will.write.it=QUOT you.SG.send.IMPER.it.to.me
         'When you write it, send it to me, I said.'
    c. *gamomigzavne=tko,   roca   dac'er=tko.*
         you.SG.send.IMPER.it.to.me=QUOT when you.SG.will.write.it=QUOT
         'Send it to me when you write it, tell him/her that.'
    d. **gamomigzavne=tko,   roca   dac'er.*
         you.SG.send.IMPER.it.to.me=QUOT when you.SG.will.write.it
         'Send it to me when you write it, tell him/her that.'

---

7 Spoken language illustrates some variation. Namely, for some speakers, (33b) does not seem to be ungrammatical but rather a variant of (33a). Similarly, for them (33d) is a possible variant of (33c).

5 History of quotative markers in Georgian

Diachronically, Old Georgian has only one QUOT enclitic, the =o that is found in clause-final position (34) (see Shanidze (1976); Sarjveladze (1997)).

(34) Old Georgian
man mactur-man tkua vidre cocxalya
DIST.NARR deceiver-NARR he.said while alive
iq'o, vitarmed šemdgomad sam-isa dyisa
he.was that after three-GEN day-GEN
ayvdge=o
I.arise.SUBJ=QUOT
'While he was still alive the deceiver said that after three days he would rise again.' (Matthew 27:63, adapted from Shanidze (1976: 149))

There are cases (35), when both coordinate clauses in the RD clause are marked by the QUOT marker =o.

(35) [romel-n-i it'q'wian]QI, vitarmed [qorc-n-i ara
who-PL-NOM they.say that flesh-PL-NOM NEG
šeisxna upal-man k'ac-ta-gan=o, aramed
he.put.AOR.them.on Lord-NARR man-PL.GEN-from=QUOT but
zec-it hkondes=o]RD.
heaven-INST he.will.have.them=QUOT
'Who say that the Lord did not put on flesh from men, but he will have it from heaven.'
(Adapted from Boeder (2002: 9), citing an old Georgian manuscript of the year 864)

The origin of the entclitic =o is not known. Some authors compare it to the interrogative particle =a that occurs post-verbally as well (36):

(36) simon, gʒinavs-a.
Simon you.are.sleeping=Q
'Simon, sleepest thou?'
(Mark 14:37, adapted from Shanidze (1976: 146))

However, the only explanation for this comparison is probably due to the morphological status of both, as enclitic. Otherwise, there is no semantic and/or etymological connection between the two.

In middle Georgian texts, the enclitic =o occurs again post-verbally. However, the word order variations allow it to be placed not only clause-finally but elsewhere too, as illustrated below in (37):

(37) Middle Georgian, adapted from Boeder (2002: 9), citing *Vepxist'q'aosani* by Shota Rustaveli
mepe-man brʒana: 'vnaxe=o mizez-i lxin-ta
King-NARR he.commanded I.saw.AOR.it=QUOT cause-NOM joy-PL.GEN
lev-isa'.
waning-GEN
'The king said: 'I have seen cause for loss of joy.''

As for the other two enclitic quotative markers, =metki (38a) and =tko (38b), they both derive from a generic speech verb *'say'* and are in use since middle Georgian (see Dzidziguri (1973)). Both forms are more or less transparent:

(38) a. QUOT (Ex. 9) Full clause (Ex. 1b)
=metki << me vtkvi
I.NARR I.said.it
b. QUOT (Ex. 16) Subjunctive form (cf. full clause in Ex. (39))
=tko << tkva
you.SG.say.SUBJ.it

(39) (šen) (is) unda tkva.
you.SG.NARR it.NOM should you.SG.say.SUBJ.it
'You should say (it).'

Example (40) illustrates the use of the instructional =tko in a text of the 12th century:

(40) Middle Georgian, from *Vepxist'q'aosani* by Shota Rustaveli, stanza 103, verses 102-103
tinatin brʒana: 'ac' c'aval, šeslva
Tinatin she.commanded now I.will.go entering
ar čemgan žam-ita. mik'itxos, hk'adre:
NEG from.me time-INST he.ask.SUBJ.for.me you.SG.dare.tell.him
iq'o=tko aka ert-ita c'am-ita'.
she.was=QUOT here one-INST second-INST
'Tinatin said: 'I will leave now; it is not time for me to enter. If he asks about me, dare tell him [that] she was here for one second.''

Note that in the middle Georgian data one can still encounter the use of the enclitic =*o* in those cases as well where the information source is the 1st person singular and where in modern Georgian one would exclusively use =*metki* (41).

(41) Middle Georgian variation, =*o* instead of =*metki*, from *Vepxist'q'aosani* by Shota Rustaveli
    a. Stanza 1145, verses 1141–1143
       ševexvec'i: '*dadumdi=o*'.
       I.urged.him   fall.IMPER.silent=QUOT
       'I urged him to fall silent.'
    b. Stanza 933, verses 930–934
       ra   *vuambo?*   *rad*   *move=o...?*
       what.NOM I.tell.SUBJ.him why I.came=QUOT
       'What should I tell him, why I came...?'

There are other middle Georgian texts that follow the new trend of using =*metki* to express the 1st person singular information source (42). This suggests that the middle Georgian period has been a kind of intermediate period until the QUOT =*metki* got its modern distribution.

(42) Middle Georgian variation, from *Rusudaniani* (XIII-XV centuries)[8]
    a. =*metki* as 'I said/*thought'
       Chapter 2, paragraph 1, line 11
       [*movaxsene*]QI: [*tu*   *mibʒaneb,*
       I.reported/told.him/her if   you.command.it.to.me
       ac've   *c'aval=metki.*]RD
       immediately I.will.go=QUOT
       'I told him/her: 'if you command me, I will go at once.''
    b. =*metki* as 'I said/thought'
       Chapter 3, paragraph 1, line 33
       [*jer*   *gamik'virda*   *da*   *meucxova*]QI:
       first   I.got.surprized and   it.seemed.strange.to.me
       [*vin*   *aris=metki?*]RD
       who   it.is=QUOT
       'First I got surprized and it seemed strange to me who (s)he was.'

---

8 Available at http://titus.fkidg1.uni-frankfurt.de/texte/etca/cauc/mgeo/rusudan/rusud.htm

c. =*metki* as 'I *said/thought'
Chapter 11, paragraph 1, lines 20–21
[*vtkvi gul-sa šina*]QI: [*bevr-s*
I.said heart-DAT inside much-DAT
sasacilo-s rasme it'q'vian iqi
funny-DAT something.DAT they.will.say.it/them there
c'aval[,] *tamaš-sa vnaxav=metki.*]RD
I.will.go game-DAT I.will.watch=QUOT
'I said in my heart: they will say many funny things, I will go there, I will watch a game.'

Example (42b) describes a situation with a surprised speaker. The enclitic =*metki* gets attached to the verb *aris* '(s)he is' in the interrogative sentence *vin aris?* 'Who is (s)he?'. The context does not rule out any of the two possible readings: (i) when the speaker utters the question and (ii) when the question arises in the speaker's mind and is not voiced as such.

Example (42c), however, is different. The QI contains the adverbial *gul-ši* 'in the heart' [=without uttering, for oneself], excluding the 'I said' reading for the QUOT enclitic. As a result, the only reading the enclitic could get in (42c), is 'I thought'.

Therefore, depending on the context, the use of adverbials and/or lexical semantics of the verbs involved in the QIs of the examples above, there can be the following readings for the QUOT marker =*metki*:
– *I said/*thought* (42a),
– *I said/thought* (42b),
– *I *said/thought* (42c).

By now I have been dealing with the bound, encliticized uses of the QUOT markers. The next section will discuss a relatively new use of one of them, namely, of *metki* that appears as an autonomous unit at the beginning of the clause and differs from the bound and postposed uses of the QUOT markers by interpretation as well.

6 Clause-initial autonomous *metki* in modern varieties of Georgian

6.1 The autonomous *metki* as 'say'

In some dialects of Georgian (43a), as well as in Tbilisi variety (43b), *metki* is attested as an autonomous lexical unit occupying the initial position in a clause (43).

(43) a. Kakhetian dialect,
    metki   gaetrie   akedan!
    QUOT   get.out   of.here
    'I told you to get out of here.'
    (From Dzidziguri (1973: 446))
  b. Tbilisi Georgian
    mamačem-i   meuneba,   ra-s   ak'etep-o
    my.father-NOM   he.is.telling.me what-DAT   you.SG.are.doing=QUOT
    da,   metki,   age, agvist'o-ši   umayles-ši   vabarep[...]⁹
    and   QUOT   see   August-in   university-in I.am.entering
    'My dad is asking me what I am gonna do and I'm like, 'See, in August I am gonna enter a university[...]''
    (From Morchiladze (2014: 52))

According to Harris and Campbell (1995: 410), the grammaticalization of *metki* in phrases like (43a) is not completed. According to the endnote 34 in Boeder (2002: 41), the particle *metki* in (43a) is considered to be at an intermediate stage between quotative particle and an autonomous verb.

In colloquial language *metki* sometimes occurs twice in a sentence as an autonomous lexical unit (at the beginning) and as an enclitic (at the end of the sentence) in order to intensify the marking of reported speech (44) (see also Topadze Gäumann 2016: 47).

(44) *metki   c'amoiq'vane   ege+c=metki.*
    QUOT   you.bring.him/her.with   MED+ADD=QUOT
    'I told him/her to bring him/her too, I said.'

Topadze Gäumann (2016: 47) reports a case, similar to example (44), where instead of the enclitic =*metki* the speaker uses the other QUOT marker, namely =*tko*:

(45) *metki   garet   davelodebi=tko.*
    QUOT   outside   I.will.wait.for.him/her=QUOT
    'I said/thought I would wait for him/her.'
    (Adapted from Topadze Gäumann (2016: 47))

---

9 The example is taken from a larger context that contains a conversation between a father and a son. The son is a footballer who got injured and was waiting for his recovery, in order to go through a selection procedure for one of the main Georgian football clubs. In this conversation the father asks the son, what his plans for the future are and the son replies that he is going to pass exams for entering the university. Thus, the initial autonomous *metki* can only get interpreted here as 'say' but not 'think'.

Although =*tko* is known from descriptive works as the instructional QUOT marker, in cases like (45) or (46), it gets employed in combination with the clause-initial autonomous *metki*. However, in such cases, it does not function as instructional quotative any more but as signaling a 1st person singular information source:[10]

(46) Posted on March 13, 2021[11]
    dyes   viq'avi   HM-ši[.]
    today   I.was   H&M-in
    metki rame   k'omport'ul   jins-s   viq'idi=tko[. . .][12]
    QUOT some   comfortable jeans-DAT I.will.buy=QUOT
    'Today I was in the H&M. I thought I would buy some comfortable jeans[. . .]'

6.2 The autonomous *metki* as '(wrongly) assume' / 'think'

In modern spoken Georgian, there is a nonstandard use of the QUOT marker *metki* with the reading '(wrongly) assume' / 'think' (see (4)-(6), (47)). It is preposed with regard to the RD clause and functions as a particle, thus, as an autonomous unit:

(47) *dzalian   ggavs,   [metki]*QI   [*šeni   da+a*]RD
    very.much she.resembles.you QUOT   your   sister+is
    Lit.: she resembles you a lot, I though she is your sister
    'She resembles you a lot, I thought/*said (s)he was your sister.' [but (s)he apparently was not]
    (Repeated from (5))

Example (48) describes the situation where a forum user inquires about a computer part and another user falsely assumes that a portable hard disk is needed. Here, the autonomous sentence-initial *metki* expresses an assumption, not an utterance:

---

10 Topadze Gäumann (2016: 48) refers to the use of =*tko* in the presence of the autonomous *metki* as doubly marked first person.
11 Available at https://forum.ge/?showtopic=35190468&view=findpost&p=57639121, (accessed March 30, 2023)
12 One of the reviewers suggested that the doubling of initial and final quotative particles points to a variation between old (postposed) and new (preposed) marking and that the use of final =*tko* points to a dialectal source (most probably Western Georgian varieties). Although it is certainly interesting to have information on the origin of separate items of this double marking (*metki*. . . =*tko*), it does not contribute to the main topic of this paper (how the autonomous *metki* (< *say*) got interpreted as *think*). Neither it helps to understand how the instructional quotative =*tko*, when combined with the clause-initial autonomous *metki*, signals the 1st person SG information source.

(48) Posted on March 24, 2021[13]
hard   disk'-i   c'avik'itxe[,]   sori   smile.gif
(Eng.)hard (Eng.)disk-NOM I.read.it   (Eng.)sorry smile.gif
metki   hard-i   unda   garedan   misadgmel-i[.]
QUOT   (Eng.)hard-NOM (s)he.wants.it from.outside attachable-NOM
'I read *hard disk*, sorry, I thought/*said (s)he wanted a hard [one] attachable from the outside[.]'

The next example (49) is also an example of false belief. There the speaker is wondering about somebody's disappearance and uses the clause-initial autonomous *metki* to mean that they were wondering by themselves (but not speaking/asking/enquiring/voicing). Namely, the interrogative sentence, *au es k'ide cocxal-i-a?* 'Oh, is this one still alive?', implies that the speaker had assumed that another person must have been dead. However, when the speaker realized that the assumption was wrong, (s)he asks another question, *metki sada-a?* 'I was wondering where (s)he was', implying their initial wondering about where the disappeared person was:

(49) Posted on March 10, 2021[14]
au   es   k'ide cocxal-i-a?
oh   this.one   still alive-MOM-COP
[biggrin.gif biggrin.gif] *metki   sada-a[?]*
[smiley   smiley]   QUOT   where-COP
'Oh, is this one still alive? [smiley smiley] I was wondering (thinking/*saying) where (s)he was.'

In yet another example (50), a forum user inquired about a place where he could sell computer parts. Others suggested a place which he thought was located near his home but, in fact, it was not. After having realized that he assumed wrongly, he used the sentence-initial autonomous *metki* to express his thought/assumption, not an actual utterance in a real time:

---

[13] Available at https://forum.ge/?showtopic=35195895&view=findpost&p=57685982, (accessed March 30, 2023).
[14] Available at https://forum.ge/?showtopic=35194111&view=findpost&p=57626166 (accessed March 30, 2023).

(50) Posted on March 23, 2021[15]
  gmadlobt... aup, vak'e-ši q'opila.
  thank.you.PL oh Vake-in it.seems.to.be
  metki gldan-ši-a es 51 sk'ola[.]
  QUOT Gldani-in-COP this 51st school.NOM
  'Thank you... Oh, it seems to be in Vake. I thought/*said this School No. 51 was in Gldani[.]'

The reading of *saying* for the clause-initial autonomous *metki*, discussed in Section 6.1, was reported at the end of the 1960s by Dzidziguri (1969: 445–446). It is difficult to determine the exact time the autonomous particle acquired the reading of *thinking*.

7 Explaining the reading 'think'/*'say'

This section gives examples of the use of the clause-initial, autonomous *metki* in different contexts, where it cannot be interpreted as *saying* but only as *thinking/wondering*.

  For instance, in (51), the speaker reports a situation where he cannot hear a voice even with his earphones on, when watching something on his computer. Later, he realizes the earphones have been connected to something else, namely to his mobile. The QUOT is used at the beginning of the clause that expresses his thought rather than his utterance.

(51) Posted on March 18, 2021[16]
  vuq'ureb, vuq'ureb[,] xma ar mesmis...
  I.am.watching.it I.am.watching.it voice NEG I.hear.it
  metki ra xdeba da uceb mivxvdi[,]
  QUOT what it.is.happening and suddenly I.realized.it
  rom q'ursasmenebi[,] romelic mek'eta[,]
  that earphones that I.was.wearing.them

---

[15] Available at https://forum.ge/?showtopic=35195894&view=findpost&p=57684510 (accessed March 30, 2023).
[16] Available at https://forum.ge/?showtopic=35195266&view=findpost&p=57661803 (accessed March 30, 2023).

>   *mob-ze   mkonia   šeertebuli...*
>   mobile-on   I.apparently.have.had   connected
>   'I am watching it, watching it, I can't hear the voice... I thought
>   'what's happening?' and suddenly I realized that the earphones
>   that I was wearing have been connected to the mobile...'

Example (52) illustrates another use of *metki* to express the commentator's wondering/thinking about the author of a blogpost.

(52) A comment on a blogpost, posted on January 14, 2012[17]
    uimee[!]   [smiley] *sanam* *bolomde* *čavedi[.]*
    oh.heck   [smiley] before till.the.end I.went.down
    metki *ra*   *sč'irs*   *hekse-s[.]* [smiley]
    QUOT   what   wrong.is Hexe-DAT   [smiley]
    ase *ʒalian* *rodis* *šecvala*
    so   much   when   she.changed.it
    c'er-is   *st'il-i=metki*   [smiley]
    writing-GEN style-NOM=QUOT   [smiley]
    'Oh heck[!] [smiley] Before I read till the end, I thought what was wrong with Hexe [.] [smiley] When did she change her writing style so much, I thought.'

Example (53) describes a situation, where the speaker walks outside his office to find out the reason why the person called *beka k'op'aliani* was visiting that day and what he wanted. Thus, the *metki* preceding the question *ra unda?* 'What does he want?' can refer to the speaker's thought but not an explicitly uttered question:

(53) Posted on July 16, 2017[18]
    kalak-is *p'rok'urat'ur-idan*   *beka* *k'op'alian-i* *iq'o*
    city-GEN prosecutor's.office-from Beka   Kopaliani   was
    mosul-i.   *gavedi.*   *metki* *ra* *unda?*
    arrived-NOM I.went.outside QUOT what he.wants.it
    aymočnda, *rom* *moc'me-ze* *zec'ol-is*   *pakt'-ze*   *iq'o[...]*
    it.appears that witness-on pressure-GEN fact-on/about he.was
    'From the city prosecutor's office there arrived Beka Kopaliani. I went out [to meet/see him]. I thought/wondered what he wanted [/was here for]. It appears that he was [here] regarding the fact of the pressure on a witness[...].'

---

17 Available at http://www.hexe.ge/2012/01/blog-post 13.html (accessed March 30, 2023).
18 Available at http://qronikaplus.ge/?p=13145 (accessed March 30, 2023).

In (54), the speaker is trying to put a name to what made him so happy that morning, before fully realizing the reason. The *metki* used there preceding the clause *ra mixaria* 'what I am glad of' can only refer to his thoughts, wonder, and not to any other explicit utterance:

(54) Posted on March 11, 2021[19]

metki	ra	mixaria		am	dilit		da
QUOT	what	I.am.glad.of.it		this	morning		and

mtel-i	sapexburto	samq'aro	ro	čvenze		
whole-NOM	football.NOM	world.NOM	PART	about.us		

ar	yadaobs	da	dasacin-eb-i		ro	ara	vart
NEG	(s)he/it.jokes	and	to.be.ridiculed-PL-NOM		PART	NEG	we.are

q'velasi[,]	ra	k'ai	grʒnoba	q'opila	turme[.]
of.everyone	what	good.NOM	feeling.NOM	it.has.been	apparently

'I was wondering what I was glad of this morning and [I realized] what a great feeling it apparently is that it is not us that the whole football world is making fun of and that we are not the object of ridicule[.]'

As it is known, Georgian QUOT markers =*o* and =*metki* can both be used with QIs based on verbs of cognitive acts or states, in addition to the verbs of speech (55):

(55)
gušin	vtkvi /	vipikre /	vigulisxme,
yesterday	I.said	I.thought	I.meant

net'av	arasrdos	movxvedriliq'avi	ak=metki
I.wish	never	I.appear.SUBJ	here=QUOT

'Yesterday I said/thought/meant [that] I wished I had never appeared here.'

However, the use when the speech verb interpretation is excluded and only the interpretation of thought is available for the autonomous *metki*, has not been discussed before.

The question is how to deal with the numerous uses of the grammaticalized autonomous QUOT marker *metki* that originates from a speech verb (*say*, see (1)) but gets an exclusively *thought* reading in modern colloquial Georgian. Can we say that along the grammaticalization cline the marker got degrammaticalized back and acquired a new lexical meaning of *thinking*? One sign of degrammaticalization

---

[19] Available at https://forum.ge/?showtopic=35187537&view=findpost&p=57627747 (accessed March 30, 2023).

for the use of *metki* could be seen in its unbound status as opposed to its use as a clitic. But that would contradict the idea of unidirectionality of grammaticalization.

Let us look at other possible similar cases of development of verbs of speech into those of thought and perception in the typological literature. Güldemann (2002) and Güldemann and von Roncador (2002) consider Shona, a Bantu language of Zimbabwe, where grammaticalazied QUOT markers originating from a speech verb acquire a new lexical reading of *thinking* (56). The phenomenon of quoted speech being interpreted as thought is not restricted to languages of Africa (see also (57)) and can be found elsewhere (cf. (58a) vs. (58b) and see (59)):

(56) Shona (a Bantu language of Zimbabwe)
    a. *nda-ti*   *uya*   *neni*
        1SG:PERF-*ti*   come:IMPER   COM:1SG
        'I said: 'Come with me!''
    b. *nda-ti*   *zvimwe*   *chi-poko*
        1SG:PERF-*ti*   perhaps   COP:7-ghost
        'I thought that perhaps it was a ghost.'
        (From Güldemann (2002: 254))

(57) Kanuri (a Nilo-Saharan language of Northern Nigeria)
     {*férònzá yèzáskána*}   *sà*   *wú-gà*
     {I have killed their daughter}   quotative.verb:3P:MED   1SG-O
     cátà
     catch:3PL.PAST
     Lit: they said/thought, I've killed their daughter, and arrested me
     'They arrested me on the charge that/ because I killed their daughter.'
     [actually, he did not]
     (Adapted from Cyffer (1974: 213))

(58) Kwaza (isolated, spoken in Brazil)
    a. *warañỹ-'e-da-tsy-re*
        work-again-1SG-POT-INT
        'Am I (going) to work again?'
    b. *warañỹ-e-da-tsy-'re-da-ki*
        work-again-1SG-POT-INT-1SG-DEC
        Lit: I say 'am I going to work again?'
        'I think I'm going to work again.'
        (Adapted from van der Voort (2002: 316))

(59) Ungarinyin (a language of the Kimberley region,Western Australia)
     anjamangarn   ngun-ngurli   a1-ma-ngarri   karnangkurr
     when   1SG.O:2SG.S.FUT-give   3MASC.SG-do-SUB   dog
     Lit.: dog saying what time you gotta chuckim mine
     'The dog thinks: 'When will you give me something?''
     (Adapted from Spronck (2015: 354))

According to Güldemann (2008: 395), acquiring a lexical interpretation by a grammatical item challenges "a strict version of the unidirectionality hypothesis of grammaticalization in that the entire scenario states that fairly grammaticalized signs like quotatives, as a result of their use in a grammatical construction, can acquire lexical properties relating to both form and meaning which they did not possess in previous stages of their development."

However, the author argues for the validity of unidirectionality, as for him, the new reinterpretation of the quotative markers is closely tied to specific grammatical contexts. As an analogy, he considers the movement verb *goes*, which gets interpreted as an utterance verb in (60) not because it acquired a new lexical meaning but because a specific context made the interpretation possible.

(60) English
     The cow goes, 'moo'.
     (Cited by Güldemann (2008: 315) (originally from Butters (1980: 306)))

Similarly, when dealing with example (61), it would make less sense to argue that the German verb *machen* 'make'[20] acquired a meaning of *uttering, saying*, than to argue for a specific constructional reading of the verb:

(61) German
     Die   Katze   macht   'Miau'.
     the   cat   makes   'meow'
     'The cat goes 'meow'.'

It has long been known that in speech different items can develop different new meanings, depending on the construction they are used in. Here comes to mind the use of the Russian imperative verb form *davaj* 'Give it!' (62a) that gets reinterpreted as 'Goodbye!' / 'Farewell!' in the contexts when speech act participants are going to

---

20 See also Güldemann (2008: 374) mentioning the use of German *machen* 'make' used when imitating sound and gesture.

depart from each other (62c). Obviously, the verb *davat'* 'to give' cannot be argued to have gained a new lexical meaning in Russian. Rather it is the reading that the verb gets in a very specific use.

(62) Russian
    a. *davaj* 'give'
       A   ty   mnogo   deneg
       PART you.SG.NOM much   money.ACC
       ne   davaj   detjam!
       NEG   you.SG.give.IPFV.it kids.DAT
       'As for you, don't give kids much money!'
    b. *davaj* 'let's'
       davaj,   postroem!
       INTERJ   we.shall.build.it
       'Let's build it!'
    c. *davaj* 'farewell!'[21]
       Nu,   davaj,   do   vstreči. . .
       INTERJ davaj   before get-together
       'Well, farewell, see you later. . .'

To argue further, I am bringing an example of a Georgian placeholder verb form *gadaimasmikna* (63) that can get all sorts of lexical readings listed in (64a) -- (64d), depending on the context (see Amiridze (2010)). It makes less sense to argue that the Georgian placeholder verb with a certain preverb (here, the preverb *gada-*) has the lexical meaning of all those verbs of Georgian that take the same preverb (see (64a) -- (64d), to list just a few). Rather, it makes more sense to argue that the placeholder verb gets reinterpreted as such, depending strictly on the context:

(63) Georgian
    gada-imasmikna.
    PV-(s)he.VERBed.it.for.me
    '(S)he VERBed it away for me.'
    (Adapted from Amiridze (2010: 75))

(64) Georgian
    a. *gada-mizida.*
       PV-(s)he.carried.it.for.me
       '(S)he carried it across [some location] for me.'

---

[21] Cited from the Russian National Corpus (Aleksej Grachev, Ardent-3. Death warrant (2000)).

b. *gada-miyeba.*
PV-(s)he.painted.it.for.me
'(S)he painted it for me anew.'
c. *gada-mic'era.*
PV-(s)he.wrote.it.for.me
'(S)he copied it for me.'
d. *gada-mit'exa.*
PV-(s)he.broke.it.for.me
'(S)he broke it (in two) for me.'
(Adapted from Amiridze (2010: 75))

The same line of argumentation could be used for the Georgian sentence-initial autonomous *metki* 'I thought/*said' (see (4), (5) as well as (48)-(54)), being derived from a speech verb but getting interpreted as a quotative referring to thought in a specific construction.[22] Probably, the same way, the grammatical item – the clause-initial autonomous QUOT *metki* – got interpreted as an item referring to thought due to a specific construction and not because it acquired a new lexical meaning.

Note that the Georgian examples are still different from the Shona case (56). If in Shona, the quotative suffix -*ti* gets a new reading (*thought*), it also retains the old one (*said*). As for the Georgian *metki* in (4), (5), (48)-(54), only the reading of *thinking* is available ('I thought/*said').

I would argue that not just the addition of a new reading can be conditioned by specific contexts (as in Shona), but losing a reading is also conditioned by specific contexts, as in Georgian, where the sentence-initial *metki* is used in cases when speaker's false/unsuccessful expectations are present. Such specific contexts of the speaker having false/unsuccessful expectations imply the preexisting process of thought and reasoning and does not necessarily require the involvement of the speech of the speaker.

8 Conclusion

In this paper I looked at the uses of quotative markers in Georgian that usually get encliticized to lexical items to express indirect reported speech. One of the markers started getting used as an autonomous grammatical element (*metki*), rather than

---

[22] This is a common strategy in languages where *say*, *think* and *want* are expressed through similar lexical elements (see Konnerth (2020)).

as an enclitic (=*metki*). It is derived from the phrase *me vtkvi* 'I said' based on the verb referring to *saying* but developed a reading of *thinking* ('I thought') as well.

The reduction of the form of the speech verb and the cliticization (speech verb >> QUOT enclitic) shows a standard grammaticalization pattern of developing a grammatical item from a lexical one. However, the latest non-standard uses of the autonomous, preposing, clause-initial *metki* that gets interpreted as *thinking* makes a grammaticalization explanation questionable.

Looking at similar data from other languages, the innovative use of the autonomous quotative *metki* can be argued to represent a case of a constructional shift of the meaning. This makes it possible to maintain the grammaticalization account of QUOT markers intact and attribute the acquired interpretation to the specific construction and contexts involved there.

Abbreviations

ACC	accusative
ADD	additive focus particle
AOR	aorist
COM	comitative
COP	copula
DAT	dative
DEC	declarative mood
DIST	distal
FUT	future
GEN	genitive
IMPER	imperative
INST	instrumental
INT	interrogative mood
INTERJ	interjection
IPFV	imperfective
MASC	masculine
MED	medial
NARR	narrative
NEG	negative
NOM	nominative
O	object
OBL	oblique
P	person
PART	particle
PAST	past
PERF	perfective
PL	plural

POT	potential
PROX	proximal
PV	preverb
Q	question marker
QI	quotative index
QUOT	quotative marker
RD	reported discourse
S	subject
SG	singular
SUB	subordinate
SUBJ	subjunctive

References

Aikhenvald, Alexandra Y. 2004. *Evidentiality*. Oxford: Oxford University Press.

Amiridze, Nino. 2006. *Reflexivization Strategies in Georgian*. (LOT Dissertation Series 127). Utrecht: LOT.

Amiridze, Nino. 2010. Placeholder verbs in Modern Georgian. In Nino Amiridze, Boyd H. Davis & Margaret Maclagan (eds.), *Fillers, Pauses and Placeholders*, 67–94. (Typological Studies in Language 93). Amsterdam & Philadelphia: John Benjamins.

Boeder, Winfried. 2000. Evidentiality in Georgian. In Lars Johanson & Bo Utas (eds.), *Evidentials: Turkic, Iranian and Neighbouring Languages*, 275–328. (Empirical Approaches to Language Typology 24). Berlin & New York: Mouton de Gruyter.

Boeder, Winfried. 2002. Speech and thought representation in the Kartvelian (South Caucasian) languages. In Tom Güldemann & Manfred von Roncador (eds.), *Reported Discourse: A meeting ground for different linguistic domains*, 3–48. (Typological Studies in Language 52). Amsterdam: John Benjamins.

Buchstaller, Isabelle. 2014. *Quotatives: New Trends and Sociolinguistic Implications*. Oxford: Wiley-Blackwell.

Butters, Ronald R. 1980. Narrative *go* 'say'. *American Speech* 55(4). 304–307.

Cyffer, Norbert. 1974. *Syntax des Kanuri: Dialekt von Yerwa (Maiduguri)*. (Hamburger Philologische Studien 35). Hamburg: Helmut Buske.

Dzidziguri, Shota. 1969. *Conjunctions in the Georgian Language*. Tbilisi: Tbilisi State University Press. (In Georgian)

Dzidziguri, Shota. 1973. *Conjunctions in Georgian*. Tbilisi: Tbilisi State University Press. (In Georgian)

Güldemann, Tom. 2002. When 'say' is not *say*: The functional versatility of the Bantu quotative marker *ti* with special reference to Shona. In Tom Güldemann & Manfred von Roncador (eds.), *Reported Discourse: A meeting ground for different linguistic domains*, 253–287. (Typological Studies in Language 52). Amsterdam: John Benjamins.

Güldemann, Tom. 2008. *Quotative Indexes in African Languages: A Synchronic and Diachronic Survey*. (Empirical Approaches to Language Typology 34). Berlin & New York: Mouton de Gruyter.

Güldemann, Tom & Manfred von Roncador (eds.). 2002. *Reported Discourse: A Meeting Ground for Different Linguistic Domains*. Philadelphia: John Benjamins.

Harris, Alice C. 1985. *Diachronic Syntax: The Kartvelian Case*. (Syntax and Semantics 18). Orlando, Florida: Academic Press.

Harris, Alice C. & Lyle Campbell. 1995. *Historical Syntax in Cross-Linguistic Perspective*. Cambridge: Cambridge University Press.

Hewitt, B. George. 1989. Review-article of Syntax and Semantics 18: A.C. Harris' Diachronic Syntax: The Kartvelian Case. *Revue des Études Géorgiennes et Caucasiennes* 3. 173–213.

Hewitt, B. George. 1995a. *Georgian: A structural Reference Grammar.* (London Oriental and African Language Library 2). Amsterdam & Philadelphia: John Benjamins.

Hewitt, B. George. 1995b. Georgian – ergative, active or what? In David C. Bennett, Theodora Bynon & B. George Hewitt (eds.), *Subject, Voice and Ergativity*, 197–211. London: School of Oriental and African Studies, University of London.

Jorbenadze, Besarion A. 1989. *Georgian Dialectology*. Tbilisi: Mecniereba. (In Georgian)

Jorbenadze, Besarion A., Manana Kobaidze & Marine Beridze. 1988. *Dictonary of Morphemes and Modal Elements of Georgian*. Tbilisi: Mecniereba. (In Georgian)

Konnerth, Linda. 2020. Recycling through perspective persistence in Monsang (Trans-Himalayan). *Functions of Language* 27(1). 55–77.

Margiani, Ketevan, Ramaz Kurdadze & Maia Lomia. 2019. *The Category of Evidentiality in the Kartvelian Languages*. Tbilisi: Tbilisi State University Press. (In Georgian)

Morchiladze, Aka. 2014. *Kemera*. Tbilisi: Bakur Sulakauri Publishing. (In Georgian)

Ramat, Anna Giacalone & Manana Topadze. 2007. The coding of evidentiality: A comparative look at Georgian and Italian. *Italian Journal of Linguistics* 19(1). 7–38.

Sarjveladze, Zurab. 1997. *The Old Georgian Language*. Tbilisi: Tbilisi State Pedagogical University Press. (In Georgian)

Shanidze, Akaki. 1973. *Foundations of Georgian Grammar, I, Morphology*. Tbilisi: Tbilisi University Press. (In Georgian)

Shanidze, Akaki. 1976. *Grammar of the Old Georgian Language*. Tbilisi: Tbilisi University Press. (In Georgian)

Spronck, Stef. 2015. *Reported speech in Ungarinyin: Grammar and social cognition in a language of the Kimberley region, Western Australia.* Canberra: The Australian National University Ph.D. thesis.

Topadze Gäumann, Manana. 2016. Mezzi di espressione dell'evidenzialità in Georgiano. Milan: FrancoAngeli.

Topuria, Varlam & Ivane Gigineishvili. 1970. Sxvata sit'q'vis martlc'eris sak'itxebi [issues in the use of quotative particles]. In Varlam Topuria & Ivane Gigineishvili (eds.), *Tanamedrove kartuli salit'erat'uro enis normebi* [Norms of the modern literary Georgian language], 161–167. Tbilisi: Mecniereba. (In Georgian)

van der Voort, Hein. 2002. The quotative construction in Kwaza and its (de-)grammaticalisation. In Mily Crevels, Simon van de Kerke, Sérgio Meira & Hein van der Voort (eds.), *Current Studies on South American Languages*, 307–328. (Indigenous Languages of Latin America 3). Leiden: Research School of Asian, African, and Amerindian Studies (CNWS).

Prapatsorn Tiratanti & Pholpat Durongbhan

9 Reported thought embedded in reported speech in Thai news reports

Abstract: Reported thought and reported speech are two categories of reported discourse, which is a presentation of anterior discourse in another context. Although both of them are regularly present in news reports, reported speech has been more frequently investigated than reported thought. This is especially true in case of studies of Thai language news reports. The current reported discourse literature consists mostly of reported speech. This study aims to fill the gap by focusing on the use of reported thought in Thai news reports. Data was drawn from 321 news articles, where 218 occurrences of reported thought were identified, and its linguistic features were analysed. Results reveal that the structure of reported thought in Thai news reports is similar to that of indirect reported thought in other languages, but without consistent linguistic markers. Further analysis included matching and analysing samples of reported thought in news articles with their original speech from the respective public interview clips to investigate the relationship between the two. This method was chosen because previous works on the English language suggest that reported thought in the press is inferred from original speech as journalists do not have access to interviewees' thoughts processes. The results of the study reveal that reported thoughts in press are not always inferred. Occasionally, the interviewees had explicitly uttered their thoughts to the press and the subsequent reporting of those utterances were simply in the form of reported speech. This phenomenon can be described as a reported thought embedded in reported speech. The research results also indicate that when a reported thought is embedded in reported speech, it becomes indistinguishable whether that thought is from the original speaker (as a thought presented in the form of speech) or the journalist (as an inferred thought reported by the narrator).

1 Introduction

The study of reported discourse[1] is a popular and familiar topic in language and literature studies. This popularity is partly because reported discourses are essen-

---

[1] The use of the term "reported discourse" can be found in other forms, such as discourse report, discourse presentation and discourse representation. They all refer to the same linguistic concept

https://doi.org/10.1515/9783111065830-009

tial features in novels (Fludernik 1993: 3), and thus, initially received much interest from researchers in literature stylistics. The subject has been extensively investigated over the decades in the fields of language and literature (Bray 2014: 222) following the development of a model of reported speech and reported thought in fiction by Leech and Short (1981: chapter 10). However, the studies of reported discourse are not limited to literature. They are also prevalent in numerous domains where language is used. Linguists and stylisticians have investigated the use of reported discourse in other text types, such as news reports (e.g., Semino and Short 2004; Urbanová 2012), scientific narratives (e.g., Pilkington 2018), and religious texts including the Bible (Al-Ameedi and Al Shamiri 2018).

Of the non-fiction text genres, news reporting is of particular interest. News texts are an informative text type with the objective of providing information to the readers, as Waugh (1995, 131–132) described that "the ostensible purpose of a news article is to convey information from journalists, who have the information, to readers, who do not, but who would like to have it. The information is assumed to consist of facts/truths about the objective/outside/referential world". The public trusts that news outlets are reliable and that reports will convey the facts truthfully to the public. Thus, journalists must attempt to show readers their commitment to relaying the truth, even though they may not have witnessed the reported events themselves. Therefore, reporters rely on the use of reported discourse – presenting utterances attained from those who were involved or observed the situation (original sources, hereafter) – by interviewing them. Reported discourse is a method that practices objectivity with the information provided (Tuchman 1972: 668), which has always been fundamental in news reporting (Mindich 1998; Schudson 2001).[2] Consequently, news texts are abundant resources of reported discourses and, thus, have been widely investigated.

Previous works on reported discourse in news texts have focused exclusively on reported speech. The explanation for this is that reported speech has long been regarded as a "default" mode for reported discourses (Short 2012: 20). As a result, research on reported speech in news reports has been conducted exhaustively, both in the area of linguistics and journalism studies (e.g., Waugh 1995; Calsamiglia

---

with a slight difference. This issue has been discussed in Short (2012). In this chapter, the words "reported discourse", "reported speech" and "reported thought" are adopted to keep consistency throughout the volume.

2 Although recent studies (e.g. Wahl-Jorgensen 2013; Harbers and Broersma 2014; Chong 2019) suggested that subjective language is unavoidable in news texts and argued that objectivity is not always predominant in news, they do not refute its existence as one of the characteristics of the news. What is highlighted in this sentence is the use of reported discourse to signify the truthfulness of the information.

and Ferrero 2003; Harry 2013; Vis, Sanders, and Spooren 2015). Current knowledge of reported speech in the press is comprehensive, including linguistic characteristics and functions. However, the term "reported discourse" is not restricted only to reported speech. Leech and Short (1981: 270) suggested that thought has also been reported in texts, and the characteristics are different from those of reported speech. While reported speech deals with the speakers' utterances in a situation, reported thought is concerned with what is in the consciousness of a person. Generally, in order to report speech, a reporter or a narrator obtains information in a form of speech and mentions it in another context. In contrast, thought is not presented evidently in interpersonal communication (Short 2012: 20), so the means of eliciting thought should not be as same as those of eliciting speech. Thus, some scholars consider reported thought to be a separate category of reported discourse that needs to be investigated further.

Notwithstanding this, literature review shows that reported thought is not well investigated in any text types (Haakana 2007: 150; Dunn 2020: 42), with previous research even more limited in the context of news reports. However, reported thought in the press contains unique features compared to reported thought in other genres. Semino and Short (2004: 135) explained that reported thought in the news could not be considered as "pure" thought presentation because it is not a "genuine thought" from its original source. The journalists can only gain information from what their original sources have said, not what they have thought. Thus, reported thought found in the news must be inferred from the speech. In other words, the journalists interpret what people think from what they said (see details later in Section 4.1).

It is worth noting that the words "infer" and "interpret" imply that there must be a process of transforming speech to reported thought in a written text. This interpretation process is an interesting feature of reported thought in the news. To the best of our knowledge, research on the process of reporting discourse in the news has been conducted mostly in the field of journalism, but rarely in linguistics. For example, Haapanen and Perrin (2017) analysed the process of reporting speech in the news. They proposed three steps to quoting in news articles, starting from content selection to reporting in news texts. Studying how original sources are transformed to reported texts from a linguistic perspective would provide an insight into the language utilised in press. Since readers receive only that which is depicted by the language of the texts, it is worth investigating reported speech and reported thought in news reports. This would provide an additional linguistic facet to the existing knowledge on news reporting.

Currently, notions of reported thought in the press are primarily concluded from English news data. Conversely, in the Thai language – the official language of Thailand located in Southeast Asia – there is inadequate research on reported thought.

The concept of reported discourse in Thai has been chiefly explained in discourse analysis textbooks (e.g., Panpothong 2013: 60–61; Angkapanichkit 2018: 248–250), with only reported speech but not reported thought being discussed. Though some research has examined reported speech in Thai news reports previously (e.g., Jiemwongsa 2017; Tiratanti and Tungviboonyakit 2019), work on reported thought in Thai news reports remains virtually non-existent. Thus, to fill the identified gap in the literature, this study is conducted within the discourse analysis framework and aims to:
1) Examine the linguistic features of reported thought in Thai news reports.
2) Investigate the relationship between original speech and reported thought in Thai news reports.

2 Methodology

The data for this study was collected from two online news websites: Thairath (http://www.thairath.co.th) and Daily News (http://www.dailynews.co.th). They are two of Thailand's most renowned and profitable news agencies (Infoquest 2020), producing both newspaper and online news content daily. In this research, online sources were analysed due to their ease of accessibility. Studies of language in the news have primarily used online data in recent years (e.g., Karlsson and Sjøvaag 2016; Lazaridou, Krestel, and Naumann 2017; O'Halloran, Pal, and Jin 2021).

The study consisted of two sections. In the first section, we randomly selected news articles from the two agencies during the study period of August to October 2019. The dataset covers 321 news stories, each article having approximately 300–500 words in length. All articles were searched manually for the use of reported thought. From 321 articles, 116 were found to have used reported thought. There were 218 instances of reported thought overall. Subsequently, these instances were closely analysed for their linguistic features (e.g., lexical items and syntactic structures). In the second section, we searched for audio and/or video recordings of the public interviews and press conferences, which produced the reported thoughts found in section one of the study. These recordings were extracted from any available online sources. A majority of the audio and video recordings were attached to the same webpage as the original news article. Not all recordings were available. Only 28 of the news articles were found to have their corresponding speech recordings. With this data at our disposal, the original speech from the recordings, and the reported thought in the news texts were examined to understand their relationship. The objective of this method was to demonstrate the similarities and differences between the original speech and the reported text, and reveal how journalists convert information from its original source into their news articles.

3 Characteristics of reported thought in Thai news reports

In this section, we will describe the linguistic features of reported thought found in Thai news reports to address our first research objective. In terms of syntactic structure, the reported thought in Thai was found to consist of a reporting clause as a main clause preceding a reported clause as a subordinate clause, as shown in (1) below. Furthermore, the position of the clauses is fixed.[3]

(1) na:j sǒm.sàk tɕʰûa wâ: rát.tʰa.ba:n tɕàʔ jù: kʰróp tʰɤ:m
    Mr Somsak believe that government will stay full term
    ├──── main clause ────┤ ├──────── subordinate clause ────────┤
    'Mr Somsak believes that the government will stay for a full term.'
                                                        (Thairath, 30 December 2019)

(1) is a reported thought, which appears in the form of a reporting clause (/na:j sǒm.sàk tɕʰûa/ 'Mr Somsak believes'), and a reported clause (/rát.tʰa.ba:n tɕàʔ jù: kʰróp tʰɤ:m/ 'the government will stay for a full term'). These two clauses are combined with a complementiser /wâ:/ 'that'. The reporting clause mentions the source of the original text as a subject (/na:j sǒm.sàk/ 'Mr Somsak') and a reporting verb as a predicate (/tɕʰûa/ 'believe'). The reported clause shows the content of the thought. In (1), the presented content is Mr Somsak's belief that the government will stay for a full term. No instance of a reported clause written with quotation marks is found in the data. Thus, it can be concluded that the structure of indirect reported thought in Thai news reports is similar to that of indirect reported thought in other languages.

    Previous research on the indirect reported discourse in several languages has proposed that it is mainly used as a summarising function. Messages expressed as indirect reports are used primarily to present the content of the original texts, not the exact expressions or wordings. The language in indirect reports is considered to be in the narrator's style and not the original format (Banfield 1973: 4–5; Li 1986: 38). Therefore, indirect reports involve some changes in syntactic patterns or lexical choices. For instance, deixis must be adjusted according to the new context, and in some languages tenses are usually backshifted. In addition to showing the structure, data in this study revealed two noticeable features in reported thought in Thai.

---

[3] Verbs presented in Thai sentences in original texts are not inflected because Thai is a non-inflectional language. However, in translation, we decided to mark all verbs in English in present forms.

Firstly, there is no tense marker present in Thai sentences. Because Thai is an isolating language, its verb forms are not inflected for such verbal categories as tense, aspect, and modality (see more: Sornlertlamvanich and Pantachat 1993; Minegishi 2011). For example, the verb /tɕʰûa/ 'believe' in (1) is not inflected in the original version. Thus, it can be concluded that tense shift is not an indirect report indicator for indirect reported thought in Thai as verbs in reported thought and narration retain the same form (no inflection). Only the meaning of the reporting verb and the sentence structure are crucial markers for signalling reported thought.

Secondly, the absence of the subject of either a reporting clause or a reported clause is another characteristic of reported thought in Thai. Thai is a radical pro-drop language, which means the inferable pronoun is possibly omitted (Neeleman and Szendrői 2007: 708; Holmberg and Pimsawat 2015: 56); thus, the interpretation of the omitted subject depends highly on the context.

(2) */pʰon.tam.rùat.ʔèːk sěː.riː.pʰí.sùt klàːw wâː jùː naj kʰân kaːn triam kaːn jaŋ mâj miː kaːn kʰɔ̌ː kʰɔ̂ː.muːn tɕàːk tʰaːŋ kaːn ʔɔ́ːs.treː.lia [ɔː'stɹeɪlɪə] tɛ̀ː tɕʰûa wâː mâj nâː tɕàʔ miː pan.hǎː pʰrɔ́ʔ pen kaːn rɔ́ːŋ kʰɔ̌ː naj tʰǎː.náʔ sùan râːt. tɕʰa.kaːn/*

'**Police General Sereepisuth says that [Thammanat's case]**[4] **is during a preparation process.** There has not been any documents requested from the Australian government yet, but **[he] believes that there should not be any problems** because the request is performed under the government authority.'

(Thairath, 24 October 2019)

Here, subject drops from (2) (bolded) are highlighted.

(2)' a. pʰon.tam.rùat.ʔèːk sěː.riː.pʰí.sùt klàːw wâː ø jùː naj kʰân
Police General   Sereepisuth   say   that ø be   in   process
kaːn.triam.kaːn
preparation
'Police General Sereepisuth says that [subject omitted] is undergoing a preparation process'
b. ø tɕʰûa   wâː   mâj nâː   tɕàʔ   miː   pan.hǎː
ø believe that not might will   have problem
'[subject omitted] believes that there should not be any problems'

---

[4] The subject in the original sentence is omitted. However, for a readable translation, the most likely subject candidade, according to our interpretation, is given in square brackets.

In these cases, readers need to infer from the context (2a) "what" is in the preparation process and (2b) "who" believes that there should not be any problems. The subject of the reported clause in (2a) is missing, while the absent subject in (2b) is that of the reporting clause. In case (2a), readers can interpret the missing piece as Thammanat's criminal case, which is undergoing a preparation process. For case (2b), readers can assume that the subject must be the same person mentioned earlier in the same sentence ("Police General Sereepisuth") because he is the only agent in the discourse who can perform the verb "believe".

The case (2b) above is relevant to this chapter as it is considered a reported thought. We can conclude that the subject of the reporting clause or reported clause is not necessarily present in the sentence. The subject omission in Thai has a consequence on the change of person deixis, which is another linguistic indicator for indirect reported discourse. Since the subject of the clause can be omitted, the shift from the first-person pronoun to the third-person pronoun is not always observable. In other words, person deixis adjustment cannot always be used to point out a reported thought in Thai.

In addition to the two structural features, reporting verbs are another important element of reported thought. Reporting verbs are key markers distinguishing reported thought from the other modes of reported discourse in narration (i.e., reported speech and reported writing). Semino and Short (2004: 38) previously regarded a reporting verb as a "reporting device". As in (1) and (2), the reported thoughts contain the reporting verb /tɕʰûa/ 'believe'. This indicates that the content which follows is what the original speaker believed. In other words, the reporting verb presents what is in the mind of Mr Somsak and Police General Sereepisuth in (1) and (2), respectively. In this study, seven verbs were identified as reporting verbs for reported thought and are presented in Table 1.

Table 1: Reporting verbs for reported thought and the number of occurrences.

Verb	Occurrences
/tɕʰûa/ 'believe'	54 (25%)
/mɔːŋ/ 'look at'	50 (23%)
/hěn/ 'see'	46 (21%)
/kʰít/ 'think'	30 (14%)
/kʰâːt/ 'expect'	26 (12%)
/sâːp/ 'know'	10 (4%)
/tâŋ kʰɔ̌ː sǎŋ.kèːt/ 'suspect'	2 (1%)
Total	218 (100%)

All reporting verbs in Table 1 have semantic implications which indicate the speaker's state of mind. According to the dictionary (Office of the Royal Society 2011), the words /tɕʰûa/ 'believe' and /sâːp/ 'know' refer to the individuals' state of mind that they have some notion or awareness of something. The words /kʰâːt/ 'expect' means that someone mindfully predicts something in their head, which is similar to the word /tâŋ kʰɔ̂ː sǎŋ.kèːt/ 'suspect', which literally means having a doubtful thought about something. For the perceptive verb /hěn/ 'see', it is a clipped word from the phrase /miː kʰwaːm hěn/ 'have an opinion',[5] which also demonstrates someone's belief. Lastly, the other perceptive verb /mɔːŋ/ 'look at', in the news context, means 'take into consideration', which is linked to a person's consciousness. Unfortunately, the aspect of semantic analysis falls out of scope of this paper; however, a detailed investigation on the semantics of reported thought would be a natural follow-up study to this research.

In summary, reported thought in Thai news reports consists of two clauses and, incidentally, shares the same structure as indirect reported thought in English. From 218 instances of reported thoughts in the data set, 7 reporting verbs were identified, with all of their meanings referring to the speaker's state of mind and awareness. Furthermore, because of the nature of the Thai language, reported thought in Thai news reports lacks tense/mood/aspect markers, and it does not always express the subject explicitly, which makes the personal deixis dependent on the context.

4 The relationship between original source and reported thought

After analysing the linguistic features of reported thought in Thai news reports, the results of the second research objective will be presented in this section, where the relationship between original speech and reported thought in news texts will be elaborated.

4.1 Reporting speech in the form of reported thought

Typically, journalists seek information using various approaches. They may arrive at the scene, talk to people, or conduct interviews. The resulting data is accumulated and selected to be reported in news articles (van Dijk 1988: 96–97). It should be

---

5 /miː/ 'have' and /kʰwaːm hěn/ 'an opinion' – the phrase /miː kʰwaːm hěn/ is clipped to /hěn/.

noted that this information could be the interviewee's speech, but never their original thoughts, to which the journalists have no direct access. Therefore, reported thought found in news texts must be extracted from the speech of the interviewee. This concept is remarked upon in Semino and Short's (2004: 135) and Semino's (2011: 298) studies, which concluded that all instances of reported thought found in the press must be "inferred reported thought".

Here, the connection between speech and thought in the news is revealed. Journalists receive information from their source in the form of speech. After that, they infer what the speaker thought or felt, then publish it as a reported thought. This type of reported thought is present in our corpus and is shown in (3).

(3) /pʰon.ʔèːk pra.jút tɕan.ʔoː.tɕʰaː naː.jók.rát.tʰa.mon.triː lɛ́ʔ rát.tʰa.mon.triː wâː kaːn kra.suaŋ ka.laː.hŏːm klàw tʰǔŋ sa.tʰǎː.ná.kaːn pʰaj léːŋ dōːj tɕʰa.pʰɔ́ʔ sa.tʰǎː. ná.kaːn tʰî: hûaj sa.něŋ tɕaŋ.wàt sùː.rin dōːj ra.bùʔ wâː krom tɕʰon.pra.tʰaːn dâj raːj.ŋaːn sa.tʰǎː.ná.kaːn maː jàːŋ tɔ̀ː nûaŋ . . . sûŋ **kʰa.ǹaʔ níː sâːp wâː mīː náːm pʰiaŋ.pʰɔː naj kaːn hâj bɔː.ríː.kaːn pra.tɕʰaː.tɕʰon léːw**/
'General Prayuth Chan-o-cha, Prime Minister and Minister of Defence, mentions the drought situation, especially in Huay Saneng dam in Surin province, that Royal Irrigation Department reports the situation consistently . . . **at the moment [he] knows that water is sufficient for the citizens.**'

(Thairath, 13 August 2019)

The bolded part in (3) is a reported thought. The journalist has presented the state of knowing something from the omitted agent (which could be interpreted as General Prayuth Chan-o-cha). In other words, the journalist reported what was in the mind of General Prayuth Chan-o-cha. One question arises here: how did the journalist know General Prayuth Chan-o-cha's thoughts, given that the only source of information the journalist had is their speech?

To further investigate this question, this reported thought was compared with its corresponding public interview clip. The result revealed that the reported text does not precisely match its original source (See Table 2), and the journalist did not present General Prayuth Chan-o-cha's speech verbatim. This was done through a process called "monologisation", a term coined by Haapanen (2017a), which refers to a complex process of transferring information from oral interviews to a written news text, where the journalist adjusts some elements. In this case, the journalist inferred that, since General Prayuth Chan-o-cha received the report, he was aware of the sufficiency of water. Thus, rather than reporting General Prayuth Chan-o-cha's original speech, the journalist decided to report his perception instead.

From (3), it is clear that there was a shift from the original speech to the reported thought. Seemingly, this phenomenon may not significantly impact the readers'

Table 2: Comparison between utterances in original speech and in reported text from (3).

Original speech	Reported thought
/kʰa.n̂aʔ ní: kɔ̂: dâj ráp ra:j.ŋa:n tɕà:k krom.tɕʰon.pra.tʰa:n wâ: lɛ̀ŋ ná:m tʰî: tɕʰáj pʰa.lìt ná:m.pra.pa: hâj kʰon naj tɕaŋ.wàt sù.rin wan ní: kɔ̂: mi: ná:m lǎj kʰâw ma: jà:ŋ tɔ̀:.nûaŋ pʰiaŋ.pʰɔ: tʰî: tɕàʔ hâj ka:n.pra.pa: pʰa.lìt ná:m.pra.pa:/	/kʰa.n̂aʔ ní: sâ:p wâ: mī: ná:m pʰiaŋ.pʰɔ: naj ka:n hâj bɔ:.rí.ka:n pra.tɕʰa:.tɕʰon lɛ́:w/
'At the moment, [I] receive a report from Royal Irrigation Department that today the water source for the production of tap water for Surin province has water running continuously, sufficient for the water plant'	'at the moment [he] knows that water is sufficient for the citizens'

understanding in this case – as the meaning derived from the speaker's speech, and the reported thought, is very similar.

In other instances, however, this research found that the inferred reported thought might influence the readers' understanding. In other words, it may give readers a different impression than they would have received from the original source. This is exemplified in (4):

(4) /pʰon.ʔè:k pra.wít woŋ.sù.wan rɔ:ŋ na:.jók.rát.tʰa.mon.tri: klà:w tʰǔŋ rûaŋ ní: wâ: **tɕʰûa wâ: ra.bɤ̀:t lǎ:j tɕùt pùan tɕʰá:w ní: "sâ:ŋ sa.tʰǎ:.ná.ka:n nɛ̂: nɔ:n"**/

'General Prawit Wongsuwan, Vice Prime Minister, mentions the current situation that **[he] believes that bombs in many places this morning "were definitely set up".**'

(Thairath, 2 August 2019)

Reading the bolded section in (4), readers can understand that General Prawit Wongsuwan believed that the bombs were set up intentionally by unknown agents. As a reported thought, this could be construed as a suggestion made by General Prawit Wongsuwan. However, after comparing the text with its corresponding interview recording, it was found that the word /tɕʰûa/ 'believe' is not present in the original source (See Table 3). In the interview, a journalist asked General Prawit Wongsuwan whether he considered the bombing as a set-up. He then replied to the journalist "[it is] definitely set-up" and that officers needed to investigate the incident further.

Much like (3), the journalist takes an extract from General Prawit Wongsuwan's speech and presents it as a reported thought – using the reporting verb /tɕʰûa/ 'believe'. The journalist first reported the original speech by deducting conversational turns, similar to the monologisation. However, the journalist did not present General Prawit Wongsuwan's utterance as reported speech but rather delivered it as

9 Reported thought embedded in reported speech in Thai news reports — **249**

Table 3: Comparison between utterances in original speech and in reported text from (4).

Original speech	Reported thought
Journalist: /raw pra.mɤːn wâː pen kaːn sâːŋ sa.tʰăː.náː.kaːn máj/ 'Can we consider [the bomb situation] as a set-up situation?'	/pʰon.ʔèːk pra.wít woŋ.sù.wan rɔːŋ naː.jók.rát.tʰa.mon.triː klàːw tʰŭŋ rûaŋ níː wâː tɕʰûa wâː ra.bɤ̀ːt lăːj tɕùt pùan tɕʰáːw níː "sâːŋ sa.tʰăː.náː.kaːn nêː nɔːn"/
Prawit: /kɔ̂ː sâːŋ sa.tʰăː.náː.kaːn nêː nɔːn/ 'definitely set-up'	General Prawit Wongsuwan, Vice Prime Minister, mentions the current situation that [he] believes that bombs in many places this morning "are definitely set up".'

a reported thought. In other words, the content of the General's statement has been turned from speech to thought through a change in the mode of presentation. This could lead the reader to understand the event differently and potentially alter their perception of the news. The reader might interpret the reported thought as General Prawit Wongsuwan's belief, but they may not interpret this thought as a certainty.

This discovery adds another aspect to the concept of monologisation – that is – the adjustment does not occur only within the domain of speech (i.e., transferring from the original speech to reported speech). Here, the journalists may receive information verbally, then report it as a thought. This demonstrates the impact of inferred reported thought on the relationship between speech and thought in the news.

This research also found instances of "pure" reported thought (a term used following Semino and Short 2004) from the original source, which had not undergone the process of the inferred reported thought. Indeed, reporters cannot access other people's minds and relay their thoughts to be presented in news articles. However, these thoughts can be conveyed in the form of speech from the original speakers themselves. Reporters can then take those words as reflections of real thoughts and report them in the news, as shown in (5).

(5) /naːj sùː.pʰa.tɕʰaj tɕʰíː tɛɛːŋ wâː mûa naː.jók.rát.tʰa.mon.triː tìt pʰaː.rá.kìt mâj săː. mâːt tɔ̀ːp kra.tʰúː dâj kɔ̂ː mâj jàːk hâj sa.rùp wâː nǐː kaːn tɔ̀ːp kra.tʰúː pʰrɔ́ʔ naː. jók.rát.tʰa.man.triː miː pʰaː.rá.kìt mâːk maːj tɕʰûa wâː naj ʔoː.kàːt tɔ̀ː tɔ̀ː paj mâj wâː naː.jók.rát.tʰa.mon.triː tɕà tɔ̀ː klàp ma tɔ̀ːp dûaj tua.ʔeːŋ rɯ̌ː mâj kɔ̂ː tɔ̂ŋ mɔ̂ːp mǎːj rát.tʰa.mon.triː tʰîː miː sùan kìaw kʰɔ̌ŋ ma tɔ̀ːp kra.tʰúː/
'Mr Supachai explains that when the Prime Minister is engaged with his business, [Mr Supachai] does not want to conclude that [the Prime Minister] refuses to answer the inquiries because the Prime Minister is tied up with piles of works. **[Mr Supachai] believes that in upcoming occasions the Prime Minister will be present to answer the questions by himself or must assign the questions to other ministers.**'

(Thairath, 14 August 2019)

The bolded section in (5) is a reported thought expressing Mr Supachai's belief. Surely, the journalist does not have access to Mr Supachai's inner cognition; still, his belief was mentioned in the news report nonetheless. Again, the question raised here is how the journalists managed to deduce that thought. By examining linguistic forms in this report, and comparing them with the original speech in the video recording, it was found that Mr Supachai's original words were: "However I believe that in upcoming occasions, I believe that the Prime Minister will be present to answer [the questions] or must assign the question to another relevant minister" (see Table 4).

Table 4: Comparison between utterances in original speech and in reported text from (5).

Original speech	Reported thought
/jaŋ.ŋaj pʰǒm kɔ̌: tɕʰûa wâ: naj ʔo:.kà:t tɔ̀:.tɔ̀: paj nîa **pʰǒm kɔ̌: tɕʰûa wâ:** na:.jók.rát.tʰa.mon.tri: kʰoŋ tɕàʔ ma: tɔ̀:p rɯ́: mâj kɔ̂: tɕàʔ tɔ̂ŋ mɔ̂:p mǎ:j hâj rát.tʰa.mon.tri: tʰân daj tʰân nɯ̀ŋ tʰîː mi: sùan kìaw kʰɔ̂ŋ ma: tɔ̀:p tɔ̀: paj/ '**However I** believe that in upcoming occasions, **I believe that** the Prime Minister will be present to answer [the questions] or must assign the question to another relevant minister'	/tɕʰûa wâ: naj ʔo:.kà:t tɔ̀: tɔ̀: paj mâj wâ: na:.jók. rát.tʰa.mon.tri: tɕàʔ klàp ma: tɔ̀:p dûaj tua.ʔe:ŋ rɯ́: mâj kɔ̂: tɔ̂ŋ mɔ̂:p mǎ:j rát.tʰa.mon.tri: tʰîː mi: sùan kìaw kʰɔ̂ŋ ma: tɔ̀:p kra.tʰú:/ '[Mr Supachai] believes that in upcoming occasions the Prime Minister will be present to answer the questions by himself or will assign the questions to other ministers.'

In (5), the journalist took Mr. Supachai's speech and accurately reported it in the news article. The comparison shows that the journalist has cut the sentence repetition and the first-person pronoun, as shown in the bolded section in Table 4. Notwithstanding these omissions, most of the original speech remains intact. It can be concluded here that Mr. Supachai himself expressed his thought in his speech, which the journalist, in turn, accurately reported in the news article. Therefore, the excerpt in (5) is an instance of reported speech where reported thought is also present. This connection between speech and thought is distinct from that which we have seen in the case of the inferred reported thought. Haakana (2007: 155–156) found a similar instance in her study of reported thought in "complaint stories" in Finnish, where a person expresses his/her thought orally as a complaint. However, reported thought in news reporting is more complex than complaint stories, since another person, i.e., the journalist, reports it again in another context.

Although thoughts can be presented clearly in original speech and no inference from the journalist is needed, some alterations still occur when the utterances are re-contextualised. In (5), the modification was a result of the distinction between spoken and written language. Spoken and written discourse have some inherently different characteristics. For example, speech is produced and processed almost simultaneously, which affords the speaker limited opportunity to plan; in contrast, written text can be prepared and edited (Cameron and Panović 2014: 21). Thus, repetition is naturally found in speech and is usually removed when presented as a reported thought in written text. Aside from this repetition characteristic, most of the original speech in (5) survives the process of re-contextualisation.

Nevertheless, it is not always true that thoughts expressed in the original speech will be directly quoted, as in (5). Our investigation concluded that, in some instances, the journalists paraphrase or summarise the main idea of the thought uttered in the original speech instead. For example:

(6) /rɔ́ːj.ʔèːk tʰam.ma.nát pʰɤ̌ːj wâː miː pra.tɕʰum sìp hâː naː.lí.ka: wan níː sûŋ sa.tʰǎː. ná.ka:n pʰák pʰa.laŋ.pra.tɕʰaː.rát jaŋ nǐaw nên **tɕʰûa wâː pʰon.ʔèːk pra.wít tɕàʔ kʰâw ma: tʰam hâj pʰák kʰêm.kʰɛ̌ŋ mâːk jîŋ kʰûn**/

'Lieutenant Thammanat reveals that the meeting is held 3PM today and the current situation of the PPRP party is going well. **[He] believes that General Prawit will make the party stronger.**'

(Thairath, 13 August 2019)

The bolded section in (6) is considered a reported thought of Lieutenant Thammanat. However, when the text is compared with the original utterance, it is found that the journalist only preserved the general idea of the reported thought. Distinct from (5), this reported thought was not presented verbatim (see Table 5).

Table 5: Comparison between utterances in original speech and in reported text from (6).

Original speech	Reported thought
/pʰɔː tʰân pʰon.ʔèːk pra.wít loŋ ma: kɔ̂ː kʰít wâː tɕàʔ pen tʰîː pʰûŋ pen tʰîː.prùk.sǎː pen làk hâj kàp pʰák pʰa.laŋ. pra.tɕʰaː.rát dâj/ 'When General Prawit becomes [a head of strategic team], [I] think that [he] will be a supporter, be a consultant, be a chief in PPRP party'	/tɕʰûa wâː pʰon.ʔèːk pra.wít tɕàʔ kʰâw ma: tʰam hâj pʰák kʰêm.kʰɛ̌ŋ mâːk jîŋ kʰûn/ '[He] believes that General Prawit will make the party stronger.'

In his original speech, Lieutenant Thammanat shared his attitude towards General Prawit's position in his political party (PPRP). In the news article, the journalist reported Lieutenant Thammanat's thought within reported speech. It can be said that the journalist did not shift the mode of reported discourse. Yet, considering linguistic choices, they did not maintain the wording and sentence structure accurately from the original speech. This is not uncommon in journalistic quoting (Haapanen 2017a), and it agrees with characteristics of indirect reported discourse in stylistic theory (Leech and Short 1981: 255–257; Coulmas 1986: 3).

As mentioned in Section 3, the reporting verb is the most significant indicator of reported thought in Thai. Although the reporting verb in (6) was changed from /kʰít/ *'think'* to /tɕʰûːa/ *'believe'*, it did not affect the mode of reported discourse as both words are reporting devices for reported thought in Thai (see Table 1). The word /kʰít/ *'think'* refers to a mental process of forming an idea in one's head (Bhandhumetha [2001] 2020: 42), and the word /tɕʰûːa/*'believe'* implies a strong notion on something (Bhandhumetha 2020: 50). Thus, semantically, both indicate an inner state of mind. Therefore, it can be concluded here that the alterations of linguistic choices in a reported clause do not have an effect on the modes of reported discourse, in contrast to the cases of the inferred reported thought.

To summarise, this section described the connection between original speech and reported thought in news articles, which can be divided into two types. Firstly, the speech from the original speaker is interpreted and reported as a thought, namely "inferred reported thought". Secondly, the speaker's thought, expressed as part of the original speech, is conveyed as reported thought within reported speech. This phenomenon can be described as "reported thought embedded in reported speech", which will be elaborated further in the next section.

4.2 Reported thought embedded in reported speech

This section will highlight the relationship between reported speech and reported thought, when reported thought is embedded in reported speech. Here, the word "embedded" is used in reference to Semino and Short (2004: 171), where they suggested that reported statements can occur in other reported discourses.[6] Short (2007: 239–241) also mentioned a phenomenon of reported speech embedded in a reported thought in fiction. Still, he suggested that further research needed to be carried out in the area of discourse embedding. This study will take into account also the phenomenon of reported thought found embedded in reported speech.

There are two kinds of reported speech where reported thought can be encountered: direct reported speech and indirect reported speech. (7) below shows the case of the reported thought, which is embedded in direct reported speech.

(7)   "*tʰâː pen kʰwaːm tâŋ tɕaj tɕiŋ kʰɔ̌ːŋ tʰân **pʰǒm tɕʰûːa wâː pʰon.ʔèːk pra.wít tɕàʔ sǎː.mâːt pʰlàk dan hâj kaːn kêː.kʰǎj rát.tʰa.tʰam.ma.nuːn naj kʰráŋ***

---

[6] For example, the utterance "it was reported yesterday that Mr Blair told overseas newspaper last week there was a clear case for one" (Semino and Short 2004: 180) shows the reported speech of Mr Blair embedded in a reported text in this news article.

níː praːsòp pʰǒn sămːrèt dâj jàːŋ nêː nɔːn pʰrɔ́ʔ pʰiaŋ kʰêː tʰân sòŋ sǎn. jaːn paj jaŋ saːmaːːtɕʰík wútːtʰíːsaːpʰaː tʰîː dâj ráp tèŋːtâŋ tɕàːk kʰaːná? rákːsǎː kʰwaːm saːŋòp hèŋ tɕʰâːt tʰâw nán saːmaːːtɕʰík wútːtʰíːsaːpʰaː tʰúk kʰon kôː rɔː faŋ sǎnːjaːn tɕàːk pʰonːʔèːk praːjút rǔː pʰonːʔèːk praː wít kan taːlɔ̀ːt weːːlaːː...." naːj tʰêːpːtʰaj klàːw
'"If it is his determination, **I believe that General Prawit can enforce a constitutional amendment to be successful because only he signals to the senators who are elected by National Council for Peace and Order, every senator is waiting for signal from General Prayuth or General Prawit all the time. . ."** Mr Thepthai said.'

(Thairath, 27 November 2019)

Direct reported speech in (7) comes with the most recognisable feature – quotation marks. However, the bolded section also shows the structure of a reported thought. It can be said that by reporting Mr Thepthai's speech with a direct quotation, the journalist also presented Mr Thepthai's thought. Thus, thought is reported as part of direct reported speech. Generally, direct speech is a method of creating an impression that the original speech is reproduced verbatim (Leech and Short 1981: 255; Short, Semino, and Wynne 2002: 499–500). It is likely that readers would interpret this reported thought to have been explicitly uttered by the original speaker (comparable to [5] and [6] in Section 4.1).

On the other hand, the reported thought which is embedded in indirect reported speech is more complex because sentences are presented without any punctuation to mark the reported text, as seen in (8).

(8) naːj tǐːjàj pʰuːnːsǐːːtʰaːnaːːkuːn tʰîː paj tɔ̂ːn ráp naːːjókːrátːtʰaːmonːtriː ráːwàːŋ kaːn loŋ pʰúːnːtʰîː tɕaŋːwàt sùːrin klàːw wâː kaːn hâj kaːn tɔ̂ːn ráp pen rûaŋ tʰîː tʰùːkːtɔŋ pʰrɔ́ʔ naːːjókːrátːtʰaːmonːtriː nam ŋópːpraːmaːn paj hâj tɕʰaːwːbâːn naj pʰúːnːtʰîː saːmaːːtɕʰík saːpʰaː pʰûːːtʰɛːn râːtːsaːdɔːn kɔ̂ː tɔŋ júttʰǔː praːtɕʰaː. tɕʰon pen sǎmːkʰan lɛ́ʔ tʰam ŋaːn júttʰǔː ʔùːdomːkaːn naj tʰǎːːná? tʰîː pen pʰûːːtʰɛːn kʰɔ̌ːŋ praːtɕʰaːːtɕʰon tʰáŋ níː **tɕʰûa wâː kaːn paj tɔ̂ːn ráp tɕà? mâj sòŋ pʰǒn kraːtʰóp tɔ̀ː kʰaːnɛːn sǐaŋ naj pʰúːnːtʰîː nêː nɔːn**

'Mr Teeyai Poonsritanakul, who receives the Prime Minister during his visit at Surin province, says that to welcome [the Prime Minister] is rightful because the Prime Minister distributes budget to the locals, the representative must adhere to the citizens and work with the ideology as being a representative of the people. By the way, **[he] believes that to receive the Prime Minister will not affect his voting score in the area.**'

(Dailynews, 20 August 2019)

The excerpt in (8) shows indirect reported speech from Mr Teeyai Poonsritanakul, who talked about receiving the Prime Minister at Surin province. However, the bolded section is considered a reported thought from its structure and its reporting verb. In this case, the reported thought and the reported speech are placed in a continuous manner. Here, the sense of "embeddedness" is not as prominent as in (7).

The reported thought embedded in indirect reported speech is perplexing. If one were to merely read the excerpt without comparison to its original source, they may not know whether the reported thought was conveyed in the original speech or inferred. In other words, there is no linguistic difference between the reported thought embedded in reported speech and the inferred reported thought. To further elaborate, in (8), it is evident that the excerpt is an utterance by Mr Teeyai Poonsritanakul. Eventually, readers will run into the reported thought in the bolded section. Here it is ambiguous whether the message in the reported thought is from the journalist's inferrence or Mr Teeyai Poonsritanakul's speech. Consequently, it is difficult to distinguish whether the statement, seen as a reported thought, came directly from the original source (the reported thought embedded in reported speech) or from an inference made by the journalist (the inferred reported thought). Further explanation is linked to the characteristics of reported thought in Thai, explained earlier in Section 3, with both types of reported thoughts sharing the same reporting verbs with no inflection for verbal categories and subject omission. Consequently, the reported thought embedded in reported speech and the inferred reported thought become visually identical.

In this section, we emphasised the association between reported speech and reported thought, in the case of a journalist reporting speech with thoughts embedded within. Certainly, the instance of the reported thought embedded in reported speech cannot be limited to the Thai language. Anyone (regardless of language) can express their thoughts through speech, and then have those thoughts re-narrated by a second party in the form of reported speech. Therefore, it is challenging to establish the boundary between these two modes of reported discourse.

5 Conclusion

Reported speech and thought were considered two separate categories in some previous studies (e.g., Leech and Short 1981; Romaine and Lange 1991; Semino and Short 2004). Their functions were found to be distinct from one another. The concept of accurate reporting is hard to determine in reported thought, and it is a significant issue in reported speech (Short 2007: 232). Moreover, the approach required to access one's speech would not be the same as the approach to accessing thoughts. Thus, it would be natural to expect that reported thought must be different from reported speech.

This research, on the contrary, emphasises the connection between reported thought and reported speech in a specific genre of text – news reports. News reporters, clearly, cannot have access to anyone's thoughts except their own. However, reported thoughts are commonly used in newspaper texts (Jucker 2006: 118). Previous research concluded that reported thoughts in the news must come from the process in which journalists interpret people's speech or expressions and present what their thoughts could be (Semino and Short 2004: 135; Walker and McIntyre 2015: 190–191). This study also shows similar instances where the status of statements has been changed from speech to thought. In other words, instead of reporting speech, journalists decided to infer thought from speech and present it as a reported thought. Thus, while reading news reports, readers will find reported speech and inferred reported thought prevalent throughout the text.

However, this study has revealed that the inferred reported thought is not the sole occurrence which shows the connection between speech and thought in the press. Apparently, reported thought can also be found within reported speech. It happens when speakers explicitly utter what they think in their own original speech; then, journalists report their speech with their reported thought embedded within. When readers examine news articles, they will find reported thought occurring as a part of reported speech. In this case, the journalist does not infer other people's thoughts. Those thoughts are expressed explicitly by the interviewee. This instance shows that reported thoughts in the press are not necessarily inferred. Although it is true that narrators cannot enter other people's state of mind and extract their thoughts, people can express their thoughts verbally. This phenomenon can also be seen in complaints (Haakana 2007) and was used as a methodology among voice-hearers (Demjén et al. 2020).

The two forms of connection between reported thought and reported speech in Thai are intertwined. Without any concrete linguistic features to point out reported discourse, they are inseparable. Reported discourse in Thai has no linguistic marking. Tense markers are not available in the language – let alone changing tenses to mark a reported clause. Deixis is not consistently adjusted, and deixis markers may even disappear completely (e.g., in the case of subject omission). The only outstanding indicator of reported discourse is the use of a reporting verb as a reporting device, which can be used to distinguish modes of reported discourse. Nevertheless, this device does not distinguish between the inferred reported thought and the reported thought embedded in reported speech. In other words, two types of reported thought in press share the same set of reporting verbs, and there is no other linguistic feature to indicate them. So, it is impossible to conclude whether reported thoughts occurring in the press are a part of the original speech or whether they have been inferred by the writers. Regardless of their inseparable linguistic features, it is worth investigating, in subsequent research, whether the inferred reported thought and the reported thought embedded in reported speech have different impacts on readers' perception of the event.

As reported thought is a less-studied mode of reported discourse, this study attempted to contribute to knowledge in this field by describing characteristics of reported thought in the Thai language and the journey from original speech to reported thought in the press. It is also possible that the relationship between speech and thought in reported discourse can be found in other languages. However, since this research examines exclusively Thai language data, the conclusion can only be applied to cases expressed in Thai. Further research in other languages could be done to confirm the presence of this phenomenon.

Appendix

Example cited

[1] *สมศักดิ์ ไม่ให้ราคาโพลหนุน "ธนาธร" นั่งนายกฯ* [Somsak ignores poll supporting Thanathorn for the Prime Minister]. *Thairath.* 30 December 2019. Retrieved from https://www.thairath.co.th/news/politic/1737293

[2] *2 กมธ. จ่อเชิญ "บิ๊กตู่" บิ๊กป้อม" ผู้นำเหล่าทัพ" แจงถวายสัตย์-งบกลาโหม* [two committees tends to invite "Gen Too, Gen Pom, and army leaders" to answer inquiries about inauguration and army's budgets]. *Thairath.* 24 October 2019. Retrieved from http://www.thairath.co.th/politic/1689611

[3] *นายกฯ ขออย่ากังวล มีแผนรับมือ หากฮ่องกงบานปลาย รพ.สุรินทร์ มีน้ำใช้พอ* [Prime Minister calms citizens with plans if Hong Kong situation gets serious – water level in Surin hospital is sufficient]. *Thairath.* 13 August 2019. Retrieved from https://www.thairath.co.th/news/politic/1636645

[4] *"บิ๊กป้อม" เชื่อระเบิดป่วนหลายจุด เป็นการสร้างสถานการณ์แน่นอน* ["Gen Pom" believes bombs to be intentionally set up]. *Thairath.* 2 August 2019. Retrieved from https://www.thairath.co.th/news/politic/1628501

[5] *กระทู้สดปมถวายสัตย์เลื่อนอีก หลังนายกฯ ติดภารกิจ ฝ่ายค้านรอถามรอบหน้า* [inquiries concerning inauguration is to postpone as the Prime Minister does not present – opposition party is to inquire in the following session]. *Thairath.* 14 August 2019. Retrieved from https://www.thairath.co.th/news/politic/1637685

[6] *ธรรมนัส เชื่อ 9 พรรคเล็กไม่ตีรวน ด้านลูกชายบุญทรง จ่อเป็นผู้ช่วยโฆษกรัฐบาล* [Thammanat believes 9 small parties are not playing tricks – Boonsong's son is expected as an assistant to government spokesperson]. *Thairath.* 13 August 2019. Retrieved from https://www.thairath.co.th/news/politic/1636371

[7] *"เทพไท" ท้า "บิ๊กป้อม" รักษาคำพูดหนุนแก้ รธน. ซี้อำนาจอยู่ 3 ป.* ["Thepthai" demands "Gen Pom" to keep his promise regarding constitutional amendment – affirms power is controlled by the Triple P]. *Thairath.* 27 November 2019. Retrieved from https://www.thairath.co.th/news/politic/1712943

[8] *ส.ส.สุรินทร์พท.ชี้หนุนอย่ายุบสภาฯ ไม่อยากให้ผลาญภาษีปชช* [Pheu Thai party representative for Surin province resists dissolution of parliament in order not to waste tax]. *Dailynews.* 20 August 2019. Retrieved from https://www.dailynews.co.th/politics/726890

References

Al-Ameedi, Riyadh T. K. & Sadiq M. K. Al Shamiri. 2018. Biblical evaluative discourse of speech and thought presentation. *International Journal of English Linguistics* 8(3). 223-238.

Angkapanichkit, Jantima. 2018. การวิเคราะห์ข้อความ [Discourse analysis]. Bangkok: Thammasat University Press.

Banfield, Anne. 1973. Narrative style and the grammar of direct and indirect speech. *Foundations of Language* 10(1). 1-39.

Bhandhumetha, Nawawan. 2020 [2001]. คลังคำ [A Thai thesaurus]. 9th edn. Bangkok: Amarin.

Bray, Joe. 2014. Speech and thought presentation in stylistics. In Michael Burke (ed.), *The routledge handbook of stylistics*, 222-236. London & New York: Routledge.

Calsamiglia, Helena & Carmen López Ferrero. 2003. Role and position of scientific voices: Reported speech in the media. *Discourse Studies* 5(2). 147-173.

Cameron, Deborah & Ivan Panović. 2014. *Working with written discourse*. London: SAGE.

Chong, Phillipa. 2019. Valuing subjectivity in journalism: Bias, emotions, and self-interest as tools in arts reporting. *Journalism* 20(3). 427-443.

Coulmas, Florian. 1986. Reported speech: Some general issues. In Florian Coulmas (ed.), *Direct and indirect speech*, 1-28. Berlin & New York: Mouton de Gruyter.

Demjén, Zsófia, Agnes Marszalek, Elena Semino & Filippo Varese. 2020. 'One gives bad compliments about me, and the other one is telling me to do things' – (Im)politeness and power in reported interactions between voice-hearers and their voices. In Zsófia Demjén (ed.), *Applying linguistics in illness and healthcare contexts: Contemporary studies in linguistics*, 17-43. London: Bloomsbury Academic.

Dunn, Cynthia Dickel. 2020. Reported thought, narrative positioning, and emotional expression in Japanese public speaking narratives. In Risako Ide & Kaori Hata (eds.), *Bonding through context: Language and interactional alignment in Japanese situated discourse*, 39-59. Amsterdam & Philadelphia: John Benjamins.

Fludernik, Monika. 1993. *The fictions of language and the languages of fiction*. London & New York: Routledge.

Haakana, Markku. 2007. Reported thought in complaint stories. In Elizabeth Holt & Rebecca Clift (eds.), *Reporting talk: Reported speech in interaction*, 150-178. Cambridge: Cambridge University Press.

Haapanen, Lauri. 2017a. Directly from interview to quotation? Quoting practices in written journalism. In Ritva Laury, Marja Etelämäki & Elizabeth Couper-Kuhlen (eds.), *Linking clauses and actions in social interaction*, 201-239. Helsinki: Suomalaisen Kirjallisuuden Seura.

Haapanen, Lauri. 2017b. Monologisation as a quoting practice: Obscuring the journalist's involvement in written journalism. *Journalism Practice* 11(7). 820-839.

Haapanen, Lauri & Daniel Perrin. 2017. Media and quoting: Understanding the purposes, roles, and processes of quoting in mass and social media. In Colleen Cotter & Daniel Perrin (eds.), *The Routledge Handbook of Language and Media*, 424-441. London & New York: Routledge.

Harbers, Frank & Marcel Broersma. 2014. Between engagement and ironic ambiguity: Mediating subjectivity in narrative journalism. *Journalism* 15(5). 639-654.

Harry, Joseph C. 2013. Journalistic quotation: Reported speech in newspapers from a semiotic-linguistic perspective. *Journalism* 15(8). 1041-1058.

Holmberg, Anders & On-Usa Pimsawat. 2015. Generic pronouns and phi-feature: Evidence from Thai. In Alison Biggs, Man Li, Aiqing Wang & Cong Zhang (eds.), *The second Asian and European linguistic conference proceedings*, 55-71. Newcastle: Newcastle University.

Infoquest. 2020. *เจาะลึกภูมิทัศน์สื่อไทยปี2563* [Discovering Thai media landscape in 2020]. Accessed from Infoquest: https://www.infoquest.co.th/thailand-media-landscape-2020/newspaper#Newspaper-1 (accessed 7 July 2021)

Jiemwongsa, Prapatsorn. 2017. *Speech presentation in Thai news reports*. Edinburgh: The University of Edinburgh MSc dissertation.

Jucker, Andreas H. 2006. "but 'tis believed that. . .": Speech and thought presentation in early English newspaper. In Nicholas Brownlees (ed.), *News discourse in early modern Britain: Selected papers of CHINED 2004*, 105-126. Bern: Peter Lang.

Karlsson, Michael & Helle Sjøvaag. 2016. Content analysis and online news. *Digital Journalism* 4(1). 177-192.

Lazaridou, Konstantina, Ralf Krestel & Felix Naumann. 2017. Identifying media bias by analyzing reported speech. In *2017 IEEE International Conference on Data Mining (ICDM)*, 943-948. New Orleans: IEEE.

Leech, Geoffrey & Mick Short. 1981. *Style in fiction: A linguistic introduction to English fictional prose*. Harlow: Pearson Longman.

Li, Charles N. 1986. Direct speech and indirect speech: A functional study. In Florian Coulmas (ed.), *Direct and indirect speech*, 29-45. Berlin & New York: Mouton de Gruyter.

Mindich, David. 1998. *Just the facts: How objectivity come to define American journalism*. New York: New York University Press.

Minegishi, Makoto. 2011. Description of Thai as an isolating language. *Social Science Information* 50(1). 62-80.

Neeleman, Ad & Kriszta Szendrői. 2007. Radical pro drop and the morphology of pronouns. *Linguistic Inquiry* 38(4). 671-714.

Office of the Royal Society. 2011. *Thai dictionary*. Bangkok: Office of the Royal Society.

O'Halloran, Kay L., Gautam Pal & Minhao Jin. 2021. Multimodal approach to analysing big social and news media data. *Discourse, Context & Media* 40.

Panpothong, Nattaporn. 2013. *วาทกรรมวิเคราะห์เชิงวิพากษ์ตามแนวภาษาศาสตร์: แนวคิดและการนำมาศึกษาวาทกรรมในภาษาไทย* [Critical discourse analysis in a linguistic perspective: Concepts and applications in discourse studies in Thai]. Bangkok: Faculty of Arts, Chulalongkorn University.

Pilkington, Olga A. 2018. Presented discourse in popular science narratives of discovery: Communicative side of thought presentation. *Linguistic and Philosophical Investigations* 17. 7-28.

Romaine, Suzanne & Deborah Lange. 1991. The use of like as a marker of reported speech and thought: A case of grammaticalization in progress. *American Speech* 66(3). 227-279.

Schudson, Michael. 2001. The objectivity norm in American journalism. *Journalism* 2(2). 149-170.

Semino, Elena. 2011. Rethinking "inferred" thought presentation: Some reflections on Palmer's "social minds". *Style* 45(2). 296-300.

Semino, Elena & Mick Short. 2004. *Corpus stylistics: Speech, writing and thought presentation in a corpus of English writing*. London & New York: Routledge.

Short, Mick. 2007. Thought presentation twenty-five years on. *Style in Fiction* 41(2). 227-243.

Short, Mick. 2012. Discourse presentation and speech (and writing, but not thought) summary. *Language and Literature* 21(1). 18-32.

Short, Mick, Elena Semino & Martin Wynne. 2002. Revisiting the notion of faithfulness in discourse report/(re)presentation using a corpus approach. *Language and Literature* 11(4). 325-355.

Sornlertlamvanich, Virach & Wantanee Pantachat. 1993. Information-based language analysis for Thai. *ASEAN Journal on Science Technology Development* 10(2). 181-196.

Tiratanti, Prapatsorn & Naphasorn Tungviboonyakit. 2019. ความแตกต่างของการรายงานคำพูดในข่าวหนังสือพิมพ์และข่าวออนไลน์ในภาษาไทย: กรณีศึกษาข่าวการเมือง [Difference between speech presentations of news reports in newspapers and online news in Thai: A case study of political news]. *Journal of Language and Linguistics* 37(2). 21-46.

Tuchman, Gaye. 1972. Objectivity as strategic ritual: An examination of newsmen's notions of objectivity. *American Journal of Sociology* 77(4). 660-679.

Urbanová, Zuzana. 2012. Direct and free direct forms of representation in the discourse of newspaper reports: Less frequent phenomena. *Brno Studies in English* 38(1). 39-54.

van Dijk, Teun A. 1988. *News as discourse.* Hillsdale: Lawrence Erlbaum.

Vis, Kirsten, José Sanders & Wilbert Spooren. 2015. Quoted discourse in Dutch news narratives. In André Lardinois, Sophie Levie, Hans Hoeken & Christoph Lüthy (eds.), *Texts, transmissions, receptions: Modern approaches to narratives*, 152-172. Leiden: Brill.

Wahl-Jorgensen, Karin. 2013. Subjectivity and story-telling in journalism: Examining expressions of affect, judgement and appreciation in Pulitzer Prize-winning stories. *Journalism Studies* 14(3). 305-320.

Walker, Brian & Dan McIntyre. 2015. Thinking about the news: Thought presentation in early modern English news writing. In Paul Baker & Tony McEnery (eds.), *Corpora and discourse studies*, 175-191. London: Palgrave Macmillan.

Waugh, Linda R. 1995. Reported speech in journalistic discourse: The relation of function and text. *Text & Talk* 15(1). 129-173.

Part III: **Reported thought as a category in its own right**

Anja Hennemann

10 Complementizer deletion in structures of reporting on thinking in Argentinian Spanish and Brazilian Portuguese

Abstract: In this paper I approach the structures Spanish [*(yo) pienso (que)* X] and Portuguese [*(eu) penso (que)* X] 'I think (that) X' from quantitative as well as qualitative perspectives. I investigate the use of these structures of reporting on thinking in conceptually oral data and in mainly informal registers. The data are retrieved from the *Corpus del Español* (CdE–Web/Dialects) and the *Corpus do Português* (CdP–Web/Dialects). The main aim of this paper is the analysis of structures where a complementizer would be expected but is not used. In this context, I debate whether this phenomenon should be described in terms of grammaticalization, pragmaticalization or constructionalization.

1 Introduction

In this paper I am concerned with a phenomenon of reported thought (RT) and reported speech (RS), i.e. when both RT and RS go hand in hand, namely in the performative use of the verbs Spanish *pensar* and Portuguese *pensar* 'think' – when these verbs of thinking encode the subject's cognitive (epistemic) attitude. Roughly speaking, I analyze utterances such as *I think (that) this is a paper by Anja* in Argentinian Spanish and Brazilian Portuguese online conversation. Even though the language analyzed in the context of this study is medially written, it is oral in character as especially in chat forums speakers write as they speak so that the language can be considered conceptually oral.[1]

---

[1] "Orality and literacy are dialectical concepts, the meaning of one term depending on the assessment of the other one. In addition, both have two aspects: a medial and a conceptual one. While mediality is trivial, the conceptual aspect is best conceived of as a continuum, thus blurring any clearcut distinction between orality and scripturality" (Raible 2002: 8967; cf. also Koch and Oesterreicher 1994: 587). For example, speeches of politicians or lectures are to be classified as medially oral and conceptually written. Conversations via WhatsApp etc. are medially written but often conceptually oral.

Acknowledgements: I thank the two anonymous reviewers for their critical questions and valuable comments, and Pekka Posio, Daniela Casartelli as well as Hans-Jörg Döhla for their general support. All remaining errors are, of course, mine.

By means of data from the *Corpus del Español* (CdE–Web/Dialects) and the *Corpus do Português* (CdP–Web/Dialects) I focus, on the one hand, on the combination of Spanish *pienso* and Portuguese *penso* with the overtly expressed subject pronoun Spanish *yo* and Portuguese *eu* 'I' as well as on its combination with the complementizer *que*. On the other hand, I investigate the omission of the complementizer in structures where one would expect a use of the complementizer, which is common for English such as in *I think this is a paper by Anja*. In doing so, quantitative and qualitative perspectives are combined. In studying the complementizer deletion in RT/RS introducing fragments such as in Spanish [*(yo) pienso* X] or Portuguese [*(eu) pienso* X] '(I) think X', I discuss whether it should be seen as a phenomenon of grammaticalization, pragmaticalization or constructionalization.

While for certain volition verbs such as *rogar* 'beg' or *suplicar* 'request, beg' the omission of the complementizer is common, predominantly in (formal) written texts (cf. Yoon 2015: 341), zero complementation for cognition verbs represents an oral phenomenon. However, to the best of my knowledge, complementizer omission in (Brazilian) Portuguese has not been investigated so far, and is thus studied as well as contrasted here with (Argentinian) Spanish.

2 Object of study

2.1 Reported speech and reported thought

Utterances like *I think (that) this is a paper by Anja* illustrate that words may embed reported thought (cf. Vygotsky 1991: 249), since the speaker verbalizes their thoughts, and reported thought represents a form of reported speech. Uttering verbally thoughts of the speaker makes RT and RS go hand in hand so that both RT and RS could be captured by the hyperonym "Reported Discourse".[2] From a syntactic point of view, the utterance above represents an example of indirect RT/RS (in opposition to direct RT/RS as in *I think: "this is a paper by Anja"*). "[D]irect speech displays the voice of the reported speaker as if the current, reporting speaker reflects it fully (cf. also Wierzbicka 1974), 'less direct' strategies increasingly signal that the voice of the reported speaker is filtered through that of the reporting speaker." (Spronck 2019: 606)

---

[2] For the proposal to summarize both RT and RS below the notion of "Reported Discourse" I thank one of the anonymous reviewers. For a discussion of the notions of reported vs. represented speech see Spronck/Nikitina (2019).

In any case, the RT/RS introducing fragment (*I think* [*that*]) and the fragment of RT/RS, i.e. the propositional content (*this is a paper by Anja*), represent parts of both direct RT/RS and indirect RT/RS (see Figure 1):

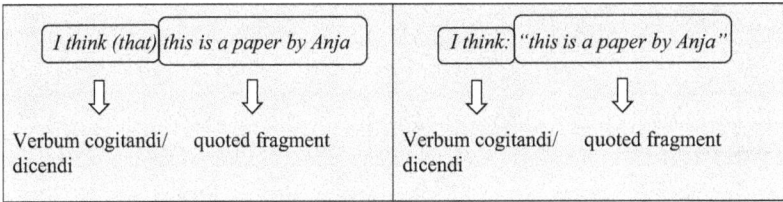

Figure 1: Parts of (in-)direct RT/RS.

RS (and RT) should not be understood as transitive/intransitive clauses (only) introduced by a specific verb of saying or thinking. Rather, RS (and RT) should be understood as a syntactic construction or syntactic class on its own (cf. Spronck 2015: 175 or Spronck and Nikitina 2019), which is comparable to expressions conveying a modal or evidential meaning (cf. Thompson and Mulac 1991). Indeed, if we look at utterances like *Maybe this is a paper by Anja* or *Obviously this is a paper by Anja* as examples containing a modal and evidential adverb, respectively, the fragment introducing the RS/RT – *I think (that)* – fulfills a similar attenuating function. This is in line with Thompson, who argues that predicates such as *think* should be analyzed "in terms of epistemic/evidential/evaluative formulaic fragments expressing speaker stance toward the content of a clause" (Thompson 2002: 125; cf. also Traugott 1995: 38–39 or Gonzálvez-García 2014) so that they are summarized under the term "stance expression" (Thompson 2002: 140). Thus, this fragment belongs to the so-called *modus* part of a sentence and not to the *dictum* part (cf. Bally 1965: 56–75). The *modus* (*I think*) – like *maybe* or *obviously* – adds a qualification to the *dictum* (*this is a paper by Anja*) and conveys the speaker's attitude (cf. also Graffi 2001: 248 or Aijmer 1997: 3).

Of course, in *I think (that) this is a paper by Anja* "the reported and the reporting clause are construed entirely from the perspective of the current speaker" (Vandelanotte 2006: 141; cf. also Vandelanotte 2009). The quoting speaker and the person about whom is reported can overlap (cf. also Bakhtin 2008: 314, 324). In other words, both the reporting and the reported clauses originate in one and the same person, in one and the same *here-now-I* system – the deictic system – of subjective orientation, called *origo*. As a point of origin, it refers to the zero point of the coordinate system of every speaking "ego" (cf. Bühler 1999: 102–103, 149; also Innis 1982: 22 or Hennemann 2013: 48, Hennemann 2020: 2), which Bühler describes as follows: "Let two perpendicularly intersecting lines on the paper suggest a coordinate system to us, O for the origin, the coordinate source[.] My claim is that if this arrangement is to represent the deictic field of human language, three deictic words must be placed where the O is, namely the deictic words here, now and I." (Bühler 1990: 117; see Figure 2)

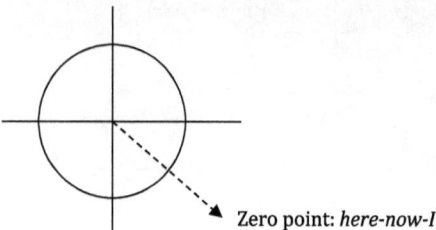

Zero point: *here-now-I*

Figure 2: *Origo:* coordinate system of subjective orientation (Bühler 1999: 102).

In examples such as *I think (that) this is a paper by Anja*, the use of the cognitive verb can be regarded as performative[3] because the speakers report on their own thinking so that "it is [. . .] the speaker's deictic centre from which both the reporting and the reported clauses are deictically and expressively construed" (Vandelanotte 2006: 139). In other words, both the reporting clause and the reported clause originate in the same zero point (see Figure 3):

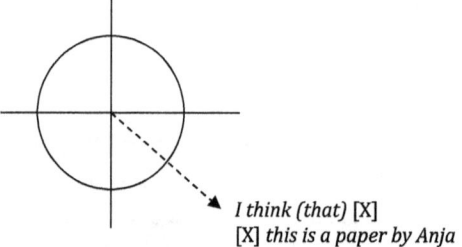

I think (that) [X]
[X] *this is a paper by Anja*

Figure 3: Deictic center for reporting and reported clause.

2.2 Performative thinking

With regard to the performative use of thinking, using the cognitive verb in the first person singular, the meanings of *I think* can be very versatile (cf. also Hennemann

---

3 However, in its modalizing/attenuating use – as opposed to its use as the bearer of the speech act – *I think* cannot be described as performative in its canonical sense.

2013: 282–302, 2016a: 102). According to Aijmer (1997: 1, 3), *I think* is "sensitive to speakers' communicative needs" and "permits, for example, extensions of meaning involving the speaker's attitudes to the hearer or to the message". Put differently, *I think* is highly context-sensitive, as also pointed out by Kärkkäinen (2003: 111): "When a token of *I think* appears in context, it becomes impossible to determine its precise semantic meaning out of context, on its own and independent of the utterance in which it occurs". Cappelli also mentions the different meaning nuances between the two poles of *think* – as "the cognitive action" and as "the result of thinking": "In the most 'literal' case, think is construed as an action, the act of thinking, and, in the most 'metaphoric' case, it is construed as the subjective result of the act of thinking, as an indicator of opinion. In between these two extremes, discourse can constrain many construals of the semantic potential of think [. . .]" (Cappelli 2007: 194).

In the following examples from Spanish and Portuguese, *pensar* is used with different meanings. In examples (1a) and (1b), the meaning of 'think' when expressing the act of thinking is illustrated, whereas in (2a) and (2b) the subjective result of the act of thinking is represented. The structural differences to be observed are the zero complementation (no complement clause) in (1a) and (1b) contrary to the use of the complementizer in (2a) and (2b). These structural differences can be related to the semantic differences in so far as the act of thinking goes hand in hand with the non-use of the complementizer:

(1) a. Spanish *Javier,* **yo pienso** *hay personas que se les sale lo malo en el internet insultando libremente a otros* [. . .] (koflaolivieri.com)
'Javier, **I think** there are people who get the bad stuff on the internet by freely insulting others [. . .]'
 b. Portuguese **Eu penso** *deve poder acompanhar todas as representações, caso contrário seria representado* [. . .] (filosofiabrasilia.blogspot.com)
'**I think** [it] must be able to accompany all representations, otherwise it would be represented [. . .]'

(2) a. Spanish **Yo pienso que** *tal vez hubieran sido algo así como espías o aurores* [. . .] (harrypotter.lsf.com.ar)
'**I think that** they might have been something like spies or Aurors [. . .]'
 b. Portuguese **Eu penso que** *é este o caminho mais adequado.* (acdematos.wordpress.com)
'**I think that** this is the most suitable way'

I think in *I think (that) this is a paper by Anja* or *I think* in *This is a paper by Anja, I think* can, for instance, be described as a phrase conveying the speaker's stance, by which the speaker also reports on their own thinking, i.e. expressing the subjective result of the act of thinking. However, depending on the context, the construction *I think* may also (predominantly) fulfill the function of a politeness strategy. In a discourse situation, speaker A may have uttered *This is a paper by Jesper*. Speaker B, in turn, is totally sure that this is a paper by Anja, but decides for attenuating the utterance in order to sound more polite. "*I think* can, for instance, be used as a strategy redressing an action threatening the hearer's negative face such as criticism or advice" (Aijmer 2002: 8; cf. also De Cock 2014: 12).[4] Regarding the Spanish and Portuguese examples ([1a] and [1b]) as well as ([2a] and [2b]), the act of thinking, when construed as an action, is usually found in structures without the complementizer *que*. Structures with the complementizer as *(yo) pienso que* and *(eu) penso que* mark the subjective result of the act of thinking, fulfilling the function of an opinion marker. However, the present study will show that complementizer deletion is also possible when expressing the act of thinking as a result.

3 Complementizer deletion

According to the *Nueva gramática de la lengua Española* (NGLE), complementizer deletion is, above all, possible with certain verbs of request and command, which require the subjunctive mood. To these verbs belong *demandar* 'demand', *suplicar* 'beg', *mandar* 'command', *rogar* 'ask/request', *pedir* 'order', *solicitar* 'request' and *ordenar* 'order' (cf. also Delbecque and Lamiroy 1999). In the following example from Argentinian Spanish, retrieved from the CdE–Web/Dialects, 'request' is directly followed by 'extend' (*hacer extensiva*) in the subjunctive mood:

(3) Spanish [...] *en caso de acceder a lo planteado **solicito haga extensiva** la presente a los Servicios Fiscalizadores de ese país* [...] (jornadaonline.com)
'in the event that you agree to the above, **I request** [that] **you extend** [Subj] this letter to the Tax Authorities of that country'

---

4 See also Vandelanotte (2004) on "distancing indirect speech/thought", which is characterized by the fact that "an initiating clause is first entered into the discourse as a straightforward claim on the part of the speaker, only to be nuanced afterwards in a sort of distancing or disclaiming afterthought (e.g. *He mailed you earlier today, he said*)" (Vandelanotte 2004: 489).

According to Brovetto (2002), zero complementation is possible when the subsequent subordinate refers to an uncertain situation, conveying an irrealis meaning. Hence, in sentences/utterances introduced by *espero* 'I hope' the complementizer may be deleted:

(4) Spanish [...] *y **espero haya** otra película más dentro de unos años* [...]
(blogs.lanacion.com.ar)
'and **I hope there will be** [Subj] another film in a few years'

However, Yoon (2015: 339) convincingly argues that the omission of the complementizer *que* is also possible if the complement conveys a realis meaning, as he illustrates with the following example:

(5) Spanish *Entonces **yo digo** ø siempre **me encantó**. De chiquilla tenía facilidad para dibujar, en vacaciones era mi hobby.*
'Then **I say** ø I always **loved** it. Since I was little, I had the ability to draw; on vacations it was my hobby' (Yoon 2015: 339; example from https://corpus.rae.es/creanet.html; oral data, Costa Rica)

As he explains, *yo digo* 'I say' "has a sentential complement that denotes a realis meaning (*siempre me encantó* 'I always loved it'), but the omission of the complementizer *que* is still possible" (Yoon 2015: 339). Hence, the statement that "in Romance [Spanish and Catalan] it is the subjunctive mood of the embedded clause that allows *que* to drop" (Llinàs-Grau and Fernández-Sánchez 2011: 12) should be formulated in a weakened manner as the complementizer can also be dropped when being followed by a verb in the indicative mood.

Instances of the structure [$V_{of\ request/command}$ + {...} + V_{Subj}], as in example (3) above, are said to be much more frequent in ancient texts than in modern ones. The described structure without complementizer can be found today in epistolary, legal and administrative language, but also in other formal varieties of written language. (cf. NGLE online). It is thus interesting that the structure [$V_{of\ cognition}$ + {...} + V] is more often found in oral and conceptually oral language.

Against the background of previous statements that complementizer deletion is bound to the subjunctive mood or an irrealis meaning in the complement as well as that zero complementation is a feature of written language and formal registers, Yoon (2015) shows that

- verbs of cognition "omit the complementizer frequently" (Yoon 2015: 350);
- "it is not necessarily the subjunctive mood, or the irrealis meaning conveyed by the indicative mood, that triggers the omission of the complementizer in Spanish" (Yoon 2015: 340);[5]
- "verbs of cognition without a complementizer normally appear with an embedded clause in the indicative mood, not subjunctive" (Yoon 2015: 344);
- "the zero complementation in Spanish actually occurs regularly in informal contexts too, but one may find more omission in formal contexts especially with the volition verb type such as *rogar* 'beg' and *suplicar* 'request, beg'. Other verb types such as verbs of cognition (e.g., *creer* 'think'), verbs of emotion (e.g., *temer* 'be afraid') and verbs of communication (e.g., *decir* 'say') appear to allow the omission of the complementizer regardless of whether the register is formal or informal" (Yoon 2015: 341);
- "some of the common factors contributing to the omission of the complementizer are, for example, (i) matrix clause subjects such as *I* or *you*; (ii) a co-referential pronoun between the complement clause and the matrix clause subject (e.g. *I think I got it right*)" (Yoon 2015: 340; cf. also Posio 2013);
- verbs of cognition such as *creer* ('think/believe'), *pensar* ('think') and *suponer* ('suppose/guess') which "occur with the zero complementizer indeed do not appear to be restricted to formal contexts (such as a public speech, formal oral interviews and newspaper articles), but they also freely occur in informal contexts (such as an informal interview and oral conversations, narrations in a novel)" (Yoon 2015: 344; also 350);
- comparing the three cognitive verbs *creer* ('think/believe'), *pensar* ('think') and *suponer* ('suppose/guess'), "*supongo* 'I suppose, I guess' shows a higher rate of omission (30.54%) than *creo* 'I think' (4.96%) and *pienso* 'I think' (10.3%)" (Yoon 2015: 343) – thus showing that complementizer deletion is more frequent with *pienso* than with *creo*.

Hence, it seems interesting a) to investigate the use of structures of reporting on thinking in conceptually oral data and also in informal registers, b) to compare the findings with the equivalent structures in (Brazilian) Portuguese, also respecting the (non-)use of the subject pronoun, and c) to discuss the phenomenon of complementizer omission in terms of grammaticalization, pragmaticalization and

---

[5] As Yoon (2015) convincingly demonstrates that complementizer deletion is not necessarily forced by the subjunctive mood in the sentential complement and since the examples analyzed in the present study did not give the impression that zero complementation is usually accompanied by the subjunctive, no further attention is paid to the interaction of complementizer omission and subjunctive mood.

constructionalization. The aims and the methodology of the present study are, however, dealt with in more detail in the following section.

4 Aims and methodology of the study

4.1 Aims

As it is not a matter of a language being or not being pro-drop, but rather a question of degree, it should be pointed out that Spanish is a more prototypical pro-drop language than Portuguese, in particular Brazilian Portuguese, where the expression of the subject pronoun is becoming increasingly frequent to the extent that it may no longer be considered a pro-drop language (cf. Posio 2021: 17 or Amaral and Mihatsch 2019). Hence, the gradual nature of "pro-drop" is taken into account.

In using a sentence-initial (or clause-initial) phrase of cognitive attitude, the following variants are possible for transmitting the information that "this is a paper by Anja":

(6) a. Spanish *(Yo) pienso que* es una contribución de Anja.
    b. Portuguese *(Eu) penso que* é uma contribuição da Anja.
       'I think that this is a paper by Anja'

(7) a. Spanish *(Yo) pienso* es una contribución de Anja.
    b. Portuguese *(Eu) penso* é uma contribuição da Anja.
       'I think this is a paper by Anja'

While different scholars have already concentrated on the investigation of the optional use of the pronoun 'I' in comparison to its non-use in the context of the speaker's thinking, on its parenthetical usage or on its epistemic or evidential nuances (cf. Aijón Oliva and Serrano 2010; Davidson 1996; De Saeger 2007; Hennemann 2016a, 2016b, 2020; Posio 2011, 2012, 2013, 2014, 2015; Schneider 2007; Vandelanotte 2006; Yoon 2015), it seems particularly interesting (i) to investigate the complementizer deletion as in examples (7a) and (7b), and (ii) to check whether the omission of the complementizer (cf. Yoon 2015) can be compared to the grammaticalization of *I think* (cf. Aijmer 1997, 2002; Thompson and Mulac 1991). At first glance, complementizer deletion is possible both with the subject pronoun *yo/eu*, as in (8a) and (8b), and without the subject pronoun ([9a] and [9b]):

(8) a. Spanish *Yo pienso son más agradables las flores, ó cuando se llevan libres, ó cuando se* [...] (tertullian.org)
'**I think** flowers are more pleasant, either when they are carried freely, or when they [...]'
b. Portuguese *Eu penso é assim, na paridade* [...] (cfh.ufsc.br)
'**I think** it is like this, in parity [...]'[6]

(9) a. Spanish [...] *por lo tanto los admiro y* **pienso** *son verdaderos revolucionarios.*
(jovencuba.com)
'[...] therefore I admire them and **[I] think** they are true revolutionaries'
b. Portuguese *Sobre o assunto eu sempre sinto aquela insatisfação e* **penso** *deve existir algo bem legal pra fazer* [...] (contracorrenteza.com)
'Regarding the subject I always feel that dissatisfaction and **[I] think** there must be something very nice to do [...]'

The main aim of the paper is to apply, but also challenge, the grammaticalization hypothesis, shown for English *I think*, to the equivalent phrases in Spanish and Portuguese. Uses of *I think* in which the complementizer *that* is deleted such as in *I think this is a paper by Anja* are described as an instance of grammaticalization (Thompson and Mulac 1991) or rather pragmaticalization (cf. Aijmer 1997, 2002): "[...] it is assumed that the distinction between main clause and subordinate clause has first become fuzzy as a result of the deletion of *that*" (Aijmer 2002: 17–18), which is illustrated by example (10b). Due to the grammaticalization/pragmaticalization of the fragment as a whole it has become possible to move *I think* into other syntactic positions – into right-peripheral (like in [10c]) or parenthetic (like in [10d]) positions (cf. Thompson and Mulac 1991: 313):

(10) a. ***I think that*** *this is a paper by Anja.*
b. ***I think*** *this is a paper by Anja.*
c. *This is a paper by Anja,* ***I think****.*
d. *This is,* ***I think****, a paper by Anja.*

---

[6] The literary translation is: "It is more agreeable to me to see them free and loose and scattered about in a grateful confusion [...]" (Apology of Tertullian, *Translated and Annotated by* WM. REEVE, A.M.).

I argue that the developmental path is better described in terms of pragmaticalization or constructionalization than in terms of grammaticalization in its "canonical" understanding. The notion of constructionalization avoids too narrow grammar definitions that would, for example, fail to consider pragmatic elements – which include the use of 'I think' (cf. Traugott 2014: 95).

4.2 Methodology

Adopting quantitative and qualitative perspectives, I am concerned with the performative use of the verbs Spanish/Portuguese *pensar* 'think', i.e. when the verb of thinking encodes the subject's cognitive (epistemic/evidential) attitude.[7] The data are retrieved from the *Corpus del Español* and the *Corpus do Português*, i.e. CdE–Web/Dialects[8] and CdP–Web/Dialects.[9]

The web/dialects part of the CdE was created in 2015–2016, and contains approximately two billion words of data, which were collected in 2013–14. These were retrieved from web pages, chat forums, blogs etc., comprising 21 different Spanish-speaking countries. The web/dialects part of the CdP also contains very recent texts of about one billion words of Portuguese, comprising the varieties spoken in Brazil, Portugal, Angola and Mozambique. Thus, these parts of the CdE and the CdP comprise texts which are not only oral in character but also contain very recent Spanish and Portuguese.[10]

Regarding the medium, communication may be phonic or graphic. As far as the conception of communication is concerned, it may be spoken or written. The combinations "phonic+spoken" as well as "graphic+written" are, of course, the most common combinations. However, as already mentioned above, this clear-cut distinction may be blurred when being confronted with, for example, lectures on the one hand and WhatsApp-conversations on the other hand (cf. Koch and Oesterreicher 1985). Hence, the "oral character" of the data analyzed in the present study represents a special kind of writtenness because the written texts incorporate certain structures from orality, which some authors call "secondary written-

---

[7] For the present study I concentrate on the verb *pensar* and not on the most common cognitive verb for each language, i.e., Spanish *creer* and Portuguese *achar*, because *pensar* is the verb which is less studied so far (cf., for instance, Hennemann 2016b, 2020, Torres Cacoullos and Walker 2011 or Yoon 2015 on Spanish *creer* or Posio 2014 on Spanish *creer* and Portuguese *achar*).
[8] https://www.corpusdelespanol.org/web-dial/.
[9] https://www.corpusdoportugues.org/web-dial/.
[10] On the general continuum between orality and writtenness, see Koch and Oesterreicher (1994: 587).

ness" or even "tertiary writtenness" (cf. Schmitz 2006: 184; Androutsopoulos 2007: 73–74). In online communication or online discourses, however, there is also a range from formal to informal texts so that the degree of orality may differ from text to text (cf. Dürscheid 2003: 39–42; Kailuweit 2009: 14). This so-called secondary writtenness is a distinctive feature for the examples of the web/dialects sections of the CdE and CdP because the other corpus sections are characterized by more formal language.

In the quantitative analysis, on the one hand, I start from the node [*pienso que*]/[*penso que*] and check the co-presence of the overtly used subject pronoun; on the other hand, I search for [*yo pienso*]/[*eu penso*] and then check the co-presence of the complementizer *que*. Thus, the structures [*yo pienso*] and [*eu penso*] are checked regarding the use of a subsequent complementizer, i.e. [*yo pienso que*]/[*eu penso que*] vs. [*yo pienso* ø]/[*eu penso* ø], whereas the structures [*pienso que*] and [*penso que*] are checked regarding the use of a preceding pronominal subject, i.e. [*yo pienso que*]/[*eu penso que*] vs. [ø *pienso que*]/[ø *penso que*]. I deal with a sample of 500 examples each of [*yo pienso*] and [*pienso que*] from Argentinian Spanish and 500 examples each of [*eu penso*] and [*penso que*] from Brazilian Portuguese. The two samples of each variety (e.g. [*yo pienso*] and [*pienso que*] from Argentinian Spanish) do not share the same set of sentences.[11]

5 Corpus analysis

As already pointed out, in this study (i) I investigate the complementizer deletion as in examples (7a) and (7b) above. In a later step, (ii) I want to check whether the omission of the complementizer is indicative of a similar grammaticalization process that accompanies the loss of the complementizer in the grammaticalization of *I think* in English (cf. Aijmer 1997, 2002; Thompson and Mulac 1991).

In terms of illustration and transparency, results where *yo pienso* or *eu penso* is not used as a RT/RS introducing fragment, i.e. if it is followed by an infinitive, combining to a complex verb, not serving to introduce (or modalize) a certain state of affairs, do not represent the object of investigation:

---

[11] Please note that metadata information about the speakers (writers) is not provided by the corpora. Hence, a certain person commenting, for example, on a Brazilian Portuguese website may not be a native speaker of Brazilian Portuguese.

(11) Spanish [. . .] ***yo pienso comprar*** *un ipad 2 64gb solo wifi, por la sencilla razón que* [. . .] (alt-tab.com.ar)
'[. . .] **I think [about] buying/I plan to buy** an ipad 2 64gb wifi only, for the simple reason that [. . .]'

(12) Portuguese ***Eu penso renovar*** *o mundo usando borboletas.* (ciencialit.letras.ufrj.br)
'**I think [about] renewing** the world using butterflies'

Furthermore, examples such as (13)–(16), where, for instance, *pienso* and *hay* or *pienso* and *debe* as well as *penso* and *deve* or *penso* and *são* belong to different clauses as the punctuation in the English translation may also demonstrate (cf. examples [13]–[14]) – *pensar* having the meaning of 'thinking *about* something' – are, of course, also not the object of investigation:

(13) Spanish *Ahora que lo **pienso hay** también otro arquetipo: la mujer ruda, que es capaz de* [. . .] (tierradecollares.blogspot.com)
'Now that I **think** about it, **there is** also another archetype: the rude woman, who is capable [. . .]'

(14) Spanish *Ahora que lo **pienso debe ser** que sólo había el No. 2 originalmente, pero* [. . .] (andaringallardo.com)
'Now that I **think** about it, **it must be** that there was only the No. 2 originally, but [. . .]'

(15) Portuguese *Meu direito de continuar pensando como **penso deve ser assegurado** por um estado laico* [. . .] (bonitaadventista.com.br)
'My right to continue thinking as **I think should be ensured** by a secular state [. . .]'

(16) Portuguese *Tudo que eu **penso são** coisas negativas* [. . .] (psicoterapia.psc.br)
'All **I think is** negative things [. . .]'

Such cases as the ones discussed above were discarded from each sample of 500 occurrences; they fall out of the envelope of variation of complementation.

5.1 Quantitative analysis for Spanish [(*yo*) *pienso* (*que*) X]

First of all, my search for the collocation [*pienso que*] in the CdE–Web/Dialects, yielded 88,210 results. I checked 500 results from Argentinian Spanish regarding the co-presence of the subject pronoun *yo* (see Table 1).

Table 1: [*pienso que*] and the (non-)use of the subject pronoun.

Total: 88,210 | Sample of 500 (100 %)	[*pienso que*]	
	With *yo*	Without *yo*
	69 (13.8 %)	431 (86.2 %)

The examples thus illustrate that the "more economic" version, the non-presence of the subject pronoun, is far more frequent than the overtly expressed pronoun. Even though several studies point out that the presence of the subject pronoun helps to anchor the speaker in (argumentative) discourse (cf., for instance, Aijón Oliva and Serrano 2010: 27), which is also the case in chat talks or forum conversation on web pages, the speakers (here writers) predominantly decide for the non-use of the subject pronoun. The reason might be – even though dealing with conceptually oral language – that medial writtenness favors the non-use of the pronouns, perhaps for reasons of language economy (when typing statements etc.).

Results containing an adverb in between *yo* and *pienso*, i.e. showing the structure [subject pronoun + adverb + verb + complementizer], were also counted:

(17) a. Spanish *Yo también* **pienso que** *el poema Instantes es una cursilería sin remedio* [. . .] (feederico.com)
'I also **think that** the poem *Instantes* is hopelessly cheesy [. . .]'
b. Spanish *Yo tal vez* **pienso que** *en julio, algún jugador se a vender y otros van a rajar* [. . .] (muyboca.com.ar)
'I maybe **think that** in July some players will sell out and others will crack [. . .]'

A look at 500 results of the structure [*yo pienso*] reveals a relatively equal distribution of the co-presence of the complementizer *que* (see Table 2):[12]

---

[12] Examples of (*yo*) *pienso* in clause-final or parenthetic position, which go hand in hand with zero complementation, are not part of the 500 results.

Table 2: [*yo pienso*] and the (non-)use of the complementizer.

Total: 19,804 | Sample of 500 (100 %)	[*yo pienso*]	
	With *que*	Without *que*
	267 (53.4 %)	233 (46.6 %)

Examples in which the complementizer *que* is abbreviated (as in 18a) or in which the punctuation does not follow the written standard (as in 18b) were also counted as the structure [*yo pienso que*]:

(18) a. Spanish *Nombre: Sandry – 24/02/2011 10:11:47* **yo pienso k** *el mejor es el masstube, es super rápido, vaja video y música* [...] (informatica-hoy.com.ar)
'**I think that** the best is MassTube, it's superfast, great video and music [...]'
b. Spanish *Luciana 2013/07/30 21:49:00* **Yo pienso, que** *Justin Bieber, es una persona muy chica, que tiene que aprender* [...] (mundotkm.com)
'**I think that** Justin Bieber is a very young person who has to learn [...]'

Summarizing, it can be stated that a) if the cognitive verb and the complementizer are combined, [*pienso que*] is more often *not* preceded by the pronominal subject, and that b) if the cognitive verb and the subject pronoun are combined, [*yo pienso*] may or may not be followed by the complementizer; 267: 233 represents a relative equal distribution of the (non-)use of subsequent *que*.

5.2 Quantitative analysis for Portuguese [(*eu*) *penso* (*que*) X]

The collocation [*penso que*] is found 57,875 times in the CdP–Web/Dialects. 500 results from Brazilian Portuguese were checked regarding the co-presence of the subject pronoun *eu*. The examples illustrate that the non-presence of the pronominal subject is far more frequent than its presence, which is, of course, very striking since the use of the subject pronoun was expected to be more frequent than its non-use (see Table 3):

Table 3: [*penso que*] and the (non-)use of the subject pronoun.

	[*penso que*]	
Total: 57,875 | Sample of 500 (100 %)	With *eu*	Without *eu*
	46 (9.2 %)	454 (90.8 %)

Just as for Spanish, results containing an adverb – or even longer phrases in between *eu* and *penso*, i.e. showing the structure [subject pronoun + {...} + verb + complementizer] – were also counted:

(19) a. Portuguese **Eu penso** também **que** deveriam criar uma galeria de imagens gratuitas [...] (blogosferalegal.com)
'I also **think that** you should create an image gallery for free [...]'

b. Portuguese **Eu penso** (e foi o motivo de ter escrito este comentário) **que**, se for [...] (ceticismoaberto.com)
'I **think** (and it was the reason for writing this comment) **that**, if it were [...]'

c. Portuguese [...] **eu** simplesmente não **penso que** seja adequado ignorar ou simplesmente relegar às notícia [...] (ars-the.blogspot.com)
'I just don't **think that** it's appropriate to ignore or simply relegate to the news [...]'

If having a look at 500 results of the same structure [subject pronoun + verb + complementizer], but starting from the collocation [*eu penso*], the picture is somehow different compared to the distribution in Spanish (see Table 2). The absence of the complementizer *que* is more frequent than its presence (see Table 4):

Table 4: [*eu penso*] and the (non-)use of the complementizer.

	[*eu penso*]	
Total: 12,681 | Sample of 500 (100 %)	With *que*	Without *que*
	202 (40.4 %)	298 (59.6 %)

Examples in which the complementizer *que* is abbreviated – as we have also seen for Spanish (as in [18a] above) – were also counted:

(20) Portuguese **Eu penso q** *é importante, entre o casal comprometido* [. . .] (esbocandoideias.com)
'**I think that** it's important, between the committed couple [. . .]'

Summarizing, the findings represented by Tables 3 and 4 are striking. On the one hand, the use of the subject pronoun was expected to be far more frequent in comparison to its non-use. On the other hand, the fact that zero complementation after [*eu penso*] is more frequent than the use of a subsequent *que* is also an interesting observation. Examples of zero complementation will be dealt with in more detail in the next section.

5.3 [*(yo) pienso* X] and [*(eu) penso* X] – cases of grammaticalization or pragmaticalization?

When treating Spanish [*yo pienso* + X] and Portuguese [*eu penso* + X] it should be highlighted that I do not refer to *yo pienso*/*eu penso* as a formulaic chunk, which is found to be used in, for instance, parenthetic position in the middle or at the end of a sentence (as in [21]) (cf. also Hennemann 2016a: 101–102), where it functions like a cognitive particle (usually surrounded by commas as in [22] and [23], but often not in oral writtenness as in [24]), which is not integrated into the syntactic structure and could be easily detached from the rest of the sentence:

(21) Portuguese [. . .] *estavamos com poucas horas em Madrid, acho que receberam informação,* **eu penso**. (ducsamsterdam.net)
'[. . .] we were only a few hours in Madrid, I suppose that they received information, **I think**'

(22) Spanish *Entonces,* **yo pienso***, María Fernanda (ella ya sabía que yo pensaba, pero fue una manera de decir le):* [. . .] (luispescetti.com)
'So, **I think**, María Fernanda (she already knew that I thought, but it was a way of telling her): [. . .]'

(23) Portuguese [. . .] *ainda é necessário perceber,* **eu penso***, que as massas têm profetas demais e de sobra.* (endireitar.org)
'[. . .] it is still necessary to realize, **I think**, that the masses have too many prophets and too much [at all]'

(24) Spanish [...] *postular que el mismo **yo pienso** acompaña todas mis representaciones, que a su vez forman un tejido sistemático, homogéneo* [...] (jacquesderrida.com.ar)
'to postulate that the same, **I think**, accompanies all my representations, which in turn form a systematic, homogeneous fabric [...]'

Instead, I refer to cases such as in (25)–(26), where Spanish *yo pienso*/Portuguese *eu penso* is used as a fragment that introduces RT/RS, followed by a subordinate clause, which is not preceded by the complementizer *que*. Or, as Thompson and Mulac (1991) show for English *I think*, these are cases, where a main clause is headed by an epistemic parenthetical. Spanish *yo pienso*/Portuguese *eu penso* is then found in sentence-initial or clause-initial position:

(25) Spanish *Javier,* **yo pienso** *hay personas que se les sale lo malo en el internet insultando libremente a otros* [...] (koflaolivieri.com)
'Javier, **I think** there are people who get the bad stuff on the internet by freely insulting others [...]'

(26) Portuguese ***Eu penso** deve poder acompanhar todas as representações, caso contrário seria representado* [...] (filosofiabrasilia.blogspot.com)
'**I think** [it] must be able to accompany all representations, otherwise it would be represented [...]'

In several papers on cognitive verbs, which also focus on these verbs and their combination with pronominal subjects, it is mentioned that "some frequently used first person singular verb forms can be analyzed as formulaic sequences which are used to express the speaker's subjective or epistemic stance" (Posio 2011: 777; cf. also Posio 2015). For example, Travis and Torres Cacoullos (2012: 739–741) analyze *yo creo* as a prefab, as a grammaticalized chunk, and explain that "*yo creo* is largely autonomous from other instances of a more schematic (subject pronoun) + verb construction" (Travis and Torres Cacoullos 2012: 741; cf. also Posio 2014) on Portuguese *acho* '[I] think' and cf. also Hennemann (2020) on Portuguese *acho* and Spanish *creo* '[I] think'):

> *yo creo* is largely autonomous from other instances of a more schematic (subject pronoun) + verb construction. Contributing to the status of *yo creo* as an autonomous unit is (1) the token frequency of the string; (2) the high proportion it comprises of all occurrence both of the lexical type *creer* and of the pronoun *yo* [...] (Travis and Torres Cacoullos 2012: 741)

Thompson and Mulac were among the first authors to treat *I think* as an output of grammaticalization, i.e. as a grammaticalized chunk because these so-called *that*-less complements "have in fact been reanalyzed by speakers as epistemic phrases, which have a degree of freedom not possible for subject-verb combinations; in particular they are 'free' to occur in other positions, just as other epistemic phrases, such as epistemic adverbs, do in English" (Thompson and Mulac 1991: 317). This freedom of syntactic position of *I think* can, of course, not be denied. However, this raises the question whether *I think* really went through a process of grammaticalization. Actually, grammaticalization – the "classical view" of grammaticalization – is described in terms of "*less freedom* in the use of linguistic expressions" (Haspelmath 1998: 318 [emphasis mine]; cf. also Kuryłowicz 1965: 52 or Lehmann 2002: 10), which fulfill new grammatical functions (Hopper and Traugott 2003: xv).

Aijmer, by contrast, is one of the first who treated *I think* as an instance of pragmaticalization, arguing against *I think* as a grammaticalized chunk by opposing the main feature of grammaticalization and the one of pragmaticalization: "pragmatic elements tend to be *optional* in the sentence while grammaticalization results in forms which are an *obligatory* part of the grammatical 'core' such as tense and mood" (Aijmer 1997: 3 [emphasis mine]). Indeed, pragmaticalization should be understood as the process, when "lexical items, such as nouns, or grammatical items (e.g. coordinators) change their category to become pragmatic items, *not fully integrated into the syntactic structure*, that have a textual or interpersonal meaning" (Grzelak 2014: 109 [emphasis mine]). Usually, pragmaticalization is associated with bleaching/loss of meaning, but since "the beginning of grammaticalization is associated with the development of new pragmatic meanings, strengthening of conversational implicatures, etc." (Aijmer 1997: 2), it seems reasonable that a strict distinction between grammaticalization and pragmaticalization is not always made (cf. Diewald 2011 on "pragmaticalization [defined] as grammaticalization" or Nicolle 2011 on "pragmatic aspects of grammaticalization"). In my view, any linguistic change is somehow bound to pragmatic needs so that certain pragmatic conditions are (somehow) always involved in any kind of development or change.[13] Within the framework of Diachronic Construction Grammar, which cannot be dealt with in detail here, Traugott (2014: 91) also explains that "some recent characterizations of grammaticalization have shifted focus to conceptualizing grammaticalization as extension", whereby "extension" refers to extended meanings of linguistic structures. She argues for changes being conceived as constructionalization, which may refer to different processes of change. According to Fried (2013: 424), construc-

---

13 See also the discussion in Heine (2018) or Heine, Claudi and Hünnemeyer (1991).

tionalization is "a process that leads to (1) the emergence of a new grammatical pattern (construction) out of previously independent material or (2) a reorganization of an existing construction, leading to an increasingly more opaque meaning of the pattern". Interestingly, the example Traugott (2014) provides, also is *I think*. Traugott's understanding of constructionalization "avoids the problem of being interpreted in terms of narrow definitions of grammar that exclude pragmatic elements such as discourse markers like *I think*; and it does not evoke definitions of grammaticalization as reduction" (Traugott 2014: 95). A change, following Fried (2013: 424), is "characterized by a confluence of factors (semantic, pragmatic, syntactic, etc.)". *I think* – seen as a pragmaticalized chunk of language – "developed into a discourse marker[14] or modal particle which is syntactically a speech-act adverbial" (Aijmer 1997: 1): "[. . .] strings such as I think which can be loosely attached to the sentence as in Bill is at home I think, are other good examples of pragmaticalization or of emergent pragmatic constructions [. . .]" (Aijmer 1997: 2)

Especially in oral conversation, "*I think* has developed a number of new functions as a response to the demands of planning and interaction with the hearer which may in their turn become conventionalized" (Aijmer 1997: 40). This is also the case for Spanish *(yo) pienso* and Portuguese *(eu) penso*. In some cases, *yo pienso/ eu penso* fulfills the function of a cognitive particle, and it could easily be detached from the rest of the sentence. It is then usually found in parenthetic position; in oral writtenness often not surrounded by commas (see examples [22]–[24] above). In its function as a cognitive particle *pienso/penso* is also used alone, i.e. without the expression of the pronominal subject:

(27) Spanish [. . .] *es la caída del cabello, un poco de inseguridad (que también **pienso** puede confundir se con los síntomas del ovario poliquístico).* (cuidatutiroides.com)
'[. . .] is hair loss, a bit of insecurity (which also, **[I] think**, can be confused with the symptoms of polycystic ovary)'

---

14 Such as *I think* (literally) represents a fragment of RT, 'I say' or 'I told you' represents a fragment of RS. No wonder that Posio and Pešková (2020: 391) also propose to consider RS introducing fragments such as (*le dije yo/digo* 'I told her*him/I say') as an independent subtype of discourse markers.

(28) Spanish *Aunque es más duro, prefiero someter me a la opinión de quien* **pienso** *puede enseñar me algo antes que hacer lo al gran público* [. . .] (dzoom.org.es)
'Although it is harder, I prefer to submit to the opinion of who, **[I] think**, can teach me something before doing it in front of the general public [. . .]'

(29) Spanish *Lo correcto* **pienso** *sería que tu médico de cabecera te pida la ecografía* [. . .] (laconsultasincita.com)
'The right thing, **[I] think**, to do would be for your family doctor to ask for the ultrasound scan [. . .]'

In each of the Spanish examples above *pienso* is not fully integrated into the syntax of the sentence, but it has pragmatic weight (cf. Davidson 1996: 543)[15] – even without being accompanied by the subject pronoun because the upcoming sequence is attenuated or modalized. The same is applicable to Portuguese *penso*:

(30) Portuguese *Adorei a sinopse do filme que* **penso** *deve ser extraordinário e, não o vou perder!* (momentos-perfeitos.blogspot.com)
'I loved the synopsis of the film that, **[I] think**, must be extraordinary, and I won't miss it'

(31) Portuguese *A o quarto dia ao deitar-me* **penso** *tinha sangue.* (vidamaislivre.com.br)
'The fourth day at bedtime, **[I] think**, I had blood'

(32) Portuguese *Minha percepção do amor,* **penso** *é a entrega, doação, renuncia, atos concretos.* (destrave.cancaonova.com)
'My perception of love, **[I] think**, is surrender, donation, renunciation, concrete acts'

---

15 Davidson (1996: 543) uses 'pragmatic weight' as a notion "that describes the ways in which subject pronouns are used to signal utterances as 'less abstract' or 'more personally relevant'". However, the cognitive verb alone (without subject pronoun) may fulfil a function of pragmatic weight because the subsequent clause is modalized/attenuated so that the modalizing/attenuating element indeed has pragmatic impact on the upcoming sequence.

While the examples above show cases of 'I think' which can be interpreted as cognitive particles in mid positions of the sentences, the following examples illustrate clause-initial uses of the same fragment, i.e. the structure [*pienso/penso* + {subordinate clause}] – behaving like a RT/RS introducing fragment without the complementizer *que*:

(33) Spanish *Estamos desarrollando materiales para e learning y **pienso** sería excelente poder explorar formas de colaborar en este proyecto [. . .]* (blogs.iadb.org)
'We are developing materials for e-learning and, **[I] think**, it would be excellent to explore ways of collaborating on this project [. . .]'

(34) Portuguese [. . .] *pois **penso** pode ser a última vez que falo com essa pessoa* [. . .] (coracaodesabedoria.blogspot.com)
'[. . .] because **[I] think** it might be the last time I talk to that person [. . .]'

(35) Portuguese [. . .] *as vezes me sinto depreciva e **penso** tem gente pior que eu.* (blogbrasil.com.br)
'[. . .] sometimes I feel depreciated and **[I] think** there are people worse than me'

(36) Portuguese [. . .] *tem treta, **penso** seria melhor um gerente ao invés de prefeito.* (plantaopolicialcn.com)
'[. . .] it's bullshit, **[I] think** it would be better to have a manager instead of a mayor'

The cases of 'I think' as an RT/RS introducing fragment without the complementizer *que*, i.e. without the subordinate clause being preceded by *que*, in sentence-initial or clause-initial position are, however, comparably rare (see examples [8a], [9a], [25] and [33] for Spanish, and [8b], [9b], [34], [35] and [36] for Portuguese).

6 Conclusion and outlook

This paper has undertaken a quantitative as well as qualitative analysis regarding the overt and covert expression of the pronominal subject and the complementizer in the structures Spanish [*(yo) pienso (que)* X] and Portuguese [*(eu) penso (que)* X] in the context of RT/RS in Argentinian Spanish and Brazilian Portuguese. RT and RS were treated together here because both categories go hand in hand in the performative use of the cognitive verb Spanish/Portuguese *pensar* 'think', which is why they could be summarized below the term of Reported Discourse.

While focusing on the combination of Spanish *pienso* and Portuguese *penso* with the overtly expressed pronominal subject (Spanish *yo* and Portuguese *eu*) as well as on its combination with *que*, the main aim of this paper was the study of structures where the use of the complementizer would be expected. In various previous studies on zero complementation it is pointed out that complementizer omission is predominantly found in written texts and formal registers. However, as also shown by Yoon (2015), this is only the case for certain verbs – for verbs of demand and command. When cognitive verbs occur without *que*, by contrast, they are part of (conceptually) oral language. Since the present study has focused on only one register – conceptually oral language – future studies could compare different oral spoken registers regarding the omission of the complementizer.

In English, sentences like *I think this was a paper by Anja* instead of *I think that this was a paper by Anja* are very common. These structures were, for instance, discussed by Thompson and Mulac (1991) or Aijmer (1997, 2002), whereby the discussion of the developmental path in terms of grammaticalization or pragmaticalization became prominent. Hence, I also discussed the different processes, arguing for describing Spanish [*(Yo) pienso* X] and Portuguese [*(Eu) pienso* X] as instances of pragmaticalization or constructionalization.

The syntactic diversity and the different meanings/functions which were illustrated for *I think* by Aijmer (1997, 2002) and Thompson and Mulac (1991) could also be shown for 'I think' in Argentinian Spanish and Brazilian Portuguese. To sum up, it can be stated that not only English *I think* but also its Spanish and Portuguese equivalents fulfill versatile functions that are even not always easy to differentiate so that I would like to propose a continuum of functions, accounting for, on the one hand, its literal meaning, referring to the act of thinking, and, on the other hand, its metaphorical meaning, when it functions as an opinion indicator, expressing the result of the act of thinking (cf. Cappelli 2007: 194). Furthermore, however, there are other pragmatic functions of *yo pienso/eu penso* such as that of a cognitive particle. When found to be used as cognitive particle, its use without subject pronoun seems to be more usual than its use with pronominal subject. Nevertheless, it should not be ignored that the use of the pronoun in (Argentinian) Spanish and Portuguese generally differ from each other. Portuguese – especially the Brazilian variety – is a less prototypical pro-drop language than Spanish.

The cases of 'I think' as an RT/RS introducing fragment without the complementizer *que*, i.e. without the subordinate clause being introduced by *que*, in sentence-initial or clause-initial position are, however, comparably rare. Hence, while there are indeed examples which can be identified as consisting of a RT/RS introducing fragment (in sentence-initial or clause-initial position), illustrating the structure [*pienso/penso* + {subordinate clause}], in most other examples *pienso/ penso* – whether accompanied by the pronominal subject or not – has moved to other syntactic positions, behaving like a cognitive particle with a modalizing/ attenuating function. Complementizer deletion can thus be seen as a consequence of this cognitive particle use. Furthermore, in [(*yo*) *pienso que*] or [(*eu*) *penso que*] the main information to be transmitted lies on the cognitive verb itself and not on the complementizer so that the complementizer itself is not absolutely necessary for the modalization/attenuation of the statement. However, future studies could deal with exactly this issue in more detail on the basis of historical data.

References

Aijmer, Karin. 1997. *I think* – an English modal particle. In Toril Swan & Olaf J. Westvik (eds.), *Modality in Germanic languages*, 1–47. Berlin & New York: Mouton de Gruyter.

Aijmer, Karin. 2002. *English discourse particles. Evidence from a corpus.* Amsterdam & Philadelphia: John Benjamins.

Aijón Oliva, Miguel Á. & María J. Serrano. 2010. El hablante en su discurso: Expresión y omisión del sujeto de *creo. Oralia* 13. 7–38.

Androutsopoulos, Jannis K. 2007. Neue Medien – neue Schriftlichkeit? *Mitteilungen des Deutschen Germanistenverbandes* 1(7). 72–97.

Bakhtin, Mikhail M. 2008 [1981]. *The dialogic imagination. Four essays by M. M. Bakhtin*. Edited by Michael Holquist. Translated by Caryl Emerson & Michael Holquist. 17th edn. Austin: University of Texas Press.

Bally, Charles. 1965 [1932]. *Linguistique générale e linguistique française*. 4th edn. Bern: Francke.

Brovetto, Claudia. 2002. Spanish clauses without complementizer. In Teresa Satterfield, Christina Tortora & Diana Cresti (eds.), *Current Issues in Romance Languages: Selected papers from the 29th Linguistic Symposium on Romance Languages (LSRL), Ann Arbor, 8–11 April 1999*, 33–46. Amsterdam & Philadelphia: John Benjamins.

Bühler, Karl. 1990 [1934]. *Theory of language. The representational function of language*. Translated by Donald F. Goodwin. Amsterdam & Philadelphia: John Benjamins.

Bühler, Karl. 1999 [1934]. *Sprachtheorie. Die Darstellungsfunktion der Sprache*. 3rd edn. Stuttgart: Lucius & Lucius.

Cappelli, Gloria. 2007. *"I reckon I know how Leonardo da Vinci must have felt...". Epistemicity, evidentiality and English verbs of cognitive attitude*. Pari: Pari Publishing.

CdE–Web/Dialects. Corpus del Español. https://www.corpusdoportugues.org/web-dial/ (accessed 10 December 2020).

CdP–Web/Dialects. Corpus do Português. https://www.corpusdoportugues.org/web-dial/ (accessed 11 December 2020).

Davidson, Brad. 1996. 'Pragmatic weight' and Spanish subject pronouns: The pragmatic and discourse uses of *tú* and *yo* in spoken Madrid Spanish. *Journal of Pragmatics* 26(4). 543–565.

De Cock, Barbara. 2014. *Profiling discourse participants: Forms and functions in Spanish conversation and debates*. Amsterdam & Philadelphia: John Benjamins.

De Saeger, Bram. 2007. Evidencialidad y modalidad epistémica en los verbos de actitud proposicional en Español. *Interlingüística* 17. 268–277.

Delbecque, Nicole & Béatrice Lamiroy. 1999. La subordinación sustantiva: subordinadas enunciativas en los complementos verbales. In Ignacio Bosque & Violeta Demonte (eds.), *Gramática Descriptiva de la Lengua Española.* Vol. 2, 1965–2081. Madrid: Espasa Calpe.

Diewald, Gabriele. 2011. Pragmaticalization (defined) as grammaticalization of discourse functions. *Linguistics* 49(2). 365–390.

Dürscheid, Christa. 2003. Medienkommunikation im Kontinuum von Mündlichkeit und Schriftlichkeit. Theoretische und empirische Probleme. *Zeitschrift für Angewandte Linguistik* 38. 37–56.

Fried, Mirjam. 2013. Principles of Constructional Change. In Thomas Hoffmann & Graeme Trousdale (eds.), *The Oxford Handbook of Construction Grammar*, 419–437. Oxford: Oxford University Press.

Gonzálvez-García, Francisco. 2014. Bringing Together Fragments and Constructions: Evidence from complementation in English and Spanish. In Hans C. Boas & Francisco Gonzálvez-García (eds.), *Romance Perspectives on Construction Grammar*, 181–226. Amsterdam & Philadelphia: John Benjamins.

Graffi, Giorgio. 2001. *200 years of syntax. A critical survey*. Amsterdam & Philadelphia: John Benjamins.

Grzelak, Szymon. 2014. Pragmaticalization of hedging markers in Japanese. *Rocznik Orientalistyczny* 67(1). 107–115.

Haspelmath, Martin. 1998. Does grammaticalization need reanalysis? *Studies in Language* 22(2). 315–351.

Heine, Bernd. 2018. Are there two different ways of approaching grammaticalization? In Sylvie Hancil, Tine Breban & José V. Lozano (eds.), *New trends in grammaticalization and language change*, 23–54. Amsterdam & Philadelphia: John Benjamins.

Heine, Bernd, Ulrike Claudi & Friederike Hünnemeyer. 1991. *Grammaticalization: A conceptual framework*. Chicago: University of Chicago Press.

Hennemann, Anja. 2013. *A context-sensitive and functional approach to evidentiality in Spanish or why evidentiality needs a superordinate category*. Frankfurt am Main: Peter Lang.

Hennemann, Anja. 2016a. El marcador *(yo) pienso (que)* y sus diferentes funciones. *promptus – Würzburger Beiträge zur Romanistik* 2. 99–120.

Hennemann, Anja. 2016b. A cognitive-constructionist approach to Spanish *creo Ø* and *creo yo* '[I] think'. *Folia Linguistica* 50(2). 449–474.

Hennemann, Anja. 2020. *Reporting on 'thinking' in Spanish and Portuguese and the role of the subject pronoun.* Online publication. University of Potsdam. https://doi.org/10.25932/publishup-47445 (accessed 01 December 2020).

Hopper, Paul J. & Elizabeth C. Traugott. 2003 [1993]. *Grammaticalization*. 2nd edn. Cambridge: Cambridge University Press.

Innis, Robert E. 1982. *Karl Bühler. Semiotic Foundations of Language Theory*. New York: Plenum Press.

Kailuweit, Rolf. 2009. Konzeptionelle Mündlichkeit!? Überlegungen zur Chat-Kommunikation anhand französischer, italienischer und spanischer Materialien. *Philologie im Netz* 48. 1–19.

Kärkkäinen, Elise. 2003. *Epistemic stance in English conversation*. Amsterdam & Philadelphia: John Benjamins.

Koch, Peter & Wulf Oesterreicher. 1985. Sprache der Nähe – Sprache der Distanz. Mündlichkeit und Schriftlichkeit im Spannungsfeld von Sprachtheorie und Sprachgeschichte. *Romanistisches Jahrbuch* 36. 15–43.

Koch, Peter & Wulf Oesterreicher. 1994. Schriftlichkeit und Sprache. In Hartmut Günther & Otto Ludwig (eds.), Schrift und Schriftlichkeit. *Ein interdisziplinäres Handbuch internationaler Forschung*, 587–604. Berlin & New York: Mouton de Gruyter.

Kuryłowicz, Jerzy. 1965. The evolution of grammatical categories. *Diogenes* 51. 55–71.
Lehmann, Christian. 2002. Thoughts on grammaticalization. Second, Revised Edition. http://www.christianlehmann.eu/publ/ASSidUE09.pdf (accessed 02 August 2020).
Llinàs-Grau, Mireia & Javier Fernández-Sánchez. 2001. Complementizer Deletion Structures: Against a Romance-English Unified Account. Research report GGT-2011-05. Universitat Autònoma de Barcelona. http://filcat.uab.cat/clt/publicacions/reports/pdf/GGT-11-05.pdf (accessed 16 August 2021).
NGLE. *Nueva gramática de la lengua española*. 2009. [Edición en línea (www.rae.es)]. (accessed 17 August 2021).
Nicolle, Steve. 2011. Pragmatic aspects of grammaticalization. In Heiko Narrog & Bernd Heine (eds.), *The Oxford handbook of grammaticalization*, 401–412. Oxford: Oxford University Press.
Posio, Pekka. 2011. Spanish subject pronoun usage and verb semantics revisited: First and second person singular subject pronouns and focusing of attention in spoken Peninsular Spanish. *Journal of Pragmatics* 43(3). 777–798.
Posio, Pekka. 2012. The functions of postverbal pronominal subjects in spoken Peninsular Spanish and European Portuguese. *Studies in Hispanic and Lusophone Linguistics 5* (1). 149–190.
Posio, Pekka. 2013. The expression of first-person-singular subjects in spoken Peninsular Spanish and European Portuguese: Semantic roles and formulaic sequences. *Folia Linguistica* 47(1). 253–291.
Posio, Pekka. 2014. Subject expression in grammaticalizing constructions: The case of *creo* and *acho* 'I think' in Spanish and Portuguese. *Journal of Pragmatics* 63. 5–18.
Posio, Pekka. 2015. Subject pronoun usage in formulaic sequences. Evidence from Peninsular Spanish. In Rafael Orozco, Ana M. Carvalho & Naomi Shin (eds.), *Subject pronoun expression in Spanish: A cross-dialectal perspective*, 59–74. Washington: Georgetown University Press.
Posio, Pekka. 2021. *A pessoa and uma pessoa*: Grammaticalization and functions of a human impersonal referential device in European Portuguese. *Journal of Portuguese Linguistics* 20 (2). 1–21. https://doi.org/10.5334/jpl.254 (accessed September 30 2021).
Posio, Pekka & Andrea Pešková. 2020. *Le dije yo, digo*. Construccionalización de los introductores cuotativos con el verbo *decir* en español peninsular y argentino. *Spanish in Context* 17 (3). 391–415.
Raible, Wolfgang. 2002. Literacy and orality. In Neil J. Smelser & Paul B. Baltes (eds.), *International Encyclopedia of Social and Behavioral Sciences*, 8967–8971. http://www.romanistik.uni-freiburg.de/raible/Publikationen/Files/Orality_2col.pdf (accessed 13 August 2021).
Schmitz, Ulrich. 2006. Schriftbildschirme. Tertiäre Schriftlichkeit im World Wide Web. In Jannis K. Androutsopoulos, Jens Runkehl, Peter Schlobinski & Torsten Siever (eds.), *Neuere Entwicklungen in der linguistischen Internetforschung*, 184–208. Hildesheim: Georg Olms.
Schneider, Stefan. 2007. *Reduced parenthetical clauses as mitigators: A corpus study of spoken French, Italian and Spanish*. Amsterdam & Philadelphia: John Benjamins.
Spronck, Stef. 2015. Refracting views: How to construct complex perspective in reported speech and thought in Ungarinyin. *Sprachtypologie und Universalienforschung – Language Typology and Universals* 68(2). 165–185.
Spronck, Stef. 2019. Speaking for Bakhtin: Two interpretations of reported speech. A response to Goddard and Wierzbicka (2018). *Russian Journal of Linguistics* 23(3). 603–618. https://doi.org/10.22363/2312-9182-2019-23-3-603-618 (accessed 01 August 2020).
Spronck, Stef & Tatiana Nikitina. 2019. Reported speech forms a dedicated syntactic domain. *Linguistic Typology* 23 (1). 119–159.
Thompson, Sandra A. 2002. 'Object complements' and conversation: Towards a realistic account. *Studies in Language* 26(1). 125–163.

Thompson, Sandra A. & Anthony Mulac. 1991. A quantitative perspective on the grammaticization of epistemic parentheticals in English. In Elizabeth C. Traugott & Bernd Heine (eds.), *Approaches to grammaticalization*, 313–330. Amsterdam & Philadelphia: John Benjamins.

Torres Cacoullos, Rena & James A. Walker. 2011. Collocations in Grammaticalization and Variation. In Heiko Narrog & Bernd Heine (eds.), *The Oxford Handbook of Grammaticalization*, 229–239. Oxford: Oxford University Press.

Traugott, Elizabeth C. 1995. Subjectification in grammaticalisation. In Dieter Stein & Susan Wright (eds.), *Subjectivity and Subjectivisation: Linguistic Perspectives*, 31–54. Cambridge: Cambridge University Press.

Traugott, Elizabeth C. 2014. Towards a constructional framework for research on language change. In Sylvie Hancil & Ekkehard König (eds.), *Grammaticalization – theory and data*, 87–105. Amsterdam & Philadelphia: John Benjamins.

Travis, Catherine E. & Rena Torres Cacoullos. 2012. What do subject pronouns do in discourse? Cognitive, mechanical and constructional factors in variation. *Cognitive Linguistics* 23(4). 711–748.

Vandelanotte, Lieven. 2004. Deixis and grounding in speech and thought representation. *Journal of Pragmatics* 36(3). 489–520.

http://dx.doi.org/10.1016/j.pragma.2003.10.003 (accessed 14 August 2021).

Vandelanotte, Lieven. 2006. Speech or thought representation and subjectification, or on the need to think twice. *Belgian Journal of Linguistics* 20. 137–168.

Vandelanotte, Lieven. 2009. *Speech and thought representation in English: A cognitive-functional approach.* Berlin & New York: Mouton de Gruyter.

Vygotsky, Lev S. 1991. *Thought and language.* Cambridge, Mass.: MIT Press.

Wierzbicka, Anna. 1974. The function of direct and indirect discourse. *Papers in Linguistics* 7(3). 267–307.

Yoon, Jiyoung. 2015. The Grammaticalization of the Spanish Complement-taking Verb without a Complementizer. *Journal of Social Sciences* 11(3). 338–351.

https://doi.org/10.3844/jssp.2015.338.351 (accessed 13 August 2021).

Daniela E. Casartelli
11 Towards a typology of reported thought

Abstract: Reported Thought, henceforth RT, has often been neglected, under the assumption that it co-patterns with reported speech. However, data from genealogically distinct languages reveals a variety of morphological properties of reported thought across the languages of the world. This first time typological analysis aims to describe reported thought as a category in its own right. Based on the morphosyntactic properties of the examples drawn from a crosslinguistic sample of 100 languages, five different morphosyntactic properties of reported thought are identified.

1 Introduction

Reported Thought, henceforth RT, has often been neglected, under the assumption that it co-patterns with reported speech (Coulmas 1986; Janssen and Wurff 1996; Lucy 1993; McGregor 1994; Reesink 1993; Spronck and Casartelli 2021 *inter alia*). RT and reported speech are two closely related morphosyntactic constructions in the languages of the world. Speech reports imply thinking about speech, but thoughts about speech do not require verbal externalization. Although RT is frequently mentioned in the literature, an independent crosslinguistic typological analysis is lacking. The present analysis presents a description of five different sub-types of RT across the world's languages. The analysis starts from the general assumption that speakers can use language to reference utterances or thoughts from others or themselves. Representing thoughts can be observed throughout the languages of the world. Thought reports are usually *framed* (cf. McGregor 1994, 2021) by a verb in the respective language that is equivalent to the English verb 'think'. *Framing* refers to the morphosyntactic structure and clausal relations of speech and thought reports. McGregor (1994: 76) notes that speech and thought reports feature two important characteristics (i) both the reported and reporting clauses are independent morphosyntactic units that can stand by themselves and (ii) that these units are structurally related. Furthermore, McGregor (1994) refers to the relation of

---

Acknowledgements: I would like to thank the University of Helsinki for funding through the project 'Language emerging from human sociality: the case of speech representation' (*3 v. tutkimusrahaa*, PI Stef Spronck), the reviewers for this chapter, the co-editors for this volume, Daniel van Olmen and Barbara Karlson for their encouragement that lead to the production of this chapter.

https://doi.org/10.1515/9783111065830-011

the reported and reporting clause as whole-whole relationship, meaning that each clause can stand independently from the other. The structural relationship between the reported and the reporting clause is one of independent units, the function of the reporting clause is to set apart the reported clause from the context. Similar to a frame of a painting in an art exhibition, the reporting clause frames the reported clause and sets it off from the other clauses in the utterance context. Consider (1) below for examples of RT in English.

(1)   1. Mary thinks "Today is a nice day".
      2. "Today is a nice day", Mary thinks.
      3. Mary thinks that today is a nice day.

In (1) in English, the verb 'think' is a complement taking verb that takes the reported clause "today is a nice day" as its complement. The complement of the matrix clause 'Mary thinks' (1a) and (1b) is direct. In (1c) the complement is indirect and headed by the complementizer 'that'. The distinction between direct and indirect complements of reported clauses is not present in all the languages of the world as in (1) for English.

In Tikar (Cameroun), indirect speech can occur without a complementizer or a verb of utterance (Li 1986: 35). Instead, the third person pronoun is used as a referent to the reported speaker as in (2)

(2)   Tikar, Northern Bantoid
      Nū,   nū   nywœl imɛ   njè
      he$_{[i]}$ he$_{[i]}$ escapes   starvation
      'He (said/thought) he's escaped starvation.' (Li 1986: 36 glosses adapted)

Examples (2) and (1) show that the grammatical strategies for expressing reported speech, be it direct or indirect, vary substantially from language to language. Furthermore, the comparison of both examples shows that neither the overt expression of a complementizer or a complement taking verb are necessary to mark speech reports. In Tikar the use of the third person pronoun referring to the reported speaker suffices to mark the speech report as in (2). However, since an overt verb of speech or thought is lacking in (2), the interpretation of the report can be either of an utterance (reported speech) or a thought. In cases where the report is under specified for its determination of speech or thought, the interpretation relies either on pragmatic inferences, or the overt expression of an addressee (cf. Spronck 2015).

In languages where a lexical distinction between THINK and SAY occurs, and reported thought and speech are overtly marked with a verb of thought or speech.

The interpretation of either reported thought or speech is therefore more clear. Consider example (3) for a thought report in Hare (Canada), with an overt verb 'think', similarly to (1b) above.

(3) Hare, Athapaskan
 goyole hurédi
 3.is.crazy 1SG.think
 'I think that he is crazy' (Rice 1989: 1297)

Following the interlinear glosses in example (3), a direct report similar to (1b) above would be expected for the Hare-English translation. In Hare however, the distinction between direct and indirect speech or thought is fuzzy when a third person pronoun is embedded in a complement clause (cf. Rice 1989: 1278). Rice (1989: 1278) notes that the direct vs. indirect interpretation of a speech or thought report depends on the pronominal elements in the reported clause, as well as the lexical properties of the complement taking verb in Slave. Examples (3) and (2) show that the distinction between direct and indirect thought or speech is language specific.

Therefore, the present crosslinguistic comparison of RT constructions requires a definition of RT that is both broad enough but also precise enough to include the variety of RT constructions across the world's languages. For the purpose of this present comparison of RT across the languages of the world, a comparative concept (Haspelmath 2010) is defined. Comparative concepts are conceptual definitions that are both broad enough to include maximal morphosyntactic variation of the phenomenon under investigation and narrow enough to focus only on the phenomenon under investigation. For the purposes of this study, a comparative concept for RT across the languages of the world is defined as follows:

(4) Reported thought constructions are morphosyntactic means of expressing thoughts from others or oneself. RTs consist morphosyntactically of an overt matrix clause (M), containing a matrix verb that can be translated as 'think', that has scope over the reported clause (R) and together form a sentential unit.

As the discussion on properties of complex clauses, e.g., reported thought continues to grow, it opens up the possibility to expand the scope of comparative concepts for lexico-semantic categories to bigger morphosyntactic units, e.g., reported clauses as defined in (4) above. The definition in (4) for RT is narrow as it excludes *defenestrated* constructions where no overt matrix clause (Spronck 2017), nor an overt verb of thinking is present. In some languages of the world reported clauses of speech or thought do not necessarily need to be framed by an overt matrix clause, nor a verb of speech or thought, as in (2). In such cases, other grammatical cues such as utterance context, overt expression of an addressee, cross-referential pronouns, or other verbs that do not exclusively convey the meaning of THINK or SAY can mark an RT construction.

The comparative concept defined for the present analysis serves the purpose of clear identification of RT in the languages sampled for this study, against other closely related constructions such as speech reports. Crosslinguistic data show that in addition to reporting speech, speakers can also explicitly report thoughts. This suggests that there is a distinction between speech and thought reporting and that the latter should be analyzed in its own right. The current analysis addresses the question whether there are shared crosslinguistic properties of reported thought in order to analyze it as a category in its own right.

The present analysis will focus on the different morphosyntactic properties of RT from a balanced sample of languages. The analysis starts off by providing a comparative concept for RT in the introduction. In section 2 the sample for the present analysis will be presented. In section 3 five distinctive morphosyntactic properties of RT with examples from the data are discussed. The analysis is completed with a discussion in section 4 and conclusion in section 5. The present analysis offers a description of different morphosyntactic properties of RT, as defined in (4), across the languages of the world, as suggested by the sample.

2 Data

This section discusses the sampling method and the sample that is the basis for the present study. The core sample for the present study consists of 100 typologically diverse languages spread across the world (see Figure 1). The crosslinguistic distribution of the languages is important for this present study, as it aims to show the variety of RT across the languages. As the variety of RT is the main criterion for this study, the sample must reflect the variation across the world's languages accordingly.

In order to reflect the crosslinguistic variety of the approximately 7000 languages of the world, typological studies make use of representative samples. Typological samples can either answer statistical questions in terms of frequency and predictability (Rijkhoff et al. 1993) or show the variety of the phenomenon under investigation (Miestamo et al. 2016). The core sample for the present study was generated as part of a PhD dissertation (Casartelli forthc.), shown in Figure 1. The core sample was constructed to show the variety of reported speech constructions and their different functions across the world's languages.

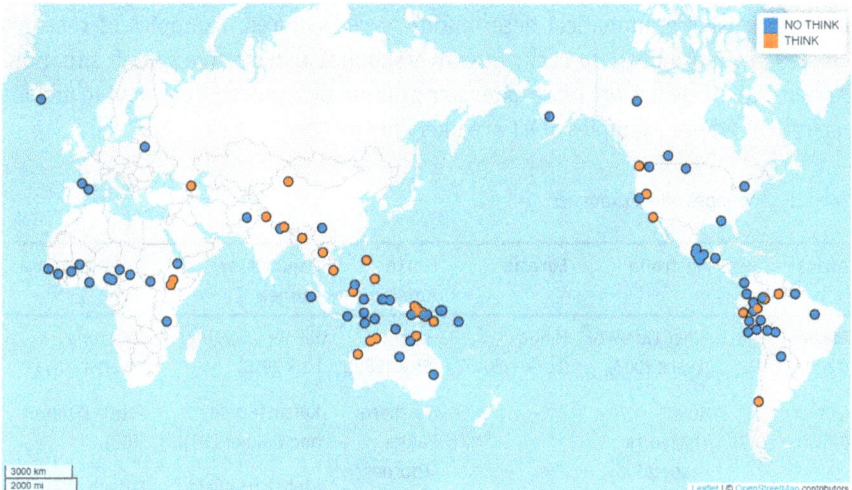

Figure 1: General sample and languages that mark reported thought.

Several data points in the sample also show a variety of reported thought expressions in the languages sampled. Based on the available data points on reported thought in the core sample, examples for the present study are chosen to provide an overview of reported thought in the languages of the world. All examples of reported thought in the sampled data show an overt verb expressing 'think', marking the thought report explicitly. Therefore, the present analysis starts from the definition of the comparative concept (4) introduced above. It serves as a definition of RT that is broad enough to include different morphosyntactic properties of RT across the languages of the world, but also narrow enough to only include RT constructions with an overt verb 'think' in the matrix clause. The comparative concept in (4) defines the clausal relations of the sampled reported thought clauses for the present analysis.

Examples of RT in the present study resemble example (3) from Hare above, or (5) from Kilmeri (Papua New Guinea) below. Both examples mark the thought report overtly with the verb 'think'.

(5) Kilmeri, Bewani Range
 Sakou umul_nek yala ko asa pi
 Sakou think.PP now I how do
 'Sakou thought: "What am I going to do now?"' (Gerstner-Link 2018: 487)

Examples (3) and (5) are drawn from descriptive grammars, i.e., maximally detailed surveys of grammatical structures for each of the sampled languages. To maximize the number of examples for reported clauses in a sampled language, more extensive grammatical descriptions were favoured. Examples of reported clauses are more likely to occur in conversational or narrative speech situations rather than in elicitation: more extensive grammatical descriptions tend to include narratives where examples of RT are likely to emerge.

Table 1: Languages of the examples.

Africa	Australia	Eurasia	North America	Papua New Guinea	South America
Maale (Amha 2011),	Bininj Gun-Wok (Evans 2003),	Hinuq (Forker 2013)	Hare (Rice 1989),	Kilmeri (Gerstner-Link 2018),	Aguaruna (Overall 2017),
Gumer (Völlmin 2017)	Kuuk Thaayorre (Gaby 2006)		Northern Paiute (Thornes 2003)	Kalam (Pawley and Bulmer 2011),	Kotiria (Stenzel 2013),
				Mehek (Hatfield 2016),	Tariana (Aikhenvald 2003b),
				Oksapmin (Loughnane 2009)	Yagua (Payne and Payne 1993)

The examples of the languages (see Table 1) discussed in the present analysis were selected to serve two purposes. First, to show the balanced crosslinguistic distribution of RT across the data and second, to show the different morphosyntactic properties of RT found in the data.

3 Reported Thought, a category in its own right

The following sections address morphosyntactic properties of thought reports in the languages of the sample. Morphosyntactic properties that are indicative of thought reports are, e.g., complement taking verbs of thinking in the matrix clause. The following sections provide a detailed analysis of five different sub-types of RT. Section 3.1 shows RT constructions where the verb 'think' overtly marks the thought report similar to the Hare example (3), and the Kilmeri example (5) above. Examples of section 3.2 focus on the verb 'think' in a serial verb construction in the matrix clause. Serial verb constructions are non-hierarchical sequences of multiple verbs that describe the same event. Section 3.3 shows converb constructions of RT with the verb 'think'. A converb functions as a subordinator or coordinator in complement clauses. In section 3.4 the analysis focuses on RT constructions with quotative markers. Quotative markers are elements that function as markers of reported clauses in reported thought or speech constructions. Section 3.5 shows the expression of RT through nominal incorporation. Nominal incorporation describes the property of verbs to incorporate nouns.

3.1 THINK in the matrix clause

With reference to the comparative concept introduced above in (4), thought reports are bi-clausal structures that consist morphosyntactically of an overt matrix clause (M), containing a matrix verb that can be translated as 'think', that has scope over the reported clause (R) and together form a sentential unit. Thought reports discussed in this analysis are framed by verbs of thinking in the matrix clause, meaning that a verb of thinking is overtly expressed and can take a reported clause as its complement.

In Bininj Gun-Wok (Australia), thought reports are framed with overt verbs of thinking that can take reported clauses as their complements. Evans (2003: 637) notes that in Bininj Gun-Wok, thought and utterance reports are direct, comparable to (1a-b) for English above. Direct reports preserve the utterance or thought as it is actually thought or spoken by the original speaker. Therefore, TAM marking, pronouns and number values in the reported clause remain as they were uttered or thought originally. In Bininj Gun-Wok, the verb in the matrix clause is usually inflected perfective or imperfective (Evans 2003: 637). In example (6) below, the matrix verb *yim* 'think' is inflected for past-imperfective, framing the thought report. The verb of the reported clause is marked for non-past (NP) tense, preserving the tense marking of the original thought. The person values in both matrix and reported clause show different object marking. While the matrix verb is marked for third person singular, the verb in the reported clause is marked for third person singular lower object (l). Lower object marking in Bininj Gun-Wok indicates the animacy hierarchy. The person values of the verbs in the matrix and reported clause are different, the agent in the reported clause and the subject of the matrix clause are not co-referential. This indicates that the original thinker in example (6) is reflecting on actions she has observed from someone other than herself.

(6) Bininj Gun-Wok, Marne
...ø-yim-i   "Ka-bu-n   kinga".
3-think-IPFV   3/3l-kill-NP   crocodile
'... she was thinking "He is killing the crocodile".' (Evans 2003: 637)

Similarly as in (6) from Bininj Gun-Wok, reported clauses preserve the TAM and pronominal marking from the original thought in Kilmeri (Papua New Guinea). In

(7) from Kilmeri (Papua New Guinea) below, the thought is framed by the matrix verb *umul* 'think' that is inflected for punctual past. The subject of the matrix clause references the author of the original thought, the older brother. Both pronouns in the reported clause are co-referential with the subject of the matrix clause.

(7) Kilmeri, Bewani Range
 ewe   umul_nek   diri   ko-pi   suloimoina
 older.brother think.PP younger.brother 1SG-POSS   extraordinarily
 mari   yala ko asa   pi
 be.sick now   I   how   do
 'The older brother thought: "My younger brother is terribly sick, what am I going to do now?"' (Gerstner-Link 2018: 487)

Matrix clauses of RTs as in, e.g., (6) or (7) above can also contain other elements such as particles that are relevant for framing a thought report. For Kuuk Thaayorre (Australia), Gaby (2006: 567) notes that in order to introduce a thought or speech report, the particle *yarriy* 'thus' is present in the matrix clause. In example (8) the particle *yarriy* 'thus' stands before the matrix verb *neegy* 'think'. The particle 'thus' always immediately precedes the predicate of an event (Gaby 2006: 570). In reports it therefore precedes the matrix verb introducing the report as follows:

(8) Kuuk Thaayorre, Northern Pama-Nyungan
 ngancn   yarriy   ngeey-m: "kee! [...]"
 1PL:EXCL(NOM)   thus   think-P.IPFV   hey
 'then we were thinking: "hey! [maybe Dad and Mum have had an accident]"' (Gaby 2006: 568)

In (8), other than in the examples discussed thus far, the subject of the matrix clause is marked with first person plural and not singular. A plural marking on the subject of the matrix clause suggests that the thought that is reported is shared between two people. In (8) the original thinkers of the reported thought and current speakers are indicated by the personal pronoun *ngancn* 'first person plural exclusive'. The content of the reported clause provides further information about the authors of the original thought. The shared thought most likely originated from siblings, as they report thoughts on their parents' state. This is sustained by the exclusive marking on the personal pronoun in the matrix clause, meaning that the speakers reference themselves but not the addressee. Exclusive marking in free independent pronouns, as in (8) reference the speakers, but necessarily exclude the addressee (Cysouw 2013). In (8) both the marking of the personal pronoun referring to the original speakers and the content of the report indicate that a pair of siblings refer to their own thoughts about their parents. The marking of the personal pronoun is a morphosyntactic property that can be interpreted unambiguously and is indicative of the authors of the thought. The content of the reported clause in (8) also indicates that siblings are thinking about their parents together at the same time.

The examples from Bininj Gun-Wok (6), Kilmeri (7), and Kuuk Thaayorre (8) above share the morphosyntactic property of framing thought reports with the verb 'think' for each respective language. Another shared property across the examples above is that the reported clause preserves the pronominal and TAM marking of the original thought in each respective language. The examples above also show that speakers can reference the actions of someone else in their thoughts as in (6) from Bininj Gun-Wok or (8) from Kuuk Thaayorre, but also address thoughts to themselves as in (7) from Kilmeri. Furthermore, another interesting observation of pronominal reference can be made in example (8) from Kuuk Thaayorre. In (8), the subject of the matrix clause is plural, indicating that the thought is shared between two people. In (8) specifically, a pair of siblings reports their shared concern about their parents, making it plausible for them to share the thought of concern together. Another observation for example (8) is that matrix clauses can contain other elements, e.g., particles that are used to frame reported clauses in addition to complement taking verbs of thinking.

3.2 RT serial verb constructions

Serial verb constructions (SVCs) have been attested in many languages in all regions of the world (Bisang 2009; Enfield 2009; Haspelmath 2016 *inter alia*). Haspelmath (2016: 292) defines SVCs as "monoclausal construction consisting of multiple independent verbs with no element linking them and with no predicate–argument relation between the verbs". Therefore, SVCs are characterized as a non-hierarchical sequence of multiple verbs that describe the same event. The following examples from different languages of the Americas and Papua New Guinea will show how thought reports can be framed with SVCs where the verb 'think' appears alongside verbs of utterance, e.g., 'say', or verbs of perception, e.g., 'hear', 'perceive', or 'think' in the examples below.

In example (9) from Hare (Canada) the verb *hurédi* expresses thought referencing the current speaker and may occur with other verbs of thinking in the matrix clause of a thought report (Rice 1989: 1297).

(9) Hare, Athapaskan
 hịdowedzíné k'e ịt desh a duhshá hurédi yerehwę
 tomorrow on bush 1SG OPT.go 1SG.think 1SG.think
 'I think I'll go to the bush tomorrow' (Rice 1989: 1297)

Example (9) shows that serialized verbs can also occur in a matrix clause that frames a reported clause. In Hare, as Rice (1989: 1279) notes, there is more than one verb for the English gloss 'think'. In (9) the verb *hurédi, think* can co-occur in the matrix clause together with the verb *yerehw* that is also glossed as 'think'. Both verbs have the same person marking but do not stand in an argument hierarchy with each other. The verbs in the matrix clause and the personal pronoun in the reported clauses marked first person singular. This indicates that the subject of the matrix clause and the subject of the reported clause are co-referential. Co-referential subject of matrix and reported clause means that the current speaker is referencing, i.e., reporting their own thoughts.

In Aguaruna (Peru) Overall (2017: 562) states that reported thought and speech constructions are cognate. In Aguaruna, complement taking verbs of speech and thought can frame speech or thought reports. Overall (2017: 562) notes that it is not always possible to clearly distinguish between thought or speech reports, as the report construction in Aguaruna is used to express both speech and thought reports. This underspecification of distinction between speech and thought reports is observed in other languages across the world as well. Especially in languages that do not have a strict lexical distinction between the verbs 'think' and 'say' as described in Voort (2002) for South American languages, (Güldemann 2008) for African languages.

The matrix clause in example (10) is on the right periphery and contains the serialized verbs 'think' and 'live' that frame the reported clause. The verb 'think' is non-finite and the verb 'live' is inflected for imperfective aspect, number and bears a different subject marker. The difference in subject marking in the matrix and reported clause indicates that the action the current speaker is thinking about is carried out by something or someone else other than himself. In the reported clause, the verb 'say' is marked with the non-temporal subordinator marker. It immediately follows the verb 'think' in the matrix clause and marks the beginning of the reported clause. The function of the verb 'say' as a subordinator in the reported clause for the matrix verb 'think' in the matrix clause is an indication that example (10) represents a thought report. Another morphosyntactic property of (10) that is indicative of a thought report is the lack of an overt reported addressee in the reported clause.

(10) Aguaruna, Jivaroan
[*wahĩ tuhã=sha wahĩ ta-wa tus] an intaima*
what but=ADD what say+IPFV-3 say+SBD+3:SS think
puha-ĩ
live+IPFV+1SG/3-DS
'as he was thinking "what's making that noise?". . .' lit. as he was thinking, saying "what says that?" (Overall 2017: 565)

As illustrated (10) a clear distinction between speech and thought reports is not always possible based on the lexical meaning of verbs of speech or thought in the languages of the world. In languages where verbs of speech and thought can equally represent speech or thought reports, other morphosyntactic properties are indicative for the distinction. Spronck (2015a) notes that the absence of an overt reported addressee in the reported clause can be indicative for the distinction between thought and speech reports. The absence of an overt reported addressee as in (10) from Aguaruna above, suggests that the speaker addresses himself, rather than speaking to an addressee. Self-addressed speech in turn suggests an internal monologue that can be interpreted as an expression of thought.

In Kalam (Papua New Guinea) similarly to example (10) from Aguaruna, reported clauses are framed by the verb 'say, speak' that can co-occur with other verbs in the matrix clause in a SVC. In example (11) from Kalam the verb -*ag* 'say' frames the reported clause and is serialized with the verbs *gos* 'think' and *n* 'perceive' in the matrix clause. The verb 'say' is marked with the same subject prior marker, indicating that the reported clause takes internal reference, i.e., the original speaker referencing himself. The last root of the serial verb construction further is marked for perfective aspect and first person singular, congruent with the same subject marker on the verb 'say'. Similarly to the examples from Hare (9) and Aguaruna (10) above, in example (11) from Kalam, verbs in the matrix clauses of thought complements can be serialized to frame the report.

(11) Kalam, Madang
"*Tap   ak   d-in!*"   *ag-i*   *gos*   *n-b-in.*
thing   that   get-HORT.1SG   say-SS.PRIOR   thought   perceive-PF-1SG
'I want that thing.' (lit. '"Let me get that thing", having said he thought.')
(Pawley and Bulmer 2011: 64)

Example (11) shows another interesting aspect of reported thought constructions. In Kalam, wanting something is typically expressed with a self-addressed speech or thought representation, as in (11) (Pawley and Bulmer 2011: 64). According to Pawley and Bulmer (2011) reported clauses that express 'want' contain an SVC where the final root is marked with first person singular hortative e. This hortative clause is in turn always a complement of the verb 'say' or 'think' (Pawley and Bulmer 2011). Example (11) shows that in some languages, the morphosyntactic structure of complement clauses in combination with specific elements in the reported clause, can be used to express a sentence meaning apart from regular quotation meaning (c.f. Spronck and Casartelli (2021) for a broader discussion on reported clauses without regular quotation meaning).

In example (12) from Kotiria (Brazil, Colombia) the Reported clause is framed by the serial verb construction in the martix clause of the verbs 'say', 'hear', 'think'. In Kotiria, SVCs are characterized by denoting a single semantic event, are realized as a single phonological word and only the last root bears inflectional markers (Stenzel 2013: 379). Stenzel (2013: 145) notes that example (12) below stems from a narrative where the narrator describes an encounter between a man and a creature. Example (12) shows the moment where the man realizes that the creature wants to harm him. The mental process of realization is morphosyntactically expressed through the reported thought construction. The reported clause contains the realization, i.e., the thought about the creature's malicious intentions. The matrix clause frames the report with the serialized verbs of perception 'say', 'hear', 'think' that describe the event of realization in (12). In Kotiria, according to Stenzel (2013: 371), the verb 'say' is the all-purpose speech verb that takes speech or thought complements. When 'say' functions as a matrix verb of a reported clause, it can co-occur with other verbs framing the same report as in (12) below following Stenzel (2013).

(12) Kotiria, Tucanoan
yʉ'ʉú+ré   a'rí+ró   chʉú-dua+ro   dí-ka
1SG+OBJ   DEM.PROX+SG   eat-DESID+(3)SG   be.PROG-ASSERT.IMPERF
dí-tho-thu+a
say-hear-think+ASSERT.PERF
'"This thing (the curupira) wants to eat me," he said to himself.' (Stenzel 2013: 145)

The final root of the matrix verbs in example (12) is marked with the perfective assertive evidential. The assertive evidential is used to express the speaker's own internalized evidence on a circumstance or the world based on their own experience of the world (Stenzel 2013: 285). The evidential marking on the final root of the matrix verbs 'think' further underlines the mental process of realization by the original speaker. Example (12) shows the simultaneous realization and expression of thought by the original speaker. He thinks about the intentions of the creature, realizes that it wants to eat him and expresses his realization to himself.

In some languages of the world the source of evidence for knowledge over a circumstance must necessarily be expressed for every utterance. In languages where the source of evidence must be stated, the grammatical category is referred to as *evidentiality* (Aikhenvald 2003a). In languages where these evidential markers are necessary, the source of evidence is part of the verbal morphology.

In Tariana (Brazil) the source of knowledge, i.e., evidence for a statement, must necessarily be expressed (Aikhenvald 2003b). The evidentiality system of Tariana has several different evidentiality markers based on how the source of knowledge was obtained, e.g., visual, non-visual, inferred or reported (Aikhenvald 2003b: 287). The reported evidential in Tariana is used to indicate, for instance, that the information has been obtained through secondhand or thirdhand knowledge. The reportative is also the preferred evidentiality marker in story-telling and narratives (Aikhenvald 2003b: 294).

Reported speech or thought constructions are an inherent part of narratives. In Tariana, direct speech complements are the most common way of marking complements of speech verbs or verbs of thinking (Aikhenvald 2003b: 553). Certain verbs in Tariana, such as -*mheta* 'think, feel' and -*awada* 'think, remember', can only take direct speech complements that contain a non-visual or inferred evidentiality (Aikhenvald 2003b: 554). In examples (13) and (14) below the reported clause is framed by the two verbs 'say' and 'think' in the matrix clause and the reportative evidential. In both examples the subject of the matrix clause and the reported clause are co-referential.

(13) Tariana, Inland Northern Arawakan
 [kaida wyaka-sika nu-nu nhua] di-a
 how.much far-PAST.INFR.INTER 1SG-come I 3SGnf-say
 dihmeta-pidana
 3SGnf+think-REM.P.REP
 '"How far did I come?" he said in this thought, he looked in vain for the road he had taken.' (Aikhenvald 2003b: 554)

The point of reference of the reportative evidential in Tariana refers, according to Aikhenvald (2003b: 288), to the point in time where the information was received. In (13) the reportative evidential is marked with remote past, meaning that the information has been received in the remote past. The person marking on both matrix verbs is third person plural, indicating that the thought originates from two people. Aikhenvald (2003b: 477) notes that example (14) stems from a Hänsel-and-Gretel type story. Similarly as in example (8) from Kuuk Thaayorre and in (14) from Tariana, the authors of the reported thought share a close bond and can therefore report a shared thought together.

(14) Tariana, Inland Northern Arawakan
 ka: wa: wa-ñale-niki na:-pida na:wada
 in.vain 1PL+go 1PL-disappear-COMPL 3PL+say-REP 3PL+think
 nha-tupe-nhe [ai paite] inau [pa:-ma]
 they-DIM:PL-FOC.A/S man one+NUM.CL:HUMAN woman one-CL:FEM
 '"We are going to disappear in vain," thought the little ones, a male and a female.' (Aikhenvald 2003b: 477)

Aikhenvald (2003b), Forker (2013) and Loughnane (2009) note that direct speech complements with verbs of thinking or speaking occur frequently in narratives. As seen for examples (14) and (13) from Tariana above, the reportative evidential occurs in reported speech or thought constructions from narratives or stories.

All examples above show that serialized verbs can occur in the matrix clauses and scope over complement clauses. In example (9) from Hare, two verbs of thinking can frame a reported clause. In (10) from Aguaruna, (12) from Kotiria, and (11) from Kalam, the serialized verbs of perception, thought, and utterance in the matrix clause scope over a reported clause. The verbs of SVCs in matrix clauses can also be marked with language specific verbal morphology, e.g., evidentiality as seen in examples (13) and (14) from Tariana.

3.3 RT converb constructions

In some languages, complex clauses require a linking element in other to frame the complement clause additionally to the complement taking verb. A linking element can be, e.g., a complementizer or a converb. Haspelmath (1995: 3) defines a converb as "a nonfinite verb form whose main function is to mark adverbial subordination". Nonfiniteness of a verb is defined as verbs that lack tense, mood, aspect marking, as well as argument agreement. Converbs are usually defined as nonfinite (Haspelmath 1995). Adverbial subordination refers to the syntactic function of converbs. They modify different verbs, clauses or sentences, excluding noun phrases (Haspelmath 1995). Clausal modification, subordination and coordination are syntactic properties that are often associated with reported thought and speech constructions (cf. Coulmas 1986) and other complex clauses. In some languages, the verb 'say' is a converb that functions as a linking element in thought reports.

In Maale (Ethiopia) converbs are often used as adverbial modifiers to a main verb (Amha 2001: 145). In (15) and (16) the converb 'say' functions as a linking element between the matrix clause and the reported clause. The aspectual marking in examples (15) and (16) below indicates the time of utterance of the reported thought in relation with the time of the reported event. The main verb in the matrix clause is marked for imperfective aspect and affirmative declarative mood in (15), while the main verb in the reported clause is marked for future imperfective aspect. In (16) the main verb of the matrix clause is marked with perfective aspect and affirmative declarative mood, as well as the main verb of the reported clause.

(15) Maale, North Omotic
táání?ízá   booka   ?áád-andá-ne   ge?-í   mal-a-ne
1SG:NOM3FS:NOM   market:ABS   go-F:IPVF-NMZ   say-CNV   think-IPFV-A:DCL
'I think she will go to the market' (Amha 2001: 175)

(16) Maale, North Omotic
?iini   ?iyátá   mádd-ó   ?ek'-is-é-ne   ge-í   mal-é-ne
3MS:NOM   3PL:NOM   work-ABS   stop-CAUS-PF-A:DCL   say-CNV   think-PF-A:DCL
'He thought that they stopped working' (Amha 2001: 149)

The converb -*í* in Maale is used to express sequential or simultaneous events in relation to the event expressed by the main verb (Amha 2001). In the examples above the converb is used to expresses the simultaneous or sequential event of thinking and reporting that thought. In both examples, the current speaker expresses, i.e., externalizes his thoughts on a circumstance he observes. In both examples (15) and (16) the reported clause takes an external reference, meaning that the agent of the action in the reported clause is not co-referential with the subject of the matrix clause.

In Aguaruna (Peru), the verb 'say' when marked with the non-temporal subordinate marker SBD and functions as a subordinator marking the beginning of the reported clause. When in this function, the subordinator immediately follows the matrix verb in the main clause. In example (17) the matrix verb 'think' in the matrix clause is preceded by the verb 'say' in its function as a subordinator in the reported clause, similar to (15) and (16) from Maale above.

(17) Aguaruna, Jivaroan
nu=ĩ   shita   shitama-ha-kawa
ANA=LOC   REDUP   crawl-APPL+IPFV-REPET+1PL:SS
i-tsɨk-cha-ta-ha=sha   tu-sa
CAUS-jump+PFV-NEG-1FUT-1SG=ADD   say-SBD+1PL:SS
anɨntaima-ta-kawa
think-APPL+IPFV-REPET+1PL:SS
'crawling and crawling there, thinking "I won't startle it"' (Overall 2017: 302)

In Gumer (Ethiopia) the converb of *bar* occurs as a complementizer with verbs of thinking including *ass* 'think' (Völlmin 2017: 169) as in (18).

(18) Gumer, Semitic
  əxʷa   iyya   mir   wə-tot   nər-ə-ßi   ba-xʷ-im
  now   1s   what   INF-work   EX-3sMs-MAL.1s   say.PFV-1SS-CV.M
  assəßt-xʷ-im.
  think.PFV-1SS-M
  'I thought: "Now, what do I have to do?"' (Völlmin 2017: 169)

The example above (18) shows that the subordinating converb and the matrix verb share the same subject (ibid.). Based on the argument agreement and tense marking on the converb, it would not fall under the definition of converbs above. However, nonfiniteness seems not to be a necessary requirement to define a converb in Gumer, as long as the converb functions as a subordinator. For the example above, Völlmin (2017: 169) notes that the converb *bar* can occur as a complementizer i.e., subordinating element for complex clauses that not only express quotation. This is indicative that the converb *bar* has lost its primary semantic meaning of 'say' and functions as a complementizer for complement taking verbs in general. In the examples from Aguaruna, Gumer, and Maale above, the converb 'say' functions as a coordinator (Maale), complementizer (Gumer), or subordinator (Aguaruna) framing the report together with the matrix verb 'think' as a reported thought. It is not uncommon in the languages of the world for the verb 'say' to lose its primary semantic meaning and function as a complementizer, or subordinator (Kouteva et al. 2019: 375).

3.4 RT with quotative markers

In some languages of the world, complements of thought or speech reports are marked with quotative markers. Quotative markers are described by Güldemann (2008: 122) as dedicated function words that frame reported clauses. Similarly to the converbs discussed in section 3.3 above, quotative markers have a limited semantic meaning of their own, but a clear morphosyntactic function. The morphosyntactic function of quotative markers to mark reported clauses may extend to mark complements of other complement taking verbs in some languages. For Hinuq (Dagestan), Forker (2013: 612) notes that the quotative enclitic =en is used to introduce complements of many types of verbs including *urezi* 'think'. In (19) the quotative enclitic is cliticized to the first base in the reported clause, immediately preceding the complement taking verb 'think'.

(19) Hinuq, Avar-Andic-Tsezic
[haɬu-s   ma?na   se=ƛen]   uryezi   Ø-iq-no   hado   uži
this.OBL-GEN1   sense   what=QUOT think   I-happen-UWPST   this   boy(I)
'What is the sense of this, he thinks.' (Forker 2013: 615)

In Hinuq, as illustrated in (19) the complement of the verb think is marked with the quotative enclitic on the first base. The quotative enclitic in the reported clause together with the complement taking verb 'think' in the matrix clause mark RT constructions in Hinuq.

In Oksapmin (Papua New Guinea), similarly to Hinuq, complement clauses of thought reports are framed by verbs of thought in the matrix clause and a quotative marker in the reported clause. According to Loughnane (2009: 412) the quotative enclitic =o attaches to the first base of the Reported clause immediately preceding the matrix verb in the matrix clause. Examples (20) and (21) show thought reports that are framed by the verb *da* 'think' in the matrix clause and the quotative enclitic =o in the complement clause.

(20) Oksapmin, Oksapmin
in   ux=ja   kin   m-ti-plox   s=o
so   3sf=O   how   make-PFV-TODF.SG   INFR=QUOT
da=x-ti-p=li=a
think=do-PFV.PER.FP.SG=REP=LINK
'"What can I possibly do with her?", he thought.' (Loughnane 2009: 343)

(21) Oksapmin, Oksapmin
jəxe   nuxul   [nix   ix=x-pat=o]   da   x-m
then   1pEX   who   like.that=do-IPFV.SG(.PRS)=QUOT   thought   do-SEQ
'Then, we thought "who is doing that" and. . .' (Loughnane 2009: 427)

In example (20) the matrix verb 'think' is further marked with the reportative evidential. The reportative evidential in Oksapmin, similarly to Tariana discussed in 3.2 above, is used i.a. in stories and narratives. The occurrence of the reportative evidential in (20) indicates that the sentence is part of an Oksapmin story or narrative (cf. Loughnane 2009: 343).

In example (21), similarly to example (8) from Kuuk Thaayorre in §3.1, the person marking on the matrix verb is third person plural, indicating that there are two original authors reporting the thought. A possible explanation for the third person plural marking in the M clause could be a collective thought that originates from a shared experience or a close bond of the speakers.

In Northern Paiute (USA), the function of the quotative marker corresponds with that in Hinuq and Oksapmin above. Similarly as in Hinuq and Oksapmin, the quotative marker in Northern Paiute marks the beginning of the reported clause. Reported clauses are marked by the quotative *mii* and framed by the complement taking verb in the matrix clause (Thornes 2003: 447). In (22) the verb 'think' takes the reported complement headed by the quotative marker.

(22) Northern Paiute, Numic
su=nɨmɨ   mogoʔni u-tuha-u   ija   owi-u   watsi-kwɨ mii
NOM=person   woman   3-under-U enter   DEM-U   hide-FUT   QUOT
sunami-na
think-PTCP
'The Indian woman went in under there. "(I) will hide in there," so (she was) thinking, (Thornes 2003: 224)

As described for examples (19), (20), (21), and (22), some languages of the world use quotative markers to mark the complement clause of thought or speech reports. In all of the examples above from Hinuq, Oksapmin and Northern Paiute, the quotative marker immediately precedes the complement taking verb of the matrix clause in the reported clause. Quotative markers are particles or clitics that are semantically bleached, i.e., do not have word-referring meaning. However, quotative markers function as framing elements indicating the beginning of the complement clause in a reported thought or speech constructions.

3.5 RT with nominal incorporation

In some languages thought reports are not overtly distinguishable from the complement taking verb in the matrix clause alone. Other elements in the matrix or reported clause may be indicative for the distinction. In Yagua (Peru) complements of the verb 'think' are infrequent in oral narrative discourse according to Payne and Payne (1990: 260). In their description, reported thought constructions use the verbalized noun 'heart', as illustrated in example (23) below. Forker (2013: 105) notes that the metaphorical representation of thoughts or emotions are frequently linked to the heart throughout the languages of the world. Example (23) from Yagua shows the internal process of the speaker thinking about an utterance of hers. At the core of her thought lies a verbal interaction with an interlocutor. That verbal interaction, i.e., direct speech is embedded within her thought. First, the direct speech of the original interaction between the speaker and her interlocutor is marked by the verb of utterance *jtay* meaning 'say'. Direct speech reports are marked by verbs of utterance in Yagua (Payne and Payne 1990: 334). That speech report is again embedded by the noun *jaachiy* 'heart' that is marked as an instrumental. The first occurrence of the noun 'heart' is marked with a verbalizer, rendering the function of the noun to that of a verb. Therefore, the verbalized noun is also inflected for mood (imperfective), tense (distant or legendary past), and person (third dual). The second occurrence of the noun 'heart' is marked as an instrumental and is co-referential with the person marking of the incorporated noun. In example (23) the verbalized noun and the co-referential nounphrase in the left peripheral matrix clause frame the construction as a reported thought as follows:

(23) Yagua, Peba-Yagua
naada-jaachiy-píiyąą-núúy-janu   jíy-jaachiy-ta   ráy   jį́įta
3DL-heart-VBLZR-IMPERF-PAST3   COR1-heart-INST   1SG:PRO   JIITA
naada-jųtay   naada-íva
3DL-say   3DL-DAT
'She was thinking in her heart. "I, yes," she$_i$ says to her$_j$.' (Payne and Payne 1990: 308)

Payne and Payne (1990: 335) note that reported clauses are framed by verbs of speech and do not require a complementizer. However, if the subject of the reported clause is not marked first or second person, but coreferential with the person marking in the matrix verb, the coreferential clitic COR1 is used. Example (23) illustrates the occurrence of the coreferential subject clitic in the matrix clause linking the thought process 'thinking in her heart' to the reported clause "I, yes". The particle *jiita* in the context of the example above (23) functions as a rhetorical underliner according to Payne and Payne (1990: 308), expressing high commitment to the utterance by the speaker. Example (23) illustrates the difference between observable speech i.e., the reported utterance and the internal domain of thought. According to Kockelman (2010: 20) the *heart* is found in many grammatical constructions metaphorically representing the internal state of mind. Example (23) shows that the meaning of the sentence has to be interpreted as a mental representation or thought of a verbal interaction that the current thinker is recalling. On the morphosyntactic level we can observe convoluted embedding of a speech report within a thought report, nominal incorporation and the metaphorical expression of thought through the heart.

4 Discussion

The present analysis has shown that languages of the world have different morphosyntactic strategies to express thought reports. In order to compare and identify reported thought constructions throughout the world's languages, a comparative concept is defined. In (4), reported thought for the purpose of the present analysis is defined as a bi-clausal structure consisting of an overt matrix clause (M), containing a matrix verb that can be translated as 'think', that has scope over the reported clause (R) and together form a sentential unit.

A common property throughout the examples discussed is the overt presence of a verb that can be translated as 'think' in the matrix clause. In some languages, reported thought constructions have metaphorical use of the heart to represent mental, or internal activities of reflection or thinking. Another distinctive property of reported thought constructions is the lack of an overt reported addressee in the reported clause. Considering the shared morphosyntactic properties of thought reports throughout the world's languages, they are comparable with those of speech reporting.

Several different strategies of framing thought reports in genealogically distinct languages of the world showed that while some languages show similar strategies, others have less frequent strategies for framing thought reports. In example (23) from Yagua the complement taking verb of the reported thought is the verbalized noun 'heart' that is translated as 'think' in English. The Yagua example shows that not all languages may have a verb to convey the meaning of thinking. The notion of thinking is however expressed with another morphosyntactic strategy that conveys the same meaning as 'thinking' in SAE (standard average European) languages, as Nikitina and Aplonova have also discussed in their chapter in the present volume. Example (23) shows that while not all languages have a distinct verb that conveys the notion of thinking, the distinction from reported thought and speech is clear. In (23) the utterance report "I, yes," she$_i$ says to her$_j$' is in turn the complement clause of the verbalized noun 'heart'. Double embeddings of thought and speech reports with distinct matrix verbs in their respective matrix clauses can be an indication for distinguishing reported thought from reported speech in the respective languages. Double embeddings of speech reports within thought reports are not a phenomenon that happens exclusively in Yagua. In Mehek (Papua New Guinea) speech reports can also be clausal complements of the complement taking verb think as in (24) below.

(24) Mehek, Tama Sepik
su   ka   hiki-m-s   ka   su   eku-m   yombo-r   naka
3SG.F   REAL think-PAST2-3SG.F REAL 3SG.F do-DEP   SIM-INF   and
i   re   eloko-m-s   ka   ke-m   nu-ra   ke-r-a
go   3SG.M.OBJ say-PAST2-3SG.F REAL PROX-M 2SG-EMP PROX-M-EMP
a   on   ke-r-a   a-tn
eat 1SG   PROX-M-EMP   eat-1SG.IMP
She thought that while she [went to the garden], she would go and say to him, "You eat this [one] and I will eat this [one]." (Hatfield 2016: 237)

Examples similar to (23) and (24) show that while languages have different strategies of framing reported clauses, it is possible to distinguish between thought and speech reports in the world's languages. What the present analysis has also shown is that more research is needed to further describe RT in the languages of the world. This first description of morphosyntactic properties of RT has limited scope, as it focuses on a specific type of clausal relations that are used to express RT as defined in (4). Further research should also take into account underspecified reported clauses in the absence of an overtly expressed matrix clause and the status of the addressee in the reported clause. Furthermore, reports that are nested in other reports as in (23) and (24) need also be part of the discussion. The crosslinguistic study of RT should be broadened to capture thought reports that go beyond the definition scope in (4), in order to obtain a more comprehensive understanding about thought reports.

5 Conclusion

The present analysis shows that despite genealogical differences in the languages of the world, expressions of reported thought cluster together with similar morphosyntactic properties. Some of these morphosyntactic properties depend on language specific verbal morphology e.g., nominal incorporation, or grammatical categories such as evidentiality. However large the variation of language specific morphosyntactic properties of RT, a closer analysis shows that RT should be discussed as a category in its own right.

This claim is sustained by the data presented and discussed throughout section 3 where five distinct morphosyntactic properties of RT have been identified. RT is usually expressed by one of the following:
1) 'think' as the only verb in the matrix clause
2) 'think' in a serial verb construction in the matrix clause

3) 'think' in a converb construction in the matrix clause
4) 'think' co-occurring with a quotative marker in the matrix clause
5) 'think' with nominal incorporation in the matrix clause

How RT is expressed in a particular language depends on the grammatical system and morphosyntactic rules of each language. Languages with similar grammatical and verbal categories express RT in a similar manner. This in turn allows for a broad-scale crosslinguistic comparison of the morphosyntactic properties of RT that has been lacking in the typological literature. It is insufficient to assume that reported thought co-patterns in all circumstances with reported speech (a closely related category no doubt) and should be therefore analysed as a sub-type of reported speech. This present analysis focuses on the expression of RT solely with the aim to open up further analysis on the subject as a category in its own right.

Abbreviations

A:DCL	affirmative declarative
ABS	absolutive
ADD	additive
ANA	anaphoric pronoun
APPL	applicative
ASSERT	assertion
CAUS	causative
CL:FEM	classifier feminine
CL:HUMAN	classifier human
CNV	converb
COR1	coreferential clitic
CV.M	m-converb
DAT	dative
DEM	demonstrative
DEP	dependency
DESID	desiderative
DIM	diminutive
DL	dual number
DS	different subject
EMP	emphatic
EX (Oksapmin)	exclusive
EX (Gumer)	verb of existence
EXCL	exclusive
FOC.A/S	focussed subject
FP	far past
FS	feminine subject

FUT	future
GEN	genitive
HORT	hortative
IMP	imperative
IMPERF	imperfective
INF	infinitive
INFR	inferred
INTER	interrogative
IPFV	imperfective
JIITA	discourse enclitic
l	lower object
LINK	prosodic linker
LOC	locative
M	main verb marker
MAL	malefactive-locative-instrumental
MS	masculine subject
NEG	negative
NMZ	nominalizer
NOM	nominative case
NP	non-past
NUM	numeral classifier
O	(primary) object
OBJ	object
OBL	oblique
OPT	optative
P.IPFV	past imperfective
PAST	past
PAST2	2nd past tense: verbal suffix indicating that action occurred a few months ago
PAST3	3rd past tense: verbal suffix indicating that action occurred in the distant or legendary past
PER	personal-factual evidential
PERF	perfective
PF	perfective aspect
PL	plural
POSS	possessive
PP	punctual past
PRIOR	prior to time of act denoted by next following verb
PRO	pronominal base
PROG	progressive
PROX	proximal
PRS	present
PTCP	participle (action nominalizer)
QUOT	quotative
REAL	realis
REDUP	reduplication
REM.P	remote past
REP	reported

REPET	repetitive
S	singular
S	subject
SBD	non-temporal subordinator
SEQ	sequential
SG	singular
SIM	simultaneous
SS	same subject
TODF	today future
U	unidentified particle
UWPST	unwitnessed past
VBLZR	verbalizer

References

Aikhenvald, Alexandra Y. 2003a. Evidentiality in Typological Perspective. *Typological Studies in Language* 54. 1–32.

Aikhenvald, Alexandra Y. 2003b. *A Grammar of Tariana, from Northwest Amazonia*. Cambridge: Cambridge University Press.

Amha, Azeb. 2001. *The Maale Language*. Leiden: Leiden University dissertation.

Bisang, Walter. 2009. Serial Verb Constructions. *Language and Linguistics Compass* 3(3). 792–814.

Casartelli, Daniela E. (forthcoming). *A Typology of Extended Meanings of Reported Speech*. Helsinki: University of Helsinki dissertation.

Coulmas, Florian. 1986. Reported Speech: Some General Issues. In Florian Coulmas (ed.), *Direct and Indirect Speech*, 1–28. Berlin & New York: Mouton de Gruyter.

Cysouw, Michael. 2013. Inclusive/Exclusive Distinction in Independent Pronouns. In Matthew S. Dryer & Martin Haspelmath (eds.), *The World Atlas of Language Structures Online*. Leipzig: Max Planck Institute for Evolutionary Anthropology.https://wals.info/chapter/39.

Enfield, Nicholas J. 2009. Serial Verb Constructions: A Cross-Linguistic Typology. *Language* 85(2). 445–51.

Evans, Nicholas. 2003. *Bininj Gun-Wok: A Pan-Dialectal Grammar of Mayali, Kunwinjku and Kune*. (Pacific Linguistics Vol. 541). Canberra: Research School of Pacific; Asian Studies, Australian National University.

Forker, Diana. 2013. *A Grammar of Hinuq*. (Mouton Grammar Library Vol. 63). Berlin & Boston: De Gruyter Mouton.

Gaby, Alice Rose. 2006. *A Grammar of Kuuk Thaayorre*. Melbourne: The University of Melbourne dissertation.

Gerstner-Link, Claudia. 2018. *A Grammar of Kilmeri*. Pacific Linguistics. Berlin & Boston: De Gruyter Mouton.

Güldemann, Tom. 2008. *Quotative Indexes in African Languages*. Berlin & Boston: Mouton de Gruyter.

Haspelmath, Martin. 1995. The Converb as a Cross-Linguistically Valid Category. In Haspelmath, Martin & Ekkehard König (eds.), *Converbs in Cross-Linguistic Perspective: Structure and Meaning of Adverbial Verb Forms – Adverbial Participles, Gerunds*, 1–56. Berlin & New York: Mouton de Gruyter.

Haspelmath, Martin. 2010. Comparative Concepts and Descriptive Categories in Crosslinguistic Studies. *Language* 86(3). 663–87.
Haspelmath, Martin. 2016. The Serial Verb Construction: Comparative Concept and Cross- Linguistic Generalizations. *Language and Linguistics* 17(3). 291–319.
Hatfield, Adam. 2016. *A Grammar of Mehek*. Buffalo: State University of New York at Buffalo dissertation.
Janssen, Theo, & Wim van der Wurff. 1996. Introductory Remarks on Reported Speech and Thought. In Theo Janssen & Wim van der Wurff, (eds.). *Reported Speech: Forms and Functions of the Verb*, 1–12. Amsterdam: John Benjamins.
Kockelman, Paul. 2010. *Language, Culture, and Mind: Natural Constructions and Social Kinds*. Vol. 10. Cambridge: Cambridge University Press.
Kouteva, Tania, Bernd Heine, Bo Hong, Haiping Long, Heiko Narrog & Seongha Rhee. 2019. *World Lexicon of Grammaticalization*. Cambridge: Cambridge University Press.
Li, Charles N. 1986. Direct Speech and Indirect Speech: A Functional Study. In Florian Coulmas (ed.). *Direct and Indirect Speech*, 29–45. Berlin & New York: Mouton de Gruyter.
Loughnane, Robyn M. 2009. *A Grammar of Oksapmin*. Melbourne: The University of Melbourne dissertation.
Lucy, John A. 1993. Reflexive Language and the Human Disciplines. *Reflexive Language: Reported Speech and Metapragmatics*. 9–32.
McGregor, William B. 1994. The Grammar of Reported Speech and Thought in Gooniyandi. *Australian Journal of Linguistics* 14(1). 63–92.
McGregor, William B. 2021. Thought complements in Australian languages. *Language Sciences* 86. 101398.
Miestamo, Matti, Bakker, Dik, & Arppe, Antti. 2016. Sampling for variety. *Linguistic Typology* 20(2). 233–296.
Overall, Simon E. 2017. *A Grammar of Aguaruna (Iiniá Chicham)*. (Mouton Grammar Library Vol. 68). Berlin & Boston: De Gruyter Mouton.
Pawley, Andrew & Ralph Bulmer. 2011 Australian National University Pacific Linguistics. *A Dictionary of Kalam with Ethnographic Notes*. Pacific Linguistics. Pacific Linguistics, School of Culture, History; Language, College of Asia; the Pacific, The Australian National University.
Payne, Doris L. & Thomas E. Payne. 1990. Yagua. In Desmond C. Derbyshire & Geoffrey K. Pullum (eds.), *Handbook of Amazonian Languages*, 249–474. Berlin & New York: Mouton de Gruyter.
Reesink, Ger P. 1993. Inner Speech in Papuan Languages. *Language and Linguistics in Melanesia* 24(2). 217–25.
Rice, Keren. 1989. *A Grammar of Slave*. Berlin & New York: De Gruyter.
Rijkhoff, Jan, Dik Bakker, Kees Hengeveld & Peter Kahrel. 1993. A Method of Language Sampling. *Studies in Language. International Journal Sponsored by the Foundation "Foundations of Language"* 17(1). 169–203.
Spronck, Stef. 2015a. *Reported Speech in Ungarinyin: Grammar and Social Cognition in a Language of the Kimberley Region*. Western Australia: Australian National University dissertation.
Spronck, Stef. 2017. Defenestration: Deconstructing the Frame-in Relation in Ungarinyin. *Journal of Pragmatics* 114. 104–33.
Spronck, Stef, & Daniela Casartelli. 2021. In a Manner of Speaking: How Reported Speech May Have Shaped Grammar. *Frontiers in Communication* 6. 1–22.
Stenzel, Kristine. 2013. *A Reference Grammar of Kotiria (Wanano)*. (Studies in the Native Languages of the Americas). Lincoln & London: University of Nebraska Press.

Thornes, Timothy Jon. 2003. *A Northern Paiute Grammar with Texts*. Eugene, Oregon: University of Oregon dissertation.
Völlmin, Sascha. 2017. *Towards a Grammar of Gumer. Phonology and Morphology of a Western Gurage Variety*. Zürich: University of Zürich dissertation.
van der Voort, Hein. 2002. The Quotative Construction in Kwaza and Its (de)Grammaticalisation. In Mily Crevels, Simon van de Kerke, Sérgio Meira & Hein van der Voort (eds.), Current Studies on South American Languages. *Current Studies on South American Languages* 3. 307–28. Leiden: Research School of Asian, African, and Amerindian Studies (CNWS).

Index

addressee 15, 26–32, 76, 81, 90, 92, 99, 103, 173, 176–178, 181, 183–184, 190, 192, 194, 214, 292, 294, 298, 300–301, 310–311
addressivity (*see also* addressee) 171, 176
affective stance (*see also* stance) 7, 141–142, 144–145, 152, 155, 157, 164–165
Aguaruna 296, 300–301, 304–306
argumentative stance (*see* stance)
at-issueness 5, 41–43, 47, 52, 54–60, 67–69

Bambara 15–16, 29–30
Bashkir 16, 19–20, 27
Ben Tey 16, 21
Bininj Gun-Wok 296–297, 299

Chuvash 16, 20–21, 22–25, 27, 32
coercion 15, 17, 23–28, 30–33
cognitive verbs 42, 46, 270, 280, 285
complementizer (*see also* complementizer deletion) 2–3, 9, 146–147, 187, 202, 263–265, 267, 268–272, 274, 276–278, 280, 284–286
complementizer deletion 2, 9, 264, 268–271, 274, 286
constructionalization 9, 47, 52, 250, 263, 264, 271, 273, 281, 282
contextualisation 47, 52, 250–251
control verbs 45
conventionalization 124, 198
converb 9, 36, 296, 304–306, 312
corpus 5–6, 9, 16, 18, 31, 35, 73, 76–77, 83, 85–87, 89–90, 93–94, 96, 98, 100, 107, 112–113, 122–123, 126–127, 147, 179–181, 193, 196–197, 200, 204, 234, 247, 263–264, 269, 273–274
corpus analysis (*see also* corpus) 5, 73, 274

dialect 6, 22, 107, 109, 112, 114, 116, 119, 120, 122, 125–129, 131–133, 135–136, 180, 185, 208, 214, 225–227, 263–264, 268, 273–274, 276, 277
discourse marker 3, 8, 32, 107–109, 112, 114–117, 119–120, 127, 130, 132, 134–135, 160, 282

ellipsis 8, 171, 174–175, 196, 198, 201
epistemic authority 73, 78, 79, 90, 94–95, 97–99, 103
equational verbs 171, 186–187, 192, 201
Erzya 171, 174–175, 179, 182–186, 188, 193, 201
Estonian 171, 174–175, 179–180, 187–188, 191, 201
eventiveness 41, 54–55, 58, 60, 63, 69
evidential reportative modal (*see also* evidentiality) 42
evidentiality 5–6, 32, 41, 47, 51, 54, 59–60, 63–64, 66–67, 78, 80, 209–210, 302–304, 311

Finnish 144, 171, 174–175, 179, 187–188, 190–191, 198, 201, 250
French 7, 115, 141–142, 147, 157, 164–165
frequency 32, 33, 94, 109, 113–114, 115–122, 124–131, 136, 280, 294

Georgian 8, 207–212, 214, 222–227, 234–235
German 2, 5, 41–44, 49–52, 54–55, 59–60, 61, 68–69, 142, 144, 175, 233
Gizey 16, 20, 26, 29
grammaticalization 3, 5, 8, 9, 20, 32, 107, 108, 109, 115–117, 119, 120, 122, 124, 131, 136, 208, 209, 226, 231–233, 236, 263–264, 270–274, 279, 280, 281–282, 285
Gumer 296, 305–306

Hare 293–296, 299, 301, 304
Hinuq 296, 306–308
Hungarian 171, 174–176, 179–180, 182–186, 188, 193, 196–199, 201

implicature 47, 64, 281
inner speech 2, 8, 19, 34, 42, 133, 141, 172, 176, 178
interactional linguistics 7, 145–146, 164

Kalam 296, 301, 304
Kilmeri 295–299
Komi 171–175, 179, 182, 193–195, 201
Kotiria 296, 302, 304
Kuuk Thaayorre 296, 298–299, 303, 307

Maale 296, 304, 305–306
matrix clause 1, 8–9, 19, 21, 24, 27–29, 49, 52, 61, 76, 85–87, 102, 146, 270, 292–293, 295, 297–305, 307–312
Mehek 296, 310–311
mental activity 17–19, 22–24, 26, 28–30, 32, 34, 135
metadiscourse 109–111
modality 5, 41, 48–49, 51, 53–54, 64, 69, 146–147, 244
morphosyntax 5, 8–9, 17–18, 23, 29, 33–35, 41, 43, 50, 69, 73, 76, 80, 85–87, 93–94, 96, 101, 108, 117, 173, 291, 293–297, 299–302, 306, 309–312
multimodality (*see also* modality) 146–147
Mwan 16, 21, 26

narration (*see* narratives)
narratives 16, 33, 85, 113, 240, 296, 303–304, 307
news reports 8, 239–243, 246, 255
nominal incorporation 297, 308–309
Northern Paiute 296, 308

Oksapmin 296, 307–308
original source (*see also* reported clause) 240–242, 246–249, 254

performative thinking 266
perspective 2, 4, 6, 73–74, 76–77, 87, 90–91, 94–102, 109, 146, 161, 241, 263–265, 273
polyphony 109, 112, 124, 128, 130, 135
Portuguese 9, 263–264, 267–268, 270–275, 277–280, 282–286
pragmatic level 43
pragmaticalization 9, 41, 43, 60, 68–69, 263, 270, 272–273, 279, 281–282, 285
presupposition 47–48, 110
productivity 114–117, 120, 131
propositional attitude verbs 41–43, 62, 68

Quechua 6, 59, 73–76, 79–82, 100
quotative (*see also* quotative marker) 3, 6, 8–9, 19–20, 24, 32, 37, 47, 55, 87, 101, 107, 109, 112, 114–115, 120, 122–136, 142–145, 152, 154–156, 164, 171–175, 180, 185–187, 192–193, 195–196, 200–202, 207–212, 215, 222–223, 226–227, 232–233, 235–236, 296, 306–308, 312

quotative index (*see also* quotative) 8, 171–172, 211–212
quotative marker (*see also* quotative) 6, 8–9, 20, 32, 107, 112, 114, 120, 121–128, 130–131, 133–136

rational stance (*see also* stance) 7, 141, 143, 145, 148–150, 152, 154–155, 164–165
reanalysis 6, 42, 62, 65–67, 125, 131, 136, 209, 281
reportative 5–6, 8, 41–49, 51–60, 62–69, 73–74, 76–81, 85–87, 89, 94, 96, 99–102
reportative mood (*see* reportative)
reported clause 9, 93, 243–245, 252, 255, 265–267, 292–293, 295–311

self-quotation 7–8, 142, 171–173, 175, 178, 181, 183, 186–187, 191–196, 198–199, 201–202
self-quotative (*see* quotative)
semantic level 48
serial verbs 300, 302, 304
Spanish 3, 6–7, 9, 55, 76, 82, 107–110, 112, 115–116, 129, 135–136, 163–164, 267–280, 282–285
speech verbs 2, 8, 24, 55, 95, 171, 174, 175, 181, 182–183, 186, 196, 198, 201, 211, 303
stance 7, 74, 79, 141, 142–145, 148–150, 152–157, 161, 163–165, 182–184, 265, 268, 280

talk-in-interaction 7, 141, 164
Tariana 210, 296, 302–304, 307
Thai 8–9, 239, 241–246, 252, 254–256
turn-taking 8, 107–108, 173–175, 196–199

Udihe 16, 19, 24, 28
Udmurt 171–172, 174–175, 179–182, 193–195, 201
Upper Napo Kichwa 6, 73–76, 79, 83, 85, 102

verba dicendi (*see also* speech verbs) 42
volitional verb (*see also* volitionality) 5, 41, 48, 67
volitionality 32, 48

Wan 16, 19–20, 22, 26

Yagua 296, 308–309

www.ingramcontent.com/pod-product-compliance
Lightning Source LLC
Chambersburg PA
CBHW050514170426
43201CB00013B/1958